E 185.615 .A84 1994

Ashmore, Harry S.

Civil rights and wrongs

DATE DUE

DEMCO 38-297

CIVIL RIGHTS

AND

WRONGS

CIVIL RIGHTS

A N D

WRONGS

A MEMOIR OF RACE AND POLITICS
1944–1994

Harry S. Ashmore

A CORNELIA & MICHAEL BESSIE BOOK

Pantheon Books   New York

8/94

28710918

Library of Congress Cataloging-in-Publication Data

Ashmore, Harry S.
Civil rights and wrongs: a memoir of race and politics, 1944–1994 / by Harry S.
Ashmore.
p.   cm.
"A Cornelia and Michael Bessie book."
Includes bibliographical references and index.
ISBN 0-679-43181-0
1. Afro-Americans—Politics and government.   2. Afro-Americans—
Civil rights.   3. Civil rights movements—United States—
History—20th century.   4. United States—Race relations.
I. Title.
E185.615.A84   1994
973'.0496073—dc20   93-30553
CIP

Book design by M. Kristen Bearse

Manufactured in the United States of America

First Edition

9 8 7 6 5 4 3 2 1

For Cousin Harold Fleming,
who understood that humor is the saving grace

The American dilemma is the ever-raging conflict between the values which we shall call the "American creed," where the American thinks, talks and acts under the influence of high national and Christian morals, and on the other hand, the values of individual and group living, where personal and local interests; economic, social and sexual jealousies; considerations of community prestige and conformity; group prejudice against particular types of persons or types of people; and all sorts of miscellaneous wants, impulses and habits dominate his outlook.

—Gunnar Myrdal,
An American Dilemma

CONTENTS

INTRODUCTION

IT HAS been fifty years since Gunnar Myrdal completed the massive study of race relations in the United States summarized in the two-volume work he titled *An American Dilemma*. I first read it in 1945 while on military leave at the end of the war in Europe, and found it a prescient reintroduction to a society that had undergone vast changes since I left it behind three years before.

Sealed away in remote training camps before being sent overseas, I had been distantly aware of increasing racial unrest as the nation passed from depression to war. But, for the first time in my life, I had been without contact with blacks, for they were not included among the thirteen thousand men who made up the 95th Infantry Division, in which I served as an operations officer. As a matter of policy, we were kept as far away as possible from the few black combat units grudgingly permitted in the rigidly segregated military services.

The nation's handful of black social scientists, along with their leading white colleagues, had been enlisted by the Carnegie Corporation for Myrdal's study, and their detailed findings reinforced conclusions I had reached in the course of a dawning career as a political writer in my native South Carolina. Politics has been defined as sociololgy in action, and I was familiar with the ground covered by the interracial teams assembled for field work in the former Confederate and border states, where the great majority of the nation's blacks were still concentrated.

One who looked closely could hardly fail to see signs of erosion in the peculiar institutions that consigned the minority race to second-class citizenship. As Myrdal put it, "Not since Reconstruction has there been more reason to anticipate fundamental changes in American race relations." He concluded that from the conservative point of view it was urgent that the Southern states

> begin allowing the higher strata of the Negro population to participate in the political process as soon as possible, and to push the movement down to the lower groups gradually. It is also urgent to speed up the civic education of these masses who are bound to have votes in the future. But the great majority of Southern conservative white people do not see the hand-writing on the wall. They do not study the impending changes; they live in the pathetic illusion that the matter is settled. . . .

For more than half a century that illusion had been sustained by a political system that denied blacks the means of challenging laws that deprived them of their civil rights. This was racial discrimination openly based on the theory of white supremacy, and, if it was deplored by moralists, it remained unchallenged, having been given constitutional sanction when the Founding Fathers accepted the imposition of slavery as a right reserved to the states.

The states' rights doctrine survived the Civil War, and the South used it to disenfranchise freed slaves and their descendants by denying them membership in the Democratic Party, whose regional dominance was so complete its nominees faced no effective opposition in general elections. But by the end of World War II the handwriting on the wall of segregation included a decree of the U.S. Supreme Court that would ultimately dismantle the one-party system. In 1944 the Court held that state primaries were an integral part of the electoral process, thus making them subject to constitutional amendments enacted after the Civil War to guarantee full citizenship for freed slaves.

A process had been set in motion that would lead to an irreparable breach in the Democratic bastion that had given the South disproportionate influence in national affairs. But my own experience provided no reason to question Myrdal's prognosis:

> The chances that the future development will be planned and led intelligently—and that consequently, it will take the form

of cautious, foresighted reforms instead of unexpected, tumultuous, haphazard breaks, with mounting discords and anxieties in its wake—are indeed small.

And this, I knew, would be the central issue I would have to deal with when the war ended in the Pacific and I returned to the Carolina upcountry as editor of the *Charlotte News*.

Haphazard breaks and discords continued to mount during the decade that followed. By 1948, when President Harry S. Truman's stand on civil rights touched off the Dixiecrat rebellion, I was situated on the front line of the partisan infighting as executive editor of the *Arkansas Gazette*. I was still there in 1957 when Governor Orval Faubus precipitated a constitutional crisis by calling out his state militia to defy a federal court's order to desegregate Little Rock's Central High School. Thereafter, my preoccupation with the race issue was shared by most of my Southern contemporaries, although not many shared my conclusions.

Any appraisal of the impact of race on American society depends on the perspective of the appraiser, and this has determined the character of the considerable body of literature that followed Myrdal's seminal work. In my contributions to the canon I have considered the civil rights movement in the context of the political developments that made it possible, and these go back to the 1930s. For actuarial reasons, my emphasis represents a minority view.

The memory of the current generation of Americans does not embrace the New Deal era, and most contemporary writers tend to dismiss, or misread, the partisan realignment that began during the administration of Franklin Roosevelt and provided blacks with their first affirmative role in shaping public policy. A leading political historian, Hugh Davis Graham, reflected the prevailing view when he placed the beginning of the civil rights movement in the late 1950s. In *The Civil Rights Era*, an examination of the "origins and development of national policy 1960–72," he conceded that there were many other plausible starting points, but rested his case on the claim that the challenge of the sit-ins in the South and the presidential election of John F. Kennedy in 1960 catapulted the civil rights issue into the forefront of national consciousness. It did this with an escalating logic and force that for the first time (since Reconstruction) forced all three branches of the federal government to confront and attempt to resolve the problems of discrimination through concerted effort. . . . The events of the 1960s shattered the old mold, and by 1972 the fundamental elements of the new order were set in place.

Most scholars now treat the shift in government priorities as a historical disjuncture. But, to a journalist who viewed the movement from the eye of the political hurricane that enveloped the South in the postwar decades, it seemed more a matter of white perceptions belatedly catching up with reality.

Over two decades litigation initiated by the National Association for the Advancement of Colored People had undermined the states' rights policy that condoned apartheid. The series of cases that culminated in the Supreme Court's 1954 ruling against segregation in public education committed the federal government to protect the civil rights of blacks wherever they were denied by the action, or inaction, of local authorities. Assurance of this kind of support released the pent-up resentment that sent masses of blacks into the streets to challenge Jim Crow.

The selective eye of television provided those outside the region with a view of the sometimes bloody encounters that followed the call for massive resistance by the political leaders of the Deep South. The dramatic scenes that appeared on the new home screens were presented as a morality play, and the reversal of the traditional identification of black with evil and white with good sustained the notion that this was just another manifestation of the benighted racial ethos deemed peculiar to the South.

If there was a radical disjuncture in the 1960s it was in the majority's perception of a social order that appeared entirely different when seen from the underside. In the nation's metropolitan areas the rising postwar tide of black immigrants had been channeled into segregated urban ghettos, and they remained beyond the ken of most whites until race riots erupted in a hundred major cities. In appraising the reaction I found little evidence of the force of logic cited by Graham:

> For the nation at large the race issue suddenly has been transmuted from an abstract moral question to a complex socioeconomic problem; from a peripheral intellectual concern to a hysterical popular obsession; from a nagging regional nuisance to a national crisis with international implications; and thereby has been elevated from cellar to stage center of American politics.

That was written in 1968, after I had settled in California as a fellow of the Center for the Study of Democratic Institutions, where I recorded my impressions of the condition of blacks outside the South in a book I called *The Other Side of Jordan*. The National Advisory Commission on Civil Disorders had just released its finding that separate but unequal communities were emerging throughout urban America, and warned that the nation must "carry through a firm commitment to massive social reform, or it will develop into a society of garrison cities. . . ." A generation later, the commitment still has not been carried through, and the steady escalation of violent crime has demonstrated the futility of relying on the criminal justice system, backed up by the military, to maintain a tolerable degree of domestic tranquillity.

It is fairly easy to measure the considerable progress blacks have made in the second half of the century. The most dramatic changes came in the South as antidiscrimination policies approved by the federal courts combined with pressures generated by the civil rights demonstrations to bring about a sea change in attitudes and practices. By the 1970s the growing black middleclass had attained status and broadened opportunities at least equivalent to those available elsewhere in the nation, and the level of racial tension was markedly lower.

But the nonviolent campaign that made Martin Luther King, Jr., a national hero never had resonance with the upheavals outside the South. The Freedom Now! banner King's followers unfurled is often cited as inspiring the generational rebellion of young middleclass whites, but the revolutionary pretensions of the New Left didn't jibe with a movement that, as the historian C. Vann Woodward noted, derived "overt support from the established government, that strives to realize rather than destroy traditional values, and seeks to join rather than overthrow the social order."

The kind of self-centered liberation that produced a drug culture, encouraged sexual promiscuity, and fostered a debased, sensual popular music was anathema to King. So was the militant stance of blacks who adopted the separatist doctrine of black power. The only aspect of the youth movement that accorded with his Gandhian principles was its opposition to the Vietnam War—and in joining the protest he parted company with mainstream black leaders and with the Democratic political leadership. The force of the civil rights movement's integrationist drive was spent before it reached the poor blacks consigned to the nation's inner cities and pockets of rural poverty.

King's eloquence, selfless dedication, and heroic presence had much to do with the raised consciousness of blacks, and that of others who considered themselves victims of discrimination because of gender, cultural identity, or sexual preference. The activist pressure groups that resulted were fueled by a passion matched by those who opposed them, and this produced an extraordinary political turbulence. There is no precise way of measuring the change in social values this reflects, but most observers agree that it has been profound.

Conventions that inhibited individual conduct have been relaxed, creating a permissiveness that has opened new opportunities of self-fulfillment for minorities and the female majority. But liberation from standards originally set by the white male establishment also had its price. If *e pluribus unum*—from the many, one—still represents the nation's goal, we have been moving away from it for two decades.

This is manifest in sharply contrasting views on the root causes of the urban crisis. Even the most fortunately situated blacks have not yet entirely escaped the effects of bigotry, and they tend to emphasize the white community's heritage of racism as the cause of the disabilities of poor blacks who suffer its most severe consequences. In their reaction to the resulting crime and violence, whites tend to place the blame on the individual rather than society.

Since television emerged as the primary medium of mass communication in the early days of the civil rights movement, it has fore-shortened perspective for the rising generation, and introduced an emphasis on pop psychology that personalizes—and usually trivializes—the coverage of social change. A case can be made that white control of the media produces bias in the treatment of news and commentary, but this is hardly the case in sports and entertainment, where the black presence is now pervasive.

The popular music industry's exploitation of the sensual, semi-literate homeboy culture of the ghetto sets the style for the young of both races, including those sequestered in affluent white neighborhoods. In reaction, the bullyboys who preside over "shock radio" talk shows promote a call-in chorus of racist bigotry. And at the far end of the cultural spectrum unbridled racial tensions on college campuses have fostered an ill-tempered debate on Afrocentrism vs. Eurocentrism in which unhyphenated Americanism seems to have been the victim of the latest academic fad, deconstructionism.

The retrospective appraisal of the cause and effect of the civil rights movement undertaken in this memoir is not intended as history; significant events and personalities are passed over lightly, heroes remain unsung, and many of those usually treated as villains turn out to be merely banal. Yet the cumulative weight of the past still shapes the political response to the changing status of blacks.

Moral considerations generated the political pressures that made possible government action to deal with racial discrimination, but for the better part of a generation they have been subordinated to the perceived self-interest of the white majority. Over time the two political parties reversed their positions, with the Democrats embracing the cause of the black minority, while the Republicans adopted a "Southern strategy" to exploit race prejudice through a commitment to turn back the gains made by the civil rights movement.

Race has always been intertwined with the economic issues that mark the ideological divide between the two parties. The laissez-faire doctrine cherished by the business-oriented Republicans was eclipsed during the Democratic ascendancy that began with the New Deal, but in the 1980s it was reinstated in its most pristine form. When Ronald

Reagan declared in his inaugural address that government cannot solve the nation's problems, because government *is* the problem, he precipitated a new round in the perennial contest between those who would employ the central government's authority and resources to deal with the problems of a society in transition, and those who would severely limit its powers and leave their resolution to the marketplace.

The strain of individualism in the American tradition combines with self-interest to ensure a populist response to libertarian rhetoric. But it has little appeal for those who have been excluded from the benefits and protections provided by government, and these make up the growing bloc of black voters who now provide the winning margin in major state and municipal elections. Playing the race card made possible the election of three Republican presidents, but it preserved Democratic majorities in both the House and Senate.

The interplay between race and politics was also instrumental in the Democrats' narrow victory in the 1992 presidential election. Bill Clinton's 43 percent plurality hardly constituted a mandate, but the 50 percent increase in the congressional black caucus provided the margin that has opened the way for national social and economic policies intended to bring about a signal change in the role of the central government.

The caucus provided a critical offset to defecting Democrats during the struggle to include basic elements of the administration program in the 1993–94 congressional budget. And the black House members stood firm when, after eight months of exhaustive preparation, the president presented a broad-based proposal for health care reform that drew fire from those who claimed it did not go far enough and those who thought it went too far.

Issues of particular concern to the black community, which bears the brunt of the worsening urban crisis, were not dealt with directly in the health care proposal, but they were implicit in it. When he appeared before Congress, the president cited the burden placed on medical facilities by "the outrageous cost of crime." And Hillary Rodham Clinton, the principal architect of the program, told House members: "We are committed, as you are, to trying to eliminate the level of violence in this country, both as a moral matter but also as a health care imperative."

There was no prospect of reducing the cost imposed by violence after the fact, the point at which the criminal justice system comes into play. The emphasis would have to be on prevention, and evidence that faith in harsh punishment as a deterrent to inner city crime was wearing thin on Capitol Hill was provided when the Senate unanimously confirmed Clinton's nominee for director of the FBI.

Spelling out the lessons he had learned in twenty years on the front line of what he called "the pandemic of crime," Louis J. Freeh, Jr., spoke out of experience as a star FBI investigator, prosecuting attorney, and federal district judge in New York. At every level of the criminal justice system he had found himself dealing with

> a distinct class of defendants who reach a certain point in their life where nothing can be done but to incarcerate them for the rest of their lives. . . . Such conditions are intolerable, and if we do not attack the root causes of crime and save our children, conditions will be even worse ten years from now, and we will again have lost most of a new generation.

As the president rounded into the second year of his term, there were indications that, in the case of health care at least, laissez-faire was beginning to lose its appeal. The opinion polls showed over 70 percent support for government intervention to provide universal coverage; only 10 percent still responded to the shibboleth of "socialized medicine" that for forty years had enabled the American Medical Association and its allies in the insurance and pharmaceutical industries to block repeated efforts at reform.

For the first time, a Clinton administration package of proposed legislation had been greeted with widespread expressions of bipartisan support, at least in principle. According to the cliché the Washington commentators adopted to express their usual skepticism, the devil was in the details and would emerge, pitchfork in hand, during a year or more of infighting that lay ahead.

But in a struggle for support from the political center the advantage passed to Bill Clinton. His temperament, lifelong study of government policy, and the experience of twenty years in elective office had cast him as a consensus-builder. His experience, which paralleled that of the black politicians brought to office by the civil rights movement, had convinced him that, while protest and confrontation may promote change in a representative democracy, it does not endure unless those divided by it can be brought together by common purpose and common sense.

Recent contributions to race relations literature cite the urgent need for a public dialogue that will deal candidly with rising levels of intolerance among members of both races. This would have to begin with recognition that racism begets racism, as demonstrated by the call for racial separatism voiced by nonpolitical black leaders as a response to the evident fact that many whites still have not put aside the traditional belief in their race's inherent superiority. This, I think, goes hand in hand with shortsighted white resistance to paying the price for dealing with the root causes of poverty even after their adverse effect on society as a whole has become inescapable.

These attitudes cannot be quickly changed, but they do not necessarily preclude resumption of government action to correct the institutional imbalance that still denies poor blacks any semblance of equality of opportunity. This was accomplished in the case of the black middleclass at a time when politicians were convinced that a majority of their white constituents would never tolerate the social changes it required. Civil wrongs that had endured since the founding of the republic were corrected, giving the black minority a voice that can now be heard at all levels of government.

The examination of the evolution of race relations in this volume will, I believe, demonstrate that there has been significant progress toward resolution of the American dilemma Gunnar Myrdal defined fifty years ago. It will also support his conclusion, and mine, that further progress toward the nation's declared goal of equal justice under law can be initiated only in the trenches of government, where Bill Clinton, arriving in Washington on the cusp of generational change, has opened a new chapter in the partisan struggle that animates the political process.

CIVIL RIGHTS

A N D

WRONGS

PRELUDE
ROOSEVELT AND THE NEW DEAL

I did not choose the tools with which I must work. Southerners, by virtue of the seniority rule in Congress, are chairmen or occupy strategic committees. If I come out for the anti-lynching bill now, they will block every bill I ask Congress to pass to keep America from collapsing. I just can't run the risk.

—PRESIDENT FRANKLIN D. ROOSEVELT to Walter White, secretary of the National Association for the Advancement of Colored People, 1933

GROWING UP in South Carolina in the years between the two world wars, I came of age in the era of political ferment that followed the election of Franklin D. Roosevelt as the nation's thirty-second president. The year he took office I entered Clemson College, painfully aware of the shattering effect of the Great Depression that gave birth to the New Deal. The comfortable middleclass life-style provided by my father, a modestly successful merchant in the state's second city, Greenville, had come to an abrupt end when he was bankrupted by the general economic collapse.

Most of my classmates had been similarly exposed to the unsettling threat of poverty, and we were aware that change was the order of the day. Yet I do not recall that in our classes or in our bull sessions there was any serious consideration of the effect this might have on what was usually capitalized as the Southern Way of Life. It was not that the peculiar institutions shaped by our Confederate heritage were unduly exalted, or even much discussed; on our remote foothill campus they were simply accepted as ordained and presumed to be immutable.

I could hardly escape the signs of social dislocation and latent political unrest when I graduated and signed on as a cub reporter for the afternoon *Greenville Piedmont* at twelve-fifty a week. Yet these portents received no serious attention at the civic club meetings I covered in return for free lunch. Looking back across more than half a century, the memory of those gatherings of the city's business and professional elite emerges as a soothing drone, a restful sound like that made by bees in honeysuckle.

I came a little closer to reality when I was assigned to the county beat, but the instruments of government, and those who administered them, were firmly set in their ways. The courthouse was a stronghold of "Yellow Dog Democrats"—those so identified since Reconstruction because of their declared willingness to vote for a yellow dog if the Democrats nominated one. The pledge provided the basis for the South's one-party politics, and among the beneficiaries were three of my cousins: John Ashmore, the county supervisor; Robert, the prosecuting attorney; and Maurice, the tax collector.

There were Ashmores of all kinds and conditions in the Carolina upcountry, but I never met a rich one. Their political prominence derived from family connections established in the two centuries since white settlers and their accompanying slaves found their westward movement halted by the barrier of the Appalachians. There were some in the lineage to be proud of, and some who were never mentioned. The Civil War historian Shelby Foote observed that in the usual Southern ancestry there were "ups and downs." In Memphis, he said, "I don't have a single friend who didn't have one distinguished personage somewhere in his background . . . and I don't know a one who didn't have some white trash in there, too."

When I asked Cousin John, who had an obvious practical interest in genealogy, just how extensive our relationships were, he was even more inclusive. "Son, the way I look at it," he replied, "we're kin to everybody in Greenville County, white or black, one way or another."

But, of course, the black members of the extended family had long since been disfranchised, and their well-being was of no official concern. The situation was no different in the private sector, where their role was limited to providing an oversupply of cheap, menial labor.

In due season I was transferred to the *Piedmont*'s senior partner, the morning *News*, and posted to the state capital in Columbia as a political correspondent. At the old statehouse the scars inflicted on the granite walls by General Sherman's artillery were left unrepaired and conspicuously marked, and a gallant Confederate cavalryman, General Wade Hampton, still stood guard on his rearing bronze charger. There, under the tutelage of the good old boys who dominated the legislature, I came to appreciate the looking-glass quality of political discourse and to understand that it is designed to reflect what the beholder wants to see. This accounted for what had begun to dawn on me as a singular fact: Race, although it had shaped so much of the nation's history, no longer had any place on the political agenda, except as a diversion.

In 1896 the U.S. Supreme Court, in its *Plessy* v. *Ferguson* decision, had interpreted the constitutional amendments enacted after the Civil War in a fashion that permitted the Southern states to legally impose second-class citizenship on the emancipated slaves, denying them basic civil rights and barring social intercourse with their white neighbors. Demography made it possible for those outside the region who deplored this kind of overt repression to treat the moral issue it raised as an abstraction—a matter beyond the reach of the political process—and it was no longer a source of partisan conflict.

The great majority of blacks were still concentrated in the Southern and border states, beyond the ken of most Americans. They continued to work the land, usually as sharecroppers, or eked out a marginal living as domestic servants or common laborers; in material terms the condition of most had not been significantly changed by the abolition of slavery. The Depression had virtually halted their migration to the great cities outside the region, where they were nominally entitled to civil rights, and they had not yet clustered in numbers sufficient to give them political leverage.

When the race issue was injected into a political campaign in the years before World War II it had the aura of an artifact. For almost half a century blacks had posed no conceivable threat to the entrenched white majority. The master-servant relationship of the slave era had been institutionalized, and the racism it embodied usually remained latent until a beleaguered politician invoked it to arouse defensive attitudes ingrained by a history that had always set Southerners apart from their fellow countrymen.

This could still produce a political eruption sufficient to divert attention from the real issues that beset Southern constituencies suffering from poverty that had not been relieved since it was visited on the region in the wake of the lost Civil War. The folk memory of Reconstruction, exaggerated as it surely was, retained enough force in the 1930s to provide comeuppance even for Franklin Roosevelt, who had become the most popular president in modern times as a result of the relief measures provided by the New Deal.

Sent down to report to the White House on Southern sentiment, Martha Gellhorn found poor whites in the Carolina mill towns talking "of the president very much as if he were Moses, and they are simply waiting to be led into the promised land." Similar soundings across the region encouraged Roosevelt to spend some of his political capital in the 1938 Democratic primaries in an effort to purge the Senate of the "Dixiecrats" who regularly joined the Republicans in blocking, or watering down, the economic and social reforms at the heart of his program. At the head of the hit list was Senator Ellison Durant Smith of South Carolina, who was running for his sixth term.

"Cotton Ed" Smith was a product of the lowcountry plantation gentry who might have stepped out of a political cartoon. At the outdoor campaign rallies where the candidates appeared in joint debate, he wore his trademark white linen suit, string tie, and broad-brimmed Panama hat. There, as he had for thirty years, he stood foursquare on the three-plank platform of the antebellum slaveocracy: states' rights, white supremacy, and tariff for revenue only. "If it was good enough for John C. Calhoun," he intoned, "it's good enough for me."

President Roosevelt made no mention of such arcane matters when he stopped off in Greenville en route to his retreat at Warm Springs, Georgia. Addressing the cheering crowd that massed around the rear platform of his railroad car, he didn't even mention Cotton Ed by name.

He simply reminded the enraptured hearers how well they had been served by the New Deal, and cited the further benefits they could expect if they replaced their senior senator with a Democrat whose support he could count on.

Cotton Ed was acutely aware that the president was dealing in the coin of the Southern political realm when he challenged his party loyalty. His response was one of the memorials I noted in a book I titled *An Epitaph for Dixie.* "The Philadelphia Story," as it came to be called, portrayed the senator's famous walkout at the Democratic National Convention two years before as an act of fealty to the faith of his fathers rather than as a protest against the renomination of the beloved Roosevelt. After implying that his two opponents were prepared to betray their heritage for a mess of political pottage, he eased onto the low ground:

> In an effort to keep this campaign on a high plane, it has been my custom to begin with the Magna Carta and trace the long struggle for individual rights that are threatened today by malefactors in Washington, D.C., masquerading as Democrats. But the other night, up yonder in Pickens County, I had started out on the fields of Runnymede and had the boys in gray halfway up the hill at Gettysburg, when an old man in the front row spit out his tobacco cud and said, "Oh, hell, Ed, tell us about Phillydelphy."
>
> So I told them. I told them about walking up to that great convention hall, and being stopped there at the outer gate— the outer gate, mind you—by a stranger who demanded to see my credentials. "Young man," I said, "if we have reached the time when the senior senator from South Carolina has to have credentials to get into a Democratic convention, I don't want in." And he stepped aside.
>
> But when I came out on the floor of that great hall it looked like a checkerboard—a spot of white here, and a spot of black there! But I kept going, down that long aisle, and finally I found the standard of South Carolina—and, praise God, it was in a spot of white!
>
> I had no sooner than taken my seat when a newspaperman

came down the aisle and squatted down by me and said, "Senator, did you know a Nigra is going to come out up yonder in a minute and offer the invocation?" I told him, I said, "Now don't be joking me, I'm upset enough the way it is." But then, bless God, out on that platform walked a slew-footed, blue-gummed, kinky-headed Senegambian!

And he started praying, and I started walking. And as I pushed through those great doors, and walked across that vast rotunda, it seemed to me that old John Calhoun leaned down from his mansion in the sky and whispered in my ear, "You did right, Ed. . . ."

The Philadelphia Story had all the basic ingredients required by the theater of the absurd that single-party politics had created in the South. The senator celebrated his victory by donning the red shirt worn by the night-riding Redeemers of Reconstruction days, posing for photographers clutching the rear leg of Wade Hampton's charger. All this no doubt shocked outlanders, and certainly the success of the run was a grievous disappointment to Franklin Roosevelt. The president's only public comment was a glum, "It takes a long time to bring the past up to the present."

Yet to the initiated, to the orator, and to the audience, there was a sort of innocence about it. Those who gathered under the chinaberry trees to whoop and holler as Cotton Ed harangued them from the flatbed of a cotton truck didn't really object to being prayed over by a Senegambian, and didn't believe Ed did, either.

The real significance of the Philadelphia Story was its irrelevance. South Carolina was as hard hit by the Depression as any state in the Union, and recovery was painfully slow from the collapse of prices and credit. In 1938 baled cotton still stood along the back roads waiting for a market, short shifts in the cotton mills crippled the economy of the Piedmont factory towns, and in the cities long lines of whites and blacks queued at relief stations for oranges and bacon. South Carolina's real problems lay in the depletion and neglect of its natural resources, and the corresponding erosion of its human resources.

Cotton Ed's opponents, Edgar Brown, the boss of the state senate, and Olin Johnson, the populist governor, where certainly aware of these issues. Yet they had to hedge their advocacy of federal action so that they did not imply deficiencies in the Southern Way of Life. Cotton Ed had headed them off by invoking the parochialism rooted in the South's unique history.

Brown provided a postmortem: "Either Olin or I could have handled Ed on the race issue, but we were both licked the day Roosevelt came out against him. The most powerful force you can turn loose in a political campaign is the voter's feeling that some outsider is trying to tell him what to do." This proved to be the case in the other Southern states, where all the incumbents on the president's hit list survived the attempted purge.

Cotton Ed would have to be classified as a demagogue by any standard definition. Yet I don't think he intended to inflame his followers, or launch them on any course of action beyond that necessary to return him to office. I doubt that he ever deliberately sought to mislead them. The oratory, with its ghostly hoofbeats of Confederate cavalry and Reconstruction era Redeemers, was an end in itself, without any direct relationship to what he would do after he returned to Washington— which would be nothing much.

In the years when Cotton Ed was in full voice, Gunnar Myrdal, examining the working of the South's one-party system from the viewpoint of a Swedish social democrat, found that "the white Southerner is—like the Negro, who is molded in the same civilization—even more of an individualist and more of a romantic than the Northerner." The result was an intense aversion to any actual exercise of authority: "The South entirely lacks the centralized organization of a fascist state. . . . The Democratic party is the very opposite of a 'state party' in a modern facist sense."

The Philadelphia Story was a relic left over from the glory days of the Old South, the mythic Dixie that had existed only in the imagination of the antebellum orators who first mounted a beleaguered minority's political defenses. Cotton Ed's litany was derived from the mighty vision held forth on the occasion of South Carolina's secession by a firebrand Charleston editor, Robert Barnwell Rhett, who predicted that a historian in A.D. 2000 would write of the Confederate States of America:

9

And extending their empire across this continent to the Pacific, and down through Mexico to the other side of the great gulf, and over the isles of the sea, they established an empire and wrought out a civilization that had never been equalled or surpassed—a civilization teeming with orators, poets, philosophers, statesmen and historians equal to those of Greece and Rome. . . .

But the glory that was Dixie lasted less than five years. This kind of high-flung oratory was embroidered upon Calhoun's defense of slavery, which depicted blacks as the "mudsill" upon which a great civilization could be erected. The dogma of white supremacy survived the lost war, but the harsh realities of Reconstruction revealed that the South, reduced to the status of a conquered province, had long since been left behind in the new industrial age that was rapidly transforming the rest of the nation.

By the time I made my way through the public schools, the consensus was that it was probably for the best that the nation had not been sundered, and this had what amounted to an official imprimatur. The history book used in the lower grades was a revision of an 1840 work by the state's most distinguished literary figure, William Gilmore Simms. In bringing the text up to date, his granddaughter Mary C. Simms Oliphant wrote:

South Carolinians were wholly mistaken in two of their most cherished beliefs: First, they felt that slave labor was necessary to the South because farming was the chief interest of this section; second, South Carolinians honestly believed that there were so many slaves that their freedom would mean that the South would belong to the black race. . . .

Time has proven how mistaken they were. We know now that we can farm successfully without slave labor, and that the freeing of the slaves has not Africanized the South. The pity is that South Carolinians had not taken the lead themselves in freeing the slaves and thus saving the country from a brother's war. Instead . . . South Carolina led the Southern states out of the union.

Mrs. Oliphant included a prescient warning to those who studied her text: ". . . to this day South Carolina has a white man's government. The welfare of two races living in one small state is a problem you will have to face when you become citizens." But this was not a problem their elders felt any compulsion to address, and three turbulent decades would pass before my generation was forced to deal with it.

The factor of race has always made it virtually impossible to apply the usual political labels in the South. Gunnar Myrdal found the region "the only place in the world where one could get a reputation for being a liberal simply by urging obedience to the law." South Carolinians had correctly used "radical" to identify the Abolitionists, and they also applied it to Republican carpetbaggers, embracing not only the dedicated souls who worked for improvement in the lot of the freedmen but also those who came South to exploit the economic opportunities always available to the unprincipled in a conquered province.

But the etymology was badly skewed when, as they usually did, proper citizens began to use the term to express their personal distaste for the excesses of Cotton Ed Smith and his oratorical cohorts. It was not only that they considered the overt display of racism unseemly; they also viewed it as unnecessary, and likely to arouse the violent reaction of poor whites that disturbed the tranquillity they cherished as the hallmark of gentility.

Those well placed in the growing cities and towns, where the power structure was now based, did not see more equitable treatment for blacks as adverse to their interests. Adherents of the "New South" doctrine propounded by Henry Grady, the influential editor of the *Atlanta Constitution*, had begun to recognize that the urban middleclass would benefit economically from the increase in purchasing power that would result from improvement in the condition of the mass of blacks.

From his editor's chair, and from lecture platforms across the country, Grady had launched a campaign to heal the wounds of the Civil War and Reconstruction by promoting a new unity of economic interest between North and South. In a famous address to the Boston Merchants' Association in 1890, he faced up to the issue raised by the South's denial of civil rights to its black population, going well beyond the legalisms employed by the Supreme Court when it restored the states' right to do so.

Second-class citizenship, he declared, was an essential check on a "vast, ignorant and purchasable vote—clannish, credulous, impulsive and passionate—tempting every art of the demagogue, but insensible to the appeal of the statesman." It was an elegant version of a Mississippi editor's explanation that it had been necessary to take the vote away from the Negro to keep white men from stealing it. And it had resonance with the Boston Brahmins in his audience whose dominance was being challenged by an influx of immigrants:

> When will the black cast a free ballot? When ignorance anywhere is not dominated by the will of the intelligent; when the laborer everywhere casts a vote unhindered by his boss; when the vote of the poor everywhere is not influenced by the power of the rich; when the strong and steadfast do not everywhere control the suffrage of the weak and shiftless—then and not till then will the ballot of the Negro be free.

Grady's doctrine left white supremacy intact, but tempered it to the Northern taste by rejecting the harsh strictures of the racist demagogues and affirming a paternalistic concern for improving the condition of the blacks. For white Southerners it combined a sentimental exaltation of the Old South with the promise of economic salvation to be found in the New. And it had a special appeal for the entrepreneurs who were beginning to replace the plantation gentry in the places of power. If these had no impulse toward social reform, they did have an immediate concern for promoting orderly economic development, and they could recognize racial strife as a threat to their interests.

A black orator of comparable skills, Booker T. Washington, embraced Grady's thesis, and gained national recognition as the preeminent leader of his race. His status was acknowledged when, as president of Tuskegee Institute in Alabama, he was invited to address a gathering of the South's business leaders at the 1895 Cotton States and International Exposition in Atlanta.

Jim Crow was now firmly in place, and Washington was recognizing reality when he conceded that the advancement of his people, and possibly their survival, depended on "making friends, in every manly way, of the people of all races by whom we are surrounded. . . . The wisest among my race understand that the agitation of questions of social equality is the extremest folly." Negroes, he said, recognize that "it is at the bottom of life we must begin," which meant mastery of the agricultural and mechanical skills taught at Tuskegee. And he, too, invoked the Old South when he assured whites that they could be

> sure in the future as in the past, that you and your people will be surrounded by the most patient, faithful, law-abiding and unresentful people that the world has seen. As we proved our loyalty to you in the past, in nursing your children, watching by the sickbed of your mothers and fathers, and often following them with tear-dimmed eyes to their graves, so in the future, in our humble way, we still stand by you with a devotion no foreigner can approach, ready to lay down our lives, if need be, in defense of yours, interlacing our industrial, commercial, civic and religious life in a way that shall make the interests of both races one. In all things that are purely social we can be as separate as the fingers, yet one as the hand in all things essential to mutual progress.

Washington's accommodating stance, and the warm reception he received from those he identified as his former masters, gave him standing throughout the nation and made him welcome in the highest circles when he traveled abroad. Republican presidents, beginning with William McKinley, accepted his recommendation of blacks for federal patronage jobs, and he was received in the White House. Then, in 1901, a new occupant of the Oval Office, Theodore Roosevelt, reportedly invited him to stay for dinner, prompting protests not only in the South but also from the dowagers who dictated social standards in the capital.

When the newspapers publicized the incident, the short-tempered Roosevelt first responded that he would have anybody he pleased to dinner. But the furor didn't die down, and word was circulated that the black visitor hadn't actually been seated at the dinner table, but had been served on a tray during a working session in the president's office, where female members of the First Family were not present. The prudent Washington refused to make any comment at all.

Tales about Booker T. Washington's famous White House meal still had currency in the South thirty years later. But the version I first heard had become a matter of amusement for those who had begun to recognize the innate irony in the kind of segregation that required separate drinking glasses for black servants who prepared and served their family's food, and when necessary provided wet nurses for their infants.

After one of his addresses, the story went, a distinguished old Confederate colonel seized Washington's hand and told him, "Booker, that was the finest speech I ever heard in my life. I just wanted to tell you I think you may be the greatest man in the United States." Modestly demurring, Washington replied, "Oh, sir, I think we'd have to say that honor belongs to the president." "Not that sonofabitch," the colonel snorted, "he's the one who invited you to dinner."

Washington was challenged from the outset by the most outstanding black intellectual of the day, W.E.B. Du Bois, who acidly termed him the "most distinguished Southerner since Jefferson Davis." He conceded that Washington had acquired the largest personal following of any member of his race, but said of the Atlanta speech, "It startled and won the applause of the South, it interested and won the applause of the North; and after a confused murmur of protest, it silenced if it did not convert the Negroes themselves."

Du Bois, born and reared in Massachusetts, was considered the successor of the militant black abolitionist Frederick Douglass. *Encyclopaedia Britannica* called him "the most important black protest leader in the United States during the first half of the century." Rebecca Chalmers Barton, appraising Du Bois's autobiography, *Dusk of Dawn*, noted that he described his Bahamas-born parents as mulatto, and said that he had absorbed "culture patterns that were not African so much as Dutch and New England." His first exposure to blacks came when he went South to begin his education at Fisk University in Nashville, where "this young Northerner in the South nurtured a race pride that was almost chauvinistic."

Du Bois went on to earn Ph.D. degrees from Harvard and the University of Berlin, developing a philosophy that in time would reflect the influence of Marx and Freud. He was a professor of history at Atlanta University when, at the height of Washington's fame, he denounced the acknowledged role model of most American blacks for his espousal of the materialistic "gospel of Work and Money." In *Souls of Black Folk* he described Washington as

> the leader, not of one race but of two, a compromiser between the South, the North and the Negro. Naturally, the Negroes resented, at first bitterly, signs of compromise which surrendered their civil and political rights, even though this was to be exchanged for larger chances of economic development. The rich and dominating North, however, was not only weary of the race problem but was investing largely in Southern enterprises and welcomed any method of peaceful cooperation. . . . Mr. Washington represents in Negro thought the old attitude of adjustment and submission.

Beginning in 1905, Du Bois made opposition to Washington his primary mission. He assembled twenty-nine like-minded blacks for a meeting at Niagara Falls, out of which came a manifesto calling for full civil liberties, abolition of racial discrimination, and recognition of human brotherhood. The "Niagara Movement" met annually thereafter, but did not achieve effective organization and influence until 1909, when white heirs of the abolitionist tradition joined with the black leaders to form the National Association for the Advancement of Colored People.

The founders included such notables as Jane Addams, Oswald Garrison Villard, John Dewey, and William Dean Howells. White philanthropists provided most of the funding for an organization committed to working for reform within the system. The wealthy Jewish brothers Joel Elias and Arthur Springarn underwrote legal action to challenge segregation in the courts, and class action suits were brought on the NAACP's behalf by an eminent Yankee, Moorfield Storey of Boston, a past president of the American Bar Association.

As editor of *The Crisis*, the magazine launched by the NAACP in 1910, Du Bois became the principal spokesman for the fledgling organization. In the years when Booker T. Washington, as Rebecca Barton put it, "walked the razor's edge between Negro pride and white prejudice," the defiantly proud Du Bois became ever more uncompromising. In his obituary comment upon Washington's death in 1915 he wrote,

> We must lay upon the soul of this man a heavy responsibility for the consummation of the Negro's disfranchisement, the decline of the Negro college and public school, and the firmer establishment of color caste in this land.

Never comfortable with the integrationist policies of the NAACP, and increasingly uncomfortable with the important role played by his white colleagues, Du Bois began insisting that change could be accomplished only through agitation and protest. He began to write off the possibility of reform through collaboration, characterizing the white man as a "blind mechanism within his own culture patterns."

Temperamentally a loner, he never joined the black radicals in the Socialist Party, and rejected Marcus Garvey's scheme to repatriate blacks to Africa, declaring that "Negroes have no Zion." But Marxist influence was evident as he began to elaborate on his ideas for a black solidarity movement led by the "talented tenth" of educated blacks. He envisioned a cooperative movement to socialize professional services and take over retail distribution in black communities, eliminating advertising and profits. This would provide jobs, and funds for resettlement of slum dwellers and the rural poor in large-scale housing projects. He conceded that his scheme was segregationist, but argued that self-segregation was better than that imposed by the whites.

A break with the NAACP was inevitable, and in 1934 Du Bois returned to his old chair at Atlanta University. There he established *Phylon: A Review of Race and Culture*, and continued his intellectual effort to deal with the contradictions of self-segregation. But he was never able to resolve the problems that would continue to frustrate those who sought a practical means of satisfying blacks' yearning for an environment in which they could order their own affairs.

Du Bois returned to the NAACP in 1944, but he was past the point of rapport with the Atlanta-born Walter White, the pragmatic integrationist who became executive secretary in 1931 and who would remain the organization's dynamic leader until his death in 1955. In 1948 Du

Bois made his final break, and retreated into the bitterness that in 1961 finally led him to join the Communist Party. Although cleared by a federal court of charges that he had become a foreign agent, he renounced his American citizenship and moved to Accra, Ghana, where he died in 1963.

Booker T. Washington and Du Bois stood at the poles of black political thought, but the debate over their differences was almost entirely an intellectual exercise. Du Bois had no support among the mass of blacks in the South, and those in the North who accepted his separatist premise were devoid of political influence. James Weldon Johnson, another notable black leader, took his philosophical stand midway between the two.

Born and reared in Florida, Johnson also began his education at Fisk, and returned there as a gray eminence in 1930 after a career as poet, novelist, and essayist that made him a leading intellectual figure in the era when Harlem served as the cultural center of black America. But he was also a man of parts who had been school principal and practicing lawyer in his native Jacksonville, had served as a U.S. consul in Central America and from 1916 to 1930 was field secretary and then executive secretary of the NAACP.

Johnson rejected all the separatist schemes that emerged in the twenties—Marcus Garvey's back to Africa movement, the Communist Party's espousal of a black soviet, and his colleague Du Bois's call for a black polity—but Johnson also rejected Washington's accommodating stance, declaring segregation in any form unacceptable. "The only salvation worth achieving," he wrote, "lies in the making of the race into a component part of the nation, with all the common rights and privileges, as well as duties, of citizenship."

The salvation he envisioned necessarily included whites. In *Negro Americans, What Now?*, written in 1934 after he had returned to Fisk, he called on blacks to "use all our powers to abolish imposed segregation, for it is an evil *per se* and the negation of equality."

White America cannot save itself if it prevents us from being saved. No self-respecting Negro American should admit even tacitly that he is unfit to be associated with by fellow humans.

Each one can stand manfully on the ground that there should be nothing in law or opinion to prevent persons whose tastes and interests make them agreeable companions from associating together, if they mutually desire to do so.

Twenty years after his death in 1938, James Weldon Johnson's integrationist view, endowed with theological and Gandhian overtones, would provide the motive power for the dawning civil rights movement, and become for a time the prevailing political doctrine in the nation, supported by virtually all black Americans and a tentative majority of whites. But any such development seemed highly improbable when I first encountered Johnson's writings in the years before World War II.

He did confirm a conviction that fed my skepticism of the mythology on which I had been nurtured. I recognized, as did Booker T. Washington, that blacks had no means of effectively rejecting the place assigned to them in Southern society. But justification of the Southern Way of Life required that whites believe, or profess to believe, that blacks were content with their lot, and I had long since rejected the notion that any human being had ever willingly accepted slavery. Johnson provided a compelling reminder that this was no less true of its successor, second-class citizenship.

Discontent was undoubtedly endemic among Southern blacks in the 1930s, but there were no detectable signs of latent unrest. Grievances were aired in local Negro newspapers, but these were usually fly-by-night enterprises ignored by the white press. Even the best fell far short of providing a channel of communication that encouraged blacks to speak frankly, even to each other, on matters that might upset the whites on whom their livelihood depended.

Although the NAACP in time would begin to fill that void, in *An American Dilemma* Gunnar Myrdal noted that the organization had "nowhere been able to build up a mass following among Negroes. The membership is still confined to the upper clases." The Urban League, the other national organization concerned with the welfare of blacks, was dismissed as inconsequential by Myrdal's colleague Ralph Bunche:

As an interracial, dependent organization it can never develop a program which will spur the Negro masses and win their confidence. It operates strictly on the periphery of the Negro problem and never comes to grips with the fundamentals of American racial conflict.

The New South doctrine propagated by Henry Grady and endorsed by Booker T. Washington was firmly in place throughout the former Confederacy and acceptable everywhere in the nation. The respectable whites who dominated Southern society translated it into a form of paternalism described by Myrdal as

a social pattern which is personal, informal, determined by whimsy and the impulses of the moment, touched by humor and sentimentality, flattering the ego, but, nevertheless, not too expensive, [it] fits ideally into the individualistic and romantic temper of the region.

Although many blacks resented the patronizing imputation of inferiority, those in the South had no choice but to accept it. Paternalism represented the liberal view on race, at least by contrast, and it was held almost exclusively by men and women who in most other respects would be considered conservative. There was no tenable political position to their left: Southerners who believed in their hearts that there should be no social distinction between the races kept their heresy to themselves, or voiced it outside the region, where it had little support but was considered harmless.

A bastardized version of the Ku Klux Klan was resurgent after the dislocations of World War I, and firebrand race-baiters still mounted the stump, but the moderates who held or sought elective office never addressed them head-on. Their tactic was to treat white supremacy as so firmly entrenched as to be politically irrelevant, and they simply ignored the dark fancies peddled by the demagogues. Their supporters would accept their silence as disassociation when South Carolina's unreconstructed governor Coleman L. Blease endorsed lynch law, proclaiming, "Whenever the Constitution comes between me and the virtue of the white women of the South, I say to hell with the Constitution!" Officeholders left it to their allies among the newspaper editors, clergy, and civil leaders to denounce Blease for such a reckless invitation to mass murder. When a mob was actually in the streets, they usually could be counted on to take a stand in the name of law and order.

In the South, as everywhere in the nation, men of property ultimately dominated the political process: planters, industrialists, bankers, utility magnates, merchants, landlords, insurance agents, and the professional men who looked after their interests. They might lose an occasional skirmish to reformers who wanted to increase their taxes or impose legal limits on their operations, but never a major battle. If some were disgusted when the demagogues fired up the poor whites with their race-baiting, they had no reason to be alarmed since they knew they would be done no real harm.

Those who controlled the economy were always able to keep men in office who shared their pragmatism and could be counted on when their fortunes might be improved by government action. Thus, in the years when Cotton Ed Smith was inveighing against his party's national leadership, the other South Carolina senator, James Francis Byrnes, was serving as Franklin Roosevelt's legislative leader, employing his formidable political skills to shepherd administration measures through Congress and, in the process, guarantee that his state got a full share of federal bounty—and possibly a little more.

A poor Irish Catholic who grew up in Charleston, Jimmy Byrnes learned the law while working as a shorthand court reporter and moved on to hang out his shingle in the industrializing upcountry. In Greenville's neighboring city Spartanburg, he converted to the Episcopal faith and established what became an unassailable political base. From 1911 to 1925 he served in the lower house of Congress, returning to Washington as senator in 1931. In 1941 his faithful service to the Roosevelt administration was rewarded by appointment to the U.S. Supreme Court, but a year later he left the bench to join FDR in the White House as director of mobilization, the most powerful domestic post in the wartime government. In 1944, had he been able to clear the nomination with the labor leader Sidney Hillman, he probably would have become Roosevelt's fourth-term vice president and successor. As it was, he served the man who got Hillman's nod, Harry S. Truman, as secretary of state.

These were milestones in the career of a national politician of the first rank, and the contrast between this sophisticated Washington insider and the Claghorn caricature presented by his colleague was absolute. Similar disparities could be seen in the congressional delegations of all the former Confederate states. There were always posturing showmen to play the role of the firebrand Dixiecrat, but the senior Southern Democrats who dominated key committees of both houses generally avoided racial matters as best they could, and when they couldn't, treated them with all the restraint they thought their constituents would tolerate. If this seemed to indicate endemic schizophrenia among electors who voted for the likes of both Cotton Ed Smith and Jimmy Byrnes, it could be attributed to the paralyzing effect of the emotionally charged issue of race on rational political alignment.

Intellectuals, who usually shared the acerbic H. L. Mencken's view of the South as a Sahara of the Bozart dominated by a reigning boobocracy, were attracted to Washington in unprecedented numbers by the New Deal's reformist zeal. They were headed by the "brains trust" Roosevelt recruited from the Columbia University faculty in preparation for his presidential campaign, and other Ivy League academicians found places in the proliferating federal relief agencies. A few were adherents to Marxist social democratic theory, but most of those characterized as leftist came out of the American tradition that can best be defined as progressive.

Although it had been amended to a degree by the mass voting blocs produced by the influx of European immigrants and the rise of labor unions, the prevailing New Deal doctrine embraced the individualism and opposition to concentrated economic power espoused by Presidents Jefferson, Jackson, Theodore Roosevelt, and Woodrow Wilson. And all of these, except the Republican Roosevelt, were Southerners who occupied places in the region's political pantheon.

Southern Democrats had a natural affinity with the progressive movement that attained influence in both parties around the turn of the century by assailing the bankers, railroads, and industrial combines that dominated the national economy. These "malefactors of great wealth," as the first Roosevelt dubbed them, were seen as natural enemies of the agrarian interests of the South, the Midwest, and the sparsely settled states beyond the Rockies. Thus Wall Street, as depicted by the cartoon figure of a bloated capitalist with a tall silk hat and a vest spotted with dollar signs, had a place along with blacks, Jews, and Catholics among the whipping boys used by Dixie demagogues to rally poor whites.

The prime targets of populist protest during the early years of the century were located in what Southerners had always considered enemy territory. In the region's only manufacturing industry of consequence, most of the early cotton mills had passed to outside corporate ownership, and those that came later were transplants from New England. The landed gentry were still politically potent, but I doubt that there was a planter in South Carolina who could have liquidated his holdings for as much as a million dollars. There was no demurrer from the political leadership when Franklin Roosevelt termed the South the nation's number one economic problem.

It was not their racial view, but their failure to live up to the progressive creed, that accounted for the president's effort to part political company with the more reactionary Dixiecrats. Memoirs by the New Deal's principal figures bear out the observation of Tom Corcoran, the wily inside operator who represented the administration in negotiations with the congressional leadership: "There *wasn't* any race problem in the thirties. When Roosevelt came in in 1933, there were more important things to worry about than civil rights."

This reading was confirmed by the black leaders assembled at the White House early in 1933 by the president's wife, Eleanor, who became, and would remain, their most insistent champion in the administration's inner circle. It was the first real contact with either of the Roosevelts for Walter White of the NAACP, who was invited along with the black college presidents Mordecai Johnson of Howard, Robert Morton of Tuskegee, John Hope of Atlanta, and Charles Johnson of Fisk.

Joseph P. Lash, a youthful protégé of the First Lady who became her biographer, recalled that "the consensus of the group was that aid programs of the New Deal should come before desegregation, especially in the South." Will W. Alexander, the South's leading white advocate of interracial cooperation, who was destined to become one of Mrs. Roosevelt's confidants, testified that when he joined the government, "we had no real doctrine, except that we were not to discriminate in the distribution of benefits. . . . In the South we accepted the fact that Negroes usually lived in their own communities so we provided projects for them—Negro projects."

In his memoir *Dealers and Dreamers*, Lash recalled that caution on racial matters, if not indifference, was characteristic of those in the cabinet usually regarded as the leading advocates of social reform. Frances Perkins, who became the first female cabinet member when she was appointed secretary of labor, "dreaded dealing with the issue," and the secretary of agriculture, Henry Wallace, who would make desegregation the principal plank in his platform when he ran for president in 1948, was described as "terribly afraid." The only exception among those of the first rank was Secretary of the Interior Harold Ickes, an aging Bull Moose progressive.

Lash offered a succinct explanation for Eleanor Roosevelt's frustration in her effort to keep racial matters on the presidential agenda: "FDR was a political broker. Eleanor was a moralist." To all such importuning by his wife and her allies the president responded with a favorite aphorism: Politics is the art of the possible. "Political realities arrested the enthusiasm for civil rights that Roosevelt, a Georgian by adoption, did not feel," Lash wrote.

In the course of his long battle to overcome the crippling effects of polio, FDR had purchased property at Warm Springs, the Georgia spa where he underwent largely self-administered therapy for months at a time. When he included Walter George, the state's courtly senior senator, on his purge list, he had him at his side as he addressed a gathering of Georgia politicians and in effect apologized, expressing deep regret at having to break with "my dear friend."

The personal style of the Hudson River patroon meshed with the aristocratic manner assumed even by the most outspokenly racist of the senior Southern Democrats. I was on hand in 1940 when the president came to Columbia in the course of his third-term reelection campaign for a flag-waving tour of the Army's Camp Jackson training center, and I noted that when he greeted the assembled notables he reserved his warmest smile and heartiest handclasp for the venerable Cole Blease.

This was perhaps a reflex, for Blease was a political has-been by that time. But the president had a compelling reason to maintain his personal relationship with the Southern political leaders who had provided the delegates that guaranteed his nomination in 1932. Cotton Ed Smith had been one of those, and, as chairman of the Senate Agriculture Committee, he was in position to remind the president of his obligations.

Rexford Guy Tugwell, one of the original brains trusters and the leading advocate of central planning in the administration, had already been labeled Rex the Red by right-wing commentators when the president decided to appoint him to a newly created senior position as under secretary of agriculture. This guaranteed Tugwell a full-blown inquisition at his Senate confirmation hearing, and he recalled that when the ordeal was over,

> FDR, smiling broadly, said to me, "You will never know any more about it, I hope; but today I traded you for a couple of murderers." I do not to this day know precisely what the deal was with Senator Smith. I suspect it was for the appointment of federal marshals with doubtful records.

That, too, was trading in the coin of the political realm as it was, and is, practiced in Washington.

Black leaders, accepting the fact that any form of desegregation that implied social equality was out of the question, continued to press for civil rights legislation where this was not a factor—notably a federal antilynching law, and a ban on the poll tax as a device for disfranchising blacks. The president remained adamant, but Eleanor Roosevelt managed to keep the black cause alive. She saw to it that talented young blacks, often those recommended by Walter White, were appointed as advisers in the relief agencies. They made up an informal "black cabinet" headed by Robert Weaver, the first of his race to earn a doctorate in economics at Harvard, who was given a place at Interior, and Mary McLeod Bethune, president of Bethune-Cookman College, who became director of the Division of Negro Affairs of the National Youth Administration.

Eleanor also found allies among white Southerners appointed to key places in the expanding bureaucracy. These were instrumental in assuring that blacks were not dealt out of the federal bounty by local administrators. Weaver, who thirty years later became the first black cabinet member, could report to the NAACP in 1939 that blacks made up 10 percent of Civilian Conservation Corps enrollment, while 390,000 were employed by the Works Progress Administration, 5,000 were teaching literacy, and 10,000 were enrolled in WPA nursery schools. Vernon Jordan, who grew up to head the National Urban League, recalled that his mother was "ecstatic" when the family was admitted to Georgia's first public housing project. It was segregated, of course, but they had never before had a place to live that was clean and warm.

The senior white Southerner in Eleanor Roosevelt's circle, Will Alexander, was also a moralist. Beginning his Methodist ministry in Nashville, he had become convinced that racism and poverty were the region's besetting twin evils. In 1919 he established the Commission on Interracial Cooperation and dedicated it to their eradication.

Alexander endowed the organization with respectability by recruiting prominent supporters among his fellow men of the cloth, including the Episcopal bishop of Mississippi, and the presidents of Baptist Wake Forest University in North Carolina and Methodist Randolph-Macon in Virginia. Appeals to the Christian conscience characterized the commission's public utterances, but factual underpinning was provided by two of the South's leading sociologists, Thomas J. Woofter, Jr., and Arthur F. Raper, who, along with their academic colleagues, undertook studies of current conditions on the racial front.

The commission, with headquarters in Atlanta and chapters in thirteen Southern states, attained a membership of seven thousand. But it was hardly more than a loose coalition of moderates united primarily by their abhorrence of the brutality represented by lynching. It is noteworthy, however, that during its twenty-four years of existence the annual total of deaths from mob violence dropped from seventy-six to three, and would never be reckoned in double digits again.

The commission went into eclipse in 1935, when it lost its prime mover. Alexander was summoned to Washington to serve as chief assistant to Rex Tugwell in the new Resettlement Administration, charged with leading landless black and white farmers out of the South's moribund sharecropping system. He raided the commission's Atlanta staff for new recruits for Eleanor Roosevelt's coterie. Among them was Clark

Howell Foreman, grandson of the publisher of the *Atlanta Constitution*, for whom the tightfisted Ickes made a place as an adviser at Interior when he was assured that his salary would be covered by a grant from the Rosenwald Fund.

Foreman, convinced that the time had come to move Southern progressives to a new plateau in their search for social justice, used Mrs. Roosevelt's political clout to bring together a set of shakers and movers with veterans of the Interracial Commission movement. The founding session of the Southern Conference on Human Welfare (SCHW) was held at Birmingham in November 1938, with Governor Bibb Graves of Alabama on hand to greet twelve hundred invited delegates, a fifth of whom were black.

Hugo Black, now a justice of the U.S. Supreme Court; his former Senate colleagues Lister Hill of Alabama and Claude Pepper of Florida, and President Frank Porter Graham of the University of North Carolina were sponsors. Included on the list were such journalistic heavyweights as John Temple Graves of the *Birmingham Age-Herald*, and Mark Ethridge and Barry Bingham of the *Louisville Courier-Journal*.

The conference convened in good order on a Sunday, and blacks and whites mingled freely on the assumption that Birmingham's segregation ordinances could be ignored in such prestigious company. The next day, however, Police Commissioner Theophilus Eugene Connor made his first appearance in the national media, arriving at Municipal Auditorium with fifteen policemen under orders to start making arrests unless the two races regrouped in separate seating. The black and white delegates "voluntarily" agreed to sit on opposite sides of the hall. The conference then voted never to hold a segregated meeting again, but "Bull" Connor had made his point, creating the headlines that forced upon the organization a race-mixing image that scared off respectable support.

Frank Graham, the Southern liberal best equipped to salvage the fledgling venture, accepted the chairmanship. He was a remarkable combination of Christian charity, old shoe country charm, sheer guts, and unswerving devotion to academic excellence, who had been conditioned by experience at beating back North Carolina's Bourbon leadership in defense of the South's least inhibited and most distinguished university faculty.

Graham stuck to the moderate line on segregation, asserting that the SCHW's purpose was to promote social justice for blacks, not social equality. Suffrage was brought completely out of the closet, however, with poll tax repeal at the top of the agenda. A vigorous lobbying and publicity campaign drew support from national labor unions and civil rights organizations, politicizing the organization in a fashion the Interracial Commission had managed to avoid. Increasingly isolated, the SCHW hung on for another ten years, but it never recovered from its early wounds and in the end served only as a refuge for the few genuine radicals visible on the Southern scene.

I had frequent opportunity to compare notes with Rex Tugwell after he returned to academia and began setting forth his analysis of the Roosevelt era in a series of highly regarded memoirs. He felt that the New Deal never lived up to its promise. Had Roosevelt been less willing to compromise with the Southern Democrats, he contended, enduring progress might have been made in reshaping the central government to deal with the structural economic and social problems brought into sharp focus by the Great Depression. Instead, there was a patchwork of short-range relief measures that never addressed the deep-seated demographic changes resulting from the transformation of an agrarian society into an industrial power of continental proportions.

But this would have meant facing up to the racial issues underlying the regional political divisions that blocked the solutions Tugwell and others advocated. And that would have required a degree of popular support for desegregation that did not exist anywhere in the nation. A graphic example was provided when Norman Thomas, the Socialist Party leader, tried to rally leftist backing for the racially integrated Southern Tenant Farmers' Union (STFU) formed by white and black sharecroppers in the plantation country of the Mississippi delta.

Stately mansions scattered along both banks of the great river still housed families that preserved the cultural patterns of the Old South. But the humane traditions of the feudal society that had its roots on the Eastern Seaboard had vanished for most of the blacks who labored in the western reaches of the Cotton Kingdom. Their fate was now determined by absentee landlords, among them corporations first formed to harvest the timber that originally covered the rich, black alluvial soil. On plantations such as the seventeen-hundred-acre spread owned by the Chapman and Dewey Lumber Company, the field hands did not deal with a genteel master in the big house, but with riding bosses who patrolled the fields on horseback.

Tyronza, in the heart of the East Arkansas plantation belt, struck Norman Thomas as *Uncle Tom's Cabin* revisited when he went there to address a group of sharecroppers. His passionate speech inspired the formation of the union that came into being in July 1934, and he became its national advocate during its brief existence. When he toured the region in 1935, resistance to the organizing effort had formed, and he encountered multiple reincarnations of Simon Legree, the depraved plantation overseer in Harriet Beecher Stowe's antislavery novel.

At a union rally in a black church at Birdsong, three dozen armed white men forced their way to the front and shouted Thomas down as soon as he was introduced. A voice bespeaking their sentiment came through loud and clear: "We don't need no Gawd-damn Yankee bastard to tell us what to do with our niggers. . . . There ain't going to be no speaking here." And there wasn't. A deputy sheriff stepped out of the mob and ordered the meeting adjourned, saying, "I cannot protect these innocent women and children." Carloads of armed thugs chased the fleeing Thomas and his companions to the county line.

The doomed union movement was a desperate response to the move by the federal Agricultural Adjustment Administration to prop up depressed commodity prices by paying farmers to decrease production. When ten million acres of cultivated cotton land were plowed under to create an artificial scarcity, the owners received compensation for the loss of the crops, while many of the tenants were deprived not only of the $216 annual cash income they averaged in 1933, but of their homes as well.

Lawyers in the Agriculture Department who drafted the AAA contracts held that they required that tenants be allowed to remain on the land and directly receive their share of government payments on the same basis that would have prevailed had the crop been harvested. But they were overruled, and the checks were sent to the landlords with no requirement for an accounting.

Thomas had attempted to plead the tenants' case with Henry Wallace, pressing for enforcement of widely ignored provisions of Section

7 of the AAA contract requiring planters to "endeavor to bring about reduction so as to cause the least possible amount of labor, economic and social disturbance." Wallace refused to concede that the AAA was at fault, and fired Jerome Frank, the department's leading lawyer, and two of his associates when they insisted that the authority provided by the contracts could and should be used to end the abuses.

Rex Tugwell sided with Frank and offered his resignation to the president, but was persuaded to stay on and head the new Resettlement Administration, which would take another approach to relieving the plight of the sharecroppers. Explaining to Norman Thomas why the landlords had prevailed, Tugwell plaintively asked, "What in the world would you do, if you had to deal with . . . such people as 'Cotton Ed' Smith and Joe Robinson?" The latter, an Arkansan, was the Senate majority leader.

When the Socialist Party's executive committee mounted a public appeal to President Roosevelt for an investigation of the "reign of terror" against the STFU, the response came from Wallace, who said it would be difficult for the federal government to step into a local controversy. "A government that has interfered as extensively as yours has in the cotton economy of the South," Thomas replied, "has a moral responsibility to act in view of the wholesale evictions I have seen with my own eyes."

Thomas tried an end run thorugh Felix Frankfurter, the influential Harvard law professor who became a Supreme Court justice, but got only an expression of sympathy. Thomas was also turned down when he urged Senator Robert F. Wagner of New York to include agricultural workers in the National Labor Relations Act, which was regarded as the unions' Magna Carta. He did persuade William Green, head of the American Federation of Labor, to join in the call for a federal investigation into "the inhuman level to which the workers in the cotton fields have been reduced." But as Thomas's biographer Harry Fleischman noted, "the unions failed to give any substantial aid to the hard-pressed Southern Tenant Farmers' Union."

Thomas finally attracted enough national media attention to the cause of the embattled sharecroppers to prompt Franklin Roosevelt to grant him a private audience. Fleischman described the result:

Thomas asked the President if he had read the AAA's Cotton Acreage Reduction Contract clause, which had allegedly been written by the manager of one of the world's largest plantations. Roosevelt said that he had not. "Would you mind reading it?" asked Thomas. "Certainly," replied Roosevelt. . . .

Roosevelt handed the contract back to Thomas, half laughing, and said, "That can mean everything or nothing, can't it?" Replied Thomas, "In this case, Mr. President, nothing. Over at the Agriculture Department they have just fired Jerome Frank, Gardner Jackson and Lee Pressman, partly because they tried to make this contract mean something."

Roosevelt, a little impatiently, interrupted Thomas and said, "Oh, Norman, I'm a damned sight better politician than you are." Thomas made the obvious retort, "Certainly, Mr. President, you are on that side of the table and I'm on this." Roosevelt ignored this and went on to say, "I know the South and there is arising a new generation of leaders in the South and you've got to be patient."

The admonition soon became moot. The widespread isolationist sentiment that had kept the country theoretically neutral after World War II began in Europe evaporated after the Japanese attack on Pearl Harbor in December 1941. As the nation plunged into the global conflict, the president told a press conference that Dr. New Deal had been replaced by Dr. Win-the-War: "The remedies that old Dr. New Deal used were for internal trouble. But at the present time, obviously the principal interest, the overwhelming emphasis should be on winning the war." After victory, reform would again be in order, "but we don't want to confuse people by talking about it now."

At a press conference of her own, Eleanor Roosevelt demurred. She was not prepared to "lay the New Deal away in lavender." Of course, it had "become rather old, rather stable, and permanent, too, in many ways," she said, but the country still needed something more than win-the-war. For the rest of her life she continued to speak out in support of social justice for the black minority, but she and her husband were gone from the White House before the race issue finally found a place on the nation's political agenda.

DIVERSION
THE UPHEAVAL OF WORLD WAR II

DEATH REVEALED: The New Deal, 10, after long illness; of malnutrition and desuetude. Child of the 1932 election campaign, the New Deal, after four healthy years, began to suffer from spots before its eyes in 1937, and never fully recovered from the shock of war. Last week its father, Franklin Roosevelt, pronounced it dead.

—*Time*, January 6, 1941

THE NATIONAL MOBILIZATION that brought victory in World War II was a watershed in the politics of race, although this would not register on the national consciousness until the Dixiecrats rallied in its aftermath for their final stand. For reasons of philosophy as well as expediency, civil rights—pressed to the point where consideration of desegregation became inevitable—had no place on the presidential agenda during Franklin Roosevelt's first two terms. In the late thirties, as he weighed the decision to run for an unprecedented third, all domestic political considerations gave way to his preoccupation with shoring up the Allies in their losing battle against the Axis.

Beneath the surface, however, attitudes were changing along with the demography that had shaped the two major political parties since the Civil War. The erosion of the peculiar institutions that gave the Old South its identity was well advanced, and revisionist historians had begun to reject the assumption that there had ever been anything approximating a monolithic Solid South. Firsthand exposure to South Carolina's hermetic political system had led me to a similar conclusion. I doubt that I would have experienced a similar revelation—certainly not as soon as I did—had I been reared in the Deep South, where the agrarian economy remained dominant and pressure for conformity was strongest.

My growing skepticism set me apart from the prevailing view, but it was not necessarily a mark of heresy in the foothill and mountain areas of the upper tier of Confederate states. Plantations were comparatively few in what we called the upcountry, and were usually much more modest than those that arose on the coastal plains and the rich, river-laced alluvial soil that stretches across Alabama and Mississippi into the delta lands of Arkansas and Louisiana and down into East Texas.

Greenville County is situated at the apex of the South Carolina triangle that thrusts into the Appalachians where the highland regions of Georgia, North Carolina, and Tennessee converge. The Piedmont section of the South, angling down along the base of the mountains, is the historic domain of the Scotch-Irish, those displaced Scots who began arriving in the 1700s from the Ulster counties of Northern Ireland. It was protestant country in politics as well as religion, and never shared the episcopal pretensions of the lowcountry, where the seaboard settlers brought with them the slave-based plantation culture fashioned in the Caribbean colonies of England and France.

At the founding of the Republic the Scotch-Irish constituted a considerable majority of the 115,534 whites who, along with 29,679 blacks, populated South Carolina above the fall line, and they were already at odds with the 28,644 whites in the lowcountry, whose plantation economy was sustained by 79,216 slaves. Until it was an accomplished fact, the upcountry's political leaders opposed secession, although they never joined with those in the mountain strongholds of North Carolina, Tennessee, and Arkansas, where Whig enclaves turned Republican and contributed troops to the Union Army.

At Clemson I had encountered *Southern Regions of the United*

States, an influential 1936 work by Howard W. Odum, the University of North Carolina sociologist who would head the Southern Regional Council when it emerged as successor to the Commission on Interracial Cooperation. Odum replaced the traditional magnolia-scented view of a monolithic South with a much more diverse regional concept. Lopping off Texas and adding Kentucky to the old Confederacy, he labeled this the Southeast—one of six cohesive regions of the United States he thought could be transformed by the new planning tools coming into use by the New Deal agencies.

Within the region, he wrote, "there were many Souths, yet *the* South. It was preeminently national in backgrounds, yet provincial in its processes. . . ." In his later writing he noted that only in the black belt and the Mississippi delta did the plantation system have primary economic importance, and even there it did not represent the way of life for the majority of whites:

> Among the important neglected factors in the interpretation of the agrarian South is that of the large number of upper middleclass non-slaveholding white folk who constituted the backbone of reconstruction and recovery. Their contributions were definitive in the regional culture. It was upon their sturdy character and persistent work that the "New South" was largely built.

Greenville in many ways epitomized the New South. The Piedmont region's proximity to the mountains provided abundant water and hydroelectric power, and some of the earliest cotton mills were established there. By 1934 there were ninety-two thousand textile workers in North Carolina, seventy thousand in South Carolina, and fifty-five thousand in Georgia. Factories transplanted from New England to exploit the abundance of cheap labor were located in self-contained villages outside Greenville's city limits, and there the companies owned the houses and supporting facilities provided for a work force made up of white men, women, and children displaced by the declining farm economy.

These anti-union redoubts made Greenville County the state's most populous, and by the time of World War I the city had proclaimed itself "The Textile Center of the South." Atop the Chamber of Commerce building an American flag made up of colored lights blinked the slogan

"My Country First, Then Greenville." This was a significant departure from the sentiment Major John William De Forest of the 12th Connecticut Volunteers noted in *A Union Officer in the Reconstruction*, an account of his experience as head of the Freedman's Bureau during the Yankee occupation of the South Carolina upcountry. He quoted a leading citizen who summed up the view that prevailed in 1866:

> I go first for Greenville, then for the Greenville district, then for the upcountry, then for South Carolina, then for the South, then for the United States; and after that, I don't go for anything. I've no use for Englishmen, Turks and Chinese.

In my time the growing city had not yet severed its ties with the agrarian past. The doomed effort to raise cotton on the exhausted red soil of the foothills went on as before. The cotton mills had provided a refuge for many of the poor whites, but one-horse farmers still tried to make a living on the few leached acres that represented the family inheritance from six generations of hard labor, and there were white and black sharecroppers on the larger tracts.

My grandparents had moved from farm to city to improve opportunities for their children, but some of my parents' siblings stayed behind on the home places. During summer vacations from grade school my older brother and I were put aboard the Piedmont and Northern interurban train and dispatched to Belton, twenty-five miles to the south, in Anderson County, where we were met by Uncle Hayne Lewis and my mother's sister Aunt Tee (for Tecora), and driven to the plantation where, in collaboration with some twenty black families, the Lewises farmed fifteen hundred acres.

Looking back, I can see that this operation was an anachronism. The rolling land, never well suited for row crops, was rapidly shedding its topsoil, and erosion was cutting gullies deep into the red earth. Cotton prices had begun the downward slide that would soon go past the break-even point, and out there in the far reaches of the section called "Possum Kingdom" you could hear the work song's mournful refrain, "Ten-cent cotton and forty-cent meat/How in hell can a poor man eat?"

But in the long days of those summer visits the old place seemed idyllic to a city boy. It was layby time, with work largely suspended in the fields, and we were each assigned a black of similar age who served as guide and protector as we roamed the fields and explored the wooded hollows. Mine was Nathaniel, and although we have been lost to each other for more than half a century, he has remained vivid in my memory. He was waiting each morning when I came out after breakfast, and at noon he shared the meal handed out to us on the back porch, where we sat on the floor among the sleeping beagles, bare feet dangling over the edge of the weathered boards.

There was a limited equality in this relationship. When we raced for some common objective or wrestled on a grassy slope, he was not expected to give quarter and usually won. In all aspects of woodcraft, and the sexual and other intriguing habits of the animal population, Nathaniel was clearly my superior, but I, in my turn, could tell him of things he had never seen and could hardly imagine. On my side the consciousness of racial difference vanished under this intimacy, but I doubt that it ever did on his, for he could not forget that when dark came on and we headed home he would pass on to a shack across the road as I turned into the big house to join those who, although they no longer had legal claim to the title, were his masters.

Yet at all levels the white and black worlds overlapped. The plantation had come down from the past typical of the upcountry pattern, comparable only in function to the great estates maintained by the lowcountry grandees. The two-story big house was plain and square, with long porches front and back; it was served by a well, a privy, and a springhouse for cooling milk and butter, lit by kerosene lamps, and heated by fireplaces and the great wood range in the kitchen. There were sheltering mulberry trees, and grass and flowering shrubs in the front yard, but the ground to the rear was mostly bare dirt where chickens, geese, turkeys, ducks, and guinea hens left deposits to be scraped off bare feet. Beyond were the smokehouse, hogpens, barns, stables, corn cribs, a shop that housed a blacksmith and a carpenter, and a commissary where the sharecroppers drew their rations. All these, like the tenant houses that dotted the fields, were innocent of paint and had long ago weathered to a soft silver gray. These were the accouterments of a self-sufficient community, and it was the only home many of the blacks had ever known.

The sharecropping system has been duly condemned as a form of serfdom that effectively bound blacks to the land and left them subject to exploitation by unscrupulous planters. Yet it was also an accommodation born of necessity in the aftermath of a lost war. Whites owned the productive land, but their capital and credit had been wiped out; freedmen, who had no other market for their agricultural skills, provided labor on loan, receiving in return subsistence and, in theory if not always in practice, a share of the profit when the crop was sold. As I saw it in the 1920s, sharecropping was producing precious little return for either party.

Uncle Hayne owned a Model T Ford, but this was the only piece of modern machinery on the place, and it was useful only for necessary trips to Belton. The roads over which he made his dawn-to-dusk tours to oversee the work in the fields were so bad he traveled by buggy. Mules drew the plows, and the planting, weeding, and picking were done by men, women, and children, so that a substantial portion of the cultivated acreage had to be kept in subsistence crops to feed the animals and the hands. One ate well in the big house, where there were bountiful supplies of home-cured meat, poultry, game, garden produce, fruits, and berries, but that was about all that could be said for the master's life-style. I doubt that any comparable investment of capital, energy, and constant worry would have produced so miserable a return in terms of cash or comfort.

The owners, no less than the tenants, were trapped. There was no way to make the operation more efficient without destroying its basic character—and this, of course, is what did happen when tractors, increasingly sophisticated farm implements, pesticides, and weed-killing chemicals began to transform all of American agriculture. This was a process that would benefit the surviving few by dispensing with the services of the many—making displaced persons of whites and blacks whose roots were generations deep in the land.

Before the wave of the mechanized future reached Possum Kingdom, Uncle Hayne and Aunt Tee had given up, and the old planter spent his last days vegetating on the front porch of a little house on the edge of Greenville. I can only assume that Nathaniel was caught up in the great diaspora that in our lifetime has denuded the Southern countryside of people and repopulated the slums of major American cities.

. . .

Blacks joined in the migration from farm to city, and, although some-what modified, the country-bred sense of community endured. In the 1920s Greenville's population was about one fourth black. The blacks worked as domestic servants and menial laborers, or found places in low-paid service trades as cooks, waiters, barbers, or porters. As best they could in their straitened circumstances, most adapted to the life-style of the whites.

Barred from better-paying jobs, they were forced to work for sub-sistence wages, with the result that Southern city dwellers of modest means could retain servants on a scale unknown in any but the most affluent households elsewhere. I have fond memories of the cook who presided over our kitchen, the nurse who tended me until my legs grew long enough to take me beyond her reach, the yardman, the washer-woman, the iceman, and assorted occasional helpers who tended to our needs. This permitted—indeed, required—a sustained personal inter-action between whites and blacks that existed nowhere else in the nation.

In the city, as it had been in the country, the relationship was that of master and servant, and the rules were laid down by the whites. But it was characterized on both sides by good manners, and this at least reflected a concern for the feelings of those in the inferior position. One of the few whippings I can remember was administered by my mother when I used the proscribed "nigger" in the presence of a black. If the pay was low and the hours long, I doubt that their treatment was any harsher than that accorded domestic servants anywhere. And certainly the professed bonds of mutual affection were something more than convenient fictions to improve the lot of the black and ease the con-science of the white.

Old Uncle Ben, a former slave, was kept on as a retainer by one of my uncles long after he had passed beyond any productive work. When he died we were dressed in our Sunday best and taken to the African Methodist Episcopal church for the funeral, and I cannot doubt that the tears that flowed down white cheeks were evidence of genuine, shared grief.

In retrospect, the social segregation implicit in the Southern Way of Life does not seem to me inherently evil. It was defensible as a necessary bridge in the Negro's passage from slavery to citizenship, which could not conceivably have been made in a single generation. What was indefensible was the white South's refusal to recognize that in practice the effort to translate custom into law did not grant to the black South any effective guarantee of human dignity.

For blacks, segregation came to mean deprivation. They did not get their fair share of the public bounty; they were not accorded equal treatment before the law; they were not allowed to participate in the conduct of public affairs that concerned them no less than their white neighbors; and they were blocked out of virtually all activities that promised economic advancement.

These conditions might have been tolerable as temporary measures, but the system that evolved with the restoration of states' rights proved to be inflexible. The effort to adjust it to changing conditions failed, and in the end it made no provision for judging a black person on the basis of demonstrated merit, but lumped the best with the worst. And it ensured its ultimate destruction by allowing blacks sufficient freedom to encourage a steady elevation of their aspirations while it stubbornly withheld the means of realizing them.

There was an element of noblesse oblige in the conventions that shaped interaction between the races, and in the romantic mythology of the Old South it had been stretched to portray slavery as a means of introducing benighted African savages to the blessings of Christian civilization. Assuming that the prevailing culture could be called blessed, this was the result, at least to a degree. In 1860 the enrollment of South Carolina's Baptist, Methodist, Presbyterian, and Episcopal denominations included 72,000 adult slaves and freedmen, and many more of the black population of about 400,000 were informal communicants.

But the notion that salvation of black souls was a primary purpose of slavery was palpably absurd, and it became more so as it was carried over to the effort to rationalize legalized segregation. The vaunted civility of Southern communities depended on the use of force when there was a real or perceived threat that blacks might seek to rise above their assigned place. There had been no real prospect of any such wholesale insurrection before the Civil War, when blacks were subject to the absolute control the political system vested in their owners. Mounted patrols of state militia—"paterollers," the blacks called them—saw to it that slaves remained within the isolated fiefdoms that made up the plantation belt.

With defeat, and the military occupation that followed, all the safeguards of the old social order disappeared. Radical policy inspired by the moral fervor of the abolitionists prevailed during the period of congressional Reconstruction that followed the conciliatory administration of Abraham Lincoln. Blacks were enfranchised, and all those who had supported the Confederacy—which meant the vast majority of whites—were disfranchised. The avowed purpose was to "put the bottom rail on top."

But few of the blacks ever achieved such elevation, and those who did found control of government still in the hands of whites—Northern "carpetbaggers" who came South to improve their fortunes, and Southern "scalawags" who were willing to suffer the opprobrium of their peers to share in the spoils of war. Not surprisingly, the displaced Southern whites proved to be unwilling to accept their assigned place on the bottom rail.

The former Confederates who saw their mission as saving the white South from perdition were called Redeemers. The leaders were the plantation gentry, and they donned red shirts or the white robes of the Ku Klux Klan as they rode forth to remove blacks from the political process. The object was intimidation, and it was not achieved without doing bodily harm. The historian Guy B. Johnson found "Reconstruction in a sense a prolonged race riot," and estimated the black death toll at five thousand. But the Redeemers were not out for vengeance; they regarded the mass of blacks as fellow victims of the new dispensation, and sought to establish a place for them that would permit the peaceful coexistence of two races they regarded as inherently unequal.

In 1984 Joel Williamson, a historian at the University of North Carolina, summarized twenty years of study of the peculiar Southern mind-set produced by its development in what he termed *The Crucible of Race*, in the title of his book. Central to his effort was definition of the usual political categories as they applied to the organic society that grew out of the fusion of white and black cultures. Williamson found the ethos that prevailed to his own day to be profoundly conservative; based on "the assumption of Negro inferiority . . . it looked quite literally to the conservation of the Negro. It sought to save him by defining and fixing his place in American society."

This was the motivation of the Redeemers, and it prevailed when Reconstruction ended with the "Compromise of 1877," the political deal between Republicans and Democrats that, in C. Vann Woodward's telling phrase, "signaled the abandonment of principles and force and a return to the traditional ways of compromise and concession." In return for withdrawal of the occupying federal troops, reenfranchised Southern Democrats accepted voting by blacks.

My grandfather Ashmore had served in Hampton's Legion, and he again answered the call when the Confederate hero became the leader of the Redeemers. They scorned the lodge hall trappings of the Ku Klux Klan and rode forth at night unmasked, identifying themselves as "paterollers" by donning red shirts. When he successfully ran for governor in 1876, Hampton set forth a platform described in a campaign brochure titled *Free Men! Free Ballots! Free Schools!!! The Pledges of Gen. Wade Hampton to the Colored People of South Carolina*.

Hampton and those of like mind who took office across the South were characterized by Williamson as liberal. They amended conservative doctrine to reject the idea of inherent black inferiority, and called for opening educational and economic opportunities to all who sought them. "As the Negro becomes more intelligent," Hampton said, "he naturally allies himself with the more conservative whites." Under his leadership there was no effort to impose demeaning segregation in public facilities.

The policy of toleration carried with it no implication of social equality for blacks, nor did it presage any relaxation of the taboo against racial amalgamation that prevailed everywhere in the United States. Liberals and conservatives alike simply dismissed the idea that freedmen constituted a threat to white supremacy. This was not raised as a political issue until the turn of the century, when it became enmeshed in the radical protest movement that exploded in all the agrarian regions of the country.

Collapse of the farm economy produced a political revolt directed against the dominant financial and manufacturing interests centered in the cities, with whom the Redeemers had become identified. When it produced a full-blown third party, the Populists, there was an effort to base the Southern wing on a white-black coalition. But the resistance of those Williamson termed Southern radicals imposed a militant anti-Negro stance on the movement that effectively limited the Populist Party as a political force to Midwestern and Western states.

The Victorian concept of female chastity as a safeguard of ethnic purity gave a powerful thrust to the radicals' insistence that blacks, freed of the restraints of slavery and encouraged by the egalitarian preachment of Yankee interlopers during Reconstruction, now constituted a threat to white Southern womanhood. Insofar as this had any relation to reality, it played on the fears aroused, particularly among isolated farm women, by the bedraggled black men who wandered throughout the region looking for means of subsistence that eluded many of those who had not succeeded in acquiring land of their own.

Most of the radical leaders were apostate planters who had come to prominence with the Redeemers. Although the nickname "Pitchfork Ben" identified him as a horny-handed son of the soil, Benjamin Ryan Tillman came of a family whose thirty-five hundred acres and eighty-six slaves placed him in the South Carolina aristocracy. But the base of the political support that enabled him to unseat Wade Hampton in 1890 was provided by his exploitation of the poor whites' ingrained antipathy for blacks.

As Hampton's successor in the statehouse and the U.S. Senate, where he served until his death in 1918, Tillman was preeminent among those who changed the benign image presented to the nation by the Redeemers. His Senate colleagues were treated to a hair-raising portrayal of black men as depraved brutes driven by "the desire to sate their passions upon white maidens and wives." Williamson cited a 1907 Senate speech by Tillman as typifying the radical response to protests against the unprecedented wave of lynchings and less organized assaults on blacks during the first quarter of the century.

When Southerners heard that a white woman had been raped by a black, Tillman proclaimed, "Our brains reel with the staggering blow and hot blood surges to the heart. . . . We revert to the original savage."

There could be no resort to law, for testimony at a trial would be a "second crucifixion" for the victim:

> I have three daughters, but so help me God I would rather find either one of them killed by a tiger or a bear and gather up her bones and bury them, conscious that she had died in the purity of her maidenhood, than to have her crawl to me and tell me the horrid story that she had been robbed of the jewel of her womanhood by a black fiend.

A Freudian would hold, I suppose, that there was no reason to question Tillman's sincerity, since his passionate defense of white womanhood was consonant with the mores of the time. Yet there is also no reason to doubt that the invocation of these horrific images provided an expedient means of maintaining a political following held together by resentment of poor whites against all the malevolent forces they perceived to be responsible for their miserable lot.

The virulent anti-Negro bias of the radical movement was never more than a transient element in Southern politics, although Williamson contended that it gained sufficient force between 1889 and 1915 to cancel out the accommodationist mind-set he defined as liberal. The result was that the old conservative credo based on white supremacy was again in full force and effect, but, if not so openly defined, this was also true throughout the nation. It sustained the resulting segregation of the races just as effectively outside the South as it did where the law required it.

The assumption that the mythology of the Old South had such a paralyzing effect on the Southern mind that it left three generations of Southerners blind to the vast changes that were taking place at all levels of their society has not yet yielded to the revisionist historians who began to challenge it in the 1930s. Williamson didn't really try to lay it to rest, and the documentation that lends *The Crucible of Race* distinction seemed to me to leave in question some of his conclusions.

By 1909, Ben Tillman was complaining in a speech to his South Carolina constituents that they were being misled by their own newspapers: "Under the lead of those editors, who were many of them in knee-breeches when we were in the throes of the Reconstruction era, the rising generation has been taught that we have no race problem and there is no possible danger from Negroes now." The editors were simply recognizing the evident fact that any possible danger of effective challenge to white dominance had ended with the disfranchisement of blacks made possible by the Supreme Court's reinstatement of the states' rights doctrine.

White Republicans in the South, with the acquiescence of their national leaders, disbanded their "black and tan" following and stopped competing with the Democrats in the general elections, paying off the black leaders by cutting them in on the federal patronage they controlled when there was a Republican in the White House. In the 1930s, when I went to cover the Republican state convention in Columbia, it consisted of a handful of well-dressed whites and blacks assembled in a lodge hall upstairs over a pool hall. When it came time to elect the state central committee there weren't enough present to fill all the places, and a black delegate put me in nomination, saying he didn't know my name but could see that I had a fine Republican face.

It followed that the criminal justice system, which had been fashioned to serve the purpose, was again fully capable of keeping blacks in their assigned place. There was no reason to doubt the ability of the police and courts to maintain the established social order. The purity of white womanhood hardly required, if it ever did, the services of men to whom the constraints of law, religious faith, or social custom had no application as far as blacks were concerned.

Major De Forest, the perceptive Connecticut Yankee who headed the Freedman's Bureau in Greenville, took note of the source of most of those who continued to be imbued with the radical faith. Among the whites he dealt with in the aftermath of the war he identified a small, aristocratic upperclass, a substantial middleclass—"semi-chivalrous Southrons," he called them—and a third group effectively cut off from both. Whites at the bottom of the social scale were epitomized by "the dull, unlettered, hopeless English farm laborer grown wild, indolent, and nomadic on new land and under the discouraging competition of slavery."

These were progenitors of the "rednecks" who, by choice or circumstance, continued to have little contact with blacks—or with more affluent whites—until my own day. Initially they were left behind when more favored countrymen found places in the expanding cities and towns. Those who populated remote mountain areas simply declared their domain off-limits to any but their own kind. The white share-croppers and marginal small farmers had no reason to traffic with blacks, and to have done so would have robbed them of the distinction a white skin provided on the lower levels of the social pecking order. And those who sought refuge in the mill villages remained isolated; the proprietors did not allow blacks in the workplace or permit them to settle in company-owned housing.

"Redneck" became the contemptuous generic term applied by more affluent whites (and privately by blacks) to the poor whites who distilled moonshine liquor on the mountain slopes, scratched out a living as sharecroppers, or prowled the lowland swamps with shotgun and fishing pole. Those whose necks grew pale when they submitted to the more disciplined life of the mill villages were denigrated as "lintheads."

W. J. Cash made heavy use of the stereotype in *The Mind of the South*, widely praised when it was published in 1941 and still generally accepted as definitive. "However much the blacks in the 'Big House' might sneer at him," he wrote, "and however much their masters might agree with them, he . . . would always be a white man. And before that vast and capacious distinction, all others were foreshortened, dwarfed, and all but obliterated." The redneck, as Cash portrayed him, was left with little more than an ambition

> to stand on his head in a bar, to toss down a pint of raw whiskey at a gulp, to fiddle and dance all night, to bite off the nose or gouge out the eye of a favorite enemy, to fight harder and love harder than the next man, and to be known eventually far and wide as a hell of a fellow. . . .

Men who fit the description did exist. They were to be found in the front ranks when a lynch mob gathered, and were admired by a sub-stantially larger number who were too inhibited to follow their lead. But Cash extended the stereotype to cover all Southern whites who could be classified as poor. "The grand outcome," he wrote, "was the almost complete disappearance of economic and social focus on the part of the masses."

Anyone attempting to plumb the psyche of the South had to deal with racism as a fact of regional life. "The story of the Negro in the South," Howard Odum wrote, "becomes, from the time of his coming to complicate the picture, the most decisive factor in the architecture of Southern culture." Cash interpreted this to mean that Southern whites, whether rich, poor, or in between, were deliberately and irrevocably yoked together in enforced ascendancy over blacks—a bond that was not weakened by the fact that the poor of both races were subject to exploitation by the upper classes.

In Cash's reading of history, Southerners were held together by what he called "the savage ideal" that emerged in the 1830s in response to the abolitionist attack on slavery. It required that dissent and variety be completely suppressed so that "men become in all their attitudes, professions and action virtual replicas of one another." He concluded that the ideal had been reinforced by Reconstruction to a point "unknown by any Western people since the decay of medieval feudalism, and almost as truly as it is established in Fascist Italy, in Nazi Germany, in Soviet Russia. . . ."

The Mind of the South was a polemic aimed at the icons of both the Old South and the New. Cash dismissed the pretensions of aristocracy among the plantation gentry as dubious, and in any case irrelevant, since they had long since been pushed aside by "horsetrading men." The new masters were typified by the "bastard barons," who in the name of progress had adapted the paternalistic plantation ethos to the textile mill villages of his native Carolina upcountry.

Cash's concerns were more aesthetic than social. He described Charlotte, where he had settled as literary critic and editorial writer for the *News*, as a "Calvinist Lhasa," hopelessly isolated from high culture by impenetrable bigotry and obscurantism, a natural haven for the poisonous Babbittry he saw as the predominant characteristic that set the New South apart from the Old. His portrayal of Charlotte had all the hallmarks of Sinclair Lewis's treatment of his fictional Zenith City, and it seemed to me to invalidate Cash's basic premise. The savage ideal could hardly be said to be in full force and effect in an urban South that was rapidly taking on the characteristics the industrial revolution had imposed on all American cities.

. . .

The black presence provided the catalyst that shaped the mind of the South as Cash read it, but blacks themselves were largely passed over in his view of the social landscape. His broadside attack on the white establishment, however, was enough to certify him as a champion of the black cause, and his biographer Joseph L. Morrison found that this became a source of embarrassment:

> He knew only too well that he was no activist; more than that he was thoroughly pessimistic about the chances for racial progress. . . . When Walter White thanked Cash on behalf of the NAACP, the author insisted that he had done nothing to deserve such gratitude.

What Cash had done was reinforce the simplified view of the South that prevailed outside the region. "His interpretation, seemingly licensed and let loose on the world by the South itself, immediately gained the high currency that it has long enjoyed," Joel Williamson wrote. "After 1941 if one needed to say something, almost anything, about the Southern ethos, he simply cited Cash and moved confidently and comfortably along."

This was impressed on me in pointed fashion, since I was in residence at the fountainhead of the abolitionist movement when *The Mind of the South* was published. As a Nieman Fellow at Harvard, I encountered a reaction not unlike that recounted by W. E. B. Du Bois, the most distinguished of the university's handful of black graduates. When New Englanders encountered him, he wrote in *The Souls of Black Folk*,

> they approach me in a half-hesitant sort of way, eye me curiously or compassionately, and then instead of saying directly, How does it feel to be a problem? they say, I know an excellent colored man in my town; or, I fought at Mechanicsville; or, Do not those Southern outrages make your blood boil? At these I smile, or am interested, or reduce the boiling to a simmer, as the occasion may require. To the real question, How does it feel to be a problem? I seldom answer a word.

In Cambridge I found that the possession of two Confederate grandfathers identified me as the other half of the problem Du Bois was not asked about. The response in my case usually involved a measure of compassion based on the assumption that my appointment to faculty status at Harvard certified an enlightened view on race, and that this must make me a pariah, if not a martyr, in my home environs. The conviction that one could not be pro-Negro without being anti-South was as firmly held among neoabolitionists as it was among the Daughters of the Confederacy.

In the Harvard community of that day, with its token sprinkling of blacks and Southern whites, there still flourished the enduring myth that Southerners and Northerners were, and always had been, divided not only by geography and conflicting economic interests but also by historically differentiated cultures and even bloodlines. In *Cavalier and Yankee* the social historian William R. Taylor described this legendary past, which had, as he noted, produced a fictional sociology:

> . . . the North had been settled by one party to the English Civil War, the Roundheads, and the South by the other, the royal party of the Cavaliers. The Yankee was the direct descendant of the Puritan Roundhead, and the Southern gentleman of the English Cavalier, and the difference between the two was at least partly a matter of blood. . . .
>
> Under the stimulus of this divided heritage the North had developed a leveling, go-getting utilitarian society and the South had developed a society based on the values of the English country gentry. It was commonly felt, furthermore, that these two ways of life had been steadily diverging since colonial times, and there were many after 1861 who believed that these characteristic differences between North and South brought on the Civil War.

This reordering of history had advantages for those who manned the rhetorical ramparts in the great debates of the antebellum era. It was easier for the abolitionists to find a substantial portion of their fellow citizens guilty of unmitigated evil if they did not have to treat them as kinfolk. The Cavalier myth left Southerners free to denounce the crass commercialism of the North and incorporate noblesse oblige into the defense of their peculiar institutions. After a hundred years the mythology was still proving useful to those who sought to exploit regional political and economic differences.

The distinguished Harvard professors to whom I turned to improve my understanding of contemporary race relations generally agreed that demographic changes now well under way were bound to have an effect on the nation's political institutions and processes. But they also agreed that, as yet, there was not enough pressure, from above or below, to bring about effective reconsideration of the pattern of legal and de facto racial segregation that existed throughout the country.

What was intended to be a sabbatical year at Harvard ended with the Japanese attack on Pearl Harbor. I had acquired a reserve officer's commission at Clemson, and in February I was ordered to Fort Benning, Georgia, to be pounded into shape for combat duty as a second lieutenant of infantry. Assigned to the 95th Division when it was activated at Camp Swift, Texas, I remained with it for the duration of the war in Europe, serving as an operations officer in the campaigns that took us from Normandy to the Ruhr.

For the first time in my life I found myself almost totally isolated from blacks. The division had existed only on paper before activation, and most of the thirteen thousand white males who filled in the ranks were assembled from all over the country. Only the top commanders and a few of the senior staff were regular army officers; the others were reservists, National Guardsmen, or brand-new products of the Officer Training Corps, and, like the enlisted draftees, they represented all but one of the nation's regional, ethnic, and class groupings.

As a matter of policy we were separated from black troops, and in almost four years of military service I had only two brief contacts with them. Although they had served with distinction in every war the nation had fought, the high command resisted using blacks for other than service troops. The Army fielded only a single black combat division, and it happened that it was located next to us when we maneuvered in the Desert Training Center in California—next being fifty miles away.

I had occasional business with my opposite number at division headquarters, where all the senior officers were white. Most considered their assignment intolerable and were trying to arrange transfers. They expressed their feelings openly in the presence of their black subordinates, and this seemed to me a more effective means of lowering morale than any ever conceived by our Axis enemies.

I had a more sustained experience with the only black tank battalion in the European Theater. The 95th Division served in General George Patton's Third Army until the last months of the war, when we were assigned to the new Ninth Army, being assembled in Holland and Belgium for the assault across the Rhine. In the course of the transfer we picked up replacements for nonorganic units that reverted to Army command.

When the orders came through, the numerical designation of the new tank battalion meant nothing to me, but it did to the division commander. Major General Harry L. Twaddle erupted when I showed him the message: "The hell they will! That's the colored outfit! They've been trying to get rid of it, and now they're going to saddle it on me to take along to Ninth Army." His protest was in vain, and next day a black liaison officer reported to the operations section—and sent a ripple through the officers' mess when I took him there for lunch. He was the first black officer we ever broke bread with, and the last.

General Twaddle, an upstate New Yorker who had spent much of his service career abroad, took occasion to explain his initial reaction to me. It wasn't a matter of prejudice, he said, but he knew that such a "reject" outfit would come with low morale and poor equipment. He was right about the equipment, but the white Virginian who commanded the battalion had passed from despair to outrage at the way his men were being treated, and he shared it with his troops. In the battles they fought under our command the black crews in the battered old Sherman tanks acquitted themselves as well as any of the armored troopers we saw in action.

At the end of the war in Europe I was a lieutenant colonel in the General Staff Corps, and shortly after V-E Day I was flown back to Washington for assignment to the Operations Division at the Pentagon, where I served until V-J Day. There must have been some black officers and noncoms in that vast labyrinth, but I don't recall seeing any.

. . .

During the years I spent in training camps and combat zones overseas I had been dimly aware of considerable racial friction in American cities, including a full-fledged race riot in Detroit. But it was not until I had renewed contacts with newspaper colleagues in the nation's capital that I began to appreciate the political impact this had on the Roosevelt administration.

With the coming of the New Deal, black voters had shifted their traditional allegiance from the party of Lincoln, and now had significant influence in the big city Democratic organizations that provided a counterbalance to the party's Southern wing. By the time Roosevelt prepared to run for a third term, the black leadership was in position to back up its appeals with political clout.

The mobilization effort launched in 1940 after the fall of France provided a sharp new focus for black grievances, and as preparation for a national draft began, Walter White handed Eleanor Roosevelt a copy of a letter addressed to Secretary of War Henry Stimson by a young NAACP lawyer, Thurgood Marshall. Listing the services that excluded blacks, Marshall warned that draftees who were denied the right to serve in any branch of the military might prefer to go to jail.

An internal memorandum from Stimson to the president, passed on by FDR to his wife, and by her to Walter White, struck the black leaders as full of loopholes. They were turned down when they sought an opportunity to discuss the issue with the War and Navy secretaries, and Eleanor sent a memo to the president urging him to intervene:

> There is a growing feeing among the colored people, and they are creating a feeling among many white people. They feel they should be allowed to participate in any training that is going on in the aviation, army, navy, and have opportunities for service. . . .
>
> There is no use going into a conference unless [the secretaries] have the intention of doing something. This is going to be very bad politically, beside being [wrong] intrinsically, and I think you should ask that a meeting be held and if you cannot

be present yourself, you should ask them to give you a report. . . .

Roosevelt agreed, and decided to preside. Walter White came away from the White House session disappointed with the response of the service representatives, but encouraged by what he regarded as evidence of the president's sympathy. One can only imagine what his reaction would have been had he had access to the private diary of Secretary Stimson, the aristocratic Republican appointed to provide bipartisan balance in the wartime cabinet. The meeting, Stimson wrote, was called only to

> satisfy the Negro politicians who are trying to get the army committed to colored officers and various other things which they ought not to do. I sent [Assistant Secretary] Patterson to this meeting. . . . According to him it was a very amusing af-fair—the President's gymnastics as to politics. I saw the same thing happen twenty-three years ago when Woodrow Wilson yielded to the same sort of demand and appointed colored of-ficers to several of the Divisions that went to France, and the poor fellows made perfect fools of themselves and one at least of the Divisions behaved very badly. The others were turned - into labor battalions.

The White House press release on the meeting with the black leaders announced that blacks would be admitted to combat units in all branches of the service, but would be segregated and serve under white officers. The black participants were outraged by the implication that they had approved such a policy. White demanded a public retraction by Steve Early, the press secretary, but all he got was a letter of apology for any embarrassment the release might have caused.

As the 1940 presidential election drew nearer, reports of black de-fections in response to the appeal of the unorthodox Republican can-didate, Wendell Willkie, began to alarm the Democratic campaign mastermind, Harry Hopkins. Summoning Will Alexander, the admin-istration's in-house expert on race relations, he relayed the bad news he was receiving from the Democratic National Committee:

Will, this fellow Willkie is about to beat the Boss, and we damn well better do something about it. . . . The President has done more for the Negroes in this country than anybody ever did since Abraham Lincoln, and you can't get word out to any of them. It looks like they are all going against him. . . . If you can, tell me what to do.

Alexander, who had been making inquiries of his own, was ready with a recommendation from Walter White for two symbolic gestures. The leaders wanted to see Colonel Benjamin O. Davis, the first black West Point graduate, appointed a brigadier general. Davis's advancement was blocked under existing policy, since black officers could serve only in three segregated units that had been maintained in regular service since the days when the black Buffalo Soldiers participated in frontier Indian campaigns. And they wanted William Hastie, the first black federal judge in modern times, who had been stashed away in the Virgin Islands, named a civilian aide to Secretary Stimson. Hopkins saw to it that this was done.

As tensions between blacks and whites mounted, Eleanor Roosevelt, who had previously accepted the limitations of existing law and custom, concluded that desegregation was the only effective approach to dealing with minority problems. Many of the things we deplore, she wrote, "are not due just to lack of education and to physical differences, but are due in great part to the basic fact of segregation, which we have set up in this country and which warps and twists the lives not only of our Negro population, but sometimes of foreign born or even of religious groups."

She expressed that view in the foreword to a proposed pamphlet reprinting a letter from a kindred spirit, Pearl S. Buck, to *The New York Times*. The publication was canceled after the December 7 Japanese attack on Pearl Harbor as Eleanor, in deference to the need for national unity, decided to become less outspoken in public. But she continued to press her husband, who now had the American war effort to justify his reluctance to give racial matters priority.

At the top of her agenda was the black leadership's demand for a guarantee that blacks would receive a fair share of the jobs being created by expansion of the industrial work force. When Sidney Hillman was appointed head of the Labor Division of the new Office of Production Management (OPM), her collaborators Will Alexander and Robert Weaver were named as his consultants on racial matters. But Alexander reported that the union leader was "very timid on the race question," which was borne out when Eleanor invited him to the White House to discuss their recommendation that a clause forbidding discrimination be inserted in all contracts handled by the OPM.

The only black leader in the AFL-CIO, A. Philip Randolph, head of the Brotherhood of Sleeping Car Porters, forced the issue by announcing a mass march on Washington to protest the exclusion of blacks from jobs in defense industries, and their humiliating treatment in the armed services. "Though I have found no Negroes who want to see the United Nations lose this war, I have found many who, before the war ends, want to see the stuffing knocked out of white supremacy and of empire over subject peoples," he said. And he asked the unanswerable question: "Why has a man got to be Jim Crowed to die for democracy?"

Fearing that such a demonstration might lead to mass violence in the edgy national capital, Eleanor agreed to the president's request that she go to New York and join with Mayor Fiorello La Guardia in appealing to Randolph to call off the march, scheduled for July 1. He refused, and she brought back La Guardia's recommendation that the president deal directly with Randolph and Walter White.

Randolph attended a White House meeting with the president and the cabinet principals, but still declined to halt preparations for the demonstration in the absence of a tangible demonstration of good faith. After stalling as long as he could, Roosevelt gave in on June 25 and issued an executive order mandating nondiscrimination in defense industries and setting up the Fair Employment Practices Commission (FEPC) to enforce it. He also announced that the Officer Training Corps would admit increased numbers of blacks, with openings for graduates being made available in all services.

Randolph canceled the march, and on July 19 the president appointed as FEPC chairman Mark Ethridge, publisher of the *Louisville Courier-Journal*. Walter White wrote Eleanor to thank her for her role in gaining the new dispensations, adding, "Mr. Ethridge has plunged in with his characteristic energy, forthrightness and courage."

But by 1942, Randolph was complaining that "both management

and labor unions in too many places and in too many ways are still drawing the color line." He called for mass protest meetings in major cities, and twenty thousand blacks turned out at Madison Square Garden, sixteen thousand in Chicago, and nine thousand in St. Louis. Randolph described them as "businessmen, teachers, laundry workers, Pullman porters, waiters and Redcaps; preachers, crap-shooters and social workers; jitterbugs and Ph.Ds."

Here for the first time blacks were acting wholly on their own to challenge the white leadership. The spontaneous movement, Randolph said, was "all-Negro and pro-Negro but not for that reason anti-white . . . a non-violent demonstration of Negro mass power." And in words that would be echoed by Martin Luther King a generation later, he proclaimed, "By fighting for their rights now, American Negroes are helping to make America a moral and spiritual arsenal of democracy."

Segregation did not end in the armed services, or in the workplace. But some, at least, of the black officers were placed in positions where they could display their capacity in competition with whites, providing a tangible answer to white prejudice—as in the notable case of the sole black fighter wing, which became the most decorated unit in the Air Corps. And, bolstered by the acute manpower shortage occasioned by the military draft, the FEPC's efforts opened jobs on assembly lines in industries previously closed to blacks.

Cities in the Midwest and West acquired substantial black minorities as the migration of blacks from the South accelerated and was channeled in new directions. This resulted in a significant increase in the black vote as party allegiance shifted. The Democrats, having carried only four of fifteen key black wards in nine Northern cities in 1932, won nine in 1936, and fourteen in 1940. By 1944 blacks had become an active and increasingly influential part of the coalition of blue-collar union members, white-collar liberals, and Southern Democratic party loyalists that ensured Roosevelt's reelection for a fourth term.

FDR, the smiling, eloquent pragmatist who brought the Democratic Party back from its long sojourn in the political wilderness, provided an enduring icon for the rank-and-file members of the coalition, but he never overcame the reservations of the black leadership. Roy Wilkins, who succeeded White as head of the NAACP, said the president could be considered a friend of blacks "only insofar as he refused to exclude the Negro from his general policies that applied to the whole country. . . . The personal touch and the personal fight against discrimination were Mrs. Roosevelt's. That attached to Roosevelt also—he could hardly get away from it—and he reaped the political benefit from it."

By the time I got back from Europe, the Roosevelts had been removed from the White House by the death of the president. The political legacy of the New Deal would be put to its first real test by Harry S. Truman, the short, blunt Missourian who said he felt like a load of hay had fallen on him when he received word on April 12, 1945, that he was in charge of a nation with a war still to win.

GENESIS
TRUMAN AND THE DIXIECRATS

The aim of the memorandum is to outline a course of political conduct
for the Administration extending from November, 1947 to November,
1948. . . . The basic premise [is] that the Democratic Party is an
unhappy alliance of Southern conservatives, Western progressives, and
Big City labor. . . . The success or failure of the Democratic leadership can be precisely measured by its ability to lead enough members
of these three misfit groups to the polls on the first Tuesday of November, 1948.

—White House memorandum, Clark Clifford, counsel,
to President Harry S. Truman, November 19, 1947

FRANKLIN ROOSEVELT died at Warm Springs, Georgia, and the funeral
train that bore his body north for a state funeral stopped along the way
to pick up distinguished mourners. Speculation as to what the elevation
of Vice President Harry Truman might portend eddied through the
Pullman cars. Cotton Ed Smith's successor, Burnet Rhett Maybank,
discussed the possibilities with a fellow Charlestonian, Earl Mazo, one
of the newspaper correspondents aboard. "Everything's going to be all
right," the senator confided to his young friend. "The new president
knows how to handle the Nigras."

The assumption that Truman was not likely to rock the boat on
racial matters was widely shared by those who had served in the Senate
with him. He had a Confederate grandfather, came from a Jim Crow

border state, and there had been nothing in his moderate voting record to alienate the Dixiecrats. But there were 130,000 black voters in Missouri when he entered politics, 20,000 of them in Jackson County, where the Kansas City Democratic machine headed by Tom Pendergast found a place for him as head of the county government.

In 1940 Truman declared in a campaign speech at Sedalia, "In giving the Negroes the rights that are theirs, we are acting in accord with the ideas of true democracy." But that same year, with characteristic candor, he told the National Colored Democratic Association in Chicago, "I wish to make it clear that I am not appealing for social equality for the Negro. The Negro himself knows better than that, and the highest type of Negro leaders say quite frankly that they prefer the society of their own people. Negroes want justice, not social equality."

"His position was the familiar one of a compassionate and fair-minded man caught between the devil and the deep on the race issue," Robert J. Donovan wrote in *Conflict and Crisis*. "This was the viewpoint, surely, of most enlightened white Americans at that time." There had been no reason for Truman to change it during his brief tenure as vice president, since it was also that of the president who made him his heir.

But a U.S. Supreme Court decision, *Smith* v. *Allwright*, handed down in 1944, was beginning to change the political equation. The Court held that the Texas Democratic primary was an integral part of the general election, and found exclusion from party registration on the basis of race unconstitutional. This sounded the death knell for the white primary, which for more than half a century had provided the principal means of disfranchising blacks in the Solid South. Roy Wilkins of the NAACP, speaking out of his experience on *The Call*, Kansas City's black newspaper, was sure the implications would not be lost on the new president. Truman, he said, was "politically astute on the race question before he ever came to Washington because the Pendergast machine was politically astute."

As the 1946 midterm national elections approached, the potential import of *Smith* v. *Allwright* was impressed on the white political leadership by the outspoken resentment of segregation voiced by black veterans returning from the war. Tension mounted as federal courts struck down the legal dodges devised to sidestep the new dispensation—including South Carolina's repeal of the state's election laws in a vain effort to establish the Democratic Party as a private club.

Reaction in the Deep South was more forthright. In a campaign speech at Laurel, Senator Theodore Bilbo urged "every red-blooded Anglo-Saxon man in Mississippi to resort to any means to keep hundreds of Negroes from the polls in the July primary. . . . And if you don't know what that means you are just not up on your persuasive measures." Eugene Talmadge was nominated governor in his state's primary after pledging that no Negro would vote in Georgia for the next four years. The only black to cast a ballot in Taylor County was shot down by four white men, and there were similar atrocities elsewhere in the state. The Ku Klux Klan was responding in its time-tested way to the defiance voiced by the politicians.

Black pickets appeared outside the White House, and fifteen thousand marched to the Lincoln Memorial, demanding, among other things, the outlawing of the Klan. Attorney General Tom Clark announced in August that he was drafting an antilynching bill for presentation to Congress when it returned from recess, and the president endorsed the move:

> Discrimination, like a disease, must be attacked wherever it appears. This applies to the opportunity to vote, to hold and retain a job, and to secure adequate shelter and medical care no less than to gain an education compatible with the needs and ability of the individual.

In September the president met with representatitves of the National Emergency Committee Against Mob Violence, made up of the leaders of more than forty religious, professional, veterans, and civil rights organizations brought together by the NAACP and the American Council on Race Relations. He declined to call a special session of Congress to act on the antilynching bill, but he agreed to create by executive order a commission to study not only mob violence but also other violations of civil rights.

Before the commission could be named, the midterm elections took place, and they proved to be a disaster for the Democrats. In addition to white resentment aroused by the president's concessions to the blacks, there were widespread protests against wartime rationing still in effect during conversion to a peacetime economy. When the voters went to the polls on November 5 they ended the control of both houses of Congress the Democrats had enjoyed since 1933. When it convened in 1947, the Eightieth Congress had Republican majorities of 246 to 188 in the House and 51 to 45 in the Senate. Many of the most effective champions of the New Deal went down to defeat, to be replaced by Republicans who would be thorns in the side of the Democratic leadership for years to come—among them Representative Richard Milhous Nixon of California and Senator Joseph R. McCarthy of Wisconsin, who won their seats by branding their liberal opponents soft on communism.

Despite the fallout from the midterm election, Harry Truman carried out his promise to set up the President's Committee on Civil Rights. On December 5 he announced the appointment of Charles E. Wilson, president of General Electric, as chairman of a distinguished interracial group made up college presidents, bishops, lawyers, business executives, and labor leaders. When their report, *To Secure These Rights*, was issued ten months later, it contained recommendations that in due course would change the contours of race relations in the United States.

As political factions began to mobilize for what would become a fundamental recasting of the old Democratic coalition, I was back in my home country, but I had moved a hundred miles north, into what was indisputably the Upper South. As state capital correspondent for the *Greenville News* I had also written on politics for the *Charlotte News*, just across the North Carolina line, and the approaching end of the war had brought an offer to join the newspaper as associate editor in charge of its editorial page. Shortly after V-J Day I returned to civilian life in the booming city that served as the financial and commercial hub of the Carolina Piedmont.

My predecessor had been W. J. Cash, author of *The Mind of the South*. The chair had been left vacant after the success of his book made it possible for him to devote full time to his literary career, only to have it cut short by his untimely death. The *News's* editorial policy, if less iconoclastic than the views Cash expressed when writing on his own, was in sharp contrast to that of its competition, the morning *Observer*, which had gained the largest circulation between Richmond and Atlanta with solid, dull news coverage and conservative editorial commentary. The *News* countered with the brash, literate output of a talented young staff assembled by owners who belonged to the local establishment but who tolerated, and sometimes enjoyed, the commotion they caused in a staid city dominated by straitlaced Presbyterians, Methodists, and Baptists.

In the prewar years I had simply reported on the political impact of changing racial attitudes that were still largely ignored in the South, although they were beginning to affect national public policy. Now I was expected to pass judgment on the stands taken by those who would have to deal with an impending social upheaval. I was soon at odds with state and local political leaders, who, while avoiding the oratorical excesses of their counterparts in the Deep South, continued to dismiss the legitimate complaints of blacks who were beginning to emerge as their constituents.

When I settled in at the *Charlotte News*, the warning Gunnar Myrdal had sounded in 1944 had been given substance by the Supreme Court ruling opening the Democratic primaries to blacks. I was convinced that the Court, having abandoned the states' rights doctrine in the case of voting, would move on to take a new look at other restrictive aspects of legal segregation. The Court was reacting to what James Weldon Johnson cited as "a series of shifting interracial situations, never precisely the same for any two generations." This, I thought, would soon have profound implications for those of my contemporaries who had begun to succeed to the places of power.

I had no illusion that many of these had come home from the war imbued with a passion for social justice. But I thought I could detect among them a new permissiveness; they seemed to me no longer prepared, as our fathers had been, to sacrifice their self-interest on the altar of white supremacy. But if, as this implied, Cash's savage ideal had been considerably watered down, public opinion still imposed limits on political action.

My colleague at the *News* C. A. McKnight once observed that if he were required to render a moral judgment on racial segregation, his Presbyterian conscience would require that he reject it, and he suspected that this was so for many Southerners. But there were no moral leaders of consequence who were prepared to force the issue, and certainly no politician could reasonably be expected to do so. This meant that those seeking to promote change—including newspaper editors—were constrained to deal with the race problem in other, more pragmatic terms.

The Supreme Court's *Allwright* decision had not spread consternation in North Carolina, as it had farther south, and I aroused no great outcry when I campaigned for the right of blacks to vote and serve on juries. A reasoned argument for justice could attract considerable support as long as there was no implication of social equality. This was certainly the case with voting, where, as I pointed out, intercourse of any sort was forbidden by law within a hundred feet of the polling place.

Early in 1947 an ebullient New Englander, Thomas L. Robinson, used his Ivy League connections with some of North Carolina's textile and tobacco barons to put together enough financing to purchase the *News* from the family that had controlled the newspaper for two generations. This, as *Time* magazine noted, aroused speculation as to whether "the new owners would turn out to be too fat to fight." Robinson sought to allay such doubts by conferring on me the title of editor.

Time cited me as "one of the South's most realistic and readable editorial writers," and sought to place me in the political spectrum:

> His campaigns (for two-party politics, racial and religious tolerance, votes for Negroes, higher pay for teachers) have established him as neither a Yankee-lover nor a deep-dyed Southerner. Ashmore . . . tempers his enthusiasm for reform with consideration of the facts of Southern life. Says he: "We hope to avoid the usual Southernisms [such as] undue sensitivity to outside criticism. . . . I am a Southerner by inclination as well as by virtue of two Confederate grandfathers, but it is high time we rejoined the union."

The new publisher, as he had promised, held to the *News*'s traditional policies, which included parsimony. My elevation in rank carried with it no increase in salary, and it did not diminish my interest in the prospect of a higher income and a wider audience. This was enhanced in some respects, and inhibited in others, by the fact that I was now firmly established in the small company of Southern editors usually called liberal, although, as *Time's* cursory treatment of my views indicated, the designation was subject to a regional discount.

Expatriation had been the usual resort for generations of Southerners with journalistic or literary ambition, but I found little attraction in the inquiries I began to receive from outside the region. One reason was temperament, which I suppose also could be construed as prejudice. New York was the capital of my trade, but my reaction to the metropolis was similar to that William Styron ascribed to his Virginian father:

> He detested New York only for what he called its "barbarity," its lack of courtesy, its total bankruptcy in the domain of public manners. The snarling command of the traffic cop, the blaring insult of horns, all the needlessly raised voices of the night denizens of Manhattan ravaged his nerves, acidified his duodenum, unhelmed his composure and his will. . . .

A more compelling reason for remaining below the Mason-Dixon line was my belief that the South was facing profound socioeconomic changes I had been consciously preparing myself to deal with. But the number of newspapers that provided the latitude I enjoyed at the *News* was limited. A case in point was provided when I received an invitation to come to Richmond to discuss the opening left at the *News Leader* by the retirement of the scholarly Douglas Southall Freeman.

I had attracted the attention of Virginius Dabney, editor of the *Times-Dispatch* and author of *Liberalism in the South*. He arranged an interview with D. Tennant Bryan, publisher of both newspapers, but an exchange of views with him and the top executive on the business side quickly established a yawning void. The newspapers' general manager, John Dana Wise, a South Carolinian who obviously hadn't read my résumé, concluded the session by observing, "I thought so—we've never had any luck with these tarheels." I headed back to Charlotte reminded of the old saw that identified North Carolina as a vale of humility between two mountains of arrogance.

As it turned out, the *News-Leader's* editorial pulpit went to James

Jackson Kilpatrick, who used it to preach defiance of rulings by the U.S. Supreme Court. In his autobiography, *Across the years*, Dabney, who had been one of the founders of the interracial Southern Regional Council (SRC), told of Wise's running campaign to force his resignation. Bryan refused to go along and tolerated the divergent views of his morning and afternoon papers until the Court ordered desegregation of the public schools. The *News-Leader* under Kilpatrick, Dabney wrote,

> carried the ball, as it were, for massive resistance. The *Times-Dispatch*, under my editorship, did not attack massive resistance, although it would have liked to do so. Neither did we espouse it actively. . . . Most of the time we simply acquiesced in it silently without making overtures on its behalf.

There were no more than a dozen major newspapers in the region that actively supported the positions on racial matters we took at the *News*. The consideration that determined policy on most of the others was summed up in a sardonic question posed by James McBride Dabbs in the SRC publication *New South:*

> Local newspapers, with exceptions so small as to be negligible, are owned, published and edited by Southern whites. Their subscribers are white; their advertisers are white. Is it not going a little far to expect complete objectivity and candor of a white Southern editor in discussing the duties of his subscribers and advertisers to members of a race that brings him no bread and butter?

The exceptions were owned by families with deep roots in their communities who waived strict balance sheet considerations and imbued their properties with an institutional sense. In the late summer of 1947 I received a phone call from the proprietor of one of these, the *Arkansas Gazette*, suggesting that I come out and discuss a top job opening there.

Like his counterpart in Richmond, the principal owner of the *Gazette* was an elegant patrician of impeccable Confederate lineage. John Netherland Heiskell's father, colonel of a Tennessee regiment in the Civil War, was a leading lawyer and judge in Memphis when he purchased a controlling interest in the Little Rock morning newspaper as a legacy for his children. Mr. J.N., as his juniors now called him, was already an experienced journalist when he took over as editor in 1902. Now, at seventy-five, he had accepted the inevitability of his succession, and was determined to arrange it so there would be no change in the institutional character he had impressed on the newspaper in the years of his stewardship.

When I arrived in Little Rock on a hot August weekend, he limited our formal discussion to a session in his cluttered office on Sunday morning, when the *Gazette* Building was deserted. He pursued his real interests in extended, often discursive conversations at his home and country club, where members of his family were brought in to look me over. He was probing to determine whether my views on public issues generally coincided with his, and were shared by Hugh Patterson, his Mississippi-born son-in-law who was moving through the chairs on the business side and would soon become publisher. In my case he had reluctantly gone outside the family to fill the place left vacant when his son, an Air Corps pilot, was killed in combat.

I, of course, was also doing some probing, and I learned enough about the *Gazette* and its proprietor to remove any reservations about transplanting my wife and year-old daughter to the big river country. Mr. J.N. was a scholarly man, and in manner a conventional one, but his ingrained sense of justice made him an unshakable civil libertarian. His views on race were those of enlightened members of his generation; he was, as Robert Donovan said of Harry Truman, concerned with justice, not social equality, which did not seem to him either desirable or possible.

His ingrained gentility had survived forty-five years of the freebooting, frontier-style political combat the *Gazette* had been engaged in since its founding in 1819. When he arrived, the dominant political figure in Arkansas was Jeff Davis, a free-swinging populist who rallied the "one-gallus boys" against the "high-collared city crowd" by using the state's leading newspaper as his favorite whipping boy. "I see an agent out there in the audience giving out that old red harlot, the *Arkansas Gazette,*" he would proclaim from the stump. "I would rather be caught with a dead buzzard under my arm, or a dead polecat."

In 1913, as a matter of poetic justice, Heiskell was appointed to serve out the deceased Davis's term in the U.S. Senate. He was there only twenty-four days, and his maiden speech was also his valedictory. He used the occasion to reassure those who feared that the spreading direct-primary movement might give undue influence to voters "dubbed with the uncouth terms 'redneck' and 'hillbilly.' " These, he said, "were the very foundation course of the strength of human society, who work at the trades of the countryside or cultivate small farms." If they were misled, the fault was "with him who perverts his talents and abuses his powers to play upon their honest hearts and open minds."

James Street, a Mississippi-born writer who apprenticed under Mr. J.N. in the 1920s, described the *Gazette* as

> a Southern lady from any angle, her Confederate limbs hidden under a Victorian petticoat and seen only in stormy weather when she kicks up her heels in an eye-catching crusade for her principles. Her tenets have made her one of the most successful journals in the world and yet her tenets are simple. What is best for humanity as the *Gazette* sees it, an honest profit is not evil, change is not always progress but never fear change, and lay not a greedy hand on the fair breast of Arkansas, point not a dirty finger.

She was about to kick up her heels again when I arrived in September to fill the role of executive editor.

I had hardly found my way around the *Gazette*'s elegant, bay-windowed limestone building when I began my own initiation into Arkansas-style political combat. It was touched off by the partisan reaction that convulsed all the Southern states when *To Secure These Rights* was released by the White House in October, 1947. In uncompromising terms the prestigious presidential committee called for the immediate end to any form of legally sanctioned racial segregation, and spelled out the federal action that would be required to achieve the goal.

The committee's unanimous recommendations included an antilynching law and federal action to curb police brutality; repeal of the poll tax and elimination of discriminatory registration requirements; denial of federal grants as a means of ending discrimination by public and private agencies; enactment of fair employment practices laws to open employment in the private sector, and establishment of a permanent FEPC; a strengthened Civil Rights Division in the Justice Department to enforce the new laws; creation of a Civil Rights Commission to exercise oversight of all government agencies; enforcement of the Supreme Court decision outlawing restrictive real estate covenants; and action to require the states to end discrimination in public and private schools and colleges.

The Truman committee's report set the agenda for the mass civil rights movement that emerged a decade later, but it hardly accorded with the political reality the president faced on the eve of a campaign for election in his own right. His reservations were evident in the special message he sent to Congress in February calling for antilynching and antipoll tax laws, and creation of a permanent FEPC and Commission on Civil Rights—measures on which he was already on record. As to the other committee proposals, he recommended only that they be subject to ongoing study by a special congressional committee. This, of course, was the standard device by which politicians sought credit for supporting legislation they knew had no hope of passage.

Truman never accepted the goal of social integration that could be inferred from the high-flown language in the committee report. His commitment was to desegregation, and was limited to putting into effect for blacks the rights and immunities spelled out in the Constitution and its amendments. Although he emphasized what would later come to be known as affirmative action, he was careful not to go beyond specified constitutional rights when he became the first president to address the NAACP:

> We cannot be content with a civil liberties program which emphasizes only the need for protection against the possibility of tyranny by the government. We must keep moving forward with new concepts of civil rights . . . not protection of the people *against* the government, but protection of the people *by* the government.

Truman expected Southerners in Congress to denounce such a stand, but he thought it limited enough to prevent any serious break in Democratic ranks. But the scales were tipped by the opening passages of his special message, in which he declared that the federal government had a duty to guarantee that the civil rights set forth in the Constitution were "not denied or abridged anywhere in our Union." That uncompromising rejection of the states' rights doctrine constituted a direct challenge to any defense of segregation that Southern ideologues might devise, and a warning shot across their bow had already been fired by the Supreme Court in *Smith* v. *Allwright*.

The reaction in the Deep South was foreordained. Robert Donovan, who was there as correspondent for the *New York Herald Tribune*, wrote that on Capitol Hill the response by members from Mississippi, Alabama, Louisiana, South Carolina, and Georgia "often exceeded the standards of what was printable in the newspapers of those days." There had never been any real prospect that the proposed legislation would be enacted, and it soon became clear that it could not even be brought to a vote. In the filibuster-prone Senate, Alben Barkley, the wily Kentuckian who served as minority leader, buried the package in committee without arousing any protest from the White House.

But there was no such restraint at the Southern Governors' Conference when it convened at Wakulla Springs, Florida. Governor Fielding Wright of Mississippi proposed a "Southern Conference of True Democrats" to formulate a course of action. Party loyalists got through a resolution calling for a forty-day cooling-off period, but Governor Strom Thurmond of South Carolina was named chairman of a committee on defense of white supremacy, and was instructed to interrogate the Democratic national chairman as to the true meaning of Truman's policies. In the absence of assurance that the president would be urged to reverse his stand, Thurmond warned, "the present leadership of the Democratic party will soon realize that the South is no longer in the bag."

The distinction in the reaction of leaders in the upper and deep Southern states began to disappear. On February 19, celebrating the hundredth anniversary of the formation of the Democratic National Committee, President Truman used a radio hookup to address Jefferson-Jackson Day dinners across the country. In Richmond, the response of

Senator Harry F. Byrd, Virginia's patrician political boss, was the assertion that the president's civil rights proposals would open the way to dictatorship. And in Little Rock, half of the 850 dinner guests walked out when his flat Missouri voice came over the loudspeakers.

By the time Truman formally notified the Democratic National Committee that he intended to run for nomination, a strategy for his defeat had begun to emerge. Meeting in Jackson, those who now identified themselves as States' Rights Jeffersonian Democrats agreed to reconvene in Birmingham after the July national convention and field a ticket of their own if the leadership did not accept the premise set forth in their declaration of independence:

> We hereby declare that the President of the United States has by his acts and declarations repudiated the principles of the Democratic Party, threatened to disturb the constitutional division and balance of the powers of government, and has thereby forfeited all claims of allegiance from members of the party who adhere to its principles.

The political battle lines were drawn, and the election of Governor Ben Laney of Arkansas as chairman of the rump party organization placed the *Gazette* at the center of the war zone.

I knew that William E. Woodruff, the Jacksonian who founded the newspaper, had nailed the Democratic banner to the masthead of the first edition back in 1819. Pondering how to deal with the governor's apostasy, I asked Mr. J.N. if the *Gazette* had ever departed the fold. He peered out of his open doorway to be sure he couldn't be overheard, leaned across the desk, and confided, "I don't like to talk about this, but the fact is we went Whig twice."

It wasn't an idle query. Party loyalty provided primary ammunition when we rolled out the heavy editorial artillery to take on Governor Laney and the Dixiecrats. On the editorial page we hammered away at the scheme to split the Democratic Party, charging that it could only improve the fortunes of the Republicans, whose hostility to all things

Southern had been demonstrated by the hardships visited on Arkansans during the years of their ascendancy.

In May the governor and I debated the civil rights issue at a Little Rock town hall meeting broadcast over a statewide radio network. Played back forty-five years after the fact, the transcript of the confrontation has a disembodied character, as it must have had for many listeners at the time. "Business Ben" Laney was a gentlemanly conservative, and if we did not exactly remain on high ground, there was a minimum of racist invective.

The governor ignored the actual content of the civil rights package President Truman had sent to Congress, and instead read out of context the most stringent passages from *To Secure These Rights*. I, in my turn, made a states' rights-*cum*-responsibilities pitch—arguing that the only answer to federal antilynching, antipoll tax, and antidiscrimination legislation was to demonstrate that it wasn't necessary, which could be done simply by carrying out, in good faith, provisions of Arkansas' own constitution.

The governor's wrath, predictably, was directed primarily against the FEPC, which was anathema to the business community: "It is the heart of the program, and they know it"—they being ideologues dedicated to the destruction of states' rights and the regulation of business. And this, he charged, would ultimately lead to the Communist ideal of total regimentation of people of all races and creeds. I replied that "they" also must include the conservative leaders of the Republican Party, who would be the principal beneficiaries of the Dixiecrats' threatened secession. "I came down here to talk about civil rights," Laney complained, "and all Mr. Ashmore wants to talk about is party loyalty." He was absolutely right.

Civility prevailed on the platform, but a member of the audience directed to me the question that was all but inevitable on such an occasion: How would I like to have my daughter marry a "nigger"? I made my standard response: A woman's choice of a husband was not the legitimate concern of anyone outside her family; surely we all could agree that intervention by the state in so intimate a personal decision constituted an intolerable violation of individual rights. The reply was hardly likely to convert diehard white supremacists, but it usually headed off a dead-end discussion of miscegenation.

A touch of sophistry is unavoidable in a media-oriented political debate, which requires loaded answers to loaded questions. Our exchange at Little Rock was a fair sample of the preliminary skirmishing over civil rights among those in the South who were warming up for the Democratic National Convention.

Truman, trying to cool the talk of partisan rebellion, continued to sidestep the civil rights issue as best he could. But pressure was also mounting on the other side. The big city Democratic leaders expressed concern when the black leadership charged that the president had reneged on a promise to ban segregation in the armed forces by failing to include such a provision in his request that Congress renew the draft and provide for universal military training.

A. Philip Randolph made another trip to Washington, and, receiving no satisfaction at the White House or on Capitol Hill, announced that he was launching the League for Nonviolent Resistance Against Military Segregation. Pledging to counsel black youths to refuse conscription, he told the Senate Armed Services Committee, "We are serving a higher law than the law which applies to the act of treason."

Democratic political tacticians began receiving warnings of wholesale defections by blacks attracted by the benign civil rights stance of New York governor Thomas E. Dewey, the virtually certain Republican nominee. These findings impressed Clark Clifford, the astute St. Louis lawyer who had served as a wartime naval aide to Franklin Roosevelt and who stayed on as counsel to President Truman. On November 19, 1947, he sent Truman a lengthy memorandum that established him as the principal architect of the coming campaign.

The president should "go as far as he feels he could in recommending measures to protect the rights of minority groups," Clifford urged, adding that even if there was "difficulty with our Southern friends that is the lesser of two evils. . . . As always, the South can be considered safely Democratic, and in formulating national policy it can be safely ignored." On the other hand, "unless there are new and real efforts, the Negro bloc, which certainly in Illinois and probably in New York and Ohio, *does* hold the balance of power, will go Republican."

Clifford's prognosis also took note of disaffection in the big city labor bloc, some of whose leaders had been put off by the strikebreaking tactics Truman had used against John L. Lewis's miners and the railway operating unions. And the beginning of the Cold War, signified by the Truman Doctrine's guarantee of American military support for European nations threatened by Communist aggression, had divided the liberal/intellectual wing of the party.

On the far left, former vice president Henry Wallace, who had been fired by Truman as secretary of commerce, denounced administration foreign policy as a "global Monroe Doctrine." His increasingly strident attacks gained him the support of the Progressive Citizens of America, made up of the remnants of the popular front that had formed around the Communist Party, U.S.A. to support the wartime alliance with the Soviet Union. Meanwhile, the anti-Communist left had organized Americans for Democratic Action (ADA), which attracted a number of New Deal stalwarts who, for reasons of policy or personality, had broken with the president.

It became evident that the maverick Wallace was setting himself up—or was being set up—to run as a third-party candidate. But the ADA liberals, like the dissident Southern Democrats, wanted to remain in the party if they could. As the July national convention approached, these strange bedfellows had united with the big city political bosses in an effort to dump Truman by drafting a candidate acceptable to all three factions—a role that would have required an ideological eunuch.

· In June, President Truman made a deal he hoped would defuse the race issue. Emerging from a White House conference, Representative John Rankin of Mississippi told the waiting reporters: "I am not without hope that the Democratic convention will reach a satisfactory agreement on civil rights. If that convention adopts the same plank that was inserted in the platform in 1944, I am assured that it will be adhered to." This meant that the platform would not go beyond pledging Congress to "exert its full constitutional powers" to protect the rights of blacks— leaving open the question of what those powers and rights really were.

By the time the platform subcommittee on civil rights met in Philadelphia on the eve of the convention, it was clear that the deal would not hold. The Dixiecrats demanded disavowal of the civil rights package the president had submitted to Congress; the liberals demanded un-qualified endorsement; and Clark Clifford sent word that the president expected the platform to honor the pledge he had made to John Rankin.

Meanwhile, those who were attempting to dump the president were frantically casting about for a candidate. For a brief, heady moment they thought they had one: General of the Army Dwight D. Eisenhower, a popular hero with no partisan political record. On July 5 the general responded to Boss Frank Hague's offer of support by the New Jersey delegation, "I will not at this time identify myself with any political party, and could not accept nomination for public office. . . ." To the political bosses, who were experts on weasel words, "at this time" did not foreclose a draft.

The president had long since recognized that Eisenhower, trading on his reputation as conqueror of the Nazi military machine, would have the inside track in a national election. Back in 1946, when he was struggling with reconversion of the wartime economy, Truman had seriously considered stepping aside. ("Sherman had it wrong," he told the Gridiron Club. "Peace is hell.") He offered Eisenhower his support, but the general, who would break out his true colors and run as a Republican in 1952, was not interested. Two years later, now committed to his own election, the president read Eisenhower's equivocal statement as Boss Hague did. When Senator Claude Pepper of Florida, an ADA adherent, announced his support of Eisenhower, Truman instructed Secretary of the Army Kenneth Royall to order the general to slam the door. Eisenhower's reply to Pepper, a Shermanesque declaration that he would not accept the nomination under any conditions, was drafted in the White House by Clark Clifford.

The stop-Truman maneuvering had reached its farcical climax when I arrived in Philadelphia to write commentary on the convention for the *Gazette*. I joined the press corps at a caucus where I found myself bemused by the array of conveners on the platform. There were James Roosevelt, chairman of the California Democratic Party; Mayor Hubert Humphrey of Minneapolis, who would become the party's most vocal civil rights champion; Mayor William O'Dwyer of New York, and Colonel Jacob Arvey, the Illinois Democratic leader, sitting cheek by jowl with Governors Ben Laney, Strom Thurmond, and William Tuck of Virginia. "Common sense had fled," Robert Donovan wrote. "Principles gurgled down the drain in a torrent of expediency. . . ."

The convention had become, as Clark Clifford described it, "the crossroads where the future of the Democratic Party, the election of Harry Truman, and the world of real politics met." Working behind the scenes, he was trying to head off an alternative civil rights platform plank the liberals planned to introduce on the floor. "Of course, almost all of them had supported the 'draft Ike' effort," he wrote, "and the platform battle was in part a continuation of that fight."

Hubert Humphrey was chosen to present the substitute plank, and he wrapped it in the rhetoric that became the trademark of the national career he launched on the third day of the convention:

> There are those who say we are rushing this issue of civil rights. I say we are a hundred and seventy-two years late. The time has arrived for the Democratic Party to get out of the shadow of states' rights and walk forthrightly into the bright sunshine of human rights.

Clifford was with the president in the Oval Office as they watched the scene unfold on one of the few rudimentary television sets that could receive the first visual broadcast of a political convention. In his memoir *Counsel to the President*, he described the reaction:

> Within an hour, most of the big city bosses, thinking President Truman was a "gone goose," and wanting to save the rest of the party in the North by carrying the black and liberal vote, swung into line behind the [Humphrey] plank. In a stunning rebuke to the President, [it] was approved by the delegates in a floor vote. Seeing the rising anger in the faces of the Southern delegates, Sam Rayburn, the convention chairman, quickly gaveled the afternoon session to a close, and sent word to the White House that it was time for the President to accept the nomination.

When the convention was called to order for the evening session, the chairman of the Alabama delegation, Handy Ellis, was recognized on a point of personal privilege. The electors who would cast the Alabama Democratic Party's votes in the Electoral College, he announced, were pledged "never to cast their vote for a Republican, never to cast their vote for Harry Truman, and never to cast their vote for any candidate with a civil rights program such as that adopted by the convention." Calling out, "We bid you good-bye," Ellis headed up the aisle, followed by half his delegation and all of Mississippi's. The Dixiecrats' third-party movement was under way.

It was two o'clock the following morning before Harry Truman got a chance to deliver his acceptance speech. The fractious delegates had wrangled throughout the evening, and he was finally nominated well after midnight—by a vote of 947½ to 263 for Senator Richard Russell of Georgia cast by Southern delegates still in the hall. And when Truman and his running mate, Alben Barkley, finally appeared on the platform, the president had to endure a final travesty.

In a scene that has lived in my memory, Emma Guffey Miller, Pennsylvania's massive Democratic national committeewoman, shouldered Sam Rayburn away from the microphone and announced that she had the honor to present the host city's special tribute to the nominee. Whereupon she pulled a cord that opened a floral replica of the Liberty Bell and released forty-eight white pigeons to serve as doves of peace.

The first thing I saw from the press pen was clouds of white feathers as some of the birds flew into the huge fans set up around the sweltering hall. The next was Sam Rayburn swinging his gavel at pigeons zeroing in on his gleaming bald head. Peace was hardly likely in that rancorous setting, but the very absurdity of the scene restored a modicum of good humor as the delegates watched each other dodge the droppings from the frantic birds.

Truman's speech, largely ad-libbed, was a partisan masterpiece that shifted attention from the controversial platform the delegates had struggled over to the one his Republican opponent, Thomas E. Dewey, stood on. The president used the Republican platform as the launching pad for a surprise announcement that brought the delegates to their feet laughing and cheering:

> On the twenty-sixth of July, which out in Missouri we call "Turnip Day," I am going to call Congress back and ask the

Republicans to pass laws to halt rising prices, to meet the housing crisis—which they say they are for in their platform.

I shall ask them to act on other vitally needed measures, such as aid to education, which they say they are for; a national health program, civil rights legislation, which they say they are for . . . extension of Social Security coverage and increased benefits, which they say they are for. . . .

It was, as the Republicans branded it, an obvious campaign ploy, but his realpolitik had put his opposition on the defensive and united his own party—or what was left of it. On July 16 the president noted in one of the memorandums he wrote to himself:

Editorials, columns and cartoons are gasping and wondering. None of the smart folks thought I would call the Congress. Dewey synthetically milks cows and pitches hay for the cameras just as that other faker Teddy Roosevelt did—but he never heard of "Turnip Day."

Two days after the Democratic convention adjourned, the Jeffersonian States' Rights Party, its title irrevocably shortened to Dixiecrat, convened at Birmingham to nominate Strom Thurmond for president and Fielding Wright for vice president. On July 23, the newly hatched Progressive Party named Henry Wallace its candidate for president. And on the day before Turnip Day, Truman announced two executive orders based on the strategy Clifford had devised for dealing with threats on the party's flanks.

The first established a fair employment practices policy throughout the federal government, with each agency head responsible for carrying it out under the oversight of a Fair Employment Board, to be set up in the Civil Service Commission. The second order declared elimination of racial discrimination in the armed services the policy of the commander in chief, and established within the Pentagon the President's Advisory Committee on Equality of Treatment and Opportunity to keep the White House informed on how it was being executed.

As anticipated, Richard Russell, indicating that he spoke on behalf of nineteen of the twenty-two Southern senators, denounced the executive orders as an "unconditional surrender . . . to the treasonable civil disobedience campaign organized by the Negroes." Thus recertified as a civil rights champion, Harry Truman would campaign on his chosen terrain.

In his message to the special session of Congress, the President asked for approval of practically all the liberal measures that had been rejected at the regular session. There was, of course, no prospect of action on any of these, and after eleven querulous days the Turnip Day Congress adjourned. Thomas Dewey's reaction was characteristic of the misjudgments that were to mark his second run for the White House: "Mr. Truman's special session is a nuisance but I do not believe it will have much effect on the election." In fact it established, and dramatized, the agenda for the populist crusade against the "do-nothing Republican Congress" that proved to be Dewey's undoing.

Civil rights could now be relegated to a peripheral place in the national campaign. The possible defection of blacks to the Republicans had been headed off, and Wallace's mystical neo-Marxism had no appeal for rank-and-file black voters, whose political leaders were cogs in big city Democratic machines. For the Dixiecrats, of course, it was the primary issue, but they were hobbled by their inability to command popular support outside their own bailiwick.

The Dixiecrat strategy turned on preventing either major party candidate from winning a majority in the archaic Electoral College, made up of delegates in numbers determined by congressional representation. The presidential candidate who wins the popular vote in a state normally receives all its electoral votes, but if there is no majority of the national electoral vote the popular vote is in effect canceled, and the choice is thrown into the House of Representatives. There, the Dixiecrats hoped, the Southern delegations should be able to see that an acceptable—that is, Republican—candidate would be seated in the White House.

Ordinarily, electors were listed on the ballot as a slate pledged to a party candidate. This had been the practice since the party system evolved, but nothing in the Constitution required an elector to accept the results of the popular vote. In four Deep Southern states—Alabama, Louisiana, South Carolina, and Mississippi—control of the party machinery allowed the Dixiecrats to list their Electoral College candidates on the ballot as Democrats although they were pledged to the Thurmond-Wright ticket.

In Arkansas, effective control of the party was now in the hands of Sidney Sanders McMath, a charismatic young liberal who had been nominated in the Democratic primary to succeed Governor Laney and was awaiting the usual pro forma certification in November. The Dixiecrats threatened to enter a well-financed racist demagogue against him in the general election if he refused to have the Democratic electors pledged to Thurmond. McMath, a World War II Marine colonel, responded to the threat in barracks-room language, and nothing came of it.

On the other flank, Henry Wallace was also having trouble getting his slate of electors on the ballot. It was evident that what Wallace called his "Gideon's army" was being used as a front by the Communist Party, and in Arkansas party members and fellow travelers were so few that the state chairman operated out of Oklahoma City. A scheme to rig the qualifications to invalidate the Wallace slate was hatched in the state-house, but was abandoned when the *Gazette* ridiculed it as hanky-panky intended to eliminate an electoral threat that could hardly be detected with the naked eye.

Wallace became an actor in the Southern sideshow to the national campaign when the Progressives decided to dramatize their commitment to the downtrodden proletariat by having the candidate go South to launch a head-on attack on segregation. The centerpiece for his campaign, like that of Strom Thurmond, was white supremacy—with Thurmond proclaiming it a God-given states' right, while Wallace attacked it as an immoral manifestation of capitalist exploitation. Although aimed from different directions, the appeal of both was directed at what Robert Sherrill identified as the electorate's "nerve strand that has been peeled slick, stretched taut between the poles of Black and White, and twanged."

Temperamentally, the two men were much alike. Each wore the blinders of the true believer, convinced that his own rectitude guaranteed the purity of his cause; each ignored the dubious company in which he found himself, refusing to entertain any suggestion that he was being used by strategists whose motives were somewhat different from his own.

Strom Thurmond was a figure out of my past. As a young reporter I had covered his court when he was a South Carolina circuit judge, and our paths had crossed in the Army. When he plunged into politics riding the wave of sentiment aroused by returning veterans, he billed himself as a liberal reformer—and at least it could be said that he was an outsider to the state's political establishment, cast in the maverick role he was to play throughout his career.

To my astonishment, he suggested that I consider resigning my post at the *Charlotte News* and becoming his campaign manager, and I don't think he ever understood why I rejected what he regarded as a golden opportunity. Politeness prevented my stating the real reason—that the humorless, stiff-necked probity that made him an honest if uncompassionate judge seemed to me to render him unfit for the give-and-take of political office.

These qualities, however, made him an ideal instrument for those who sought to divert Southern votes from Harry Truman. Thurmond laced his oratory with biblical quotations, and subjected those loath to leave the Democratic fold to the judgment of the church at Laodicea: "I know thy works; thou art neither cold nor hot. . . . So then because thou art lukewarm, and neither cold nor hot, I will spew thee from my mouth."

As it turned out, I dealt with both third-party candidates face to face. Wallace, who refused to speak to a segregated audience, would have been accommodated in Little Rock had he accepted the traditional site for campaign speeches, the band shell in a city park where there was no permanent seating and blacks were free to stand among the whites. But, to dramatize the Jim Crow issue, his handlers sought booking at a municipal auditorium, and when the segregation rule was waived, finally got a rejection from a downtown hotel.

These absurdities outraged J. N. Heiskell's libertarian sensibilities. His position was that any qualified candidate for president had a right to speak in Arkansas, and the people had a right to decide for themselves whether they wanted to hear him. To that end he announced that the *Gazette's* powerful radio station would provide Wallace free time, and when the manager objected, he told him he need have nothing to do with it except to clear airtime, since, to my surprise, he would have me interview the candidate so the program could qualify as news.

Wallace arrived in Little Rock in a near-paranoid state, having been greeted by thrown eggs and vegetables at his other Southern stops. In the course of our broadcast I followed up his usual strictures against Truman's foreign policy and the South's segregation practices by encouraging him to discuss the real revolution that was transforming the South under policies formulated during his tenure as Roosevelt's secretary of agriculture. On that familiar ground he relaxed and responded with an ease and eloquence that prompted the station manager to pass in a note suggesting that we extend the session to a full hour.

Watching from a third-floor window as the candidate departed, I saw his flying wedge of bodyguards hustle him into the waiting limousine provided by a black funeral home. The limousine remained at the curb while the police motorcycle escort took off with sirens keening. The driver had turned on the radio to listen to the broadcast, and the battery was dead. The last I saw of Wallace, he was helping the trailing press photographers push off the old Cadillac.

It may have been, as he said, the century of the common man, but his uncommon campaign placed him beyond the ken of those who were the object of his concern. His doctrinaire handlers had him expounding the pomposities of radical cant, which did not come naturally to him, and when he followed his own bent he floated off into opaque mysticism. So far as ordinary blacks were concerned—and working-class whites, for that matter—he was speaking in an unknown tongue.

A few weeks later, Strom Thurmond came to town, and his handlers demanded equal time. I tried, as I had with Wallace, to steer him into discussion of issues outside his narrow campaign litany, but to no avail; it was clear that he saw me as one of the lukewarm souls spewed out of the company of loyal Southerners. As we came out of the studio, we learned that lightning had struck the transmitter and we had been off the air for about a third of our discussion. Some of the local Dixiecrats charged that their candidate had been denied a full hearing, but Thurmond never joined in the complaint. It would, after all, have been unbecoming to concede the possibility that a heavenly thunderbolt had worked in favor of the infidels.

The national Democratic effort consisted primarily of the storied transcontinental whistle-stop tour during which the plain-spoken president appeared on the rear platform of his campaign train to address thousands of ordinary citizens who greeted him with cries of "Give 'em hell, Harry!" He won only 49.5 percent of the popular vote, but it was enough to give him the electoral majority that confounded the political experts. In his memoir Clark Clifford, taking due credit, explained how it happened:

> Certainly Dewey's arid personality and his passive, overconfident campaign gave President Truman an easier target than anyone anticipated. The defections of both Wallace and Thurmond also gave President Truman an unexpected opportunity to present himself as the true heir of FDR. . . . Black Americans rallied to the Democrats in record numbers, and actually provided the margin of victory for the President in several key states. In short, the pieces of the puzzle had for the most part fallen into place in November of 1948 much as we had hoped when preparing the strategy memorandum a year earlier.

In the South the damage control effort by the Democratic loyalists confined the party bolt to the four Deep Southern states. The rump parties came out even in the popular vote—1,169,021 votes for Thurmond, almost all of them in the South; 1,157,172 for Wallace, almost all of them outside the South. Summarizing the result, I termed the Dixiecrat rebellion one of the most conspicuous failures in American political history:

> The thirty-eight electoral votes accorded Governor Thurmond in South Carolina, Alabama, Mississippi, and Louisiana are meaningless, for in those states the Dixiecrats had seized the election machinery and presented their candidates in the guise of regulars. Elsewhere in the region the Dixiecrats ran under their true colors and could not muster sufficient support to throw a single Southern state into the Republican column.
>
> Yet the Dixiecrats did have a considerable importance. Although they tried to be polite about it, it was quite clear that they were in fact the anti-Negro party. . . . The case they presented to the Southern voter was a familiar one. They appealed to his prejudices and played upon his fears. They hurled the

reckless charge that election of either major candidate would mean Negro domination of the South, and for good measure added the allegation that the federal civil rights program endorsed by both the Democrats and Republicans is Communist in nature and inspiration.

I was overly optimistic in predicting that the election meant that the race issue was no longer a certain ticket to public office for any demagogue unprincipled enough to use it. But, bizarre as it often was, the partisan process had stripped away obfuscation, forcing genuine divisions over policy to the surface and eliminating those who sought to sabotage the party from within.

In the long run this would benefit Southern blacks, but it also demonstrated that in national politics the civil rights cause aroused little enduring support. Both parties employed it as a political gambit—the Democrats to hold together their shaky coalition in the big cities, where the black vote was a factor; the Republicans to harass the Democrats by exploiting issues that raised mass opposition among whites where their own party had no support to lose.

It followed that civil rights quickly disappeared from the national agenda in the face of the compelling issues that engulfed the Truman administration. During the next four years the president had to deal with the Communist takeover of China; the North Korean invasion of South Korea; development of the thermonuclear arsenal made possible by the hydrogen bomb; and the rearming of Western Europe to contain the expansion of Soviet influence. His response made him the world's leading anti-Communist, but it offered no protection against Republican charges that his administration was soft on conspirators whose unAmerican activities posed an internal threat—this despite the fact that his rout of the Wallace Progressives had demonstrated the impotence of the radical left.

To create bipartisan support for military operations in Asia and Cold War in Europe, Truman had to make concessions to the conservative coalition that remained in place in Congress even though the Democrats regained control of both houses. "Trying to make the Eighty-first Congress perform is and has been worse than cussing the Eightieth," he complained. "A president never loses prestige fighting Congress, but I can't fight my own Congress. There are some terrible chairmen in the Eighty-first."

In his 1949 State of the Union message, Truman again urged enactment of the civil rights package. But he was disarmed, and he knew it. "I've kissed and petted more consarned S.O.B. so-called Democrats and left-wing Republicans than all the presidents put together," he wrote. "I have very few people fighting my battles in Congress as I fought FDR's."

How few was demonstrated when Vice President Barkley used his authority as presiding officer to uphold a change in the Senate rules that would have allowed two thirds of the members to halt the filibusters the Dixiecrats employed to block action on civil rights measures. Senator Russell forced a floor vote, and the Barkley ruling was rejected, 46 to 41—with 23 Republicans and 3 Western Democrats joining the 20-member Southern bloc.

"Generally speaking, the Democrats were paper tigers on civil rights issues," Robert Donovan wrote. "The defeat of Barkley's ruling . . . mocked hopes inspired by the civil rights plank in the 1948 Democratic platform and by Truman's victory. It obliterated any chance of any major civil rights legislation in his second term."

STALEMATE
THE REPUBLICAN ASCENDANCY

I am convinced that the Supreme Court [*Brown*] decision set back progress in the South at least fifteen years. . . . It's all very well to talk about school integration—you may also be talking about social disintegration. Feelings are deep on this, especially where children are concerned. . . . We can't demand perfection on these moral questions. . . . And the fellow who tells me we can do these things by force is just plain nuts.

— PRESIDENT DWIGHT D. EISENHOWER, quoted by
Emmet John Hughes, *The Ordeal of Power*

A WEEK AFTER Harry Truman's famous victory at the polls, I was in New York's historic Town Hall defending the honor of the South. "What Should We Do About Race Segregation?" was the question before the house in a national radio debate, also carried on the rudimentary ABC television network. Hodding Carter, editor and publisher of the *Mississippi Delta Democrat-Times*, and I faced Walter White, executive secretary of the NAACP, and Ray Sprigle, a white *Pittsburgh Post-Gazette* reporter who had darkened his skin and traveled "underground" through the Jim Crow South disguised as a black.

Sprigle led off by proclaiming that in four weeks as a pseudo-Negro he had found that "wanton, inexcusable, capricious murder walks the streets and highways of the Southland, dogging the heels of ten million black men—women, too—and pouncing whimsically, with or without provocation." Walter White was far too seasoned a hand to indulge in such vulnerable oversimplification. He stuck to the high ground, setting forth the NAACP's basic argument in terms impossible for Carter and me to refute:

> There can never be any equality within the framework of seg-
> regation. Denial of equal educational and economic oportunity,
> disfranchisement, the ghetto, and the humiliation of the human
> spirit are the inescapable consequences of segregation. At the
> same time, a false sense of racial superiority is bred among those
> who do the segregating. The second consequence of segregation
> and the evils that grow out of it is the steadily lowered prestige
> of the United States among the two thirds of the people of this
> earth who are colored, and also among many white peoples.

Hodding Carter was the only editor of a Mississippi daily newspaper who had demonstrated that he was "acutely aware of, and actively opposed to the discriminations that are still practiced in the South." He used that record as preface to rejection of President Truman's civil rights program as "a windmill attack upon certain diminishing results of racial antipathies rather than upon the causes." I rested my case on the recent rout of the Dixiecrats:

> With their ballots the voters of the South declared race a dead
> issue in the great majority of the Southern States. . . . Seven
> hundred thousand Negroes were qualified to vote in the South
> last Tuesday, and so far as I know most of them did vote. . . . In
> eighty years, only a moment in the sweep of history, the Negro
> has moved within sight of his traditional goal of proper civil
> rights.

The sophistry in my arguments was exposed in exchanges with Walter White. But his most telling charge was leveled in the form of a question addressed to me in the course of our informal discussions offstage: "You know segregation has to go. Why don't you admit it? There you are, six feet tall, blond, blue-eyed, a certified Confederate WASP. You've been a colonel in the Army, you've been in combat. What are *you* afraid of?" It was calculated needling. The Georgia-born White knew that physical courage was essential to a Southerner's self-image. And he knew that I knew he had earned the right to ask the question.

His fair skin and sophisticated style permitted him to pass the color bar unnoticed, and as an investigator for the NAACP he had employed Sprigle's undercover technique in reverse. In 1919 he used press credentials provided by the *Chicago Daily News* to cover postwar violence in the Mississippi Delta plantation belt. At Elaine, Arkansas, the shooting of a white deputy by a black man brought in federal troops, and the soldiers moved through the countryside taking into "protective custody" every black they could find, except those who were shot for resisting arrest, or seeming to. Looking over the files of my newspaper, I later wrote:

> The *Gazette* reported that twenty-five blacks and five whites were killed at Elaine. On the basis of his undercover investigation, White published reports that set the black death toll nearer to two hundred. Twenty-five years later James Street, recalling the slaughter in a memoir, wrote: "No one knows to this day just how many folks were killed." But one thing is certain: no representative of the *Gazette*, in that day or in my own, was ever subjected to personal danger as intense and protracted as that faced by the young investigative reporter from the NAACP during the weeks he spent among the inflamed citizens of that God-forsaken backwater.

The optimism I expressed at Town Hall for further progress on the race relations front dwindled rapidly as Harry Truman's ability to advance domestic programs in Congress was steadily dissipated during his last years in office, and finally was reduced to a rearguard action to protect reforms put in place in the New Deal era. Party loyalty declined along with presidential prestige, and by midterm the civil rights coalition that ensured the 1948 Democratic victory was coming up short in every test.

It was still possible for the movement to obtain impressive endorsements outside the South; in January 1950, 4,000 delegates from 33 states convened in Washington for a national mobilization in support of the civil rights agenda. But although this was ostensibly an interracial effort, more than 3,000 of those attending represented NAACP chapters; the CIO sent 383, the AFL 119, B'nai B'rith 350, the American Jewish Congress 185, the ADA 60, and assorted church groups 200.

The sole accomplishment of the mobilization was to leave behind in Washington a permanent lobby called the Leadership Conference on Civil Rights. Roy Wilkins of the NAACP, emerging as the movement's leading political strategist, insisted that to achieve maximum impact its efforts should be concentrated on a single piece of legislation, and FEPC was endorsed as "the most fundamental of all pending civil rights bills." The Leadership Conference deployed its forces on Capitol Hill, but the mere threat of endless debate by iron-tongued Southern senators guaranteed the measure's demise. It was clear that the votes necessary to invoke cloture were not to be had.

"Most of the principals in the parliamentary farce now going on want to keep the FEPC issue alive for campaign purposes in the coming Congressional elections," Arthur Krock wrote in *The New York Times*, suggesting that even President Truman could be counted among the *farceurs*. The NAACP magazine *The Crisis* dished out condemnation with an even hand: ". . . neither the Republicans nor the Northern Democrats can blame the Dixiecrats. Cloture on FEPC was blocked by Northern and Western senators of both parties, nine Republicans and twelve Democrats." That pattern was to prevail until 1957, when an FEPC bill finally made it out of committee and had to be done to death in open voting.

The only significant civil rights measure to survive the impasse was desegregation of the armed services, which the president achieved through executive orders that placed it effectively beyond the reach of Congress. Even so, it required a great deal of internal pushing and shoving to bring it about in the face of the outspoken opposition of the star-spangled generals and admirals entrenched in the Pentagon.

As Army chief of staff, General Eisenhower declared the armed forces unready "spiritually, philosophically or mentally to absorb blacks and whites together." Even after the order was in effect, his successor, General Omar Bradley, insisted that the Army "is not out to make any social reforms. The Army will put men of different races in different companies. It will change that policy when the nation as a whole changes it."

Truman appointed Solicitor General Charles Fahy to head a compliance committee, and throughout 1949 Fahy wrestled with Louis Johnson, the president's appointee as secretary of the newly created Department of Defense. Johnson, Clark Clifford noted, "confined his support of desegregation to empty rhetoric, and fought the very existence of the Fahy committee." The Navy and now independent Air Force reluctantly yielded, but the Army did not begin to move until the president, assuming the mantle of commander in chief, issued direct orders that forced his military subordinates to choose between compliance and resignation.

The new dispensation took effect while the armed services were engaged in what was euphemistically called a "police action" in Korea, where a massive American expeditionary force, under the flag of the United Nations, fought Communists. Whites at the front were fighting in a country where they were themselves an ethnic minority. There were no social amenities to protect against black intrusion, and under the stress of common peril they welcomed the support of troops of any color who seemed to know what they were doing. Patriotism had a restraining effect on the far larger number who served in support roles.

Mobilization for what became a protracted war effort even caught up with me. I had been automatically reassigned to the Army reserve at the end of World War II, with my lieutenant colonel's commission now in the General Staff Corps. Strictly a wintertime soldier with no interest in playing war games, I had ignored occasional communiqués from reserve headquarters until one arrived ordering me to Camp Chaffee, Arkansas, for two weeks' active duty.

I reported at Chaffee's artillery replacement center along with a thousand or so raw draftees who represented the weekly quota shipped to Arkansas from induction stations in surrounding states. The busy headquarters had no use for a temporary, supernumerary operations officer, so I was issued a Jeep and told to look around the sprawling reservation and prepare a staff analysis of the thirteen-week basic training cycle. As it turned out, my uniform, which relieved me of the suspicion normally aroused by a nosy newspaperman, gave me the opportunity to have an inside view of the process involved in the creation of the nation's first racially integrated fighting force.

Upon arrival at Chaffee a white youth from a Jim Crow state would find blacks sharing his sleeping quarters, standing naked beside him in the shower, and sitting at his elbow in the mess hall. Even more shocking, he would find himself not only taking orders from blacks, but, in the hard-nosed Army way, also being dressed down by them. Yet, as far as I could see, the racial mixture was producing no more disciplinary problems than I had encountered when we put an all-white infantry division through the same training cycle.

It was, of course, an inherently abnormal situation as far as the draftees were concerned. All sorts of unprecedented things were happening to them, and the sudden absence of the color bar was only one more manifestation of a drastically changed life-style dictated by a hierarchical command structure in which they were at the lowest rung.

Off-duty, blacks and whites tended to group with their own kind, but those who chose to eat or drink together attracted no special attention. An Army post in those days was still a male preserve; except for a few nurses and WACS, there were no women around to complicate social relationships. In the nearby towns military police records indicated that disturbances were fewer and less severe than they had been in World War II, when Chaffee was all-white.

At the bar in the officers' club I checked my impressions with the regulars and reserve retreads who clustered there when the sun crossed the yardarm. One of these was a Louisiana-bred major who spoke out of experience with the lone World War II black division. "This is the only way to handle the problem," he said. "Trying to make a fighting force out of Nigra troops under white officers no longer gets the job done. And if you're going to draft white kids for combat you sure as hell can't let the black ones stay home."

The major didn't think the white draftees were having any great difficulty in adjusting. "It shakes them up at first," he said, "but they begin to realize that they can work and fight alongside a Nigra, or under one, without having any close personal contact if that's the way they want it. The main thing is what it does for the Nigras. It gives them the kind of self-confidence a soldier has got to have if he is going to put his ass on the line. And once they get it they average out about like the whites—about the same percentage of yardbirds, ordinary Joes, brown-noses, and beavers who are going to work hard to go up through the ranks.

"There are some problems, of course. A commander who wants to discriminate can still get away with it to some extent—and the other side is that Nigras are likely to holler 'discrimination' any time they fall short. But, hell, that's the way it is with whites, too. If your superiors have got it in for you for whatever reason you're liable to get old in grade, like I'm doing—and it just ain't human nature for anyone to admit he was passed over for due cause."

This was the prevailing view among scores of officers and noncoms I talked with. There were some who bitched, talked fondly about the good old days of Jim Crow, and let their prejudices show in dealing with blacks. But I found none who thought there was any possibility that the policy would be reversed, and few who believed it should be. Harry Truman had erected an enduring monument to his embattled administration.

As the 1952 election drew near, the president's popularity was at a low ebb, and the Democrats were in serious disarray. The Dixiecrats' bolt had not affected the party's control of state and local government even in the states they carried, but direct support of the Republican presidential ticket was now being urged by Southern dissidents. The move was masterminded by James F. Byrnes, the embittered elder statesman who had returned from Olympus to be elected governor of South Carolina virtually by acclamation.

The Democratic high command moved to meet the threat when the annual Southern Governors' Conference met at Hot Springs, Arkansas, in November 1951. Sid McMath, as host governor, loaded the program with Washington heavyweights led by Speaker Sam Rayburn, a prime example of loyalty to the party of his fathers. And to smoke out the opposition he asked me to deliver an address on civil rights— a subject, he had discovered, that had never before been publicly discussed at the conference.

In my remarks at the opening luncheon I acknowledged the dilemma facing governors whose white constituents opposed the civil rights measures embraced by both political parties. They now faced a majority of voters not yet willing to accept blacks as equals, and a growing minority no longer willing to settle for anything less:

> The practical problem before the South is to preserve social segregation while at the same time meeting the conditions of a Constitution and a national tradition which demand that full civil liberties and full equality of opportunity be extended to all citizens without discrimination. If I read the election returns correctly, a considerable majority of the people of the United States have come to believe that this cannot be done, and therefore to support, or at least accept, a federal program of legislation that is clearly aimed at the immediate end of segregation.
>
> So far we have attempted to meet the constant assault on segregation largely by negative means. We have fought back, sometimes successfully, but our weapons have been those of an embattled political minority, and they are poor things at best. . . .
>
> We must recognize, first of all, that in fundamentally public activities—and the test here would be their support by tax funds—the Negro must either be treated without official prejudice or in absolute, incontrovertible fact be provided with separate but equal facilities. When we have done this we can argue, and I think be heard sympathetically, that we have met the stated commitments of citizenship, and we may then insist that matters involving the private relationship between the two races are, and should be, beyond the reach of the law.

When I finished, the only applause came from the lone Republican governor, Theodore McKeldin of Maryland; the Democratic loyalists grouped around Governor McMath; and my colleagues at the press table. Herman Talmadge of Georgia stalked out at midpassage, and when John Popham of *The New York Times* asked Governor Byrnes for comment the shocked response was, "Why, I believe I know that boy's family!"

I had not expected to make any public converts. The prospect of political mayhem had attracted a swarm of political writers to Hot

Springs, and in their presence these elected officials could hardly be expected to endorse views that not only were offensive to many of their constituents but also were implicitly critical of their own conduct. The real significance lay in the fact that the reaction was so restrained. The recruiting effort by Byrnes and Governor Allen Shivers of Texas, who rode shotgun, was stopped cold by McMath's strategy; a year later they were the only two Southern governors to support the Republican presidential ticket publicly. The GOP landslide stopped short of the Southern heartland, reaching only to Virginia, Tennessee, Florida, and Texas.

Republican leaders, looking for a charismatic candidate to exploit what they called the mess in Washington, took up the quest dissident Democrats had launched four years before. It was assumed, with reason, that General Eisenhower had turned down the proffered nomination only because it came from the wrong party.

He had retired from the Army to accept the presidency of Columbia University, where his indifferent administration bolstered the suspicion that he considered it a temporary sinecure. In 1951 he was called back into service as supreme commander of the Allied forces mustered into the North Atlantic Treaty Organization. This put him back in the public eye, and Republican leaders began openly wooing him. In early 1952 he allowed his name to be entered in the New Hampshire Republican primary, and in June he resigned his NATO command and formally entered the race.

I had been situated too far down the chain of command even to catch a glimpse of the general when I served under him, but in the fall of 1951 I was exposed to his famous grin and considerable charm. A dozen members of the American Society of Newspaper Editors were selected by the Pentagon for a conducted tour of NATO dispositions, and at our first stop we were invited to an informal luncheon with Eisenhower at his Versailles headquarters outside Paris. He was still nominally uncommitted, but there wasn't any doubt why we were there. Rotated into chairs at the affable general's side, we tried to draw him out on his political views. It was a frustrating exercise; he was already wrapped in the cloak of bland generalities he wore when he mounted the stump.

Moderate Republicans led by Thomas E. Dewey masterminded the general's successful nomination campaign against Senator Robert A. Taft of Ohio, champion of the isolationist Old Guard. On the Democratic side the most likely contender was Governor Adlai Stevenson of Illinois, the eloquent patrician who had pushed through major reforms in his state's notoriously corrupt government. President Truman offered his support, but Stevenson was reluctant to accept it. He liked his present job, was certain to be reelected, and doubted that any Democrat could win a national election.

The 1952 party conventions in Chicago were the last to be dominated by delegates selected by state party organizations. Only a minority of states, most of them small, then required that presidential candidates run in their primaries. Truman predicted that the primary results would be "just eyewash when the convention meets." True to form, the party bosses got together to deal out the two contenders who had picked up delegates by popular vote, Senator Estes Kefauver of Tennessee and Governor Averell Harriman of New York. The noncontender, Adlai Stevenson, still protesting that he was a candidate only for reelection as governor of Illinois, was nominated on the third ballot.

Stevenson's soaring welcoming address had touched off a well-prepared draft movement, and he topped it with a memorable acceptance speech in which he pledged to talk sense to the American people. In the euphoria of the moment it was possible to believe that the ruptured party had been united by coupling a nominee from Abraham Lincoln country with a Deep Southern running mate, Senator John Sparkman of Alabama. But Stevenson was comitted to the civil rights platform he had helped fashion four years before, and in circulating among the Southern delegations I found it evident that the rift had only been papered over.

In the 1952 election civil rights played only a minor role as a campaign issue. The Democrats, trying to heal their party's wounds, had obvious reasons for downplaying it, and the Republicans had nominated a candidate who was hardly disposed to pay even lip service to the demand for federal action to end racial discrimination. In *Eisenhower: Captive Hero*, Marquis Childs recalled that in 1948 the general had laughed when liberal Democrats started wooing him. He was, he told a reporter, a strong believer in states' rights:

> . . . if he had to name any single individual whose outlook he agreed with it would probably be Senator Harry F. Byrd of Virginia. The idea of using the police power of the federal government to enforce, say, an anti-lynching law was abhorrent to him, since he was convinced that to turn federal authority to such an end would be disastrous.

Adlai Stevenson had compiled an impeccable record as a civil libertarian when he practiced law in Chicago, and as governor had sponsored a state FEPC law and desegregated the state parks and the Illinois National Guard. It was assumed, or at least hoped, that this would be enough to hold the big city black vote while he maintained an accommodating stance with the Southern wing of the party.

Trying to maintain that precarious balance caused a split among the volunteers who flocked to Stevenson headquarters in Springfield to help prepare the torrent of oratory the candidate would be required to spout as he barnstormed across the country. The writers who worked out of makeshift offices in the local Elks Club included a faction led by the Harvard historian Arthur Schlesinger, Jr., one of the founders of ADA, who pressed for a Truman-style give-'em-hell campaign. For temperamental as well as tactical reasons, Stevenson resisted, as did those who worked on speeches for Southern consumption. The "Moonlight and Magnolia Team," as the "Elks" derisively referred to them, had established their own redoubt at the St. Nicholas Hotel when my friend David Cohn, a talented Mississippi essayist, asked me to help out with speeches for the first foray across the Mason-Dixon line.

I had planned to join the campaign press corps for the pass through Louisiana, Florida, and Tennessee, and arranged to spend a few days in Springfield before picking up the caravan in St. Louis. My first personal encounter with Stevenson, over a ritual toddy at the fusty old governor's mansion, confirmed the favorable impression I had taken away from Chicago. He was one of the great conversationalists of the day—witty, perceptive, often ironic at his own expense—with a curiosity and willingness to listen rare among politicians of his stature.

He considered himself his best speechwriter, and was frustrated that he now had to rely on others for input he always tried to reshape when time allowed. In discussing what I might contribute, he warned that he would make no statement on civil rights before any audience that he could not repeat anywhere he spoke. The convention draft, he felt, had left him free of obligations to any special interest. That was true enough, but it did not insulate him against the pulling and hauling of the contending factions within his own entourage, nor did it help in dealing with party leaders whose help he needed.

Stevenson's own essentially moderate view on racial matters was not satisfactory to either side. The northern party leaders were hardly pleasured when he appeared before their followers to deplore what he called the "sledgehammer approach," contending that in the end coercive measures would be harmful to both races. And his Confederate antecedents, which permitted him to turn up kinfolk everywhere he went in the South, did not allay the suspicions of such political satraps as his Georgia cousin Richard Russell, who remained convinced that he must have made some kind of civil rights deal with Harry Truman.

When I arrived in St. Louis to sign on the press plane I found my friend Ralph McGill of the *Atlanta Constitution* trying to head off trouble on the racial front. James Hicks of Harlem's *Amsterdam News*, one of two blacks among the scores of correspondents, had just discovered that New Orleans' segregation laws had prevented the campaign's advance man from booking rooms for them at the Roosevelt Hotel. Arrangements had been made to put up the two at the home of a black college professor, and the more Hicks thought about it, the angrier he became.

The next morning McGill and I sat with him on the flight to Oklahoma City. Our efforts to cool him down were to no avail; by that time he had made up his mind to make a public issue of his exclusion. When we landed I warned Arthur Schlesinger, who was with the candidate, and called George Chaplin, who had been my city editor on the *Piedmont* and was now editor of the *New Orleans Item*. I urged him to assure the hotel manager that two black reporters would never be noticed in the confusion attending the arrival of two planeloads of bedraggled journalists and politicians. George sighed, and said that under ordinary circumstances the ordinance could be waived—but the owner of the Roosevelt was a dedicated Dixiecrat who would be delighted with an opportunity to embarrass Stevenson.

On the flight from Oklahoma City McGill made his last, best effort to placate Jimmy Hicks. How would it be, he asked, if he and Ashmore stayed with him at the professor's house? It didn't work, and Hicks went to the press room at the Roosevelt to announce his withdrawal from the campaign entourage. Before the reporters could get to Stevenson for comment, we were on our way to a rally in Beauregard Square, and he had no reason to go beyond the passage in Dave Cohn's speech draft:

> As you know, I stand on the Democratic Party platform with reference to minority rights. I have only one observation to make on this subject, one that must sadden you as it saddens me. It is that, after two thousand years of Christianity, we need discuss it at all.

Most of the correspondents wound up in the French Quarter after the rally, and Jimmy Hicks's protest got little more than a paragraph or two in the national press.

The speech in Nashville the following night was one to which I had been the principal contributor. I have always appreciated the appraisal of Stevenson's biographer John Bartlow Martin, who was one of the ablest of the Elks and who shared their bias against moonlight and magnolias: "Like all Southern speeches it was very long and contained a recitation of Stevenson's Southern ancestry; the crowd expected and liked it. . . . It was a skillful speech."

I left the campaign party at Nashville and had no further contact with the candidate except to send along an occasional suggested speech passage. In retrospect, I doubt that Stevenson's position on civil rights made any significant difference in the outcome. If he did not emphasize it, he certainly did not conceal it, and those on both sides who were sensitive on the subject surely knew where he stood. His own conviction came through in a speech to a mixed audience in Richmond. "I should justly earn your contempt if I talked one way in the South and another elsewhere. I do not attempt to justify the unjustifiable, whether it is anti-Negroism in one place, anti-Semitism in another—or, for that matter, anti-Southernism in many places. And neither can I justify self-righteousness anywhere."

The election was a Democratic rout. Eisenhower won 55.1 percent of the popular vote, giving him a 442 to 89 electoral sweep. The new president's personal popularity had enabled him to run far ahead of his party, but his coattails were long enough to give the Republicans majorities in both houses of Congress. Eisenhower had no mandate to deal with issues that had not been raised—and in the case of civil rights he would do his best to minimize the responsibility that was finally thrust on him.

"When the administration took office," Robert Donovan wrote, "it was plunged into the whirlpool of Korea, China, the budget . . . and a hundred and one other things. Somehow no one gave much thought to the special problems of the Negro, and practically nothing was done about this politically very sensitive matter." But a great deal of thought was being given to it in another branch of the federal government.

In its stately marble quarters on Capitol Hill, the U.S. Supreme Court had been dealing with cases that were pushing the justices toward fundamental reconsideration of the nation's policy on race relations. Without attacking the separate-but-equal doctrine, NAACP lawyers had sought redress in the Jim Crow states through court orders requiring that public facilities available to blacks be brought up to the standards of those provided for whites. In the process they had managed to force a significant breakthrough at the top of the educational structure.

In a Maryland case a state court held that the Constitution's equality standard could not be met by paying the tuition of blacks attending professional schools at universities outside the state's jurisdiction. Since the cost of establishing a separate law school at Maryland's black state college was prohibitive, the only alternative was to lower the color bar. The precedent resulted in court-ordered desegregation at the graduate level in other border states.

Outside the Deep South this became standard practice without arousing any great outcry. In 1947, although he expressed strong misgivings, Governor Laney made no move to block the University of Arkansas' voluntary enrollment of a black student in its law school, and one, who was almost as distinctive because she was female, in its medical school. But the blacks involved were only a tiny minority among mature white classmates, who usually lived off-campus. The issue of social equality was not effectively raised, as it inescapably would be if desegregation were ordered at lower levels of the educational structure.

The NAACP was represented in court actions by aggressive young black lawyers, many of whom had been educated at leading Ivy League schools under the out-of-state tuition scheme. They had the counsel of leading constitutional experts who made up the 187-member Committee of Law Teachers Against Segregation in Legal Education—practically all of them white. In June 1950 a total of 43 of these joined with NAACP state and branch presidents to consider a basic change in litigation strategy recommended by Thurgood Marshall, head of the semi-autonomous NAACP Legal Defense and Educational Fund.

Marshall's proposal for a head-on attack on separate-but-equal raised a good many questions among the black leaders and their white supporters. "I certainly would not have had the courage to go after segregation per se," Louis Pollack, a future dean of Yale Law School, recalled. "Certainly not at the public school level." Marshall had the courage, and he carried the day, emerging from the strategy session to announce, "We are going to insist on nonsegregation in American education from top to bottom—from law school to kindergarten."

By the end of the year NAACP lawyers were moving ahead with five public school cases covering the range of segregation laws in force in the eighteen jurisdictions where separate schools were required or permitted. When they reached the Supreme Court they were combined to provide the basis for the historic ruling that took its title from *Brown v. Board of Education*, the Topeka, Kansas, case that was the first to be filed on appeal.

In the spring of 1952, while the cases were pending, I was one of the speakers at a gathering of three hundred lawyers, social scientists, and civil rights leaders assembled for a colloquium at Howard University in Washington. In my address to the preponderantly black audience, as I had before to the Southern governors, I warned that advocates on both sides of the central issue raised by *Brown* were in danger of misreading public opinion, citing as a prime example the declaration in the colloquium's prospectus: "Negroes are determined, and all but the most reactionary whites are resigned to the fact, that enforced segregated schools must go in the very near future."

The reality, I insisted, was that a substantial majority of whites in the South were a long way from being resigned to the abandonment of segregation in the public schools. It would be a grave mistake to assume that Governor Byrnes did not enjoy the support of his South Carolina constituency when he declared that he would sooner abandon public education than lower the color bar in a single school.

I could, as most of the justices no doubt would, concede the moral argument, but that did not dispose of the fact that the Supreme Court was faced with the problem of fashioning a ruling that would not prove to be unenforceable. Professor John P. Frank of Yale Law School put it bluntly: "A judge cannot be blamed if he shrinks from precipitating a race riot." There were also cautionary voices on the black side, but they were silenced by the passionate response of the young lawyers on the NAACP team. "Shall the Negro child be required to wait for his constitutional rights until the white South is educated, industrialized and ready to confer these rights on his children's children?" James Nabrit demanded. The answer in the brief the NAACP subsequently filed was a resounding "no."

Oral arguments in the *Brown* cases were heard by the Court in December 1952, and the reaction of the justices made it clear that their verdict would have momentous consequences for public education. If *Plessy* survived, black schools would have to be made demonstrably equal as well as separate, and enforcement of such an order would impose heavy financial and administrative burdens on school districts ill prepared to assume them. If the decision went the other way and the Court ordered desegregation, the emotionally loaded problems confronting responsible local school officials would be without precedent.

The officers of the Ford Foundation's Fund for the Advancement of Education concluded that the foreseeable results of the pending Court action deserved the kind of attention they were not getting from the educators upon whom the burden would fall. To begin with, there was little reliable information on the actual disparities within the dual systems. Statistical data involving black schools had been so neglected, and frequently doctored, that the official records provided only a limited basis for estimating what would be required to revamp the system.

Early in 1953 the board of directors of the Fund, chaired by retired Supreme Court justice Owen J. Roberts, authorized its president, Clarence H. Faust, to offer a blank check to any appropriate institution in the South willing to undertake a comprehensive look at the structure of biracial education. The project was deemed urgent, since at least preliminary findings should be available when the Court made its ruling—now expected at the end of the 1953–54 term.

The Fund had established an experimental teacher training project in Arkansas, and as a trustee of Arkansas State Teachers College I had come to know Faust. He stopped in at the *Gazette* to discuss the problems he was encountering as he made the rounds seeking a home for the dual school project. By June it was evident that the undertaking was too politically charged to obtain the sanction of the trustees and admininistrators of any public or private university in the region, although a number of individual scholars were willing and anxious to participate.

The Fund concluded that it would have to administer the project directly, and I was asked to sign on as director. Faust brushed aside my lack of scholarly credentials, and the fact that I could not take leave from my newspaper duties; the Fund met those objections by recruiting experts to do the research and establishing a coordinating staff in Atlanta. Within days forty social scientists and legal scholars on various campuses had begun to sift through the available data and extract additional facts from those charged with administering the dual school systems.

It was stipulated that "the Fund will not undertake to argue the case for or against segregation in public education. . . ." But it was impossible to insulate the project against the qualms of the nervous school officials with whom we dealt. In order to assemble the chief state school officers in Atlanta to review our findings we had to hold the meeting in secret at an isolated suburban resort and guarantee that in case of a leak we would deny that any of these elected officials had ever been present when the possibility of desegregation had even been mentioned.

I had begun the project assuming that my principal obligation would be to edit the several volumes to be published by the University of North Carolina Press. But it soon became evident that my scholarly colleagues were not going to get their material in shape for publication in time to be of use to those who would immediately be affected by the Supreme Court decision.

The need for a summary of their findings initiated my association with Harold Fleming, a young Georgian who had come home after graduating from Harvard to take a job with the Southern Regional Council that led to a distinguished national career in the civil rights field. We had drafted Fleming for the Atlanta coordinating staff, and I put him to work under forced draft extracting pertinent excerpts from the voluminous research I could rework.

I did manage to hold to the neutral role enjoined by the Fund, and the report was generally accepted as authoritative. But it seemed to me that anyone who read my account of the path the South had followed since the beginning of public education in the past century, and considered the implications of the changing demographic patterns revealed by pages of tables and graphs, could not doubt that time was running out for the rigidly segregated society hammered into place eighty years before. In the concluding paragraph of the summary volume, *The Negro and the Schools,* I wrote:

> In the long sweep of history the public school cases before the Supreme Court may be written down as the point at which the South cleared the last turning in the road to reunion—the point at which finally, and under protest, the region gave up its peculiar institutions and accepted the prevailing standards of the nation at large as the legal basis for its relationship with its minority race. This would not in itself bring about any great shift in Southern attitudes, nor even any far-reaching changes in the pattern of biracial education. But it would redefine the goal the Southern people, white and Negro, are committed to seek in the way of democracy.

It took more than two and a half years for the Supreme Court to pull itself together and render a unanimous decision reversing the states' rights doctrine that had determined the federal government's civil rights policies since the end of Reconstruction. In the light of all that has followed, it was not inappropriate that the historic ruling resulted from a political deal made by a professedly nonpolitical president.

At the 1952 Republican convention, Earl Warren, the three-term governor of California, had stepped aside as a favorite son candidate to make way for Eisenhower's nomination, and had been promised the first appointment to the High Court. The opening came with the sudden death of Chief Justice Fred Vinson on September 8, 1953. The sixty-two-year-old Warren, who had spent all but three years of his career in public office, was unquestionably a politician, and this proved to be an asset as he undertook to bring the divided Court together.

When he took office, four of the justices were committed to over-turning the separate-but-equal precedent, but four others were hesitant to face the practical consequences and couched their reservations in terms of legal doctrine. In his memoir *The Court Years*, Justice William O. Douglas noted that the leading theorist, Felix Frankfurther, was brought around by the feeling that "if a practical politician like Warren thought we should overrule the 1896 opinion, why should a professor object?"

The school desegregation edict the new chief justice persuaded his contentious brethren to support was necessarily an exercise in moderation. It could be judged radical only by those who held extreme opinions of their own, or, as in the case of President Eisenhower, were far removed from the reality of race relations as they existed at midcentury. There was, of course, a profound moral component, an affirmation of the requirements of simple justice. But Warren imposed his own un-pretentious style on the opinion, instructing his clerks that drafts offered for consideration should be "short, readable by the lay public, nonrhetorical, unemotional, and, above all, nonaccusatory."

And that was how *Brown* came down. In simple, straightforward prose, the opinion reviewed the development of public education from the rudimentary state that characterized it when the constitutional issue was first raised:

> Today [education] is a principal instrument in awakening a child to cultural values, in preparing him for later professional training, and in helping him adjust normally to his environment. In these days, it is doubtful that any child may reasonably be expected to succeed in life if he is denied the opportunity of an education. Such an education, where the state has undertaken to provide it, must be made available to all on equal terms.

> We come then to the question presented: Does segregation

of children in public schools solely on the basis of race, even though the physical facilities and other "tangible" factors may be equal, deprive the children of equal educational opportunities? We believe that it does. . . .

To separate them from others of similar age and qualifications solely because of their race generates a feeling of inferiority as to their status in the community that may affect their hearts and minds in a way unlikely ever to be undone. . . .

Any language in *Plessy* v. *Ferguson* contrary to this finding is rejected. We conclude that in the field of education "separate but equal" has no place.

It is doubtful that the findings of the Ashmore Project had any direct influence on the Court's decision, although Justice Roberts, who wrote the foreword to *The Negro and the Schools*, indicated that page proofs had been available to his brethren. But it did play a significant role when the justices, having united on the moral issue, turned their attention to the thorny political problems that had to be dealt with in implementing the historic decision. The Court called for new briefs and oral argument, and invited the attorneys general of all the affected states to participate. Another year would pass before the mandate to desegregate the public schools took effect.

DEFAULT

EISENHOWER VS. THE SUPREME COURT

. . . if he had gone to the nation on television and radio telling the people to obey the law and fall in line, the cause of desegregation would have been accelerated. Ike was a hero and he was worshipped. Some of his political capital spent on the racial cause would have brought the nation closer to the Constitutional standards. Ike's ominous silence on our 1954 decision gave courage to the racists who decided to resist the decision ward by ward, precinct by precinct, town by town, and county by county.

—ASSOCIATE JUSTICE WILLIAM O. DOUGLAS,
The Court Years

THE *BROWN* DECISION produced an automatic roar of defiance in the Deep South, but across most of the Jim Crow states responsible political leaders held their tongues, and not a few indicated that they felt sure the ruling would be accepted as the law of the land. In bellwether Virginia, Governor Thomas B. Stanley announced that he would convene a meeting of local and state officials "to work toward a plan that shall be acceptable to our citizens and in keeping with the edict of the Court. Views of leaders of both races will be invited." Most Southern newspapers deplored the decision as premature, but counseled calm, and some predicted ultimate acceptance. Leading churchmen spoke out approvingly, and the organized denominations endorsed the ruling as morally correct.

In Little Rock, the school board, with the evident approbation of the local establishment, announced, "It is our responsibility to comply with federal constitutional requirements and we intend to do so when the Supreme Court of the United States outlines the methods to be followed." In the border states, and areas in the upper South where the proportion of black to white students was small, a process of voluntary desegregation began that eliminated Jim Crow in 750 districts.

The more or less favorable reaction involved a mixture of conscience and pragmatism. The Court ruling stiffened the resolve of those who recognized the inherent injustices of the segregated society, giving them a practical reason to shake off the stifling conformity imposed by local mores. And the industrializing South had begun to create a business community whose leadership recognized the adverse economic consequences of explosive racial confrontation.

In the course of the Ashmore Project I had discussed with a number of leading industrial managers and promoters the possibility that the Court might order an end to segregated schools. The reaction of C. Hamilton Moses, the evangelical president of Arkansas Power & Light, was typical. Moses, who employed the style of a country preacher on behalf of the private utilities' crusade against the "creeping socialism" of public power, was shocked when I told him I thought the Court would overturn *Plessy.* "They can't do that!" he said, "Why, the folks in the country won't stand for it." But suppose they do order desegregation and there is widespread racial trouble? "Oh, my God, no!" Moses cried. "If the Klan starts riding again we'll never sell another bond issue on Wall Street." Would he, then, be prepared to speak out publicly on behalf of law and order? None of those I talked with was willing to go that far—but there was little doubt that they would be using their influence behind the scenes, at least so far as it didn't entail undue political risk.

By any of the measures we used to sound public opinion there appeared to be considerable latent support for an orderly adjustment to the requirements of *Brown.* What was missing in the year of suspense that followed the Court's initial ruling was effective local leadership to rally support for the school officials who would have to carry out the Court's mandate. I was convinced that this would begin to emerge in response to a call to civic duty from President Eisenhower. A pillar of the Southern establishment could hardly reject a moral appeal from a conservative war hero with popular support so widespread he was regarded as above partisan politics.

There is no way to know whether that judgment was correct, for President Eisenhower rejected any and all requests that he lend moral support to the Supreme Court's decision. There is evidence that he tried to shape the briefs filed by the Justice Department to support the separate-but-equal doctrine, and succeeded in keeping them noncommittal. In 1958, sitting beside Virginius Dabney at a Washington dinner, he confided, "I went as far as I could, but was unsuccessful," and added, "The worst damn fool mistake I ever made was appointing Earl Warren chief justice." He refused to offer any public judgment of his own on the merits of *Brown*, and when he couldn't avoid being involved in its consequences, said only, "I think it makes no difference whether or not I endorse it."

Inside the Supreme Court the niceties of constitutional theory gave way to questions of community attitudes—how adamant they were in the affected districts, and the extent to which they might be modified by court action. The issue was central to Chief Justice Warren, who saw the Court's task as devising implementing decrees that would "give the district courts as much latitude as we can, and as much support as we can."

Warren had taken along *The Negro and the Schools* when he went on vacation, and it addressed the problem the Court would face in effecting what Justice Frankfurter called the "imposition of a distant will." I had written:

Interest in the public schools is universal, and it is an interest that directly involves not only the taxpayer but his family, and therefore his emotions. . . . It is axiomatic that separate schools can be merged only with great difficulty, if at all, when a great majority of the citizens who support them are actively opposed. No other public activity is so closely identified with local mores.

In *Simple Justice*, a definitive account of the year-long deliberations that followed *Brown I* and culminated with *Brown II*, Richard Kluger noted that "the attorneys general of the South read those words, underlined them, and called them to the attention of the Court in the briefs submitted for the final rounds in *Brown*." In doing so the Southern advocates extrapolated my assertion of the obvious to support the contention that it would be impossible to comply with any desegregation order until a great majority of the citizenry agreed that the move was desirable. This, in effect, would have made compliance voluntary, postponing it for, as the Virginia brief put it, "a now indeterminable period."

This line of argument ignored passages in *The Negro and the Schools* dealing with recently desegregated school districts. "One thing that stands out in these case histories," I had written, "is the frequency with which those who have had experience with integration—professional educators and laymen alike—have steeled themselves for a far more severe public reaction than they actually encountered."

My own conclusion, left unstated in the book, was that a formula that allowed reasonable latitude for school officials charged with merging the dual systems would prove acceptable in the border states and the upper South. Experience there would demonstrate that the pattern of social relationships would not be dramatically altered by the proximity of the two races in the classroom, and this in time would reduce the resistance in the Deep South, where lawyers were already preparing for a generation of litigation.

This was the essence of the memorandum I sent to Attorney General Richard W. Ervin of Florida when he retained me as a consultant in the preparation of his state's brief. I argued for a decree that would leave it up to each school district to draw up a plan for compliance. The elongated state of Florida provided a sampling of the varying proportion of black and white population, and attendant community attitudes, to be found in the region as a whole—ranging from those of the Deep South in the upper tier of cracker counties to those of transplanted big city Jewish neighborhoods in resort and retirement communities farther down the peninsula.

It was unrealistic to assume that such diverse school districts could proceed toward the goal at the same pace. The test to be applied in federal district court by a judge familiar with local conditions should not turn on the degree of desegregation at any given stage of the transition, but on whether the district was proceeding in good faith. The draft brief concluded:

> In its decision of May 17, the Supreme Court has put to a new test the essential machinery of democracy, which must protect the rights of the minority while recognizing the desires of the controlling majority. With the patience and forbearance of the courts, we believe the State of Florida can meet the test. We plead only for a chance to work out our own solutions under the terms of legal precedents and decrees that recognize the realities before us.

This, it turned out, was exactly what Chief Justice Warren had hoped for—a response that accepted the principle set forth in *Brown* and pleaded only for concessions of time. It would commit local officials to compliance while relieving the federal district courts of the necessity of assuming the assignment powers of local school boards. These conditions were met in *Brown II*, the decree handed down on May 31, 1955. I cannot, however, claim that my pleading had any direct bearing on the outcome, for it never found its way into the proceedings.

Attorney General Ervin thanked me kindly and wrote that "we were able to work in some of your material at the last minute." But the few phrases that survived were totally out of context, embedded in a turgid, contentious disquisition intended to demonstrate that the Supreme Court had "projected an immediate inrush of turbulent ideas" that might cause "a tornado which would devastate the entire school system." The brief proposed a legal gauntlet described by Richard Kluger as epitomizing the evasive legal tactics being devised across the South:

> Under it, even the most ungainly camel in Islam would have had an easier time passing through the eye of a needle than a black child getting into a white school in Florida. . . . Throughout this obstacle course, the burden of proof would have rested entirely upon the Negro petitioner, while local and state officials would have had a vast repertoire of vague and arbitrary standards

at their disposal to thrust into the desegregation machinery anywhere along the line and jam it.

That horror chamber of legal restraints, as Kluger termed it, provided
the final irony in my brief career as a legal counsel. Everything I had
proposed was resoundingly refuted by the official Florida brief's conclusion: "The Court stands not in need of the whip and the scourge of
compulsion to drive our people to obedience. . . ."

While the Ashmore Project was in progress, the NAACP launched a
parallel study of community attitudes under the direction of the brilliant
black psychologist Kenneth Clark, whose findings on the effect of racial
discrimination on children received judicial notice in *Brown I*. The
report of Clark's team of social scientists filled an entire issue of the
Journal of Social Issues, a publication of the American Psychological
Association, and in sum agreed with our conclusion that there was very
little affirmative support for desegregation among white patrons of the
affected schools. However, Clark contended that, when faced with the
absence of an effective alternative, people could be expected to change
the way they acted before they changed the way they thought—and that
actual experience would tend to allay fears rooted in prejudice.

This was in line with my own thinking. But Clark's recommendation
that the NAACP should take an uncompromising stand on implementation ignored a key point in his own findings: Such changes in the
hearts and minds of men could take place only after they had been
persuaded to accept the condition—that is, desegregation—that would
make them possible. To bring this about, Clark cited the necessity for
"a clear and unequivocal statement of policy by leaders with prestige."
Responsible authorities would have to be willing to "deal with violations,
attempted violations and incitement to violations by a resort to the law
and strong enforcement action." This meant that they must refuse to
"engage in, or tolerate subterfuge, gerrymandering or other devices for
evading the principles and the fact of desegregation."

But as Earl Warren was acutely aware, leaders with prestige who
occupied critical positions in regard to the enforcement of Court orders—beginning with the president—had not so far been willing to

provide unequivocal support for *Brown*. And there could hardly have been more convincing evidence of willingness to tolerate legal subterfuge than the briefs before the Court filed on behalf of Southern officialdom.

Thurgood Marshall was divided in his own mind over the strategy of basing the NAACP position on a demand for immediate desegregation. Some of his key advisers had serious reservations. William T. Coleman, Jr., a black former law clerk of Justice Frankfurter, after going over a draft brief based on the Clark material, warned that it would not persuade the Court and would irritate the justices: "We would be much better off under a decree which would permit the States to file for Court approval plans which would permit . . . gradual effective transition."

To follow that advice, Marshall would have to modify the position he had taken in the first round of argument, when he insisted that delay of complete desegregation would be a denial of justice. In asking Coleman and others in his inner circle for advice, he conceded, "It will, of course, not do us any good to take the exact same position we took last year. On the other hand, I am not certain what position we should take this year."

He was wrestling with that dilemma when I had an opportunity to discuss the implications of *Brown* with him. This came about in the fall of 1954, when we participated in a panel discussion at the annual *New York Herald Tribune* forum at Hunter College. The neoabolitionists who made up the audience were generally euphoric about the consequences of the Court's desegregation ruling, and I found myself cast in my usual cautionary role. In our exchanges on the platform Marshall challenged anything I said that might be construed as gradualism.

We both had post-*Brown* findings to support our positions. The NAACP had commissioned Kenneth Clark to check on reactions in school districts that voluntarily desegregated. My last service to the fund as we closed out the Ashmore Project was to establish the Southern Education Reporting Service at Nashville under an interracial board made up of leading newspaper editors and educators. I had persuaded C. A. McKnight, my successor as editor of the *Charlotte News*, to head the project, and he was on hand for the Forum discussions.

Marshall and I continued the argument over implementation when the platform guests repaired to the elegant Fifth Avenue apartment of the *Herald Tribune*'s proprietor, Mrs. Helen Reid. As the gathering, generously fueled by alcohol, grew more relaxed, Marshall assumed his ironic homeboy manner, and our exchanges took on a leaven of Southern-style kidding. We wound up at one end of the long drawing room leaning against a grand piano, where McKnight, an accomplished amateur jazz pianist, had been persuaded to the keyboard.

Several drinks later, Marshall grinned and said, "Oh, the hell with this. We're never going to get anything settled this way. I tell you what— let's Indian-wrestle two out of three." By this time the distinguished assemblage had gathered around the piano, and McKnight announced that he would accompany our historic encounter with an original composition titled "Nigger-loving Boogie." With the jazz aria thumping in the background, the big lawyer had no difficulty in putting my forearm down.

But it was a different story when he insisted in his closing argument before the justices, "There is nothing before this Court that can show any justification for giving this interminable gradual adjustment." When the justices convened on April 16, 1955, for their final conference before announcing their verdict, Kluger noted,

> Earl Warren, presiding, showed in his opening remarks that he had picked and chosen eclectically from the blended caution and resoluteness of the Justice Department brief . . . from the canny ruminations of Felix Frankfurter, from the fervent fears of the Court's Southern contingent—Black, Reed and Clark— and from the most astute outside commentators on the problem, such as Harry Ashmore.

When *Brown II* came down on May 31 it contained only seven paragraphs. Written by the chief justice on behalf of the unanimous Court, it reaffirmed the "fundamental principle that racial discrimination in education is unconstitutional," and warned the courts below that "it goes without saying that the vitality of these constitutional principles cannot be allowed to yield simply because of disagreement with them." Community attitudes were not mentioned as such, but they were obviously included among the "variety of obstacles" to be taken into account by federal judges sitting as courts of equity. The opinion employed somewhat convoluted language to provide flexible guidelines:

Full implementation of these constitutional principles may require solution of varied local school problems. School authorities have the primary responsibility for elucidating, assessing and solving these problems; courts will have to consider whether the action of school authorities constitutes good faith implementation of the governing constitutional principles.

The order remanded the test cases to the district courts "to take such proceedings and enter such orders and decrees consistent with this opinion as are necessary and proper to admit to public schools on a racially nondiscriminatory basis with all delibereate speed the parties to these cases." The "deliberate speed" oxymoron infuriated some of the young NAACP lawyers, who felt that *Brown II* nullified the famous victory they had won the year before. But Thurgood Marshall, as I had expected, was far more philosophical.

He had used his eloquence and force to argue for a rigid time scale for compliance, but he hadn't really expected to get one. He was too experienced, and too pragmatic, to contend that white public opinion was going to yield automatically to what was now declared to be the law of the land. There was going to be plenty of litigation ahead, but now he had precedent on his side and, presumably, the full weight of the federal government. Two days after the decision was announced, he had a long telephone conversation with his old friend Carl Murphy, publisher of his hometown *Baltimore Afro-American*, who told him he thought the Court had provided the means to whittle away the last vestiges of *Plessy*. Marshall agreed:

> I'm sure of it. I was telling the guys up here—the guys kept on woofin' and I told them—I said, you know, some people want most of the hog, other people insist on having the whole hog, and then there are some people who want the hog, the hair, and the rice on the hair. What the hell! The more I think about it, I think it's a damned good decision.

The NAACP team, Marshall said, would go after recalcitrant school officials state by state, wherever there was lack of good faith compliance: ". . . those white crackers are going to get tired of having

Negro lawyers beating 'em every day in court. They're going to get tired of it. . . ."

At Indianola, Mississippi, fourteen leading citizens had "met and counseled together on Black Monday"—that being the day the Supreme Court handed down *Brown I*. Thus was born the loose confederation of segregationist organizations called White Citizens' Councils that spread across the South in the following months. The first chairman, Robert P. Patterson, a Leflore County planter, condemned the traditional night-riding violence of the past and pledged that the councils' opposition to school desegregation would be carried out by lawful means. The founders' legal expert, Judge Thomas Pickens Brady, specifically disavowed the Ku Klux Klan: "They hide their faces because they do things you and I wouldn't approve of."

What the councils would approve of was spelled out in the wake of *Brown II* when the NAACP moved to initiate five test cases in Mississippi. At Yazoo City fifty-three black parents petitioned the local school board for an immediate end to segregation, and a mass meeting of white citizens was assembled in the high school auditorium to discuss the matter. Young Willie Morris, a senior at the University of Texas home for summer vacation, recognized all of the dozen prominent men who sat on the platform. "Some of them were fathers of my best friends, men I had known and admired and could talk to on a first-name basis," he wrote in his memoir *North Toward Home*. In the audience he saw his father sitting with a neighbor. And from the back of the hall he heard rebel yells and shouts of "Let's get the niggers!"

The chairman quickly stilled the clamor. The white citizens of Yazoo City, he said, would neither commit nor condone violence. He then outlined the procedure to be followed in protecting the Southern Way of Life. Employers of blacks who signed the petition would fire them, and if they were tenants their landlords would evict them. Wholesalers would cut off supplies and credit to the black retailers, and black customers would be turned away by white merchants when they sought to buy goods. The chairman, obviously on advice of counsel, noted that this action was not being undertaken on behalf of the local Citizens'

Council, but represented the spontaneous reaction of the white community as a whole.

On the legal front, the federal district courts were still in a holding pattern. In three of the *Brown* cases—those from Kansas, Delaware, and the District of Columbia—the school districts began moving toward compliance. In Virginia the judge sitting on the Prince Edward County case held that "apparent inaction on the part of the defendants does not necessarily show noncompliance." And in the South Carolina case a three-judge panel provided an interpretation of *Brown II* that would set the pattern of pleading in hundreds of cases to come:

> What has been decided, and all that has been decided, is that a state may not deny to any person on account of race the right to attend any school that it maintains. . . . The Constitution, in other words, does not require integration. It merely forbids discrimination. It does not forbid such segregation as occurs as a result of voluntary action. It merely forbids the use of governmental powers to enforce segregation.

This ruling, it seemed to me, would take the heat off schools in those areas where white resistance was strongest—for these usually were also the areas where blacks were least likely to press for their newly declared rights. If the process were allowed to run its natural course for a few years, with prodding from the NAACP limited to strategically determined venues, I thought it likely that patterns of compliance would spread southward from the border states, bypassing depressed rural areas while the separate school systems in the more sophisticated and permissive larger cities were being merged.

An example was provided by Hoxie, Arkansas, where the unanimous vote of the elected school board opened the way for twenty-five black students to join the thousand whites in the local high school, thus ending the awkward and expensive practice of shipping the students to a neighboring district with a black high school. The mayor of Hoxie explained why the town's leaders had reached their decision: "It's the law of the land, it's inevitable, it's God's will, and it's cheaper." James McBride Dabbs of the Southern Regional Council observed that "the time is ripe for change when justice and expediency meet."

But the Citizens' Councils did not limit their activity to communities where they were able to arouse majority support. They began moving against any white leaders who, in their favorite derogation, bowed the neck and bent the knee to federal authority. Amis Guthridge, an obscure Little Rock lawyer, arrived in Hoxie with bundles of Citizens' Council literature and began urging that the school patrons had an obligation to God, their country, and the white race to resist the actions of their elected officials.

As the tone of protest demonstrations became increasingly militant, the school board sought support from the only official agency available, and what had begun as voluntary action came under federal jurisdiction. A district judge issued an injunction against those attempting to interfere with the operation of the public schools.

The Eighth Circuit Court of Appeals upheld the district court, ruling that this attempted deprivation of constitutional rights could not be sheltered under the First Amendment guarantee of free speech. The injunctive power of the federal courts was increasingly called upon as segregationist demonstrators became more and more aggressive. In Clinton, Tennessee, in the first manifestation of mass violence, a roving agitator named John Kasper wound up in jail for contempt of court.

Precluded from inciting their followers to physically bar the admission of blacks, the Citizens' Council leaders turned to a campaign of harassment against white leaders who accepted federal jurisdiction. At Hoxie this included a suit in state court charging school board members with financial misconduct, and anonymous threats to the school superintendent menacing enough to cause his resignation.

The council movement was never to attract a mass membership; by its own claim, active supporters at the high point ranged from a hundred thousand in Alabama downward to only twenty thousand in Texas. The failure of whites to flock to the activist banner did not, of course, mean that there were not many more who shared the desire to maintain the segregated school system. It was to these the council addressed its relentless propaganda campaign, aimed not so much at making dues-paying converts as at silencing any who dared dissent from its insistence that the Southern political leadership must present a solid front against the federal courts.

Senator James Eastland of Mississippi emerged as the principal spokesman for the cause, calling for "a united movement for the preservation of America under a constitutional form of government." The Supreme Court, he said, had bowed to

> pressure groups bent upon destruction of the American system of government and the mongrelization of the white race. . . . The Court has responded to a radical, pro-Communist political movement in this country. . . . We in the South cannot stay any longer on the defensive. This is the road to destruction and death. We must take the offense.

In their effort to keep the movement respectable, the council leaders continued to disavow violence. But they found it impossible to draw a clear moral distinction between old-fashioned night-riding and the kind of brutal economic reprisal they advocated. The orators could not attract the kind of crowds that turned up at their public rallies if they toned down the rhetoric below the level of a battle cry. Speaking in Alabama, Jim Eastland stayed on what in that league could be called high ground, but neither he nor any other speaker disavowed the unsigned handbill circulating through the audience, a parody of the Declaration of Independence that began, "When in the course of human events it becomes necessary to abolish the Negro race, proper methods should be used. Among these are guns, bows and arrows, slingshots and knives. . . ."

A red and black full-page advertisement in the *Montgomery Advertiser* was signed by a state senator, Sam Englehardt, as executive secretary of the Citizens' Councils of Alabama. "There are only two sides in the Southern fight," it proclaimed, "those who want to maintain the Southern way of life and those who want to mix the races. There is no middle ground for moderation . . . that middle ground has been washed away by the actions of the NAACP in seeking to destroy the freedoms of the Southern white man." The broadside ended with assurance that "there is no hate or animosity in this organization," but this was of little comfort to the few moderates still visible in the Deep South.

. . .

As the 1956 presidential election approached, it was evident that President Eisenhower was not going to abandon his professed neutrality on the school desegregation issue. His reaction to the turmoil in the South was to dismiss it as the work of radicals on both sides, equating the demand of blacks for their declared legal rights with white militants' defiance of the courts. The deteriorating situation seemed to me to cry out for a national leader who would assume the role Eisenhower rejected, that of a conciliator who would use the great moral prestige of the presidency to encourage white and black leaders to seek solutions within the area of practical compromise left open by the Court. And I thought Adlai Stevenson, the likely but still undeclared Democratic candidate, had the temperament and political connections the role required.

Shortly after *Brown II* came down I sent him an editorial from the *Gazette* in which I argued that it was urgent that he abandon his Hamlet posture and make it clear that he expected to be nominated again in 1956. This stung him, as I knew it would. "Does it strike you that 'coyness' is what the other fellow does while you yourself are engaged in the honorable pastime of 'playing them close to your chest'?" he replied.

The exchange continued through the summer, culminating when I charged that he had a moral obligation to the Democratic Party, and to the country, to declare his intention of standing for the nomination before the field became cluttered with other hopefuls. If he was willing to do his duty as I saw it, he replied, was I willing to join the effort? When I paid him an overnight visit in Libertyville in August he told me he was beginning to assemble a small staff to plan for the campaign, and asked me to join him as soon as I could arrange to take leave from the *Gazette*.

In September, committed to serve until next summer's Democratic convention, I moved my wife and grade school daughter to a tall, gloomy Victorian house near the University of Chicago campus. My title was personal assistant to the unannounced candidate, and at a press conference Stevenson defined my role as providing advice on "substance, issues, and problems." I was also expected to provide a conspicuously non-Ivy League persona in Stevenson's immediate entourage, and establish an informal relationship with the media. The term had not yet been coined, but as the correspondents began to arrive at our downtown headquarters I soon realized that I had become a spin doctor.

We began preparing for a rematch in which Stevenson could deal with the record compiled by a sitting president rather than having to contend with the smiling image of an apolitical hero. Then, in late September, Eisenhower suffered a heart attack, casting doubt on his ability to run for reelection. The Democratic nomination, which had seemed Stevenson's by default, suddenly became a real prize. Estes Kefauver put on his coonskin cap and announced that he would be back on the primary trail, and Harry Truman, never reconciled to what he considered Stevenson's toplofty approach to practical politics, announced his neutrality in such a way as to encourage Averell Harriman, who again stood by, waiting for a deadlock to develop.

The effect of this was to accentuate the North-South division in the party, and this would now have to be dealt with in terms of the specific issues raised by *Brown*. The shape of things to come emerged at a November press conference at which Stevenson announced that he would enter the primary marathon, beginning with Minnesota. Asked if his endorsement by so many Southern Democrats didn't indicate that he had compromised his views on civil rights, he responded with a short, flat denial. Commenting on a statement by Senate majority leader Lyndon Johnson that the Supreme Court had removed civil rights from the political arena, he said that ought to be the case, and he hoped it would be. It was, of course, wishful thinking.

I would later be credited—or charged—with selling Stevenson on the moderate position on school segregation he adopted and saw interpreted by his critics as the kind of gradualism that could no longer be supported—in public, at least—by black leaders. In fact, before we had even discussed the points that had to be dealt with in the wake of *Brown*, he had plucked sensitive nerves by announcing opposition to legislation sponsored by Harlem's Representative Adam Clayton Powell to withhold federal aid from school districts that did not desegregate forthwith. The measure carried little practical weight since there was then no significant federal funding for public schools, but it had high symbolic importance for Democratic liberals.

In July, speaking to the National Education Association, Stevenson had endorsed both federal aid to education and *Brown II*:

And I hope that what is good for all will not be lost to all by any linking together of the school aid and desegregation issues, which would delay realization of our hopes and expectations on either or both these vital fronts. In the long run segregation and discrimination, like other obsolete heritages, will yield quickly to the general advance of education.

Hubert Humphrey, the Senate's leading advocate of both federal aid to education and civil rights, wrote to praise the NEA speech, and pointed to the political reality: There was no way to get an education funding bill out of the House without the Powell amendment, and no way to get an amended bill past the Senate. But the emotional quotient on both sides of the race issue had now reached the point where this could not be treated as a signal that compromise was in order. Stiff red necks were being matched by stiff black ones—and white liberals far removed from the scene of actual collision in the South tended to be even more adamant than the blacks. The issue would dog the Stevenson campaign all the way to November.

The Minnesota primary looked like a setup, so much so it encouraged our fond belief that a solid victory over Kefauver would relieve Stevenson of more than token participation in the other contests to follow. He had the formal endorsement of the state Democratic organization and the active support of Humphrey and Governor Orville Freeman. And Minnesota, with only a small black population concentrated in Minneapolis and St. Paul, hardly seemed a place where the race issue should have a high priority. I still remember the only black I ever saw at a rally outside the Twin Cities. A February blizzard was tugging at his Russian-style fur hat when I encountered him at the entrance to a snowbanked town hall up in the Iron Range country. "Man," he said, taking note of my accent, "we sure a long way from home."

But the mere presence on the stump of the tall, shambling Kefauver raised the issue. He became a living populist symbol, cast in the role of David arrayed against an establishmentarian Goliath, and in Minnesota this evoked the glandular, sentimental response to civil rights that had helped make Humphrey the state's leading political figure. So as these disparate figures barnstormed across the frozen countryside, the impassive, soft-spoken man from Andrew Jackson country, with little more than a passing mention of race, turned the issue against the unhappy warrior from Abraham Lincoln country, who saw no reason to mention it at all. When the votes were counted on March 20, Kefauver had won handily, and now the contest would go down to the wire, with the decision turning on the June primaries in California and Florida.

On our first swing down the West Coast I was greeted at San Francisco with a grim warning from Franklin Williams, the NAACP's West Coast representative. He rejected the point Stevenson had been making throughout the campaign, that implementation of *Brown* required interracial understanding and could not be achieved by coercion. At a minimum, he demanded endorsement of the Powell amendment and a pledge to use any other means necessary to root out Jim Crow. Otherwise, he promised, the black vote in the primary would go to Kefauver.

Blacks were not yet numerous enough in California to constitute a major bloc vote, and they did not have the political organization this threat implied. And Kefauver, if anything, had been less specific than Stevenson on *Brown*. The fact was that Williams's influence was greater with the reflexive white liberals who were then riding high in California's amorphous Democratic Party than it was in the black wards of San Francisco, Oakland, and Los Angeles. But, as was demonstrated at the Democratic Council convention at Fresno, this only made the issue more acute.

Before that volatile audience Stevenson elected to take the high ground. John Bartlow Martin, who had joined the campaign entourage, said of the speech, "It was lofty, thoughtful, and almost nobody in California liked it." Kefauver, following with his standard denunciation of fat cats and special interests, rang all the right bells, and Martin noted that Stevenson buttons were falling like autumn leaves. Growing increasingly testy under the pressures of nonstop campaigning, Stevenson gave his own verdict on the speech, which was largely his handiwork: "Here among these intense young liberals it missed its mark. Evidently what they want to hear about is civil rights, minorities, and Israel, and little else, and certainly no vague futures."

In Los Angeles, before a black audience, one sentence emerged clearly from remarks that most of those present could hardly hear: "I will do everything I can to bring about national unity even if I have to ask some of you to come about it gradually." Bill Lawrence of *The New York Times*, standing beside me in the back of the jam-packed hall, exclaimed, "He's blown it," and I knew that interpretation would dominate the reports in the national media by the accompanying pack of correspondents.

There was also trouble on the other flank. I flew to Washington in March when I got word that Strom Thurmond, now in the Senate, was circulating a "Southern Manifesto" on Capitol Hill. It had little substance, denouncing *Brown* as an abuse of judicial power and declaring that the 101 senators and representatives who finally signed would "use all lawful means to bring about the reversal of this decision, which is contrary to the Constitution." Since Kefauver had refused to sign, the manifesto would hurt Stevenson in the remaining primaries, but I elicited only expressions of sympathy and sighs of resignation from his supporters on the Hill. When I asked Senator Olin Johnson of South Carolina if he couldn't at least urge his colleague to delay release of the manifesto, he replied, "It's no use trying to talk to Strom. He believes that shit."

As we came to the end of the primary trail, civil rights took on critical importance in Florida. Some of our people were convinced that Kefauver was privately making promises on civil rights that went far beyond his public position. I never believed that this was true, but the fact was that neither candidate had any control over what his local supporters were saying. "On the word-of-mouth level, Kefauver's people are undoubtedly making hay with the ain't-nobody-here-but-us-Confederates approach to segregation," I wrote in a report to Jim Finnegan, the national campaign manager. "In the cracker country the standard technique is a broad wink and the question, 'Who do you think can handle them niggers better, a city fellow from Illinois or a country boy from Tennessee?' "

At the end of March I sent a memorandum to Stevenson appraising the deteriorating situation in the South. The irreconcilables, who now included the latter-day Confederates, some of the black leaders, and those I called Madison Avenue abolitionists, would not be swayed no matter what he said. He could shore up support for his moderate stand only by driving home two essential points:

(1) To the Southern leaders: You can stand anything but a party bolt, and the only man who can head it off is Adlai Stevenson. (2) To the Negro and liberal leadership: The worst thing that can happen to the American Negro in 1956 is a Southern bolt which, regardless of the outcome of the presidential election, will bring racists to power in many of the Southern states and keep them there for many years to come.

At the end of the calamitous California foray, Stevenson wrote me a tart note: "I think the time has come to get some of this stuff straight and I wish you would put in my hands as promptly as possible a draft statement with respect to (1) desegregation, (2) voting, and (3) violence." I tried, as did every other member of the staff, and he had voluminous input from outside advisers. The problem was summarized by John Bartlow Martin:

He could not forget that what he said in California would be read in Florida. It was the most dangerous issue of all, the one that could defeat Stevenson in the primaries. It was at the same time the issue that could rescue him, for it might appear to the Democratic managers at convention time that only Stevenson could prevent the party from being torn apart by the race issue.

When we came back to California in April for a major Los Angeles speech, Stevenson had melded all the drafts into his own words, and fleshed out his basic position with his usual eloquence:

Like most Northerners, I feel that the Supreme Court has decreed what our reason told us was inevitable, and our conscience told us was right. The Supreme Court said *what* is to be done. The question of *how* we will effect this transition in an orderly, peaceful way remains to be settled. The question is not going to settle itself. And the longer we drift the greater the danger— the danger from those who would violate the spirit of the Court decision either by lawless resistance or by undue provocation.

Here, for the first time, he took the issue directly to Eisenhower, urging that the president immediately call together white and black leaders for a full and open discussion of the means by which compliance with the Court decision could be brought about. He renewed the charge in a New York speech, citing the president's failure even to acknowledge his call:

> The presidency is, above all, a place of moral leadership. Yet in these months of crucial importance no leadership has been provided. The immense prestige and influence of the office has been withheld from those who honestly seek to carry out the law in a gathering storm and against rising resistance. Refusing to rise to this great moral and constitutional crisis, the administration has hardly acknowledged its gravity.

Eisenhower never responded to Stevenson's challenge on the race issue, nor to any of the others he raised. As it turned out, he didn't need to. By 1956 the revolution in mass communications had begun to transform the political process. Television now reached into the great majority of American homes, and coaxial cable linked the stations together. The networks provided direct, nationwide coverage of the campaign, and candidates could control segments of airtime through paid advertising.

As TV became the primary medium of communication, Madison Avenue merchandising techniques could be employed to substitute image for substance—a practice ideally suited to the smiling general, whose hands-off, board chairman style of administration distanced him from the controversies engendered by the cabinet officers who actually ran the government. The need to generate the emotional response TV campaigning made possible frustrated the cerebral Stevenson, who resisted any effort to substitute platitudes for reasoned argument.

When I left the campaign after we narrowly won the primaries in California and Florida, the polls showed Stevenson running well behind Eisenhower. Returning to help work the delegates at the Chicago convention, I found no optimism among the party leaders, who tried to put the Democratic coalition back together by nominating Estes Kefauver for vice president. The Republican victory in November was no surprise—but the margin was a grim portent for the future. Eisenhower carried the popular vote, 35.5 million to 26 million, and the electoral vote, 457 to 73. Stevenson won only in Missouri and six Southern states.

Eisenhower would continue to ignore the ominous response to school desegregation that had made possible his triumph in traditional Democratic strongholds. But he had less than a year to go before his hand was forced by a constitutional crisis as grave as any the nation had faced since the Civil War. The only surprise for me was the site. The showdown came where I had least expected it, at Little Rock.

TRANSITION
THE KENNEDYS AND KING

In 1953 John Kennedy was mildly and quietly in favor of civil rights legislation as a political necessity consistent with his moral instincts.

In 1963 he was deeply and fervently committed to the cause of human rights as a moral necessity inconsistent with his political instincts.

—THEODORE C. SORENSEN, *Kennedy*

In 1955, when the U.S. Supreme Court handed down *Brown II*, Governor Orval Faubus of Arkansas issued as moderate a statement as any made by a major Southern officeholder:

> It appears that the Court left some degree of decision in these matters to the federal district courts. I believe this will guarantee against any sudden dislocation. . . . Our reliance now must be upon the good will that exists between the two races—the good will that has long made Arkansas a model for the other Southern states in all matters affecting the relationship between the races.

Running for reelection in 1956, Faubus handily defeated the most effective of the state's diehard segregationists, James D. Johnson, who charged that the governor was about to subject Arkansas to the horrors of race-mixing. In 1957, when eight Southern states enacted statutes reasserting the states' rights the Supreme Court had invalidated, Faubus offered no encouragement to supporters of the so-called State Sovereignty Commission approved by his own legislature.

This revival of the pre–Civil War doctrine of nullification was inspired by the Citizens' Councils' call for "massive resistance" to school desegregation. It was given a historical gloss by James Jackson Kilpatrick of the *Richmond News-Leader*, who reached back to the Kentucky-Virginia interposition resolutions of 1798. The right to reject the authority of the Supreme Court, he said, "rests in the incontrovertible theory that ours is a union of sovereign states, that the federal government exists only by reason of a solemn compact among the states. . . ." That compact, he proclaimed, was abrogated when the Court attempted to interpose its will between that of the people and their state government.

In an interview with *Time*, Kilpatrick attempted to provide sociological underpinning for his legal theory: "The Negro is fundamentally and perhaps unalterably inferior; he is also immoral, indolent, inept, incapable of learning and uninterested in full racial equality. The segregationist South has no guilt about keeping the Negro in his proper place—that is to say, in separate schools."

Faubus, who always insisted that he was not a racist, never endorsed the old dogma of white supremacy. And in July, after the rambunctious legislators had gone home, he rejected a demand by the Citizens' Council that he employ the new "sovereignty" legislation to interpose his police powers and halt the desegregation of Little Rock's Central High School, due to begin in September. "Everyone knows no state's laws supersede a federal law," he said.

Over in Mississippi, Senator Eastland complained bitterly: "In Arkansas, where the governor will not take action, racial integration has already started. . . . If the Southern states are picked off one by one under the damnable doctrine of gradualism I don't know if we can hold or not." That was the signal for resistance leaders across the Deep South to concentrate their powers of persuasion, and intimidation, on Orval Faubus. His office at the state capitol was subjected to a mounting barrage of telegrams and telephone calls.

On August 22 Governor Marvin Griffin of Georgia arrived in Little

Rock to address the first local Citizens' Council rally to attract more than a handful of the faithful. He was accompanied by Roy Harris, the colorful publicist who served as president of the Citizens' Councils of America. While Griffin sat beside him nodding agreement, Harris outlined the steps deemed necessary to preserve the Southern Way of Life. Georgia's governor, he declared, unlike Arkansas's, was prepared to turn out his State Highway Patrol and National Guard to bar any black child from attending any white public school, and he would enlist in their support every right-thinking, red-blooded white Georgian.

Faubus did not attend the rally, but he put up Griffin and Harris in guest quarters at the governor's mansion. Before they departed for Atlanta, they had achieved their objective. Twelve days later, on the night before Central High School opened for the fall term, Faubus ordered his National Guard troops to seize the school grounds and secure them against invasion by nine black children.

Faubus needed a threat of violence to justify his interposition, and he did his best to provide it. Before school opened he testified in state chancery court in support of a Citizens' Council–inspired plea for an injunction suspending the School Board plan. Without identifying the source, he said he had been told that white and black students had been found in possession of revolvers, and he had other evidence of impending trouble he was not at liberty to divulge.

Nor did he divulge it in federal court when his hand was called by Judge Ronald Davies, who had access to a voluminous report compiled by FBI agents who had found no evidence of impending mob action. Judge Davies directed the School Board to proceed as scheduled, and the only injunction in effect was his order forbidding interference by "all persons in any manner, directly or indirectly."

When the black children were turned away by armed soldiers acting under the governor's orders, the legal excuses he had used to justify defiance of the federal court had run out. "The issue," I wrote in a front-page *Gazette* editorial, "is no longer segregation vs. integration. The question has now become the supremacy of the government of the United States in all matters of law. And clearly the federal government cannot let this issue remain unresolved no matter what the cost to this community."

The bizarre developments that followed made it clear that it was still an issue President Eisenhower was loath to face. The United Press reported from Washington: "Attorney General Herbert Brownell, Jr., was without any immediate strategy or policy to pursue." One of the capital's most influential power brokers, Philip Graham, the Southern-born publisher of *The Washington Post*, moved into the vacuum in an effort to promote a negotiated settlement. His increasingly frenetic campaign was described by David Halberstam in *The Powers That Be*:

> He became a self-appointed manager of the Little Rock crisis. He was on the phone day and night to everyone: the White House; presidential advisors Sherman Adams and Maxwell Rabb; Nixon; Bill Rogers [the deputy attorney general]; Harry Ashmore, the Little Rock editor; Brooks Hays, the Little Rock Congressman; black leaders Thurgood Marshall and Roy Wilkins. Trying to think of anyone Ike might listen to. Calling on his White House reporter, Eddie Folliard, to pass on notes to Ike. Calling Ike's friends to get him to move. Trying to move Faubus a little, wondering what might affect Faubus, thinking of Truman. Truman was a good Baptist and a traditionalist, maybe Truman would call Faubus. But who would call Truman? Brooks Hays, that's who. Hays was a national lay Baptist leader and so Graham called Hays to call Truman to call Faubus. . . .

Hays made the call to Truman, and another to Sherman Adams, thus becoming the link between the two parties. It was a sad case of miscasting. Thoroughly honorable, highly intelligent, richly humorous, and devoutly Christian, Hays was, despite his fourteen years in Congress, still something of a political innocent—entirely too trusting to deal with the devious Faubus and the hot-eyed men who were now breathing on his neck. His great concern, he wrote in *A Southern Moderate Speaks*, was that Faubus "not be driven into the arms of the few extremists in the Southern governors' group." Faubus, of course, was already there.

It took Hays three days to persuade the governor to accept Sherman Adams's condition that he initiate the request for a meeting and publicly acknowledge his "desire to comply with the order that has been issued by the District Court in this case. . . ." By this time Eisenhower was operating out of his vacation headquarters on the golf course of the

Newport Country Club in Rhode Island—a resort of America's biggest rich, which, as one reporter pointed out, seemed an unlikely place from which to deal with desegregation since it did not admit blacks, Jews, Catholics, or poor Protestants.

Hays, who accompanied Faubus to Newport, wrote in his diary: "It seems to me that time, not substance, presents the difficulty. The governor is not opposed to the School Board decision being carried out, he simply thinks that a delay is essential to the maintenance of peace." That, in essence, was the proposition Faubus presented to Eisenhower, who responded sympathetically.

But Attorney General Brownell was also on hand to remind the president that the School Board plan was not in the province of the executive, but under the jurisdiction of the federal courts. The existing order, he pointed out, had allowed three and a half years to work out a plan to admit nine black high school children, and another six years to complete opening the grades. On its face, this was the minimum any district court could conceivably approve without abandoning the Supreme Court mandate altogether.

When formal statements were issued after the meeting, it was clear that Brownell had prevailed. Faubus's statement, duly cleared by Sherman Adams, echoed the only public statements the president had ever made in regard to *Brown*:

> I have never expressed any personal opinion regarding the Supreme Court decision of 1954 which ordered integration. That is not relevant. That decision is the law of the land and must be obeyed.
>
> The people of Little Rock are law-abiding, and I know that they expect to obey valid court orders. In this they shall have my support. In so doing it is my responsibility to protect the people from violence in any form. . . .

The president responded with an expression of confidence that the governor intended to "respect the decisions of the United States District Court and to give his full cooperation in carrying out his responsibilities in respect to those decisions."

The Newport Compact lasted just six days. The National Guard troops remained in place, and the black children stayed out of school until Judge Davies called a hearing on the procedure required to implement the agreement. Faubus's attorneys appeared, declined to offer testimony or argument, and walked out after declaring,

> The position of the respondent, Governor Faubus . . . must be firm, unequivocal and unalterable. The governor of the state of Arkansas cannot and will not concede that the United States in this court or anywhere else can question his discretion and judgment as chief executive of a sovereign state when he acts in the performance of his constitutional duties.

The commander of the National Guard troops testified that his orders from the governor were to continue turning away black children who sought admission to any white school. Judge Davies reached the inescapable conclusion that Faubus was deliberately defying his court and ordered him to cease and desist. That night Faubus ordered the troops removed and departed for the Southern Governors' Conference at Sea Island, Georgia, where he received the warm embrace and hearty congratulations of his host, Marvin Griffin.

The next morning, September 23, a semblance of the mob Faubus had been predicting finally materialized at Central High. The black students, entering school under the protection of city police, were jeered by whites of assorted age and sex assembled at the main entrance, along with upward of a hundred newsmen, who in the seething confusion were never able to determine how many were activists and how many were curious bystanders. Little Rock's fire chief had been pressured into refusing use of his equipment for mob control, and the dispirited police, denied the usual backup support by state forces, were spread thin around the four-city-block campus. The assistant police chief in charge, Eugene Smith, concluded that it would be impossible to cover all possible entrances when classes broke for lunch and hundreds of students came pouring out of the building. Shortly before noon the black children were taken out through a back door.

At the *Gazette* my office took on the atmosphere of one of the combat command posts I had manned in my days in the infantry. Most of the out-of-town correspondents were working out of our city room, and I was handling phone calls from all points on the compass, including a number from Phil Graham. One of these, in which he transferred me to Deputy Attorney General William Rogers, was referred to in news reports that gave rise to the durable myth that I was responsible for the dispatch of the federal troops President Eisenhower ordered into Little Rock the following day.

Asked for my appraisal, I told Rogers the city police had done all they could and that the situation was now beyond their control. Tension in the community was at flash point, inflammatory rumors were spreading, and the situation was likely to grow worse unless there was an unmistakable show of force. I have no idea whether this influenced Rogers; in any case, the same information was surely pouring in from the scores of FBI agents who had been sent in to augment the resident force.

Another Washington call came from Senator J. William Fulbright. Our friendship had survived his signing the Southern Manifesto, but it had been many months since he had consulted me on a political matter. Now he asked what I thought he should do, and I suggested that he call Faubus at Sea Island, urge him to make state forces available to maintain law and order, and announce the result when, like everybody else who had tried, he failed to get a satisfactory answer. Well, he said, he was leaving for England that afternoon to deliver a series of lectures at Oxford, and he thought it would be best to avoid a statement of any kind until his return.

Days later, after the federal troops had restored order to the beleaguered city, Fulbright's assistant John Ericson called to report that the senator had completed his assignment at Oxford and would soon be heading home. He could no longer avoid making a statement on the Little Rock crisis, and he had asked Ericson to see if I had any suggestions. Tell him, I said, that he might as well enroll for the second semester.

The Battle of Little Rock ended abruptly when President Eisenhower was finally persuaded to remove the Arkansas National Guard from the governor's command and replace the state troops at Central High with a detachment of the 101st Airborne Infantry flown in from Fort Campbell, Kentucky. In terms of actual casualties it hadn't been much of a fight. Two black newsmen and a hapless black passerby had been beaten; three white reporters and two photographers had been manhandled; there were twenty-five arrests at the school site, and a few others were brought in for creating disturbances elsewhere.

However, the psychic damage was heavy. The television and still cameras sought out the naked face of hatred, and certainly it had been on display. The pushing and hauling of a few hundred frenzied men and women were magnified in the consciousness of the world to the point where Little Rock became the symbol of brutal, dead-end resistance to the minimum requirements of racial justice.

The impression still lives that the city was the site of sustained race rioting so widespread the U.S. Army had to be called in to put it down. The fact is that no one, black or white, then or later, was injured seriously enough to require hospitalization. The only role for the Army was to provide unmistakable evidence that, after all his vacillation, President Eisenhower was finally prepared to see that the orders of the federal courts were carried out.

The brief encounter, treated by the national media as high drama, was reduced to an oversimplified morality play. The villain's role was assigned to Orval Faubus, and under the glare of television lights his wily hillbilly persona became a caricature as he discovered that sophisticated outlanders of the press corps, no less than rednecked voters, could be diverted by sheer preposterosity.

He set the tone for his endless press conferences when a hard-nosed interrogator charged that his lawyers' defiant withdrawal from Judge Davies's hearing contradicted the pledge of support for *Brown* he had issued at Newport. He had agreed to that statement, he said, only because the president's men insisted on it. "Just because I said it," he added, "doesn't make it so."

That, I think, was an entirely candid response. I never questioned Faubus's assertion that he was not a racist; it was unabashed expediency, not conviction, that determined his course. Among the hundreds of writers who have appraised his character, I thought Robert Sherrill came closest in *Gothic Politics in the Deep South:* "There is in Faubus's makeup a weakness that, in moments of pressure, makes him act seldom from logic, often from fear, and even more often from whatever the last stress happens to be before action is demanded of him."

When he became convinced that he could not hold his rural support in a third-term race for reelection against a segregationist candidate, he grabbed the doomed strategy the Citizens' Council leaders were pressing on him. Under stress, he adopted the segregationist party line, assailing his few visible opponents as Communist mongrelizers, and employing the full force of his office to support the Citizens' Council's effort to silence the *Arkansas Gazette* by organizing a boycott that cost the owners millions of dollars.

The campaign of intimidation orchestrated from the governor's office kept the Little Rock community in turmoil, but it did not silence the *Gazette* or force the withdrawal of the black students who had become national celebrities as the Little Rock Nine. But it was not possible to maintain a normal educational program in a besieged school surrounded by armed guards, and in May the school board went back to federal court to plead that in the face of continued harassment by the state government, it was powerless to carry out the further desegregation required by its original plan.

A local federal judge granted a stay, but the Circuit Court of Appeals promptly handed down a 6-to-1 opinion barring any further delay: "We say that the time has not come in these United States when an order of a federal court must be whittled away, watered down, or shamefully withdrawn in the face of violent acts of individual citizens. . . ." Asked for reaction, President Eisenhower said his feelings were exactly the same as they were when he called out the troops. So, said Orval Faubus, were his. But a month later the Supreme Court had the final word when all nine justices interrupted their summer recess to hear a final appeal for a delay in the desegregation of Central High.

Under pressure to find some way out of the impasse, the school board had rejected the counsel of its regular attorney, A. F. House, who had from the outset warned of the futility of resistance. Judge House was replaced by Richard Butler, a lawyer willing to contest the ruling of the Circuit Court of Appeals. In oral argument, Butler pleaded:

> The point I am making is this, that if the governor of any state says a U.S. Supreme Court decision is *not* the law of the land,

the people of that state, until it is really resolved, have a doubt in their mind and a right to have a doubt.

Chief Justice Warren replied:

I have never heard such an argument made in a court of justice before, and I have tried many a case over many a year. I never heard a lawyer say the statement of a governor, as to what was legal or illegal, should control the action of any court.

Interpositon was formally interred by the unanimous Court ruling that followed.

Now Faubus played the last card in the Citizens' Council deck. The legislature had included in the Sovereignty Commission legislation a measure empowering him to close desegregated public schools and transfer their assets and tax income to private academies. In September he used it to order all Little Rock high schools shut down, and directed the school board to lease their buildings to the newly created Little Rock Private School Corporation. The Supreme Court responded with another unanimous ruling holding that "evasive schemes for segregation cannot be used to nullify Court orders."

Cut off from the school system's assets, the effort by the private school corporation to sustain a valid program without tax revenue was doomed from the outset. The closing of the three public high schools left 3,261 white students and 1,069 blacks without access to an accredited institution unless they chose to leave the city—as hundreds of the more affluent did.

In November the school board members declared the situation hopeless and resigned, forcing a series of special elections in which the local establishment finally rallied to provide a crushing defeat for the Citizens' Council slate supported by Faubus. In September 1959, the Little Rock schools opened with the desegregation plan in full force and effect.

The defeat of the segregationists in Little Rock resulted from a political fusion reminiscent of the one forged by the Redeemers—a coalition of the country club set and the black community. Not all the whites could be assigned such exalted status, but that's where the leadership came from. This working relationship continued after the crisis subsided and spread to the lesser cities of the state. The salt-and-pepper voting bloc grew in effectiveness until it overwhelmed the rural populists, bringing to the governor's office as Faubus's successor a multimillionaire Republican socialite, Winthrop Rockefeller—the only Arkansas mountaineer, I once observed, who owned his own mountain. As the number of black voters increased throughout the region the coalition was replicated in the Deep South, finally bringing to an end the decade of demagoguery and confrontation still to come.

As the threat of mob resistance receded on the school front, the focus of national media attention shifted to the effort to end segregation in places of public accommodation—buses, lunch counters, hotels, theaters, swimming pools, golf courses, and the like. This phase of the civil rights movement was launched by blacks on their own motion, and carried forward under leaders who emerged from black churches to stage-manage mass confrontations with the white leadership.

The demand for access to facilities that were often privately owned raised issues that had not been dealt with in the court action that followed *Brown*. Here federal intervention in the face of counteraction against the demonstrators was not automatic, for it was not court orders but traditional trespass laws that were being violated. By taking their cause outside the courtroom the black leaders raised the issue of justice above the distracting tangle of legalisms, and the dramatic street rallies that followed impressed it on the national consciousness in moral terms.

The fact that Southern blacks now marched under their own leadership has been construed as a parting of the ways with white moderates who were attempting to contain the threat of violence implicit in the widespread popular support for massive resistance to school desegregation. This notion became prevalent among a generation of scholars and writers too young to have had personal experience with the movement. In the *Encyclopedia of Southern Culture*, brought forth in 1989 by the University of Mississippi, Professor Gary L. Williams, who contributed the article "Journalists, Modern South," described the handful of Southern newspaper editors who supported compliance with *Brown* as

> Lost Causers of a (mild) sort, too. Paternalistic, defensive, past-haunted in spite of themselves . . . they have been enthralled by Southern consciousness and its traditionalism [and] thrown

off balance by the assertiveness of the "New Negro" . . .
Journalistic proponents of the Modern South found themselves
not so much leading a reform movement as tagging along in
hopes of making such a movement palatable to moderates in
Dixie. . . . They were accustomed to leading, not following,
and were thus dismayed by the activism of the New Negro.

The depiction of the embattled editors as displaced leaders was absurd
on its face; prior to *Brown* there was no desegregation movement in the
South, nor could there have been as long as the Supreme Court upheld
the separate-but-equal doctrine. The idea that we were trying to make
compliance palatable, however, was eminently correct. If there was to
be any significant movement toward ending segregation it would require
at least the acquiescence of the controlling white majority.

Recognition of this reality was reflected in the agenda of the seminal
protest movement Martin Luther King, Jr., launched at Montgomery,
and it shaped the strategy he devised when the year-long bus boycott
touched off a widespread uprising against the overtly demeaning aspects
of apartheid. While the issue was drawn on the streets, King never forgot
that the impasse was not resolved until NAACP lawyers obtained a
Supreme Court ruling declaring Montgomery's bus segregation ordinance unconstitutional. Victory came only when federal intervention
combined with economic pressure to force capitulation by the city's
white leadership.

The bus boycott was an introduction to the real world for King,
whose boyhood was sheltered by the status of his father, one of Atlanta's
most respected black ministers. The younger King received his minis-
terial training at a white seminary in Pennsylvania, and a doctorate in
theology from Boston University. In his memoir *Stride Toward Freedom*
he described his reaction when he assumed his first pastorate in the
"Cradle of the Confederacy," where seventy thousand white citizens
fondly believed they enjoyed a good relationship with fifty thousand
blacks:

I found the Negro community the victim of a threefold mal-
ady—factionalism among the leaders, indifference in the educated group, and passivity in the undereducated. All these

conditions had almost persuaded me that no lasting social reform could ever be achieved in Montgomery.

The outraged response to the arrest of the eminently respectable black seamstress Rosa Parks when she refused to yield her seat to a white bus passenger proved King wrong in the last assumption, but he had correctly appraised the conditions he would have to deal with as he became the leader of a national protest movement. His first task was to persuade middleclass blacks to place at risk the hard-earned respectability and economic security they had gained by passively accepting the standards set by the white community. He did so by appealing to the deep religious faith that provided a bond with the mass of powerless poor blacks who bore the brunt of the system's oppression.

The gospel preached in black churches was compatible with King's commitment to nonviolence, which had become the bedrock of his personal philosophy in the course of his graduate study of Mahatma Gandhi's crusade to end colonial rule in India. It was basic to the strategy King presented to the young ministers who attended the founding meeting of the Southern Christian Leadership Conference (SCLC) in Atlanta early in 1957. Within a month ninety-seven black preachers from ten states had responded to his call, and SCLC began to make a place for itself alongside the old-line black and interracial organizations.

"Nonviolent resistance emerged as the technique of the movement, while love stood as the regulating ideal," King wrote. "Christ furnished the spirit and motivation, while Gandhi furnished the method." In every public utterance he held forth the vision of the "beloved community," and when his followers threatened to reply in kind to white harassment, he repeated a variation of the injunction he addressed to hundreds of restive blacks, some of them armed, who rallied around his Montgomery parsonage after dynamite exploded under the front steps:

> We must love our white brothers, no matter what they do to us. We must make them know we love them. Jesus still cries out in words that echo across the centuries, "Love your enemies; bless them that curse you; pray for them that spitefully use you." This is what we must live by. We must meet hate with love.

Remember, if I am stopped this movement will not stop, because God is with the movement. Go home with this glowing faith and this radiant assurance.

The invocation of religious faith shared by both races aroused some passive sympathy beyond the color bar, but there were few whites among the seventy thousand who by 1961 had picketed, sat in, or marched to protest segregated facilities in more than a hundred Southern and border state cities. Thirty-six hundred of these demonstrators wound up in jail.

The crusade launched by SCLC made King a national celebrity, and he quickly learned to exploit the access to the media his new status provided. In February 1957 he sent a telegram to President Eisenhower urging him to convene a White House conference on civil rights comparable to those he had sponsored on education and juvenile delinquency. The message concluded with a touch of nonviolent pressure: "If some effective remedial steps are not taken we shall be compelled to initiate a mighty Prayer Pilgrimage to Washington." There was no response, and the first black protest march on the capital was scheduled for May 17, the third anniversary of *Brown*.

King had now received his secular anointment, a cover story in *Time*, and the black leadership threw its resources behind the pilgrimage. There on the steps of the Lincoln Memorial were A. Philip Randolph, Roy Wilkins, Adam Clayton Powell, and Mordecai Johnson surrounded by celebrities from show business and sports: Ruby Dee, Harry Belafonte, Sidney Poitier, Sammy Davis, Jr., and Jackie Robinson. *The Washington Post* estimated that twenty-five thousand people, mostly black, were assembled on the Mall when Mahalia Jackson's powerful voice rolled out, "I've been 'buked, I've been scorned." The climax came in King's peroration, which was more supplication than demand:

Give us the ballot—and we will transform the salient misdeeds of bloodthirsty mobs into abiding good deeds of orderly citizens.

Give us the ballot—and we will fill the legislative halls with men of good will.

Give us the ballot [now the crowd was chanting the opening line with him]—and we will place judges on the benches of the South who will do justice and love mercy.

Give us the ballot—and we will quietly and nonviolently, without rancor and bitterness, implement the Supreme Court's decision of May 17, 1954.

King's speech, Harlem's *Amsterdam News* said, "established him as the number one leader of sixteen million Negroes in the United States. . . . At this point in his career the people will follow him anywhere." But the pilgrimage didn't succeed in opening the door at the White House. The best the administration would offer in response to Congressman Powell's importuning was a meeting with Vice President Richard Nixon and the cabinet's lonely liberal, Secretary of Labor James P. Mitchell. King found the vice president polite, cool, and noncommittal, and the secretary unwilling to go beyond a recitation of existing programs presumed to benefit blacks. "The forces of good will failed to come through," King told his followers.

It was not until the closing days of the Eisenhower regime that King finally received an invitation to the White House. The other black leaders present relied on him to make an eloquent appeal for federal support. The president listened politely, but his only response came when he walked King to the door, murmuring, "Reverend, there are so many problems . . . Lebanon, Algeria. . . ."

Even had he been so inclined, such aloofness from the mounting racial crisis in the South was no longer possible for any Democrat seeking to succeed Eisenhower. In the course of the hard-fought 1960 presidential election, the winner, John F. Kennedy, initiated a relationship with Martin Luther King that was instrumental in rallying the black voters who ensured his narrow victory over Vice President Nixon. King, in turn, acquired what amounted to an open line to the Oval Office.

Now living in Atlanta, where he had established the headquarters of SCLC, he took no active part in the campaign, but he was in touch with his friend Harris Wofford, the white Washington lawyer who served as Kennedy's civil rights adviser. One night in October, after a meeting in downtown Atlanta, King drove his car into De Kalb County, a Ku

Klux Klan stronghold, to take the distinguished Georgia author Lillian Smith back to Emory University Hospital, where she was undergoing treatment for cancer. The sight of a black man and a white woman sitting alongside each other on the front seat was enough to bring about his arrest. He was convicted of driving without a Georgia license and was released on probation. But after his arrest during a sit-in at an Atlanta department store, the probation was revoked. King was promptly sentenced to six months at hard labor and spirited off to a state prison.

His frightened wife appealed to Wofford, who had Jack Kennedy respond with a personal call. Coretta King announced to the press that the Democratic contender was at work seeking her husband's release, and added, "I have heard nothing from the vice president or anyone on his staff."

The candidate's brother Robert, who served as campaign manager, did some discreet telephoning to local Democratic leaders, who saw to it that King was promptly released. With the national media present in force, he was greeted by a cheering throng at Ebenezer Baptist Church, where his staunch Baptist father announced from the pulpit that he was withdrawing his previous public endorsement of Richard Nixon: "I had expected to vote against Senator Kennedy because of his religion. But now he can be my president, Catholic or whatever he is. . . ."

When the popular vote was counted a month later, Kennedy had won by fewer than 120,000 votes of nearly 69 million cast, but he had carried the electoral vote, 303 to 219. Black votes had provided his winning margin in Illinois, Michigan, Texas, South Carolina, and possibly Louisiana. Loss of the electoral vote of only the first two states would have meant his defeat.

When Harris Wofford introduced King to Jack Kennedy early in the campaign, the young preacher came away from the meeting with an affirmative impression. But he told Wofford he thought Kennedy lacked "a depthed understanding" of civil rights issues—what a less formal man would have called a gut feeling. I had a similar view, based on casual acquaintance with the Massachusetts senator that began in 1956 when he was seeking a place on the presidential ticket as Adlai Stevenson's running mate.

A degree of detachment was perhaps inevitable for the scion of a wealthy Boston family, his Catholic heritage tempered by an uppercrust New England education. Theodore C. Sorensen, his chief Senate aide and White House counsel, wrote in his memoir *Kennedy:*

> Contrary to some reports, Kennedy was not converted to this cause [civil rights] by the eloquence of some persuasive preacher or motivated by his own membership in a minority group. . . . As a senator he simply did not give much thought to this subject. He had no background or association or activity in race relations. He was against discrimination as he was against colonialism or loyalty oaths—it was an academic judgment rather than a deep-rooted personal compulsion.

Clark Clifford, who became one of his most perceptive intimates, noted that Kennedy displayed "a useful pragmatic cynicism toward events and people." He came to the office, Clifford thought, endowed with "something rare and valuable in a politician—a sense of irony." These qualities were on display when the newly elected president met with black leaders and their liberal supporters.

"Nobody needs to convince me any longer that we have to solve the problem, not let it drift on in gradualism," he told them. "But how do you go about it? If we go into a long fight in Congress, it will bottleneck everything else and still get no bill." He would appoint blacks as judges and ambassadors, give them policymaking positions in the subcabinet, and increase their percentage in top- and middle-level civil service jobs. But no package of civil rights legislation would be sent to Congress.

During the campaign, in chiding Eisenhower for failure to use his executive powers to deal with racial issues, he had cited examples that went well beyond this limited agenda:

> For example, the president could sign an executive order ending discrimination in housing tomorrow. Second, the president could compel all companies which do business with the government—and, after all, that is nearly every American company—to practice open, fair hiring of personnel without regard to race, creed, or color. . . . In addition, the Department of

Justice can pursue the right to vote with far more vigor. . . . So I would say that the greater opportunity is in the executive branch without congressional action.

Liberals construed this as a campaign promise, and it came back to haunt him. Kennedy did create the President's Committee for Equal Employment and put Vice President Johnson in charge, but there was no provision for effective enforcement, and the stroke of the pen that would presumably end discrimination in housing was not forthcoming. Instead, the president adopted the strategy King had advocated when he addressed the Prayer Pilgrimage. The primary emphasis would be on extending the franchise, still denied to the mass of powerless rural blacks despite Supreme Court rulings outlawing the white primary.

Although it was glossed over during the star-struck era that followed inauguration of the glamorous new administration, the president's approach, implemented by his brother Robert as attorney general, produced an increasingly corrosive division of interest among the civil rights leaders. The emphasis on voting rights was of little consequence in the North, where the franchise was generally available. King stood apart from the disgruntled main-line leadership when he declared:

> The central front . . . we feel is that of suffrage. If we in the South can win the right to vote it will place in our hands more than an abstract right. It will give us the concrete tool with which we ourselves can correct injustice.

The jaundiced view from the left was voiced by Victor Navasky, who wrote in *Kennedy Justice*, "The trick was to encourage the inevitable integration, but never at the cost of disturbing the social equilibrium." He went on to characterize the effort to secure the franchise for Southern blacks as a means of curtailing the civil disobedience campaign, "diverting the energy of civil rights workers from direct confrontation with Southern 'law.' "

It was true that the policy meant that in practice the administration would intervene only when the equilibrium already had been disturbed by overt violation of federal court orders. And the approach did involve practical political considerations; recalcitrant though they were on racial matters, Southern Democrats had contributed materially to Kennedy's election, and in Congress they were leading supporters of his Cold War foreign policy. But there were also constitutional restraints against broad-scale intervention. These were set forth by Burke Marshall, chief of the Justice Department's Civil Rights Division:

> We do not have a national police force. There is no substitute under the federal system for the failure of local law enforcement responsibilty. There is simply a vacuum, which can be filled only rarely, with extraordinary difficulty, at monumental expense, and in a totally unsatisfactory fashion.

Robert Kennedy, in an address at the University of Georgia Law School, pledged the administration to pursue amicable, voluntary solutions to problems of racial discrimination wherever possible. But, the new attorney general warned, "if the orders of the [federal courts] are circumvented, the Department of Justice will act. We will not stand by and be aloof. We will move."

The *Atlanta Constitution* praised the speech, which was not surprising, since Kennedy had consulted Ralph McGill on what to say. "Never before in all the travail of bygone years," McGill wrote, "has the South heard so honest a speech from any cabinet member." And Georgia-born Louis Martin, the black strategist at the Democratic National Committee, reported to the attorney general that it had evoked a similar response in the North: "Congratulations are pouring in from brothers everywhere, here and abroad, If you keep up this way, one of these days I might be able to go back home."

It was an auspicious beginning, but as it turned out neither the black leadership nor the white resistance movement was involved at the inception of the first major racial crisis the Kennedys faced. It was touched off by James Meredith, a stubborn, self-starting loner who was attending the black state college at Jackson when he was inspired by President Kennedy's inaugural address to apply for admission at the University of Mississippi.

"I am an American-Mississippi-Negro citizen," he wrote to the registrar that night. "With all of the occurring events regarding changes in our educational system in our country in this new age, I feel certain this application does not come as a surprise to you. . . ." Surprise or not, it was summarily rejected.

The NAACP took up Meredith's cause, and he managed to run the gauntlet set up by unreconstructed federal judges in Mississippi. His court appeal was rejected twice in district court and four times at the appeals level before Supreme Court justice Hugo Black intervened to order him admitted. Ross Barnett, described by Robert Sherrill as "bone dumb," was perhaps the only Southern governor disposed to ignore the lessons taught by Orval Faubus's experience with interposition. Appointing himself acting registrar, Barnett personally refused to enroll Meredith.

Standing at the entrance to the university administration building at Oxford, he adorned the occasion with one of the *non sequiturs* for which he became famous. The would-be student was the only black within half a mile when he arrived surrounded by a platoon of U.S. marshals. "Which of you is James Meredith?" the governor politely inquired. Satisfied that he had the right man, he read a decree barring him from the campus "now and forevermore." The circuit court of appeals responded by giving Barnett a week to purge himself of contempt on penalty of jail and a running fine of ten thousand dollars a day.

Robert Kennedy initiated one of the protracted telephone negotiations that were to occupy him during the thousand days of his brother's truncated administration. Bowing to the threat by the circuit court, the governor pledged that there would be no violence when Meredith returned to the campus, and promised to provide state police to preserve order. But Barnett kept reneging on the agreed arrangements, which at one point called for a fake confrontation in which U.S. marshals would display unloaded weapons to demonstrate on television that he had stood firm to the bitter end.

Jack Kennedy moved in, reserving network television time for an address to the American people and sending word to Barnett that he was going to recite the full record of the futile effort to negotiate a settlement. The governor responded by offering still another deal—to arrange to have Meredith enrolled in Jackson and taken secretly to the campus by a back way while he and the lieutenant governor decoyed the mob that had assembled at Oxford. The president agreed, and at the end of the conversation turned in wonder to his aides: "Do you know what that fellow said? He said, 'I want to thank you for your help on the poultry program.' "

Now the comedy was over and the tragedy began. Barnett reneged still again, abruptly withdrawing the state police he had agreed to provide to hold back the mob surrounding the U.S. marshals at the administration building. When the state force departed at nightfall, cries of "Kill the nigger-loving bastards" sounded loud and clear, and the marshals had to resort to tear gas. Then came a rain of Molotov cocktails, iron bars, bricks, and jagged projectiles from shattered concrete benches—and finally, rifle fire.

After two hours of siege the president sent in the army units he had placed on standby alert. The state's National Guard had been federalized, and the first unit to arrive was Mississippi's own Troop E of the 108th Armored Cavalry. The commanding officer was a nephew of Oxford's most illustrious citizen, William Faulkner, whose fiction included no more savage a scene than the one enacted just down the street from the old family homestead.

The casualty list included 166 marshals, among them 28 wounded by snipers' bullets. Forty members of Troop E were struck by missiles or shotgun blasts, including Captain Faulkner, who suffered two broken bones. There were two fatalities, one a white citizen of Oxford who may have been a bystander, the other a correspondent for Agence France Presse, who was executed by bullets in the back of his head. Although not a single shot was fired by the federal forces, Ross Barnett placed the blame for the riot on the "inexperienced, nervous, trigger-happy" marshals.

When it was all over at Oxford and James Meredith was attending classes on the subdued campus, the Mississippi State Senate passed a resolution declaring "complete, entire and utter contempt for the Kennedy administration and its puppet courts." But the display of pique only provided evidence that the dead-end politicians had nothing else to say. The Kennedys had demonstrated in practice the policy the attorney general had set forth at the University of Georgia. They would play along with Southern officials trying to save face with segregationist constituents, but they would not tolerate violence.

The Justice Department allowed the contempt-of-court citation against Barnett to become moot, eliciting a dissent from Judge Minor

Wisdom, who thought the court should have enforced it: "To avoid further violence and bloodshed all state officials, including the governor, must know that they cannot with impunity flout federal law."

In fact the lesson had been learned, at the statehouse level at least. Resistance would continue for a while, but those in high office would be careful to keep a safe distance from the bullyboys who employed the last resort of violence. After Oxford, rhetorical defenders of the Southern Way of Life found it prudent to acknowledge their obligation to maintain law and order, and ostentatiously look the other way when it broke down.

The president and the attorney general were also prepared to rely on court orders where lawsuits might remove restrictions on voting rights, but there were practical limitations on their effectiveness. The civil rights legislation pushed through in 1957 by Senate Democrats led by Lyndon Johnson had given the Justice Department authority to initiate court action if it could be shown that only a small percentage of eligible black voters was allowed to qualify—as in the case of Mississippi, where fewer than 15 percent were on the rolls in seventy-four of eighty-two counties. But it was clear that court orders would be of little avail where ignorance, apathy, and fear were the primary factors keeping blacks away from the polls.

In the Deep South, and in rural areas elsewhere, a grass-roots education project would be required to teach illiterate and semiliterate blacks how to meet legitimate registration requirements, and to assure them they could count on federal support in cases of overt intimidation. This was the point pressed on the Kennedy administration by Stephen Currier, head of the Taconic Foundation. My old friend and collaborator Harold C. Fleming played a prominent role in the effort after resigning as executive director of the Southern Regional Council to establish the Potomac Institute, a capital think tank funded by Taconic.

The president and attorney general were happy to support the effort led by Currier to line up other foundation support for the project, which would relieve the administration of the necessity of seeking a congressional appropriation to fund the undertaking. The White House blessing helped Currier obtain the endorsement of the major civil rights organizations, and a total of $783,000 was contributed by the Taconic, Field, and Edgar Stern foundations.

The Voter Registration Project was organized by the Southern Regional Council under the direction of Wiley Branton, one of the first black graduates of the University of Arkansas Law School. The SCLC collaborated in setting up a residential training school for field workers in Georgia headed by two of King's key aides, Andrew Young and Wyatt Tee Walker.

The Kennedy strategy was compatible with King's commitment to nonviolence in SCLC's continuing campaign to desegregate places of public accommodation. Targets of opportunity were selected where there was a reasonable expectation of gaining concessions without a dead-end confrontation, making possible informal negotiations between local white leaders and emissaries sent from Washington to invoke the prestige of the White House.

But the tactical restraints King's moderation required were scorned by the impetuous young leaders of the lunch counter sit-in movement that in 1960 developed spontaneously on black college campuses in North Carolina. They made a bow to their elders in titling their organization the Student Nonviolent Coordinating Committee (SNCC), but they rejected the proffered role as the youth division of SCLC and insisted on full autonomy.

In the spring of 1961, against the advice of the SCLC leadership, members of SNCC—Snick, as they called it—joined the "Freedom Rides" sponsored by the Congress of Racial Equality (CORE), a Northern antidiscrimination organization headed by the black Quaker pacifist James Farmer. Whites were included in the teams CORE sent across the Mason-Dixon line to challenge Jim Crow on interstate buses and at their terminals. The Freedom Riders proceeded in fairly good order through the upper South, but when they crossed into Alabama the local police stood aside while men and women of both races were brutally assaulted by white mobs.

King arrived on the scene and entered into protracted negotiations with Washington, demanding the kind of federal usurpation of local authority the administration was reluctant to undertake. The president's response was to insist that the Freedom Rides be called off to prevent further violence, a request that was promptly rejected by young John

Lewis of SNCC, who recruited black student volunteers in Nashville and headed for Birmingham.

Although the Justice Department sent in marshals to protect King and a churchful of his followers when they were besieged in Montgomery, Robert Kennedy's main effort was aimed at enlisting the support of state authorities to assure safe passage for the Freedom Riders as they moved on to Mississippi. The attorney general made a deal with Senator James Eastland, who guaranteed that there would be no violence when the buses pulled into the station at Jackson. The Freedom Riders would be arrested on charges of traveling "for the avowed purpose of inflaming public opinion," but a bail bond fund had been prearranged and they would be released unharmed. Robert Kennedy, who had agreed in return to call for a cooling-off period, was profoundly shocked when King and Farmer refused to go along. Freedom Riders continued to arrive in Jackson until they filled the local jails and spilled over into the notorious Parchman state prison farm.

"It's a matter of conscience and morality," King explained to the attorney general in one of their interminable telephone conversations. "They must use their lives and their bodies to right a wrong." On this score there was no meeting of minds. "You know," King said of the Kennedys, "they don't understand the social revolution going on in the world and therefore they don't understand what we're doing." Robert Kennedy in his turn questioned whether the Freedom Riders really had the best interests of their country at heart: "Do you know that one of them is against the atom bomb?—yes, he even picketed against it in jail."

The Kennedys' pragmatism was endorsed in the opinion polls; Gallup showed 63 percent disapproval of the Freedom Rides on principle, but 70 percent approval of the use of U.S. marshals to protect the riders—with a reading of 50 percent in the South. And *The New York Times*, bespeaking liberal sentiment, opined: "Nonviolence that deliberately provokes violence is a logical contradiction."

King had always recognized that the primary purpose of action on the ground was to produce reaction in Washington, as it did in this case, although not in the fashion he demanded. The attorney general petitioned the Interstate Commerce Commission to strengthen regulations requiring the end of segregation in interstate terminals, and the

Justice Department began systematic enforcement in railway stations and airports as well as at bus depots.

The mob attacks on the Freedom Riders portrayed on the nation's TV screens aroused popular support for CORE's subsequent Freedom Highway campaign to desegregate motels. The threat of a national boycott that would involve sympathetic white travelers was enough to bring around the big chains, and at the close of 1962 Farmer proclaimed that blacks "could now drive along the nation's highways secure in the knowledge that they could find a place to dine and spend the night."

King had not lost his faith in reconciliation in the course of his jousting with the power structure, but his innocence had been tempered. "Freedom," he wrote, echoing the great black abolitionist Frederick Douglass, "is never given voluntarily by the oppressor; it must be demanded by the oppressed."

At Birmingham, he demonstrated what he meant when he contended that nonviolence did not have to be passive, adopting tactics more in line with the civil disobedience practiced by SNCC. The aggressive demonstrations SCLC launched to force downtown department stores to desegregate their facilities and hire black clerks produced scenes of police brutality burned into the nation's consciousness by network TV cameras. No American then alive is likely to forget the snarling police dogs and fire hoses that greeted thousands of schoolchildren when they marched, singing, into the city's central shopping district—and these scenes have since become leading items in the repertory used in TV treatment of civil rights issues.

King himself wound up behind bars, where he wrote an eloquent reply to local white ministers who termed him an "outside agitator" and deplored what they termed his un-Christian extremism. The Apostles, he noted, were also outside agitators, and Jesus was considered "an extremist for love." As always, he closed his epistle from the Birmingham jail on a redemptive note:

One day the South will know that when these disinherited children of God sat down at lunch counters they were in reality standing up for what is best in the American dream and for the most sacred values of our Judeo-Christian heritage.

Birmingham touched off a nationwide wave of reaction that forced the Kennedys to recognize that they could no longer temporize with such overt manifestations of racism. On June 11, 1963, the president in a TV address to the nation joined King on the high moral ground, saying the issue raised by the black protesters was "as old as the Scriptures . . . and as clear as the American Constitution."

For the first time his emphasis was on justice rather than law and order. Citing the great disparity between the condition of the white majority and the black minority, the president asked: "Who among us would be content with the counsel of patience and delay?"

The fires of frustration and discord are burning in every city, North and South. Where legal remedies are not at hand, redress is sought in the streets, in demonstrations, parades and protests which create tensions and threaten violence. . . . We face, therefore, a moral crisis as a country and a people. It cannot be met by repressive police action. It cannot be left to increased demonstrations in the streets. It cannot be quieted by token moves or talks. It is time to act in the Congress, in your state and local legislative body, and, above all, in our daily lives.

He closed with a pledge of support for legislation that would go beyond the issue of individual rights and address the denial of equal economic opportunity. On June 19 the package, worked out in collaboration with Vice President Johnson, was delivered to the Congress.

This met the demands of the Northern black leaders for a truly national civil rights strategy, but the president had serious reservations when A. Philip Randolph persuaded the major civil rights leaders that it was time to organize a mass march on Washington to help persuade Congress to enact the proposed legislation. Kennedy called the leaders to the White House, where he told them, "We want success in Congress, not just a big show at the Capitol. Some of those people are looking for an excuse to be against us. I don't want to give any of them a chance to say, 'Yes, I'm for the bill but I'm damned if I'll vote for it at the point of a gun.' "

To overcome divisions in their own ranks, the leaders had already agreed to stay away from Capitol Hill and avoid direct confrontations, but Randolph, Farmer, and King told the president they were determined to march. King observed, "Frankly, I've never engaged in any direct action movement which did not seem ill-timed. Some people thought Birmingham ill-timed." Kennedy grinned at his brother Robert and added, "Including the attorney general." Recognizing that there was going to be a march on Washington anyway, the president publicly endorsed it as a proper manifestation of the people's right to petition their government.

On August 28, 1963, a quarter of a million people from all parts of the nation, fifty thousand of them white, gathered on the mall before the Lincoln Memorial. All the leading figures in the civil rights movement were on the platform, but by common consent the day was Martin Luther King's. The "I Have a Dream" speech that rolled out across the airwaves has now become as familiar as the Gettysburg Address of the Great Emancipator whose brooding bronze image loomed behind the inspired young preacher. I recorded my own impressions in a book called *Hearts and Minds*:

> I was the only Southerner in a group that watched the march on television in California. When King had finished sketching his vision of the beloved community there was not a single wisecrack to be heard from these often brittle sophisticates, and I doubt that there was a dry eye among them. Yet I think that I, like all Southerners, was touched in a different way—in my case, not so much by King's implied promise of absolution for guilt inherited from slave-owning forebears, as pride that this man, so uniquely one of the South's own, had become, for the moment at least, the nation's chaplain.

The addresses by Kennedy and King marked the valedictory of the Southern phase of the civil rights movement. There would still be confrontations with last-ditch defenders of the Southern Way of Life, but these would be largely confined to Alabama and Mississippi, and were aptly described by Ralph McGill as guerrilla fighting among the ruins of the segregated society. The basic problem of opening the mainstream to a mass of black citizens incapacitated to varying degrees by the racist imprint on American society remained to be dealt with, and now it would have to be faced where it still had not even been acknowledged—in the great cities outside the South.

MIDPASSAGE
THE DEMOCRATIC ASCENDANCY

We have all argued that the Supreme Court decision of May 1954 is not the law of the land. But everyone must agree that it is the fact of the land. Interposition, sovereignty, legal motions, personal defiance have all been applied—and all attempts have failed. As we meet, South Carolina is running out of courts. . . . We of today must realize the lesson of one hundred years ago, and move on for the good of South Carolina and our United States. This should be done with dignity. It must be done with law and order. It is a hurdle that brings little progress to either side. But the failure to clear it will do us irreparable harm.

—GOVERNOR ERNEST F. HOLLINGS, farewell address,
South Carolina General Asssembly, January 9, 1963

By THE BEGINNING of Jack Kennedy's third year in office the militant segregationists were beginning to lose political control in all but two of the Southern states, Alabama and Mississippi. Elsewhere massive resistance effectively ended when the governor of South Carolina warned his legislators that they had fallen back to the last ditch. Conceding that legal devices for delaying compliance with *Brown* had been exhausted, Fritz Hollings made way for my alma mater to serve as a latter-day Appomattox Courthouse.

In January 1963, Clemson University admitted its first black student, Harvey Gantt, a graduate of Charleston High School who had won a national merit scholarship and decided he wanted to be an architect. He had first accepted the offer the state used to buy off black applicants to its professional schools, making up the difference in tuition costs for those who agreed to go elsewhere. But at Iowa State University he quickly discovered that the absence of official discrimination was no barrier to race prejudice. It was cold in Ames, he was lonely, and as a practical matter he concluded that if he was to pursue his chosen profession back home he'd be better off going to school with his future colleagues.

Gantt turned to the NAACP, and after a year of litigation a federal court ordered his admission to Clemson. By the time he arrived on campus the state had mobilized its resources to ensure that there would be no vestige of the racist extravaganza that had marked James Meredith's entry into the University of Mississippi. "Clemson," Fred Powledge wrote in *Free at Last?*, "had become the example of proper school integration, and Ole Miss the aberration."

Unlike Meredith, who attended class accompanied by an armed federal marshal and withdrew at the end of his first term, Gantt was fully accepted by his classmates. After earning his degree he established a successful architectural practice at Charlotte, where he was twice elected mayor by a substantial majority of white voters, and was narrowly defeated in a race for the U.S. Senate as the Democratic candidate.

Looking back on his experience at Clemson, Gantt told Powledge he thought he had finally prevailed because the political leadership was dominated by fellow Charlestonians: "I always said you could appeal . . . to their manners if you couldn't always appeal to the morality of the situation." The lawsuit, he concluded, was simply a charade intended to demonstrate to diehard constituents that the leaders had been sincere in their opposition. "Once that was done, then they could sit back and say, 'Now we're not going to do what Mississippi did.' "

The Supreme Court orders requiring desegregation of institutions of higher learning had been stripped of ambiguity, but this was not the case with those involving the public schools. Districts with a relatively low proportion of blacks to whites usually merged the separate schools with little difficulty, but in those where black enrollment exceeded what had come to be regarded as the "tipping point" of 30 percent, "all deliberate speed" had been reduced to a snail's pace.

"The race problem," Justice Robert Jackson once observed, "would be quickly solved if some way could be found to make us all live up to our hypocrisies." Had that been possible, the thorny matter of enforcing the Court's desegregation orders would have been taken care of by the final injunction of the landmark ruling:

> The responsibility for achieving compliance with the Court's decision in these cases does not rest on the judiciary alone. Every officer and agency of the government, federal, state and local, is likewise charged with the duty of enforcing the Constitution and the rights guaranteed under it.

But a decade would pass before the executive and legislative branches joined in the effort to merge the dual school systems. Initially, the judiciary, which had no enforcement powers of its own, had to rely on state and local authorities to carry out court orders, and most, when not openly hostile, were inhibited by the political risk involved.

This accounted for the ambiguity of the guidelines set forth in *Brown II.* Although the original decree clearly required establishment of a unitary school system, the means of achieving it were left open. The lower courts were charged with fashioning implementing decrees, and the Supreme Court let stand the precedent set in the South Carolina case, which held that a segregated school district was under no compulsion to change its attendance patterns unless black children sought admission to a white school.

The resulting "freedom of choice" policy provided that any qualified black petitioner must be admitted to a white school if there were a vacancy in an appropriate classroom, but in the absence of such a demand segregation would be considered voluntary and allowed to continue. In practice this preserved segregation through involuntary inaction, since black children could only cross the color bar one at a time, and subterfuge could be challenged only by going to court. It could be safely assumed that no white children would exercise their freedom of choice to attend the generally inferior black schools.

This had the effect of removing the most sensitive of the civil rights issues from the political agenda. In the South, court-ordered school desegregation was too limited to arouse widespread white reaction, and blacks were concentrating on securing the franchise and gaining access to employment and places of public accommodation. Outside the region it was still assumed that *Brown* had no application to school districts where segregation had never been required by law.

By the 1960s I was viewing these developments in a somewhat longer perspective than that available on the front lines in Little Rock. *The Negro and the Schools* had attracted the attention of Robert Maynard Hutchins, the former president of the University of Chicago who, as associate director of the Ford Foundation, had been instrumental in setting up the Fund for the Advancement of Education. In 1954 he had become president of the Fund for the Republic, another Ford offshoot, which had been given fifteen million dollars to advance the cause of civil liberties and civil rights.

Hutchins asked me to join the Fund's board of directors, described by Eric Sevareid in a CBS broadcast as "a group of the most responsible, respectable, and successful business and professional men in the country . . . banded together in a herculean effort to roll back the creeping tide of what is known as McCarthyism."

I could hardly match the prestige of my colleagues, but I had other credentials. The board had been without a Southern member since Malcolm Bryan, an Atlanta banker, resigned upon discovering that the philanthropy was committed to controversial action on the racial front. The Fund had become a primary source of support for the South's beleaguered interracial organizations as the McCarthyite equation of civil rights with Communist-inspired subversion dried up their local funding, and the more conventional national foundations were intimidated by the furor. Dwight Macdonald noted that "philanthropoids" tended to be "timid beasts, and when they are frightened by some small but vocal minority, they envelop themselves in clouds of public relations."

I, of course, already had been branded. As the anti-Communist hysteria began to abate in Washington, the professional witnesses who testified before congressional investigating committees found a market for their wares among the segregationist politicians and publicists in the South. Orval Faubus was a leading purveyor of the propaganda message in Arkansas, and I became a primary target.

When the editor of a segregationist weekly threatened to sue the *Gazette* for libel because I had called him a liar, I suggested to our counsel, A. F. House, that we file a countersuit on the ground that the plaintiff's newspaper regularly charged me with un-American activities. Judge House's negative response was not entirely ironic: "I don't think I'll have any trouble proving in court that he's a liar, but I'm damned if I'll waste my time trying to convince an Arkansas jury that you're not a Communist."

Racial tension, while still widely regarded as primarily confined to the South, was rising everywhere blacks had become numerous, and Hutchins concluded that the Fund had been dealing only with its surface manifestations. Racial discrimination, he contended, was only one of the basic issues posed by unprecedented currents of change that affected the whole of American society:

> Our situation has changed too fast for our ideas, and so our ideas have degenerated into slogans. . . . Most of us retain individualistic, liberal ideas, but we live in a bureaucratic culture. It remains to be seen whether we can make our ideals applicable to our culture, or whether we can make our culture conform to our ideals.

Hutchins recommended to the board that the Fund's grant-making activities be terminated and its remaining resources be used to establish a new "think tank" to appraise the impact of rapidly changing technology and demography on the nation's institutions and processes. When the Center for the Study of Democratic Institutions opened at Santa Barbara, California, in the fall of 1959, I was offered an appointment as a senior fellow.

The reopening of the Little Rock schools and the restoration of the *Gazette*'s lost circulation and advertising freed me to move on, and I signed on as a half-time consultant. But before I could settle down among the scholars and experts assembled in those salubrious surroundings, I was committed to spend some months among the black migrants who were now clustered in the inner city neighborhoods of New York.

. . .

The assignment that developed into a sequel to *An Epitaph for Dixie* called *The Other Side of Jordan* originated with Robert M. White III, who had been summoned from his family's newspaper in Mexico, Missouri, to see if he could rejuvenate the ailing *New York Herald Tribune*. He was struck by the fact that none of the New York dailies paid more than cursory attention to the city's black population, which now stood at 20 percent and was rapidly increasing as displaced farmworkers streamed in from the rural South.

These blacks shared the upper end of Manhattan with Puerto Ricans and were spreading across both the East and Hudson rivers to encroach upon white ethnic enclaves in the other boroughs and the New Jersey river towns. Accompanied by a knowledgeable black guide, James Booker of Harlem's *Amsterdam News*, I spent the spring of 1960 in neighborhoods more densely populated and as thoroughly segregated as any I had known in the South.

When my old friend Ralph McGill of the *Atlanta Constitution* learned that I had accepted White's assignment, he sent me a remarkably prescient letter. His observations would be commonplace today, but few then recognized that the technological revolution that made blacks surplus population in the agricultural South was also reducing the market for unskilled, entry-level labor in the old industrial centers:

> We are developing a dangerous segment of population of youthful age that won't be able to find employment. To be sure race enters into it and aggravates it. The Puerto Ricans, the Italians, the Jews and the Negroes all have their clashes in New York and Chicago, but it grows largely out of idleness, frustration and economic lacks. These unemployed and uneducated thousands can, at best, hold fringe jobs. If they get married, they can't support a wife; so they drift into petty crime and then into major crime.

The political implications of this massive demographic shift were pointed up by the nation's most conspicuous black politician, Adam Clayton Powell, Jr., when I interviewed him in the pastor's study at Harlem's

Abyssinian Baptist Church. The sybaritic Powell, who was also New York's lone black congressman, smoked a Havana cigar and sipped imported brandy while he elaborated on his reaction to the civil rights movement.

"In the South it's the middleclass and upperclass Negroes, the preacher, the teacher, the student, and they're fighting for the golf course and the swimming pool and the restaurant and the hotel and the right to vote. But when you leave the South, where only one third of the Negroes now live, you have a revolution of the masses. Not the classes. And that revolution is interested in schools, housing, jobs. And civil rights legislation will not help them at all."

Powell exploited the antiwhite sentiment that was gaining ground in Harlem, but he also warned that "the day the Negro changes from nonviolence to violence, he is finished, and the black revolution has to start all over again at some future date." This reading of political reality made no impression on another minister who was soon to eclipse the prodigal congressman as a center of media attention.

At a Harlem restaurant I was introduced to the politics of rage in an extended interview with Malcolm X, the intense, born-again ex-convict who presided over Temple Number Seven of the Nation of Islam. I was, like most of those who faced him in the years to come, impressed by the young minister's obvious intelligence and steel-edged drive. Just over six feet tall, whip-thin, with a bronze complexion and close-cropped, rust-colored hair, he had been called "Detroit Red" in his earlier incarnation as a numbers runner, dope peddler, pimp, and second-story man. I wrote of that encounter:

> His scorn for white liberals and fellow-traveling blacks in the civil rights movement made Adam Clayton Powell's strictures sound like accolades. Anyone who expected blacks to improve their lot in a white-dominated society was "integration-mad," and if he wore a black skin he was a "house nigger" for the whites. Any black intellectual who challenged Black Muslim doctrine was written off as "Uncle Thomas, Ph.D." In our several hours of conversation he was always on the offensive; any topic I tried to introduce was bent to fit his litany—the white man was the devil, his God was false, his professed com-

mitment to justice was a part of the "tricknology" he used to delude blacks. . . . I could not doubt his sincerity when he punctuated this diatribe with a reiterated "I *believe* in anger."

This was a doctrine of separatism, at the other pole from Martin Luther King's espousal of integration, and it was beginning to gain credence among black intellectuals. Two of the most gifted of these, James Baldwin and Lorraine Hansberry, coined a battlecry for the countermovement when they asked, "Who wants to integrate with a burning house?" The politics of rage, I discovered, dispensed with answers to questions as to how it was proposed to go about creating an autonomous, economically self-sufficient polity within a society dominated almost 10 to 1 by whites. The response was a version of the answer Fats Waller gave when asked about the meaning of jazz: If you've got to ask, you'll never know.

If one listened only to what was being said by black orators in Harlem's public places, there was no reason to question the verdict of the black journalist Louis E. Lomax, who in 1959 declared in a *Harper's* article that "the NAACP is no longer the prime mover of the Negro's social revolt. This revolt, swelling underground for the past two decades, means the end of the traditional leadership class."

At the corner of Seventh Avenue and 125th Street, which served as Harlem's Hyde Park, the dismissal of the interracial movement's black leaders was laced with a sharp edge of anti-Semitism. The scene was dominated by the preachment of various sects of black nationalists whose speakers mounted folding stepladders to harangue the passersby. The tone, and much of the vocabulary, was that of a white Citizens' Council rally. "The Jew-dominated NAACP is no friend of yours," was a frequent refrain.

The revolt was aimed at those who, with the patronage of wealthy white liberals, in the 1920s and 1930s had made Harlem the cultural capital of the national black community. Those were the years of the "Harlem Renaissance," when sophisticated New Yorkers made pilgrimages uptown as they would to an exotic tropical country. Jazz had just been discovered, and Harlem had a dozen glittering supper clubs and scores of more modest establishments where the Prohibition law and other restrictions on sinful proclivities could be bent for a price.

In his memoir *The Big Sea*, Langston Hughes, a poet and essayist who gained recognition in those years, recalled it as the time "when the Negro was in vogue." This led to the acceptance of talented black musicians and literary figures in intellectual circles downtown, but the genuine, if limited, racial interaction among artists and their patrons did not extend to the whites who sat at ringside tables uptown staring at the black customers as if they were "amusing animals in a zoo."

> The Negroes said: "We can't go downtown and sit and stare at you in your clubs. You won't even let us in your clubs." But they didn't say it out loud, for Negroes are practically never rude to white people. So, thousands of whites came to Harlem night after night, thinking the Negroes loved to have them there. . . .

The clubs, and the white voyeurs, had disappeared by 1960, when I spent days and a good part of many nights in Harlem. But in what had become a self-contained small city there was still evidence of the politeness Hughes cited. "In the brightly lighted commercial districts, where the humdrum business of life goes on," I wrote,

> a man with a white skin had no difficulty making innocent passage. If he is looking for trouble he can probably find it, and wind up carved like a Thanksgiving turkey. But if he minds his own business he will be treated with courtesy and respect—the special, almost painful politeness that any close-knit community reserves for the identifiable stranger in town.

There was misery and squalor behind the streaked tenement windows that looked out on garbage-strewn streets where swarms of yelling, pink-heeled children ran untended, and the red skein of violence ran through the varied fabric of life in Harlem, as it did in every big-city ghetto. But it was a place where there was still a sense of community, and the fact that it was ebbing was the primary concern of the indigenous black leadership.

. . .

Retaining Harlem's unique identity was very much on the mind of J. Raymond Jones, known throughout the borough of Manhattan as "The Fox." No one, I noted after spending an evening with him, would have mistaken him for anything but a politician, and a very successful one:

> He has the look—the gray hair shading now into white, the subdued and impeccable tailoring, the sense of presence that comes of sitting frequently at head tables. He smokes cigars, and they come from Havana. His drink, in which he indulges sparingly, is an esoteric brand of Scotch for which bartenders have to reach in the bottom shelves. His conversation is rich in personal anecdote, and laced with earthy humor.

Had he been born Irish or Italian, Ray Jones might have been the leader of Tammany Hall by then. Born black in the Virgin Islands sixty years before, he had made it as far as membership in the Democratic organization's executive committee. Named leader of Harlem's key Thirteenth Assembly District in 1944, he had cemented his position by bringing Adam Clayton Powell back into the fold after the mercurial congressman bolted the party in 1956, shocking Harlem by posing with a smiling President Eisenhower on the White House steps. Asked about a report that it cost the Republicans fifty thousand dollars to arrange the conversion, and the Democrats a hundred thousand dollars to get Powell back, Jones said, "Certain financial arrangements have to be made to pay the legitimate cost of any political campaign."

In preparation for the coming elections, Jones had just arranged a deal that brought together Powell and Manhattan's black borough president, Hulan Jack, and scuttled a slate of Puerto Rican candidates for local office. He explained that the resulting Powell-Jack United Harlem Leadership Team was a natural result of the attack on Tammany by insurgent liberal Democrats that had weakened the control of the party boss, Carmine De Sapio.

"Put Jack's and Powell's groups together and we swing 20 percent of the votes in Manhattan," he said. "Swing those votes right and we ought to wind up with 20 percent of the jobs. If we do that we don't need the Puerto Ricans—and anyway the break with them makes Carmine nervous, and that's good for us.

"When the leaders run again, Carmine is done. I plan to be around to help pick up the pieces. I've seen control of this town pass from the Irish to the Italians. Anybody who can count votes ought to be able to figure out that the Negro's turn is coming—if not for control, at least for a bigger share of the pot."

Jones, who had spent his life working within the system, dismissed the separatist plaint of the Muslims and other black nationalists as nonsense. But, although he expressed none of the scorn for the main-line leadership voiced by Malcolm X and Powell, Jones considered most liberal reformers irrelevant. Of the effort to have the Census Bureau drop all racial identification, he said, "Silliest damned thing I ever heard of. How am I going to bargain for the Negroes if I can't prove where they are?

"A lot of our people listen too much to sociologists. Sure, the white liberal leaders in the past have done a lot of things that needed doing. But why did they support antidiscrimination laws and public housing and all the rest? Because the Negro vote has been growing steadily and they couldn't ignore it. I say it has grown big enough so that Negroes can take over their own show."

Jones displayed no emotional response to the dramatic civil rights movement in the South. There were no significant black votes there yet, and in his political calculus this was what counted. Yet, while we talked, events were shaping up there that would make him a key player in the coming return of the Democrats to power in Washington.

In October, when the presidential contest hung in the balance, Jack Kennedy staged a Constitutional Rights Conference in New York and used the occasion to deliver a speech in Harlem with Adam Clayton Powell at his side. Following up, Louis Martin, the black strategist at the Democratic National Committee, seized upon Kennedy's intervention to secure King's release from a Georgia prison as a means of energizing black voters in the big cities. Black preachers would spread the word in the churches, but Martin, who once said no black could survive in politics as long as he had without becoming a cynic, knew it would also be necessary to turn out the bars and pool halls. His kindred spirit

Ray Jones responded with a drive that gained momentum right up to Election Day.

Harris Wofford, who headed the Civil Rights Section at Kennedy headquarters, gratefully noted the result in his memoir *Of Kennedys and King*:

> On election day, the wily, street-wise Harlem Democratic leader, Ray ("the Fox") Jones called me to say that . . . there had been a massive turnout of Negroes for Kennedy throughout New York, and that he wanted to take his hat off to the Civil Rights Section, about which he had at first been skeptical. "It was like a symphony," he said, "working up to a great last movement."

The only major figure among the national civil rights leaders who maintained his base in Harlem was the Pullman porters' union chief, A. Philip Randolph, who, at seventy, had attained the status of elder statesman. He had arrived during the Renaissance, but played no role in it since he had come up from Florida endowed with an ascetic lifestyle impressed on him by his father, a circuit-riding AME preacher. "My home was almost Calvinistic," he said. "It was rigidly moralistic, and rigidly supervised. I never saw a bottle of whiskey, nobody used profanity, and there was no playing on Sunday."

He had made a career for himself in what were then the virtually lily-white ranks of American labor unions. In the 1930s, when he became head of the segregated Brotherhood of Sleeping Car Porters, its 35,000 members accounted for almost half the total black membership of the American Federation of Labor. The porters' union, which also included dining car cooks and waiters, was still all-black in 1960 except for a few whites on the Canadian lines. But Randolph was using its solidarity as the base from which to speak out on behalf of the 1.5 million blacks who had gained union membership in the years since he pressured President Roosevelt into establishing the first Fair Employment Practices Commission.

At the 1959 AFL-CIO convention Randolph had precipitated a floor debate on racial discrimination that drew a challenge from an outraged President George Meany: "Who the hell appointed you the guardian of all the Negro union members in America?" The old porter's answer to the old plumber was the formation of the Negro American Labor Council, which he had just announced when I interviewed him on a quiet Saturday morning at his headquarters in a shabby old Harlem office building.

He was looking forward, he said, to what might well be his last great battle, but he was in a reminiscent mood, recalling others when the issues had been more personal and immediate. "I used to go into the South when you had to hide out to have a union meeting, even if it was segregated. You weren't even safe in a church. I've been in Memphis when Boss Crump's police would come right up to the pulpit and give the order for the organizers to be out of town before the sun set. You knew they meant it, too.

"What we're up against now is something different. Oh, there is still race prejudice in the unions, sure. But on top of that there is the fact that whites have always run most of the unions, and if we are going to move up on the inside it means that somebody has got to move over. Nobody ever likes that.

"But that time has run out. We've got to fight now to get our full rights within the unions, and not only in justice to our own people. I say that what really weakens the union movement is its own practices of discrimination; as long as that goes on we are disarmed before our enemies.

"And there's another, maybe a bigger reason."

Unlike the Harlem leaders I had interviewed who looked on the Freedom Marches in the South as essentially irrelevant to the issues facing blacks in the urban ghettos, Randolph had identified with the movement from the time of Martin Luther King's bus boycott in Montgomery. And Randolph had just been literally dragooned by the young black college students who had launched sit-ins at segregated lunch counters in North Carolina. His face lit up when he told me about being taken off a train by a student delegation that had found out his travel schedule and came aboard unannounced at an operating stop.

"They scared the life out of the porter, and he tried to keep them out. I think he even told them I wasn't on the train, but they knew better, and they just pushed him backward into my compartment. He kept saying, 'For the Lord's sake, boss, don't go with these people. They're wild!'

"But they told me they had a car waiting, and they needed me on their campus, and they would take me on to Charlotte to meet my appointments. It was the sit-ins they wanted to talk about, of course. They already had them going in two cities and were planning more.

"So I went with them, and when we got there the whole auditorium was full of students and they had been waiting for hours. The president and some of the faculty came to greet me, and they looked pretty nervous, and I guess I couldn't blame them. That whole place was full of electricity. You could feel it.

"I got up to talk to the students, and when I looked out over those young faces, there wasn't but one thing I could say. I told them I would do what I could to help. That's what I'm doing now—trying to help the best way I know how."

In the early years of the Kennedy administration the return of activist government to Washington served to reenergize the Democratic organizations in the great cities—which included the black political leadership. This had the effect of containing the spread of the Muslim and black nationalist movements among rank-and-file blacks. But the resentment of black intellectuals at the rebuffs and condescension they encountered at the hands of prejudiced or insensitive whites continued to make emotional converts to the separatist cause,

In 1963 James Baldwin generated shock waves when he exalted the politics of rage in his polemical book *The Fire Next Time*. The "torture, castration, infanticide, rape, death and humiliation" suffered by blacks at the hands of whites, he contended, had imbued the Negro with a hatred of the white man so deep that

it often turned against him and his own, and made all love, all trust, all joy impossible. . . . The Negro's experience of the white world cannot possibly create in him any respect for the standards by which the white world claims to live.

He sought to distance himself from the overt racism implicit in the preachment of Malcolm X, but he conceded that things are as bad as the Muslims say they are—in fact they are worse, and the Muslims do not help matters—but there is no reason that black men should be expected to be more patient, more forbearing, more farseeing than whites; indeed, quite the contrary.

White liberals who professed sympathy for the integrationist cause were characterized by "incredible, abysmal and really cowardly obtuseness." And Baldwin rejected Martin Luther King's commitment to nonviolence, declaring that it was considered a virtue only because whites did not want their lives, their self-image, or their property threatened.

Baldwin's status as an artist brought him an invitation to a White House dinner, and afterward Arthur Schlesinger, Jr., now an aide to President Kennedy, took him to his home to meet with a group of white civil rights activists, including some then holding positions in the government. "He seemed to regard them as worse than Southern bigots, who at least were honest enough to admit that they, like all white men (by definition), hated the Negro," Schlesinger wrote in his memoir, *A Thousand Days*.

But Baldwin's passionate eloquence titillated the whites who kept *The Fire Next Time* high on the bestseller lists, and it prompted Robert Kennedy to seek out his views on the role he envisioned for the government in dealing with the racial polarization he cited. Kennedy set up an informal meeting at his New York apartment, and invited Baldwin to bring along other blacks he thought the attorney general should hear.

Along with such notable figures in New York's black community as the sociologist Kenneth Clark, Lorraine Hansberry, Lena Horne, and Harry Belafonte, the gathering included Jerome Smith, a young Freedom Rider who had been severely beaten in the course of the foray through the South. Smith opened the session by declaring that being in the same room with Robert Kennedy made him feel like vomiting. When Kennedy expressed resentment at what he took to be a gratuitous expression of personal contempt, the others rallied around Smith. Three hours of what Schlesinger described as noncommunication followed, in the course of which there was talk of sending arms into the South. The shocked Kennedy described his reaction:

They didn't know anything. They don't know what the laws are—they don't know what the facts are—they don't know what we've been doing or what we're trying to do. You couldn't talk to them as you can to Roy Wilkins or Martin Luther King. They didn't want to talk that way. It was all emotion, hysteria. They stood up and orated. They cursed. Some of them wept and walked out of the room.

What disturbed Kennedy most was the lack of support by those in the group who later took him aside to assure him that they respected what he was doing for the black cause. One who had been a dinner guest at his Hickory Hill home said, "Of course, you have done more for civil rights than any other attorney general." When Kennedy demanded to know why he hadn't spoken up when he was being pilloried, the reply was, "I couldn't say that to the others. It would affect my relationship with them. If I were to defend you, they would conclude I had gone over to the other side."

This struck me as a sad echo of the rationale members of the white establishment in the South employed to explain why they felt it necessary to remain silent in the face of unwarranted attacks on those who were attempting to bring about an orderly transition to a desegregated society. Summing up interviews with Harlem's black intellectuals and political leaders in *The Other Side of Jordan*, I had concluded that "it is no more possible to conduct a rational debate on the race issue within the [northern] Negro community than it is within the impassioned and disturbed white community of the South."

The Negro leader who tries immediately finds himself assailed on the ground that he has joined the white enemy camp to shore up his own status in the larger community—and it is further argued that in the rarefied atmosphere of the national interracial movements he has lost touch with the Negro masses. In an earlier time, when Negro ministers and educators spoke for the colored community in seeking concessions from the dominant whites, the term of opprobrium was "Uncle Tom." . . . Today it is "phony liberal"—and it applies not only to Negroes who deal with whites in high places, but also to the whites with whom they deal.

I used Baldwin's confrontation with Bobby Kennedy as the point of departure later that summer when *Look* magazine, prompted by rumblings in the ghettos, asked me to appraise the situation on the race front. The encounter had provided striking evidence of the gap between rhetoric and reality that was now being redefined along North-South lines: Baldwin, a native New Yorker with no personal experience in the South that produced Martin Luther King, had emerged as the most adamant spokesman on one side, paired off against Governor George Wallace of Alabama, who was now the most conspicuous defender of the Southern Way of Life. Neither, I predicted, could prevail, although both could, and doubtless would, cause a good deal of trouble:

> The feudal system [Wallace] seeks to maintain has been falling apart under its own weight for more than a generation. . . . Those in Alabama whose power is recognized in the title Big Mules are still balky, but they have decided to get back to making money.
>
> Mr. Baldwin can lend momentum to the drive for Negro rights, but he can produce neither the millennium nor the holocaust. His tortured eloquence flutters the intellectuals and his revolutionary words thrill the alienated of all complexions. But the mass of American Negroes do not reject the existing social order, seeking only to share fully in its bourgeois blessings.

An actual resort to violence would be suicidal for a minority vastly outnumbered by whites, who had total control over the means of forcible subjection. Yet, as Malcolm X had divined, the threat of violence could provide effective pressure on the white leadership. Whether consciously or not, the militant blacks were taking a leaf from the book of the Southern segregationists who had employed the same tactic in rallying support for massive resistance.

It was, however, a tactic that could backfire, as it had when the Southern leaders proved unable to restrain the more agitated of their followers. Martin Luther King's commitment to nonviolence, I pointed out, was dictated not only by his vows of conscience but also by a tactical sense honed by experience:

> So long as violence is directed against peaceful Negro dem-onstrators, elementary standards of justice backed by Federal guns are automatically on their side. Let Negroes initiate the attack, or even reply in kind, and the balance will shift—and without this essential support Negroes will again be a helpless minority in an aroused white community.
>
> Martin Luther King not only subscribes to, but has given real meaning to the battle cry of the movement: No white man has a right to ask a Negro to wait any longer for equality. But, as a practicing Christian, Dr. King has to recognize that every white man has a right to insist that the quest for equality not be marked by a trail of blood.
>
> It is on this critical point that Dr. King had to part company with a good many of those who have lately swung aboard the freedom train. He speaks for justice. They cry out for vengeance.

By 1963 the Kennedy administration had endorsed measures that greatly broadened the government's approach to the plight of poor blacks, and, despite the fulminations of the militants, the mass of those in the big cities still responded to the conciliatory message voiced by King in the March on Washington. There was no echo of the confrontation with Bobby Kennedy when main-line black leaders gathered at the White House in August to plan their lobbying effort in support of the civil rights package the president had sent to Capitol Hill.

Lyndon Johnson, the acknowledged master of congressional cal-culus, was asked to sum up the prospects. Pointing out that a filibuster was inevitable in the Senate, and could be ended only by a two-thirds majority vote, the vice president ticked off the numbers:

> We have about 50 votes in the Senate, and about 22 against us. What counts are the 26 or so votes that remain. To get those votes we have to be careful not to do anything that would give those who are privately opposed a public excuse to appear as martyrs.

Three months later those figures were altered by a genuine martyrdom— that of John Fitzgerald Kennedy. At Dallas on November 22 an assassin's bullets brought an end to the brief regime of the gallant young president, and launched the myth that would preserve the romantic aura of Camelot for the generation then coming of age. In death he acquired a political leverage he had never known in life.

Five days after the state funeral, Lyndon Johnson went before a joint session of Congress to declare:

> No memorial oration or eulogy could more eloquently honor President Kennedy's memory than the earliest possible passage of the civil rights bill for which he fought so long. We have talked long enough in this country about equal rights. We have talked for one hundred years or more. It is time now to write the next chapter—and to write it in the books of law.
>
> I urge you again . . . to enact a civil rights law so that we can move forward to eliminate from this nation every trace of discrimination and oppression that is based upon race or color. There could be no greater strength to this nation both at home and abroad.

It required both the anguished memory of Jack Kennedy and the formidable presence of the first Southern president since the Civil War to secure passage of the legislation that finally brought an end to legal segregation in the United States. John and Robert Kennedy had been committed to the cause, but theirs had been an abstract, patrician approach. To Lyndon Johnson the issue was rooted in his inner being; he had experienced poverty, and the scorn of the more fortunate, and had seen firsthand its effects on poor blacks and Latinos.

His parochial Texas style was in sharp contrast to the urbane sophistication of the late president, but the black leaders credited him with the "depthed understanding" King found missing in the Kennedys. "I had always felt that if I turned on the radio and heard the president of the United States speaking with a Southern accent I would panic," Whitney Young of the Urban League said of his reaction to news of the succession. "But I did not feel that way at all. I felt by that time that Lyndon Johnson would do exactly what he did."

Johnson's sensitivity to the effects of racial bigotry also extended to white Southerners who, whether or not they shared it, were affected by its consequences. As vice president he had replied to a White House request for advice on how the president should respond to continuing defiance in parts of the Deep South:

> The hell with confronting those people. But I think he ought to talk frankly and freely, rather understandingly and maybe fatherly. He should stick to the moral issue and he should do it without equivocation. . . .
>
> If your President just enforces court decrees, the South will feel that it has yielded to force. But if he goes down there and looks them in the face, these Southerners at least respect his courage. They feel that they are on the losing side of an issue of conscience.

For Johnson a moral appeal was a matter of political tactics, which also required the application of a horse trader's skills. He used both in steering the civil rights package around the usual committee blockade in the House, which passed the measure by a vote of 290 to 130 on February 10, just two weeks after it reached the floor. In the process he had strengthened the enforcement provisions of the original bill and added FEPC.

In the Senate, breaking the inevitable filibuster required six months of relentless arm-twisting. It was July before the leader of the opposition, Richard Russell of Georgia, conceded defeat, paying tribute to the president's use of "the full weight of his powerful office and the full force of his personality—both of which are considerable. . . ." In an aside to Johnson's aide Bill Moyers, Russell said, "You tell Lyndon Johnson that I've been expecting the rod for a long time, and I'm sorry it's from his hand the rod must be wielded, but I'd rather it be his hand than anybody else's I know."

When the time came to invoke cloture, the president had mustered 71 votes, four more than needed. After 115 amendments were defeated on the floor, the Civil Rights Act of 1964 passed by a vote of 73 to 27. The measure transferred the burden of initiating action in school desegregation cases from black plaintiffs to the attorney general, and authorized the Justice Department to initiate class-action suits. This became the principal means used to end discrimination in housing, employment, and public accommodations, now specifically outlawed by act of Congress.

There were also provisions intended to strengthen protection of voting rights, but these proved to be inadequate, and it was on this key issue that Johnson faced down the militant segregationists when they made their last stand in the redoubts of Alabama and Mississippi.

In November 1963, Wiley Branton, director of the Southern Regional Council's voter registration project, reported that only 3,871 blacks had been added to the voting rolls in Mississippi after two years of effort, and announced that funds budgeted for the state would be diverted to areas where real progress was under way. The Council commented: "Here every datum of economics and every fact and twist of history have conspired to keep white people deeply and oftimes harshly resistant to change, and its Negro people ill-equipped for it."

The joint Council of Federated Organizations (COFO) formed by SNCC, CORE, and the NAACP had gotten nowhere in its effort to overcome the obstacle course set up to deny blacks the ballot. COFO's charismatic moving spirit, the Harlem-born, Harvard-educated Robert Parris Moses, conceived the Freedom Summer Project to bring in students from outside the region to support his flagging troops. Nine hundred volunteers responded, most of them idealistic young white men and women from uppercrust campuses in the North and West.

The arrival of what most white Mississippians regarded as Yankee interlopers touched off a renewed wave of Klan-style terrorism. Twenty-nine black churches went up in flames, and there were more than a thousand arrests of COFO workers, eighty beatings, and six violent deaths. Backwater Neshoba County contributed a textbook example of collaboration between the Klan and local authorities when a team of two white New Yorkers and one native black disappeared after being arrested on a speeding charge.

President Johnson responded with platoons of FBI agents headed by J. Edgar Hoover, who established an office for himself at Jackson. A U.S. Navy search team finally unearthed the battered bodies of the missing men buried under an earthen dam. Hoover, who with good reason had been considered less than sympathetic to the black cause, declared that the six-week search had been hampered by "water moccasins, rattlesnakes, and rednecked sheriffs, and they are all in the same category as far as I am concerned." Johnson promised to continue using all the means at his command to end the reign of terror.

In Alabama, a SNCC-led voter registration campaign at Selma encountered Sheriff Jim Clark, a Bull Connor–style practitioner of head-knocking intimidation. The protracted standoff brought in King, who along with John Lewis of SNCC organized the famous march from Selma to Montgomery. Lewis suffered a fractured skull and scores of marchers were wounded when the first attempt to cross the Alabama River was turned back by the sheriff's deputized posse of mounted men and George Wallace's state troopers.

Lyndon Johnson summoned Wallace to the White House for an application of the fatherly persuasion he had recommended to Jack Kennedy. Nicholas Katzenbach, who had succeeded Robert Kennedy as attorney general, described the exchange:

> He [Wallace] was . . . trying to tell the President that it was his responsibility to turn off the demonstrations. President Johnson's response was, "You know, George, you can turn those off in a minute." He said, "Why don'cha just desegregate your schools?" He said, "You and I go out there in front of those television cameras right now, and you announce you've decided to desegregate every school in Alabama." Wallace said, "Oh, Mr. President, I can't do that, you know. The schools have got school boards; they're locally run. I haven't got the political power to do that." Johnson said, *"Don't you shit me, George Wallace."*

Wallace's state troopers not only stepped aside, but federalized Alabama National Guardsmen provided an escort for the procession of hymn-singing blacks, accompanied by a sprinkling of white supporters, who finally made their march across the Black Belt to Montgomery. There, with twenty-five thousand followers massed in the square flanked by the

Capitol, where the Confederacy was founded, and the Dexter Avenue Baptist Church, where he had launched the historic bus boycott. King renewed his prophecy: "We are on the move now—no wave of racism can stop us."

The president instructed Katzenbach: "I want you to write the god-damnedest toughest Voting Rights Act you can devise." Johnson went up to Capitol Hill to present the bill in person to a special session of Congress, and his Texas twang lent special emphasis to his peroration:

> What happened in Selma is part of the larger movement which reaches into every section and state of America. It is the effort of American Negroes to secure for themselves the full blessing of American life. Their cause must be our cause, too. Because it is not just Negroes, but really it is all of us who must overcome the crippling legacy of bigotry and injustice.
>
> And we shall overcome.

By that time Johnson had been elected president in his own right in the landslide victory he construed as a mandate to launch a War on Poverty, in which the key battlegrounds would be outside the South.

PINNACLE

JOHNSON AND THE GREAT SOCIETY

. . . in the teeming racial ghettos, segregation and poverty have intersected to destroy opportunity and hope and to enforce failure. The ghettos too often mean men and women without jobs, families without men, and schools where children are processed instead of educated, until they return to the street—to crime, to narcotics, to dependency on welfare, and to bitterness and resentment against society in general and white society in particular.

—Report to the President,
National Advisory Commission on Civil Disorders,
March 1, 1968

B<small>Y THE TIME</small> the Republican candidates squared off in the 1964 presidential primaries it was evident that the coalition held together by the personal popularity of President Eisenhower had not survived the defeat of Richard Nixon. The America First isolationists who dominated the party before World War II had never really made their peace with the moderate internationalists. And now Theodore White noted the welling up of

wordless resentments, angers, frustrations, fears and hopes . . .
a mood entirely different from the mood of the Taft conservatives of the forties and fifties who had wanted simply to hold

175

the country still; the new mood of the primitives insisted that the course of affairs be reversed.

Civil rights became a determining issue as the dissidents rallied behind a flag-waving libertarian from the Far West who had once suggested that the country would be better off if the effete Eastern Seaboard states were sawed off and allowed to float out to sea. When the field narrowed to two contenders they could not have more neatly represented the party's two wings had they been chosen by a Hollywood casting director.

Nelson Rockefeller, the urbane governor of New York, was the grandson of the founder of one of the nation's great fortunes, whose inheritance included among its beneficiaries the National Urban League. Senator Barry Goldwater of Arizona, a man of more modest but still substantial means, was the grandson of one of the storied pioneers who had pushed back the frontier largely on their own and imbued their descendants with faith that any man could fashion his own destiny if the government didn't get in the way.

Goldwater, of Jewish descent and an admirer of the tribal culture of Arizona's Indians, could hardly be classified as a racist. But his abiding contempt for big government allied him with the states' rights segregationists in the Senate, and he was a conspicuous opponent of the Civil Rights Act of 1964. Any government action that smacked of social reform was likely to unbridle his acid tongue, and he was not disposed to listen to the professional handlers and spin doctors who had begun to take over campaign management for both parties.

At first he refused to support the organization of the National Draft Goldwater Committee, and when seven thousand partisans turned out for a Washington rally in July 1963, their hero was not there to greet them. But the promoters brought him around by employing his own style, declaring that they would "draft the sonofabitch whether he wanted to run or not." In January he announced that he would enter New Hampshire's kickoff primary.

A World War II pilot who then held a major general's commission in the Air Force Reserve, Goldwater came out firing. On the stump he questioned the dependability of the intercontinental missiles upon which the bipartisan doctrine of deterrence depended, urged the use of atomic weaponry by NATO commanders, and proposed rescinding recognition of the Soviet Union and withdrawal from the United Nations if mainland China were admitted. On the domestic side he advocated abolition of the income tax, sale of the Tennessee Valley Authority, and voluntary status for Social Security. The Eisenhower administration, he said, had turned out to be just "a dime-store New Deal."

Rockefeller, who disagreed on every count, faced Goldwater in the primaries and stayed ahead in the quest for commitments in Republican strongholds in the East and Midwest. But the caustic Arizonan rounded up defecting Democrats in the South and West, and when he edged out Rockefeller in the California primary he was within sight of the nomination. The moderates launched a draft of their own and persuaded the reluctant Governor William Scranton of Pennsylvania to pick up the banner.

Goldwater's opposition to the Civil Rights Act of 1964 was a prime factor in moving Scranton, another genteel inheritor of wealth and status conditioned by the party's abolitionist tradition. He launched a frantic, last-minute quest for delegates to add to those Rockefeller released to him. But when the convention opened in San Francisco on July 13 it was clear that the Goldwater faction was in charge, and the odds had become insurmountable.

Any lingering doubt was dispelled when President Eisenhower delivered a speech that had been drafted by his aides as an elder statesman's appeal for party unity. The old soldier had inserted into the text a passage of his own studded with racial code words that produced a roof-raising response from the Goldwater partisans:

> . . . let us not be guilty of maudlin sympathy for the criminal who, roaming the streets with switchblade knife and illegal firearms seeking a helpless prey, suddenly becomes upon apprehension a poor, underprivileged person who counts upon the compassion of our society and the laxness or weakness of too many courts to forgive his offense.

When Nelson Rockefeller took the podium to propose amendments to the hard-line platform draft, the modest ripple of applause was drowned out by a chorus of boos and catcalls. When he could be heard, the New Yorker charged that in the primary campaign he had encountered the kind of infiltration and takeover of established political organizations employed by Communists and Nazis, and declared that such extremist tactics had no place in America. "It was as if Rockefeller were poking with a long lance and prodding a den of hungry lions," White wrote.

The regional shift in control of the party was evident when rebel yells greeted South Carolina's vote to clinch the Goldwater nomination. The new standard bearer's acceptance speech was a states' rights litany, excoriating the central government and all its works, exalting rugged individualism, and concluding with the defiant declaration that was to be remembered as his campaign trademark: "Extremism in the defense of liberty is no vice! . . . Moderation in the pursuit of justice is no virtue!"

While the Republicans headed for what White called a rendezvous with disaster, the Democrats were making room in their strained coalition for newly enfranchised black voters who would offset defecting Dixiecrats. George Wallace, saying it was time to send the party's national leaders a message, entered Democratic primaries outside the region, attracting 34 percent of the vote in Wisconsin, 30 percent in Indiana, and 43 percent in Maryland. The results shocked those who still assumed that racism ended at the Mason-Dixon line, but it neither surprised nor disturbed Lyndon Johnson.

Depth polls commissioned by the president demonstrated that what came to be termed white backlash against the Democrats' identification with the black cause was being more than offset by Republican crossovers disillusioned by their party's swing to the far right. While Wallace attracted ethnic voters in Wisconsin's working-class neighborhoods, Republican dairy farmers flocked to Johnson. In Maine, long a GOP bastion, what Johnson's pollster termed "frontlash" gave him 77 percent of the vote, and nationwide 50 percent of those who had voted for Nixon in 1960 were leaning toward Johnson. By June the Gallup poll showed the president taking 81 percent of the vote against Goldwater, and Harris gave Johnson 74 percent.

Those figures would have been altered had the unrest that flared in black ghettos with the coming of hot weather not been damped down by a campaign orchestrated from the White House. The President and

Robert Kennedy, still serving as attorney general, used all the resources available to the incumbent to lean on main-line black leaders and their liberal white supporters. All the national organizations except CORE and SNCC agreed to suspend protest demonstrations until after the election.

Barry Goldwater on his own initiative suggested to the president a private compact to eliminate overt exploitation of the race issue in the general election. Johnson agreed, and Goldwater held to his pledge, rejecting his handlers' pleas for use of TV ads featuring inflammatory film clips of rioting blacks assaulting whites on the streets of New York.

As the Democratic convention approached, Johnson was so certain of nomination by acclamation that he saw no need to balance the ticket with a conservative vice president, and named the party's leading exponent of civil rights, Hubert Humphrey, as his running mate. But when the delegates convened at Atlantic City in August, the reason SNCC had refused to join in the pledge to suspend demonstrations became evident. There was to be one more—on the floor of the convention.

Confrontation began at the meeting of the Credentials Committee, which since 1948 had wrestled with questions of party loyalty posed in the wake of the Dixiecrat effort to scotch the nomination of Harry Truman. This time a black delegation representing the Mississippi Freedom Democratic Party (MFDP) demanded to be seated in place of the white delegation duly elected in the state's Democratic primary.

Barred from participating in the regular primary by rigged registration procedures, the MFDP had conducted what amounted to a straw vote to name its delegates. Although it didn't have a legal leg to stand on, it had a powerful moral argument—and, when it came down to it, the old issue of party loyalty, since there was good reason to believe that the regular organization was prepared to deliver the state's electoral votes to Barry Goldwater.

This left the national party leadership in the awkward position of upholding its standing procedure while trying to avoid the embarrassment of a legalistic rejection of MFDP. The problem was compounded by the fact that the regular delegation was led by Governor Paul Johnson, whose idea of a knee-slapping campaign joke was to identify the initials of the NAACP as standing for "niggers, apes, alligators, coons, and possums." "Are we going to seat a delegation headed by a man like that?" demanded Joe Rauh, the white Washington civil rights lawyer who argued the case for MFDP.

Lyndon Johnson sent in his first team, headed by Hubert Humphrey and the CIO's Walter Reuther, and after three days of maneuvering, a compromise was worked out that won the endorsement of the leaders of SCLC, NAACP, CORE, and the chairman of the MFDP, Aaron Henry. It provided that the regular Mississippi delegates would have to take an oath to support the national ticket; two MFDP delegates would be given full voting, which meant speaking rights; and the others would be seated as honored guests.

In addition to these symbolic gestures, the compromise resolution gave the blacks a solid victory in its provision that at the Convention of 1968, and thereafter, no delegations would be seated from states where the Party process deprived citizens of the right to vote by reason of their race or color. But it did not satisfy a band of young blacks led by Stokely Carmichael of SNCC. When the resolution was adopted without opposition they linked arms, shoved the sergeants at arms aside, occupied the Mississippi seats, and staged a raucous sit-in on the floor of the hall. "When the convention resumed deliberations three turbulent hours later," Thomas R. Brooks wrote in *Walls Come Tumbling Down*, "the sympathy won by the upright stance of the MFDP . . . had been all but wiped away by the intransigence of a handful of militants."

The incident had no effect on the 1964 campaign, but it foreshadowed the course of events that by the next presidential election had ended the forward thrust of the civil rights movement.

Throughout the campaign Barry Goldwater scrupulously avoided overt appeals to racist sentiment, but blacks and their white sympathizers had no doubt where he stood on issues of paramount concern to them when he declared:

> One thing that will surely poison and embitter our relations with each other is the idea that some predetermined bureaucratic

schedule of equality—and worst of all a schedule based on the concept of race—must be imposed. . . . That way lies destruction.

Lyndon Johnson also made only passing mention of race, wrapping the programs he had initiated to redress discrimination in his vision of a reunited America with a renewed commitment to the common good. But, speaking at a campaign rally in New Orleans, he coupled an appeal to the Dixiecrats' better nature with a stern warning:

> Whatever your views are, we have a Constitution and we have a Bill of Rights, and we have the law of the land, and two thirds of the Democrats in the Senate voted for it and three fourths of the Republicans. I signed it and I am going to enforce it . . . and I think any man who is worthy of the high office of President is going to do the same thing. . . .

Both Goldwater and Johnson spoke with the passion of commitment, but the Republican candidate looked backward to a simpler America, while the Democrat held forth a vision of the "Great Society" the nation's abundance could now provide. He first used the term in a statesmanlike commencement address at the University of Michigan, but he endowed it with evangelical fervor in his stump speeches. At Pittsburgh he proclaimed:

> So here's the Great Society. It's the time—and it's going to be soon—when nobody in this country is poor. It's the time—and there's no point in waiting—when every boy and girl will have all the education that boy and girl can put to good use. It's the time when there is a job for every boy who wants to work. It's a time when every slum is gone from every city in America, and America is beautiful. It's the time when man gains full domination under God of his own destiny. It's the time of peace on earth and good will among men.

Johnson's masterful campaign produced the greatest popular vote margin in history, 43,126,506 to 27,176,799, and carried all but 6 states. The home folk gave Goldwater Arizona, and states' rights sentiment prevailed in the Deep South—Mississippi, Alabama, Louisiana, South Carolina, and Georgia—but even here the margins were narrow. In the Senate the Democrats gained 2 seats, bringing the total to 68, and 37 new Democratic congressmen provided a margin of 295 to 140 in the House. The Republicans gained one governor for a total of 17, but lost more than 500 seats in state legislatures, losing control of both houses in 12 states.

With due discount for the ineptness of the effort mounted by the divided Republicans, the president was entitled to regard his landslide victory as a mandate to implement his vision of a Great Society. In anticipation he had assembled task forces of scholars and experts to make recommendations for government action in the fields of education, urban problems, the environment, and transportation. They provided the basis for the blizzard of legislation that enveloped Congress in the early months of 1965.

In a spurt of activity that surpassed that of the first hundred days of the New Deal, the Department of Housing and Urban Development was created, headed by the nation's first black cabinet officer and charged with literally rebuilding the nation's cities; the federal government was given responsibility for improving public education from kindergarten through college; Social Security was expanded to cover basic health services, including hospitalization; economic development programs were launched to create new jobs; and the FEPC was strengthened to ensure that blacks and women got their share.

Hugh Sidey, Time's White House correspondent, described how it was done: "Johnson would zero in on a congressman or a senator to get what he wanted. . . . I would be amazed at some of the devices he would use. He would lie, beg, cheat, steal a little, threaten, intimidate. But he never lost sight of his ultimate goal, his idea of the Great Society." Willard Wirtz, who stayed on from the Kennedy administration as secretary of Labor, said of the result, "When you think of what happened in 1965, you turn around two centuries. Just take civil rights and women, to mention two—he turned the whole country around."

Most of these programs were broad-range, intended to benefit the great majority of citizens, and they were implemented through federal departments working in traditional fashion with state and local agencies. But the president had also declared a "War on Poverty," and this embraced economic as well as political issues and required the expenditure of federal funds in a fashion the expansion of civil rights had not.

The cluster of programs intended to deal with the special problems of those below the poverty line embodied an approach outlined by President Kennedy in a 1961 message to Congress concerned with an increase in juvenile delinquency that seemed "to occur most often among school dropouts and unemployed youth faced with limited opportunities and from broken families." He proposed that the federal government support experimental programs that would "reach deeply into the experiences of every day life in deprived families and local communities." Congress responded with an appropriation of ten million dollars a year for three years.

To develop implementing legislation, Kennedy established the President's Committee on Juvenile Delinquency, made up of the attorney general, as chairman, and the secretaries of Health, Education, and Welfare, and Labor. This gave Robert Kennedy a leading voice in the development of poverty programs that ultimately included Head Start for pre-school children; VISTA, a domestic Peace Corps; the Neighborhood Youth Corps to provide part-time jobs for teenagers; Upward Bound to prepare disadvantaged youth for college; and the Community Action Program to coordinate welfare activity and provide legal aid.

The President's Committee on Juvenile Delinquency did not resolve the inevitable conflicts among the departments and agencies involved in the development of these programs. The Department of Labor wanted to place the main emphasis on job creation, while advocates of community action programs sought "maximum feasible participation" by the poor in the creation and management of their own affairs. Walter Heller, chairman of the Council of Economic Advisers, pushed for basic reform in Aid to Families with Dependent Children, contending that both economic and social costs would continue to mount so long as the welfare system was limited to providing subsistence for the socially unfit, since they would continue to multiply unless means were developed to equip and motivate the able-bodied to become productive members of society.

In recounting the background of the War on Poverty, Daniel Patrick Moynihan, who as assistant secretary of Labor supported Heller's view, cited the unresolved turf battles between those who wanted to use existing local institutions to carry out the programs and those who insisted on radical changes in order to place control in the hands of the beneficiaries. The result was that when President Johnson took over he was presented not with "a choice among policies so much as a collection of them."

To establish order among the warring factions Johnson created the Office of Economic Opportunity (OEO) as an umbrella organization, and to head it brought over the director of the Peace Corps, Sargent Shriver, the most idealistic member of the Kennedy clan. But the in-fighting continued, and the issues posed by the concept of the community action advocates were still unresolved when the OEO faded into history.

It can be seen in retrospect that some of the programs were ill-conceived and others maladministered, and the record has been used to attack the underlying premise of the War on Poverty. But these pioneering projects were so malnourished that it is impossible to appraise fairly the potential of the first effort to use the resources of the federal government in a concerted effort to salvage the salvageable among those clustered below the poverty line.

By the time the poverty programs were on the launching pad, dis-integration of the South Vietnamese Army faced the president with a fateful choice of abandoning the anti-Communist regime his predecessors had propped up, or increasing the American military force and giving it a combat role. Secretary of Defense Robert McNamara, strongly urging the latter course along with virtually all the holdovers from the Kennedy administration, proposed that the reserves be mobilized and taxes increased to cover the cost of the expanded military effort. But this would have required action by Congress, and the president de-murred. In July 1965 he told his inner circle:

I don't know much about economics, but I do know the Con-gress. And I can get the Great Society through right now—this is a golden time. We've got a good Congress and I'm the right President and I can do it. But if I talk about the cost of war the Great Society won't go through, and the tax bill won't go through. Old Wilbur Mills [the Arkansan chairman of the House Ways and Means Committee] will sit down there and he'll thank me kindly and send me back my Great Society, and then he'll tell me he'll be glad to spend whatever we need for the war.

Sargent Shriver had projected an annual OEO budget of sixteen billion dollars, only to end up with two billion. The president had been assured by the Pentagon, Shriver recalled, that an investment of twenty billion in Vietnam would allow him to end the war by December 1966: "The idea was that we had to fight *this* war this year. Next year we'd get to the war on poverty. I think I knew then that 'next year' wasn't going to come."

The civil rights crusade for social justice that inspired the War on Poverty had a magnetic attraction for idealistic university students outside the South who were growing restive under the bland conformity that characterized middle-class America in the postwar decades. These incipient rebels were especially inspired by the example of their peers in SNCC who defied their more cautious elders to mount a militant campaign of their own.

A direct connection was made by students at elite institutions who volunteered for service in Mississippi during Freedom Summer. Radicalized by their front-line experience, they returned imbued with a romantic aura that made them leaders of what was called, with at least rhetorical justification, a generational revolution. In the year of Lyndon Johnson's triumph at the polls, the Northern version of the student sit-ins was touched off at Berkeley when University of California campus police arrested Mario Savio, a Freedom Summer veteran who defied regulations to recruit Friends of SNCC in a restricted area. Before the year was out, student protest had become a national phenomenon.

The youth movement was bifurcated from the outset. Some of the students who rebelled against standards of behavior enforced by university administrators acting *in loco parentis* considered themselves founders of a counterculture. They seemed to be, as Milton Viorst put it in *Fire in the Streets*, "convinced that the defining characteristic of America was hypocrisy. The generation took delight in being personally unkempt, using vulgar language, living in filthy pads. This was truthful. This was authentic. . . ."

Those who called themselves hippies practiced nonviolence, but their profession of universal love embraced a hedonism that could not have been farther removed from the self-sacrificing precepts of Martin Luther King. The other branch of the youth movement was more disciplined and a little more coherent. It adopted the title New Left to indicate its independence, but it was hard to distinguish its agenda from that of the neo-Marxist Old Left it scorned for working within the system.

"Unlike the young black in civil rights," Viorst observed, "the white student had no identifiable self-interest in promoting his cause. For better and worse his concerns were less practical than moral, his goals not reformist but often millenarian." The ambition to escape from poverty was foreign to both wings of the movement. The hippies adopted the trappings of the poor, and the New Leftists sought to identify themselves with the blue-collar working class, but for most this abnegation was tempered by the fact that they continued to have available the resources of their middle-class families.

The University of California at Santa Barbara became a key outpost of the youth rebellion in the years after the Free Speech Movement erupted at Berkeley, and most of the junior fellows and a few of the seniors at the Center for the Study of Democratic Institutions were sympathizers, if not active supporters. Their idealism was appealing, but it seemed to me that such an amorphous collection of professed free spirits could not be considered part of the civil rights movement, but in fact was an aberration.

It simply was not possible for these youths to make effective connection with the black leaders who were generally credited with inspiring the confrontational tactics they adopted. Martin Luther King was appalled by the sexual promiscuity and use of narcotics exalted by the hippies as a form of protest, and the militant young blacks who took over the leadership of SNCC were scornful of the revolutionary protestations of peers far removed from the real dangers they faced. Stokely Carmichael voiced their contempt in *Black Power: The Politics of Liberation in America:*

. . . many young middle-class white Americans, like some sort
of Pepsi generation, have wanted to "come alive" through the
black community and black groups. They have wanted to be
where the action is. . . . They have sought refuge among blacks
from a sterile, meaningless, irrelevant life in middle-class America. They have been unable to deal with the stifling, racist,
parochial, split-level mentality of their parents, teachers,
preachers and friends. Many have come seeing "no difference
in color," they have come "color blind." But at this time, and
in this land, color is a factor and we should not overlook or
deny this. The black organizations do not need this kind of
idealism, which borders on paternalism.

As it turned out, the youthful rebellion produced no basic changes in
the nation's institutional structure, nor did it bring about any redistribution of income and its corollary, power—indeed, a convincing case
can be made that reaction against its excesses moved the political establishment in the opposite direction. However, it did have a profound
cultural effect, producing a college generation that, although it lapsed
back into conformity as it came to maturity, remained far more socially
permissive than its predecessors. This enhanced the upward mobility of
middleclass blacks, but it tended to isolate further the mass of poor
blacks, who still constituted a considerable majority.

In an address at Howard University in June 1965, Lyndon Johnson took
note of what was beginning to be recognized as a black underclass
separate and distinct from those who had begun to move into the mainstream. "In far too many ways American Negroes have been another
nation, deprived of freedom, crippled by hatred, the doors of opportunity
closed to hope," he said. Now the nation had responded to the call for
simple justice, and "the courts, the Congress, the President and most
of the people have been the allies of progress. . . ."

But freedom is not enough. You do not wipe away the scars of
centuries by saying: Now you are free to go where you want,
do as you desire and choose the leaders you please.

You do not take a person who, for years, has been hobbled by chains and liberate him, bring him up to the starting line of the race and then say, you are free to compete with the others, and still justly believe that you have been completely fair.

Thus it is not enough to just open the gates of opportunity. All our citizens must have the ability to walk through those gates.

The nation, he said, was now entering the second and most profound stage of the battle for civil rights, and he committed the government to seek means to guarantee "not just equality as a right and a theory but equality as a fact and as a result." The president concluded by announcing that he was calling an interracial White House conference of community leaders, scholars, and experts to deal with the issues he had touched on. The 1947 report of the Truman commission that established the agenda of the civil rights movement had been called "To Secure These Rights." The theme of Johnson's conference would be "To Fulfill These Rights."

Patrick Moynihan had contributed most of the substance of the Howard University speech, including a passage that reflected a central conclusion based on his sociological studies of the urban poor that pointed up the difference between the situation of inner-city blacks and that of other past and present ghetto dwellers:

Perhaps most important—its influence radiating into every part of life—is the breakdown of the Negro family structure. For this, most of all, white America must accept responsibility. It flows from centuries of oppression and persecution of the Negro man. It flows from long years of degradation and discrimination, which have attacked his dignity and assaulted his ability to provide for his family. . . .

Unless we work to strengthen the family, to create conditions under which parents will stay together—all the rest, schools and playgrounds, public assistance and private concern, will never be enough to cut completely the circle of despair and deprivation.

The text of the presidential address had been read in advance to Martin Luther King, Roy Wilkins, and Whitney Young, all of whom praised it, and it was generally applauded in the black community. But in the weeks that followed, the political atmosphere underwent an abrupt change with the leak to the media of one of the hundred numbered copies of a confidential internal memorandum in which Moynihan had elaborated on the pathological condition of the black family,

The document the press labeled the "Moynihan Report" drew upon government statistics that demonstrated a marked increase in illegitimate births among black teenagers as evidence of family disintegration and the declining status of the black male. It was not a new theme for the erudite young cabinet officer. He had developed it a year before in an article published in *Daedalus*, the journal of the Academy of Arts and Sciences.

But the internal memorandum, Harold Fleming noted, was without the compassionate rhetoric of the Howard speech or the buffering of conventional scholarly language. Fleming, who had participated in the *Daedalus* symposium, and had heard Moynihan discuss its implications in a closed session at the Potomac Institute, characterized the memorandum as "a stark, unadorned portrait of a people trapped in a brutal and dehumanizing 'culture of poverty' that had perhaps become fatally resistant to customary remedial action."

Moynihan's thesis has since become part of the conventional wisdom, but in the 1960s the leaked memorandum, sensationalized by the media's treatment, aroused a storm of protest from main-line black leaders, including some of those who had cleared the presidential address. Whitney Young of the Urban League complained, "One can't talk about the pathologies of Negroes without talking about the pathologies of white society. If Negroes are sick socially, then whites are sick morally." James Farmer of CORE was bitter:

> As if living in the sewer, learning in the streets and working in the pantry weren't enough of a burden for millions of American Negroes, I now learn that we've caught "matriarchy," and "the tangle of Negro pathology." . . . By laying the primary blame for present-day inequalities on the pathological condition of the

> Negro family and community, [the Moynihan Report] has pro-
> vided a massive academic cop-out for the white conscience. . . .

The accusation that Moynihan had absolved whites and "victimized the victim" hardly stood up, since he had pointedly identified racism as the root cause of the urban crisis. But his explanation that his intention had been to stimulate federal agencies to face up to the special problems besetting poor blacks was rejected or ignored. The storm of protest silenced most of the black and some of the white scholars who had applauded his *Daedalus* article.

Moynihan already had aroused enmity on the left by taking issue with those on the OEO staff who shared the youth movement's obsession with the most extreme version of participational democracy. Their insistence on "maximum feasible participation" by the poor to give them control of the poverty agencies had obvious appeal for the radical black separatists, who could hardly concede the hard fact cited by Moynihan— that in the worst of the ghettos the extended family, which traditionally had provided a stable base for black communities, had been eroded to the point where community in any institutional sense no longer existed.

There was not even a pro forma defense of Moynihan from the White House, and he resigned, ostensibly to run for president of the New York City Council. But there was no way the disgruntled president could cancel the White House conference Moynihan had been instrumental in inspiring. It was postponed until the spring of 1966, with a face-saving announcement that some two hundred experts would be assembled for a planning session in November.

A. Philip Randolph was honorary chairman when the group met, but even his august presence wasn't enough to quell the rumors of dissension. Mary McGrory's *Washington Post* column was headlined: "Moynihan Conspicuously Ignored: The Non-Person at the Conference." And Evans and Novak wrote:

> The gap between the civil rights movement and the Johnson
> administration is wider than ever. A carefully planned effort to
> inject a new realism regarding the plight of the Northern Negro
> was a failure.

Looking back on the Howard University speech, Harold Fleming, who served as associate director of the White House conference that finally took place a year later, concluded that "an eloquent presidential call for racial equality heralded a series of events that ultimately splintered the civil rights consensus." But the Moynihan controversy became a footnote when an eruption of violence in the black ghetto of Los Angeles touched off what came to be called the "long, hot summers."

The year before there had been serious flares of racial violence in New York, but these were quickly contained. J. Edgar Hoover had become obsessed with the idea that the rioters were inspired by radical leaders of the youth movement bent on enlisting the black lumpenproletariat in a grand revolutionary design, but his agents found no evidence of such a conspiracy in the scattered outbreaks during the summer of 1964. The FBI report concluded:

> The common characteristics of the riots was a senseless attack on all constituted authority without purpose or objective. . . . [The] mob violence was dominated by the acts of youths ranging in age to the middle twenties. They were variously characterized by responsible people as "school dropouts," "young punks," "common hoodlums," and "drunken kids."

This was the pattern of the eruption in a Los Angeles neighborhood called Watts. It came as a surprise, since blacks in California, where most had arrived since the beginning of World War II, were considered better off than anywhere else in the country. They enjoyed full political rights, and the Urban League rated Los Angeles first among major cities in terms of housing, employment, and available amenities. The unemployment rate among the city's 500,000 blacks was only 7.9 percent, less than double that for whites.

But in Watts, the poorest of Los Angeles's nine black districts, 30 percent of the young males were jobless, and it was these who ran through the streets chanting a slogan adopted from a local disk jockey, "Burn, baby, burn!" The spontaneous combustion was touched off by a routine police arrest, as would be most of those that followed. Before order was restored six days later, a National Guard force of 14,000 had been brought in to impose a curfew over a 46-square-mile area. The casualty list stood at 34 killed and 898 wounded, most of them black; property losses were estimated at $45 million. The pattern would be repeated in 4 cities in 1965, 21 in 1966, and 75 in 1967.

The sad, simpleminded motivation for the saturnalia of arson and looting during the long, hot summers was exemplified in a touching story told by Martin Luther King. When he and Bayard Rustin went to Watts to see if they could help quell the fever, they were greeted by an exultant youth who proclaimed, "We won!" Rustin responded, "How have you won? Homes have been destroyed, Negroes are lying dead in the streets, the stores where you buy food and clothes have been destroyed, and people are bringing you in relief." The happy vandal replied, "We won because we made the whole world pay attention to us. We made them come."

Shocked members of the white establishment did come to the aid of Watts and the other charred ghettos. Expansion of public services brought some relief; Watts, for example, got a new Martin Luther King Hospital and Medical School. There and in other cities leaders in the private sector encouraged the location of sales, services, and manufacturing facilities to provide access and jobs for inner-city residents. The federal OEO projects, undernourished as they were, enabled some of the inhabitants to pull themselves above the poverty line, and philanthropists provided seed money to establish or expand social services within the isolated ghetto communities.

The rescue squads from the private sector proceeded on the assumption that market forces could provide employment, which would make any black who was willing to work a self-sustaining member of society. The public and philanthropic agencies usually recognized that the situation was not quite that simple, but their attempts to devise programs to meet the special needs of the socially handicapped were undercut by the rapid decline of support for the civil rights movement.

There had been widespread expectation among both races that once they were free of the legal barriers of segregation black migrants from the South would begin to be assimilated into the larger society, as had been the religious and ethnic minorities they often replaced in the inner cities. To an extent, the "melting pot" scenario proved applicable to those who had adapted to middleclass standards and values. Most of these had lived for a generation or more in urban communities in the South and were equipped to take advantage of improved educational opportunities, and job openings provided by fair employment laws. But to offset the latent racism their color aroused they had to accede to terms that set them apart from the illiterate and semiliterate blacks who were counted among the working poor. And by choice or circumstance, most maintained no effective connection at all with the blacks huddled below the poverty line.

This was the underclass that was to be dealt with in what the president had called the second phase of the civil rights movement. Its cause and effect were described in the later writing of Richard Wright, whose *Native Son* became the first bestseller by a black author. He was one of those who wound up on Chicago's blighted South Side in the course of the great diaspora from the Mississippi delta.

> We, who were landless on the land; we, who had barely managed to live in family groups; we, who needed the ritual and guidance of institutions to hold our atomized lives together in lines of purpose; we, who had known only relationships to people and not relationships to things; we, who had our personalities blasted by two hundred years of slavery and had been turned loose to shift for ourselves—we were such a folk as this when we moved into a world that was destined to test all we were, and threw us on the scales of competition to test our mettle.

The civil rights movement foundered when it came North and encountered the class stratification that had been overcome in the South by the unifying effect of indignities visited upon all classes of blacks. Throughout the 1960s the anti-integrationist black nationalism espoused by Malcolm X and his intellectual fellow travelers gained ground in the ghettos, although only a small minority actually converted to the Black Muslim faith. In his history of the civil rights movement, *Freedom Bound*, Robert Weisbrot cited the trend as built on inescapable political logic:

Civil rights legislation had exhausted the original demands of the movement, and its leaders had to expand their own concerns in order to retain a constituency. Johnson's War on Poverty had anticipated the shift in black priorities and helped for a time to keep leaders within the Democratic fold. As disappointment with the antipoverty programs mounted, though, black critics increasingly doubted whether patchwork reforms could justify their faith either in the President or in the existing social and political system.

Against this background Martin Luther King's effort to employ SCLC's precepts to create a mass integrationist movement in Chicago was destined for failure. And CORE, which had its roots in the North, began to abandon its interracial character under pressure from black chauvinists; in 1965 James Farmer, the instigator and one of the heroes of the Freedom Rides, was forced to resign when he resisted the effort to purge CORE of its white officers and board members.

Raising the consciousness of downtrodden blacks had been a prime objective of the civil rights movement. "When they spoke to a white person, their backbones seemed to crumple. They seemed to diminish," Coretta King wrote when she first encountered the poor blacks of Montgomery. Her husband made the head-high march the symbol of the movement. "We can straighten up our backs and walk erect now," King told the humblest of his followers. "We are walking to freedom in dignity." His own steadfastness in the face of massive intimidation provided an enduring refutation of the white supremacist assumption of inherent black inferiority.

But black consciousness as manifested in the inner cities of the North and West had now risen to a point where communication between the two races began to break down. James Farmer had complained that the Moynihan Report would provide an excuse for abandonment of the effort to redress the social damage racism had caused. But most whites needed no such rationale. As Weisbrot noted,

> To many citizens the spectacle of civil rights veterans spurning integration and white supporters appeared ungrateful and peculiarly ill timed. Television, radio and journal accounts de-

picted Negroes everywhere as politically triumphant, gaining sweeping federal legislation and antipoverty programs with the aid of a thoroughly reconstructed Southern President. Few black activists, however, shared this roseate view of the movement's progress or prospects.

This was a bitter pill for white supporters of the civil rights cause to swallow, and many never succeeded in doing so. In an introduction to *Witnesses for Freedom*, Rebecca Chalmers Barton's volume of biographical essays on black writers, Alain Locke, the Howard University poet and philosopher who was a leading figure in the Harlem Renaissance, noted that white liberals had to overcome two barriers in attempting to appraise black attitudes. The first was their own pride and prejudice, and, having overcome that, they were surprised to

> discover beyond that another—the minority group's inner barricade of defensive self-protection, which with the generations may have piled itself up into a spite wall of stubborn and resentful alienation.

White complaints about ingratitude provided a prime example of the paternalism bitterly resented by those who articulated the mounting anger in the ghettos. The arrogance that was the hall mark of white racism had begotten its black counterpart.

Lyndon Johnson said after the Watts riot, "It is not enough simply to decry disorder. We must also strike at the unjust conditions from which disorder largely flows. . . . We must not let anger drown understanding." But as hot weather brought on annual outbreaks of violence in inner cities from coast to coast, it was evident that his War on Poverty programs had proved to be too little and too late. Doris Kearns, then a White House aide, recorded his private reaction: "God knows how little we have really moved on this issue, despite all the fanfare. As I see it, I've moved the Negro from D+ to C−. He's still nowhere. He knows it. And that's why he's out in the streets. Hell, I'd be out there, too."

If the black youths torching the ghettos were to escape from the debilitating culture of poverty they would need jobs, but most did not have the minimum communication skills and motivation required for employment in the private sector. Providing these essentials was the primary mission of the War on Poverty, and there had been some successes. But white reaction against the spread of violence eroded the political support the president needed to increase and, where needed, redirect the antipoverty programs.

By 1966, when there were twenty-one outbreaks officially recorded as "civil disorders," appropriation bills for OEO were saddled with restrictive riders. "Backlash continued to stalk the corridors of Congress in the debate over antipoverty legislation as talk of law and order crowded out discussions of destitution in the ghettos," Robert Weisbrot wrote. In the congressional campaigns that fall Gerald Ford, the House minority leader, sounded the theme for the Republicans:

> How long are we going to abdicate law and order—the backbone of civilization—in favor of soft social theory that the man who heaves a brick through your window or tosses a fire bomb into your car is simply the misunderstood and underprivileged product of a broken home?

In the midterm elections Republicans replaced forty-seven incumbent Democrats in the House and three in the Senate.

Stymied on the political front, Johnson sought to enlist the business community, making the point that the most immediate need was for what it could provide, entry-level employment. He created a new agency, JOBS (Job Opportunities in the Business Sector) as a catalyst, and NAB (National Alliance of Businessmen) as a support organization.

Fifteen chief executives of corporations of the status of Coca-Cola, Mobil Oil, Safeway Stores, ITT, and Alcoa were persuaded, or dragooned, to serve as the executive committee of NAB, with Henry Ford II as chairman. Assembled for a White House luncheon, they were subjected to a characteristic charge by the president:

> We've looked at every kind of job program—government manpower training programs, the Job Corps, vocational training programs and retraining programs. And we've found [that] what

works best is what you do best: on-the-job training. We're faced with the hard core unemployed. You all are going to have to teach them how to wash and stay clean, how to read and write. All the things everyone around this table got from their mommies and daddies. Only these people don't have mommies and daddies. Or if they do their mommies and daddies can't read or don't know how to help. . . .

Anticipating the inevitable ideological objections to burdening the private sector with what his Republican successors would contemptuously label social engineering, Johnson gave the corporate executives an eminently pragmatic reason why they should undertake affirmative action programs of their own:

The economy has been so good to you that you can afford to give a little back. You can put these people to work and you won't have a revolution because they've been left out. If they're working, they won't be throwing bombs in your homes and plants. Keep them busy and they won't have time to burn your cars. . . . I need your commitment to make taxpayers out of these taxeaters.

The blue-ribbon National Advisory Commission on Civil Disorders concurred, warning that the United States was "moving toward two societies, one white, one black—separate but unequal." But when its report was published in March 1968, Johnson, unable to meet its key recommendations for expanded government programs, or even to maintain those in place, largely ignored it. Liberals, whose distrust of the free-wheeling Texan had resurfaced, accused him of yielding to the resurgent right wing that threatened his pending reelection.

A bitter indictment was brought by the talented novelist John Hersey, author of an impassioned chronicle of the Detroit riot, *The Algiers Motel Incident.* The explosion there in July 1967 represented a considerable escalation over Watts. In six days of street fighting thirty-seven blacks and three whites were killed, two thousand, mostly black, were wounded, and arsonists touched off fifteen hundred fires. As police control broke down, whites joined blacks in what Walter Reuther called the first integrated looting, contributing to the $350 million in property losses. The situation remained out of control until the president sent in regular army troops.

Hersey concentrated his reportage on the action of a posse of fifty city police, state patrolmen, and National Guard troops who raided a motel in search of snipers. The incident emphasized the point he thought had been glossed over—the sexual element of racism, as exemplified by the white officers' brutal reaction to the discovery of white women consorting with black men:

> I believe it to be at the very core of racism. If real progress is to be made, it cannot be made simply by expenditures of funds, even in great sums, on "programs"; racism must be educated or coaxed or wrenched or stamped out of the centers of injustice and grievance—namely out of police forces, courts, legislatures, unions, industry, schools, the civil service, and the bureaucracy of welfare.

Lyndon Johnson, if he had deigned to reply, might have asked just how he was expected to go about educating, coaxing, wrenching, and stamping out racism except through the kind of measures he had initiated. And the bitterness that had begun to engulf him was surely enhanced by Hersey's charge:

> The spectacle of this man running for cover from the conclusions of the Commission which he created . . . was not only disgusting; it was positively inflammatory, for it denied the very thesis of the report. The Texan seemed to want to deny the charge of white racism.

Even considering the passion of the moment, the indictment was absurd on its face. Lyndon Johnson was the first president to face up to the prospect cited in its conclusion by his Commission on Civil Disorders:

> A democratic society cannot depend upon force as its recurrent answer to longstanding and legitimate grievances. This nation cannot have it both ways. Either it will carry through a firm

commitment to massive and widespread social reform, or it will develop into a society of garrison cities where order is enforced without due process of law and without the consent of the governed.

Twenty-five years would pass before another president undertook a comparable effort to rally the political support such a commitment required. In the meantime, the steadily rising urban crime rate constituted what Mayor John Lindsay of New York termed a permanent, year-'round long, hot summer.

REALIGNMENT
NEW COALITIONS FOR BOTH PARTIES

The marvel of American politics previously had been its ability to channel passion into peaceful choice of directions. In 1968 hate burst out of the channel, and hate, whether from student ideologues, unabashed white racists or black extremists, incubated further hate, loosing lunatics, gunmen, rock-throwers and club-wielders.

—THEODORE H. WHITE, *The Making of the President 1968*

LYNDON JOHNSON seriously unbalanced the national budget when he sought to protect his War on Poverty by avoiding the formal congressional approval necessary for a tax increase to cover costs of the Vietnam escalation. But he did even more damage to his political prospects when he forfeited the possibility of activating military reserve units, which also would have required action on Capitol Hill. Without this considerably less painful means of providing additional manpower, he had to place the burden on the draft machinery left in place after World War II.

Draft quotas, which could be set by executive order, had remained low after Korea, with deferment available for categories of eligible young men, including college students. Now the rapid increase in troop requirements forced the president to sharply curtail these automatic exemptions. As the troop buildup began in Vietnam, the prospect of arduous combat duty in the jungles of Southeast Asia had an immediate impact on the campuses, where enrollment in graduate and professional schools had offered a pleasant and possibly useful refuge from the draft for those who could afford the time and money.

The traditional antiwar cause, primarily supported by those moved by pacifist religious convictions and by idealistic supporters of the United Nations, had been embraced by the hippies and New Leftists as part of their general protest against the established order. Now it began to attract support from students, faculty, and parents moved primarily by self-interest, and with little or no sympathy for the rest of the radical agenda.

On the surface, the movement retained the confrontational style of the civil rights movement. Impassioned young orators proclaimed the intention of college students to force a change of policy by filling the jails to overflowing, as Martin Luther King's followers had done in the Deep South. Across the country thousands responded by publicly burning their draft cards as a presumed invitation to arrest.

The thought of what was likely to happen to these white, middleclass youths in a federal prison became a matter of concern to Willard Gaylin, a physician on the faculty of Columbia University who was also an adjunct professor at Union Theological Seminary. He found that his apprehension was shared, for more pragmatic reasons, by Myrl Alexander, director of the Federal Bureau of Prisons, who recognized that "the brutalizing of a congressman's nephew would capture headlines in a way that routine rapes and slashings in a typical prison population had not."

Twenty-five years later, Gaylin recalled the results when, with Alexander's backing, he began visiting prisoners incarcerated for defying the draft. In three years of research he found that only seventy political war resisters were imprisoned in the entire country:

> Where were all the rest? They were utilizing the loopholes and dodges that were built into the Selective Service Act to protect the children of the middleclass. Even when most influential middleaged men supported the war, they were making sure that their sons did not serve. I did not have one friend, one colleague

or patient who had a child serving unwillingly in Vietnam. How did they get out? They wriggled through the loopholes that had been created for them.

In 1967 the student anti-Vietnam protest was converted into a full-fledged political movement by a spellbinding organizer who began recruiting sympathetic faculty members to lead "teach-ins" on college campuses from coast to coast. As a student leader at the University of North Carolina, Allard K. Lowenstein had been a crusading president of the National Student Association, an experience that remained central to his development as he went on to serve as a leader of Students for Stevenson, assistant to Eleanor Roosevelt at the United Nations, and aide to Hubert Humphrey in the Senate. After establishing a law practice in New York, Lowenstein found time to devote his talents to youth-oriented liberal causes, including the Mississippi Freedom Democratic Party.

Committed to working within the system, Lowenstein had concluded that the only way to force President Johnson to reverse course and negotiate a peaceful settlement in Vietnam was to threaten him with opposition in the Democratic primaries, and to deliver it if necessary. This appeal brought straight-arrow students flocking to the cause in numbers that swamped the long-haired militants and turned off the black radicals.

The rising tide of popular opposition to the Vietnam War also swamped the civil rights movement, already beset by white backlash against continuing outbreaks of ghetto violence. In the South the restive youngsters in SNCC made their final break with Martin Luther King when Stokely Carmichael took over the leadership. Forcing the resignation of John Lewis, an unyielding advocate of nonviolence, Carmichael openly rejected the goal of integration and spurned political coalition. The voter registration drive in Alabama was converted into a tool for creating a separate Black Panther political party. "To me," Carmichael said, "the only good thing the vote could do was wreck the Democratic Party and spring off a revolution in America."

The collaboration of SCLC and SNCC ended in the course of a

demonstration in Mississippi, where Carmichael's followers tried to replace the familiar call for Freedom Now with a chanted demand for Black Power. King rejected the ploy, declaring that "black supremacy would be equally as evil as white supremacy." The direct challenge to King resulted in a precipitous decline in support for SNCC. By mid-1967 the headquarters in Atlanta was closed, and the *Constitution* estimated that its scattered active members numbered no more than 150. "SNCC, like Carmichael, is a melancholy story," Ralph McGill wrote:

> From its beginning in North Carolina, through the Freedom Rides, the Freedom Schools, and the long contests with segregation before the public accommodations law, SNCC was an inspiring organization. I do not think I have ever seen any more courageous, any sweeter or more dedicated lot of young people. They endured jails, abuses, brutalities. Some were killed. When Carmichael opted for the anti-white Black Power group he cut them off. . . .

A native of Trinidad described by his admirers as "the magnificent barbarian," Carmichael had a brief run as a media star, entrancing the radical chic with his revolutionary rhetoric. His followers in what became the Black Panther Party gravitated to the extreme wing of the youth movement, and some went underground with the Weathermen when that remnant professed fealty to the Maoist dictum that power grows out of the barrel of a gun. They appeared on television wearing black military-style berets and waving rifles, but when actual violence erupted in the ghettos it was evident that even there their posturing was, to use one of the youth movement's favorite derogations, irrelevant.

The Black Panthers were destined for the scrap heap of history, King wrote in his final testament, *Where Do We Go from Here?*:

> It claims to be the most revolutionary wing of the social revolution taking place in the United States. Yet it rejects the one thing that keeps the flame of revolution burning, the ever-present flame of hope. When hope dies, a revolution degen-

erates into an undiscriminating catchall for evanescent and futile gestures.

Yet hope was dimming for King himself. He could not join the young militants; if only one black voice could still be heard speaking out against violence, he said, it would be his. But by that token he found it increasingly difficult to support the Vietnam War, and in the end he split with the main-line black leaders—and with Lyndon Johnson. After months of searching his conscience he took the pulpit at Riverside Church in New York to proclaim, "We are committing atrocities equal to any perpetrated by the Vietcong. The bombs in Vietnam explode at home—they destroy the dream and possibility for a decent America."

At the president's behest, Roy Wilkins of the NAACP and Whitney Young of the Urban League joined Vice President Hubert Humphrey in pleading with King to temper his protest. On a cruise down the Potomac aboard the presidential yacht they argued that his identification with the anti-Vietnam movement would alienate the political support so essential to further black progress. But King could not be moved. "I could never again raise my voice against the violence of the oppressed in the ghettos," he said, "without having first spoken clearly to the greatest purveyor of violence in the world—my own government."

King joined the Spring Mobilization of church, pacifist, Old Left, and New Left groups opposing the Vietnam War, and the Reverend James Bevel of SCLC served as organizer of a demonstration staged at United Nations Plaza. Asked about the political implications of including radical contingents with main-line support groups, Bevel replied, "We're going to get to the left of Karl Marx and left of Lenin. We're going to get way out there, up on that cross with Jesus." That was the tone of the address King delivered to a throng estimated by the police at 150,000.

The reaction in Washington was immediate and pointed. Carl Rowan, a black journalist who had served as director of the U.S. Information Service, charged in his newspaper column that King had created "doubt about the Negro's loyalty to his country." Rowan referred to allegations of subversive influence in SCLC being systematically leaked to journalists by J. Edgar Hoover and his men: "I report this not to endorse what King and many others will consider a 'guilt by association' smear, but because of the threat that these allegations represent to the civil rights movement."

As he had been before the election of John F. Kennedy, King was again beyond the official pale. In June, when Lyndon Johnson finally convened his beleaguered White House Conference on Civil Rights, a subordinate member of SCLC was accorded vice-chairman status, while the founder and paramount leader of the mass movement was left off the program and invited to attend only as a guest.

The Center for the Study of Democratic Institutions could no more avoid the Vietnam issue than it could the divisive turbulence among supporters of civil rights. Robert Hutchins was a gray eminence of the antiwar movement who advocated an international rule of law to restrain the nationalism that had always propelled sovereign nations into armed conflict. As the nuclear arms race raised the specter of worldwide holocaust, his first priority went to seeking a means to prevent World War III.

Hutchins saw in *Pacem in Terris*, the dramatic 1964 encyclical of Pope John XXIII, a possible breakthrough in the Cold War. The Vatican's overture aroused great interest in Moscow, where it was viewed as a conciliatory gesture from the ideological citadel of Western anticommunism. But normal diplomatic channels were still frozen by the postwar chill, and there was no follow-up in Washington or in the European capitals. Hutchins concluded that the only way to pursue the opening would be through an East-West dialogue on a wholly unofficial basis.

To that end he proposed a great convocation in New York to bring together political, intellectual, and spiritual leaders from both sides of the Iron Curtain to address as individuals an agenda based on "the requirements of peace" set forth by Pope John. In February 1965 the center convened what *Life* described as "an extraordinary assemblage of the world's shakers and movers. The guest list would have done credit to a U.N. charter meeting or a state funeral. . . ."

I had ended a stint as editor in chief of *Encyclopaedia Britannica* and returned to the center full-time as executive vice president, and when planning for *Pacem in Terris* began I became the principal organizer. The convocation was conceived as a public relations exercise that might reopen a popular dialogue on the central issues of the Cold War. To clear the way for the kind of delegates who inspire widespread media coverage, I found myself again operating in political circles here and abroad.

When U.S. Supreme Court justice William O. Douglas, the center's board chairman, and I called on President Johnson to urge that he deliver the opening address, the Vietnam War had not yet become a burning issue. But, as we would discover, the president already viewed the deteriorating situation in South Vietnam as posing a stark choice between direct military intervention and abandonment of the failing government his predecessors had supported for more than a decade. Throughout the fall Justice Douglas continued to press his old friend but found that "he dodged, ducked and evaded the proposition, changing the subject and finally shunting me off to the staff that was instructed to sabotage me politely."

The opening address at the *Pacem in Terris* convocation was delivered by Vice President Hubert Humphrey, but it hardly served as a keynote. By February 1965, when two thousand delegates from twenty nations convened in the Great Hall of the United Nations to receive the blessing of Secretary-General U Thant, the massive troop buildup had begun, and the air war had been extended across the border into North Vietnam. Humphrey's evasive, noncommittal speech, he told me, was not the one he wanted to deliver but the only version he could clear with the White House.

Public reaction to the *Pacem in Terris* convocation was generally favorable. In the aftermath I saw a good deal of U.N. Under Secretary Ralph Bunche, who, on pragmatic as well as moral grounds, shared King's conviction that the cause of racial justice had become inextricably linked with the Vietnam issue. Before he undertook the diplomatic career that earned him a Nobel Prize, Bunche had served as Gunnar Myrdal's principal black assistant when they traveled through the South conducting research for *An American Dilemma*. He spoke out of that experience when he contended that the gains made by the civil rights movement could not possibly survive the political divisions that were now rending the electorate.

Bunche was an influential voice among those who urged that the dialogue the center had initiated be expanded to include both North and South Vietnam. Hutchins agreed, and with the assistance of European leaders who joined in the planning for a projected *Pacem in Terris II* in neutral Switzerland, arrangements were made for emissaries from the center to discuss the convocation with leaders of the North Vietnamese government. I was chosen for the mission, along with my old friend William Calhoun Baggs, editor of the *Miami News*, who was now a member of the center's board.

The mission to North Vietnam in the first week of 1967 was undertaken with the State Department's blessing under an agreement that we would travel secretly and probe for an opening for official negotiations in the face of Hanoi's rejection of the president's reiterated offer to go anywhere at any time to seek a negotiated settlement—a proposition North Vietnam president Ho Chi Minh refused to consider without cessation of the bombing. In the North Vietnamese capital, where the air raid sirens provided frequent reminders of America's near-total air superiority, we had a candid two-hour exchange with the venerable Ho in which he indicated that arrangements could be made for unconditional official talks on the basis of reciprocal suspension of aggressive military action.

This apparently was considered a significant concession when we reported the discussion in detail to Under Secretary of State Nicholas Katzenbach; Assistant Secretary William Bundy; and Ambassador Averell Harriman, the president's designated peace negotiator. A letter to Ho over my signature was drafted in collaboration with Bundy, who was in charge of Southeast Asian affairs, indicating that "senior officials of the State Department" were interested in moving secret discussions to the official level.

When the air strikes were renewed and escalated after suspension for Vietnam's Tet holiday, we discovered that while the conciliatory letter inviting further discussion at the official level was being prepared in the State Department, a message was going forward from the White House that hardened the prior demand for what Hanoi regarded as a formula for surrender. Sent over the president's signature through diplomatic channels, this communication was in Ho's hands well before he received the one I had signed.

This was a clear act of duplicity, and it was compounded in the weeks that followed as we began to run into evidence in Washington and foreign capitals that our effort to line up participants for *Pacem in Terris II*, now set for May in Geneva, was being undercut despite the administration's ostensible approval of the undertaking.

The campaign orchestrated from the White House to discredit the convocation had given me a place on Lyndon Johnson's list of pariahs when I met one afternoon in Geneva with a far more prominent one— Martin Luther King, Jr. We sat alone in a lounge at the Hotel Inter·Continental discussing our shared memories of a South that lay beyond the ken of most of the assorted dignitaries who wandered by. The impression he left with me was one of abiding sadness.

His resolve to press ahead with his Gandhian quest for social justice was unshaken, but he saw the movement he had founded engulfed by the tide of violence rising in the jungles of Southeast Asia and on the streets of our great cities. He made the connection when he addressed the convocation. "I criticize America because I love her, and I want to see her standing as a moral example to the world," he said. But that was not possible while she continued to wage a war that "exacerbated hatred between continents, and, worse still, between races."

By the fall of 1967 the mainstream media were citing the "credibility gap" occasioned by the discrepancy between the president's profession that he was seeking a negotiated settlement in Vietnam and his evident commitment to a military resolution. The administration's sabotage of *Pacem in Terris II* was a case in point, and I felt it relieved me of any obligation to continue observing the confidentiality Bill Baggs and I had agreed to when we were used as informal emissaries. In September I published a full account of the affair in the inaugural issue of *Center Magazine*.

When the article was released to the press it created headlines from coast to coast, causing such a furor that before the day was over the State Department felt constrained to issue a lengthy official rejoinder and schedule a press conference for Secretary Bundy. The publicity tended to identify me with the Vietnam protest movement in a way I had neither sought nor desired.

The vicious personal attacks on the president seemed to me uncalled for, since the nation had become embroiled in the conflict under Cold

War policies put in place under President Eisenhower and enhanced by President Kennedy. "But if Vietnam cannot fairly be called Lyndon Johnson's war," I wrote in the *Center Magazine* article, "responsibility for the fact that it now dominates all United States policy, foreign and domestic, is inescapably his."

I had been close enough to Johnson in the past to sense the agony this consummate wheeler-dealer must be suffering as he found himself facing a political dead end. And I had no doubt that he shared my dismay that the hardships and hazards on the front lines of the miserable jungle war were being borne primarily by blacks, Southern rednecks, and big-city ethnics—young men without the influence and affluence that enabled their middleclass peers to dodge the draft.

The antiwar movement, in which the loyal majority had been drowned out by the militant posturing of the radical fringe, had no prospect of pressuring Lyndon Johnson into anything that could be construed as an American surrender. "I could think of nothing more likely to harden Johnson's resolve," I wrote, "than pickets

> outside the White House chanting, "Hey, Hey, LBJ, how many kids did you kill today?" unless it was those who gladdened J. Edgar Hoover's heart by shouting, "Ho Ho Ho Chi Minh, NLF is gonna win" as they ran through the streets baiting policemen and trashing public facilities and private property.

The television cameras, which focused on the street demonstrations as they increasingly crossed the line into physical violence, made it difficult to distinguish between the radicals and those who were bent on rallying political support to bring about change within the system—whose numbers were rapidly mounting as the body bags came home from Vietnam and the commanders at the front kept calling for additional reinforcements. But both at the fringe and in the center of the movement, blacks, with the notable exception of Martin Luther King, were conspicuous by their absence.

The Black Power militants rejected the invitation to join the umbrella National Mobilization Committee to End the War in Vietnam, and few blacks of any persuasion showed up in Chicago for the December

1967 meeting of the anti-Johnson Conference of Concerned Democrats organized by Allard Lowenstein. The campus "teach-ins" had been a resounding success, and by spring Lowenstein was seeking a candidate to lead this potential army of middleclass youths in a Democratic primary campaign to unseat Lyndon Johnson. The role was urged on King at an April meeting in New York, where Lowenstein was joined by James Wechsler, editor of the *New York Post*, and Norman Thomas, an elder statesman of the Old Left, in arguing that the civil rights leader's personal prestige would give political focus to the antiwar movement. King declined, but left no doubt that he would support the effort to replace the president.

Lowenstein took his recruiting mission to Capitol Hill, and there he found his man—a brilliant iconoclast, Senator Eugene McCarthy of Minnesota. A senior Democrat who had served in Congress since 1948, McCarthy functioned as an astringent critic of public policy rather than as a leader of causes. His complex ego drive did not involve the usual politician's quest for personal power, and he continued to function primarily as a critic after he announced at the end of November that he would challenge the president in selected primaries, beginning with New Hampshire in March.

I was then chairman of the advisory council of the California Democratic Party, a fairly high-powered group of nonofficeholders, most of whom shared my view that in Vietnam we were fighting the wrong war in the wrong place for the wrong reasons. I had known McCarthy since we worked together in the 1956 Stevenson campaign, and when he called to ask for my support I was happy to endorse him—which caused the state chairman, on instructions from the White House, to scuttle the advisory council. Another friend, Blair Clark, a former head of CBS News, had become McCarthy's campaign manager, and I joined him for a swing with the candidate from Sacramento to San Francisco and down to San Diego. The turnout was impressive, although McCarthy, in conventional terms, wasn't.

The senator was equipped with a sharp wit and, when he bothered to use it, considerable charm, but there was no passion in his cool, detached indictment of administration policy. The mechanics of the campaign bored him, and so did most of the local politicians he was supposed to spend time wooing. The momentum for his running start was provided by the army of student supporters recruited by Lowenstein;

they were able to tap into the vein of antiwar protest that now extended far beyond the campus.

To distinguish themselves from the radical fringe of the antiwar movement they "came clean for Gene," sloughing off the counterculture trappings in vogue among the collegiate young. Beards were shaved off, hair was cut, and thousands of neatly dressed, mannerly young men and women turned out along the campaign trail to ring doorbells, pass out literature, and staff state and local headquarters.

In its first test at the polls this anti-Vietnam insurgency all but upset a sitting president assumed to have a lock on the nomination. Johnson led in the New Hampshire primary, but McCarthy polled 42.4 percent of the vote and won twenty of twenty-four convention delegates. With McCarthy write-in votes in the Republican primary factored in, Johnson had run only 203 votes ahead of his challenger in a rock-ribbed conservative state.

The demonstration of the president's vulnerability was enough to prompt another contender for the anti-Johnson vote to enter the primaries, Robert Kennedy, now a U.S. senator from New York. Kennedy presented a vivid contrast to McCarthy. Once he declared against the Vietnam War, the charismatic brother of the martyred president won the immediate endorsement of Martin Luther King, and a surge of support from his followers. The increasingly bitter contest between the two Irishmen would continue down to the wire in the California primary, creating further turmoil within the ranks of the already fatally divided Democratic party.

The implications of this rising tide of opposition were not lost on Lyndon Johnson, who could project voting patterns as well as any man alive. While he was still maintaining his unyielding public posture, he drafted Clark Clifford, Harry Truman's gifted campaign tactician, as secretary of defense to succeed the disheartened Robert McNamara. After a rigorous reappraisal of the failing military effort in Vietnam. Clifford initiated secret meetings for the president with a select group of "wise men"—top foreign and defense policy officials in preceding administrations—who reversed their previous Cold War positions and recommended a negotiated settlement.

Bill Baggs and I had no inkling of any of this when we received an indication that Hanoi was interested in reopening the channel that had been set up before the *Pacem in Terris* convocation, but it no doubt accounted for the civil reception we received when we reported the new feeler to the State Department. A second mission was promptly endorsed, and we again agreed to keep the contact secret until we had returned and reported the result—and, as a matter of importance to us, had a chance to appraise the official reaction.

We had just arrived in Hanoi on March 31 when Johnson removed himself from the 1968 presidential race. The unequivocal withdrawal came in an address to the nation delivered from the Oval Office on the eve of the Wisconsin primary. As a tangible gesture toward a new opening for negotiation, the president announced that the aerial assault would be pulled back to the lower section of North Vietnam, but this was conspicuously less than the bombing halt North Vietnam had demanded, and the senior functionaries we dealt with remained skeptical. It required three days of protracted discussions to convince them that for a man of the president's overweening pride, abandonment of the presidential contest had to be regarded as an act of political self-immolation.

We kept the State Department informed through neutral diplomatic channels, and were finally able to report that we had received an aide-mémoire that confirmed in writing the willingness of the North Vietnamese to participate in negotiations that opened the way for the Paris peace talks. On our last night behind the lines, our host, Hoang Tung, editor of *Nham Dan*, the official government newspaper, came to the old villa where we were quartered to gently break the news that Martin Luther King, Jr., had been assassinated. Our reaction was described in *Mission to Hanoi*, the book Baggs and I coauthored:

> We were, in that dim dining room with its awkward French bourgeois furnishing, literally on the other side of the globe from the scene of the gentle King's death, and it felt as though we were on the far side of the moon.
>
> We had both known King well . . . and we could hear him again at *Pacem in Terris* in Geneva, proclaiming . . . words singularly fitting for this place on this day:
>
> " . . . North Vietnam and/or the National Liberation

Front . . . may have understandable reasons to be suspicious, [but] life and history give eloquent testimony to the fact that conflicts are never resolved without trustful give-and-take on both sides."

In a brief stop in Tokyo on the flight back to Washington we first heard details of the aftermath of King's death from the American ambassador. In bitter commemoration of the apostle of nonviolence, spontaneous riots had flared in the black ghettos of cities across the nation. The worst of these was in the national capital, where nine blacks were killed and martial law imposed. A curfew was in effect when we were met at Dulles International Airport by a State Department aide and driven into the city:

We rolled in awed silence down the broad avenues, past the White House, up 16th Street to our hotel in the heart of the downtown district. An occasional police car prowled past, or a military personnel carrier with armed troops, but nothing else moved. Down the whole length of 16th, from Lafayette Square to Scott Circle, past the grand hotels, the Soviet embassy, the University Club, only one pedestrian was in sight, a single defiant Negro with no one to accost and, until a patrol car came by, no one to accost him.

It was the end of the era in which the civil rights movement changed the contours of the nation's race relations under the leadership of Martin Luther King and the patronage of Jack Kennedy and Lyndon Johnson.

When the contest for the Republican nomination got under way, there were indications that the party had begun to recover from the wreckage left in the wake of the Goldwater debacle. Richard Nixon, who in 1964 had described what was left of the Republican constituency as "religious, recidivist, and reactionary," had been rejuvenated and was the acknowledged front-runner.

After his narrow loss to John F. Kennedy in 1960 he had gone home to California to enter the 1962 governor's race, only to find his bid undermined by extreme right-wing influence on the state Republican organization. He kept his feeling of betrayal bottled up, blaming the media for his loss to the ebullient Democrat Pat Brown, but in a distraught farewell press conference indicated that he was retiring from politics.

That seemed to be confirmed in 1963, when he moved to New York and accepted a senior partnership in a Wall Street law firm. The wealth and status that came with the job restored his self-confidence, and he became an effective practitioner of corporation law as well as a "rainmaker" whose connections from his vice presidential years brought in wealthy clients.

The political juices began flowing again as he contemplated the disintegration of the Democratic coalition under the impact of anti-Vietnam War protest and white backlash. With funding provided by wealthy Republican moderates, he embarked on a "Congress '66" barnstorming tour that covered thirty thousand miles and took him into eighty-two congressional districts. His success in rallying support for local candidates played a major role in Republican gains in the midterm elections—forty-seven seats in the House and three in the Senate. And it ensured that Richard Nixon would have renewed support from grateful GOP state leaders for another run for the presidency.

His principal opponent was George Romney, the pro–civil rights governor of Michigan, who had the backing of Nelson Rockefeller and was leading in the opinion polls. But the earnest, deeply religious style that bespoke Romney's sincerity made him a dull campaigner and left him open to ridicule. Governor James Rhodes of Ohio, a fellow Republican, said in retrospect, "Watching George Romney run for the presidency was like watching a duck try to make love to a football."

Romney sought to capitalize on antiwar sentiment by calling for neutralization of the warring factions in Vietnam, but that was territory already staked out by Democrats opposing Lyndon Johnson. When Romney accounted for his earlier support of the war effort by saying that he had been brainwashed by the military brass, Eugene McCarthy observed, "I would have thought a light rinse would have been sufficient." As the primary season opened, a poll of voters in bellwether New Hampshire showed Nixon leading Romney, 64 to 12 percent. In February, after months of dogged campaigning in the state, Romney was trailing Nixon by 6 to 1 and gracefully withdrew from the contest.

Cleaving to his centrist line, Nixon went on to handily carry primaries in Pennsylvania, Indiana, Wisconsin, and Nebraska. In the final contest, in Oregon, he won decisively over his most formidable remaining opponent, Ronald Reagan, the Hollywood actor turned politician who had corralled California's rampant conservatives to win the governorship they had denied the former vice president.

Reagan had inherited Goldwater's mantle, and with it had come the blessing of many converted Dixiecrat leaders in the South who now controlled the state Republican parties. But delegates were still to be had there by negotiation, and Nixon arranged a closed meeting in Atlanta with a group of party leaders headed by Senators Strom Thurmond of South Carolina and John Tower of Texas.

Here civil rights, not Vietnam, was the primary issue, and Nixon moved far enough to the right to bring Southern Republican leaders into the fold. He avoided endorsement of segregation in principle, but assured them that he considered the *Brown* decision in need of reinterpretation by the kind of strict constructionists he would appoint to the Supreme Court; that he thought busing to achieve school desegregation was wrong; and that he didn't think federal funding should be withheld from districts that didn't achieve racial balance. That, plus the tough law-and-order line he had begun to take in the primaries, proved to be sufficient.

Nixon had a majority of the delegates in his pocket when the Republicans met in Miami in August. He defused the antiwar issue by joining the two outspoken doves Romney and Rockefeller in seeing to it that the platform's Vietnam plank pointed toward negotiation and away from further military intervention. The result was termed by Theodore White a masterpiece of political carpentry.

Nixon won the nomination on the first ballot with 692 votes, against 277 for Rockefeller and 182 for Reagan. Nixon had patched together a coalition that would take him to the White House—with the assistance of a third-party movement so far to the right it permitted him to stay in the political center, or as close to it as a Republican could be expected to come.

Nixon's benefactor was George Wallace, who in his first inaugural address as governor of Alabama had announced the platform he would stand on throughout his career in national politics: "I draw the line in the dust and toss the gauntlet before the feet of tyranny, and I say, 'Segregation now—segregation tomorrow—and segregation forever!' "

In 1964, when he made an abortive run against Lyndon Johnson in the presidential primaries, his sharp-tongued denunciation of the "pointy-headed liberals" who favored civil rights had drawn a significant response from blue-collar voters in northern states. Four years later, out of office because of the term limit in Alabama's constitution, Wallace had his wife, Lurleen, elected governor and deployed skilled operatives from his political machine to place him on general election ballots from coast to coast.

By the summer of 1968 his American Independence Party had met the legal qualifications in forty-nine of the fifty states, and the Wallace ticket included a four-star hawk, Curtis LeMay, as his vice presidential running mate. When Wallace support edged up toward 20 percent in the national polls, the media could no longer ignore him, and sensation-prone reporters were fascinated by the broadside populist attack based on his thesis that "there's not a dime's worth of difference between Republicans and Democrats."

Money rolled in to finance his travels along the trail of political scorched earth he blazed through white working-class neighborhoods in the major cities. The people, he proclaimed, were fed up with "the sissy attitude of Lyndon Johnson and all the intellectual morons and theoreticians he has around him." Faulting the president's prosecution of the Vietnam War, he said, "I think we've got to pour it on. We've got to win this war." General LeMay, who had headed the Air Force's Strategie Air Command, provided a formula for quick victory, urging that nuclear weapons be used to "bomb the North Vietnamese back to the Stone Age."

Campaigning in Cicero, the suburb where Martin Luther King's Chicago crusade had foundered, Wallace expanded his target list beyond the long-hairs, anarchists, intellectuals, and bureaucrats to include "these newspaper editors that look down their nose at every workingman in Cicero, on every workingman in the United States, and call them a group of rednecks or a group of punks because we want to defend America."

The attack on the "lyin' newspapers" was a tactic Southern demagogues had long used to discount media criticism their inflammatory oratory invoked, and it helped Wallace reach across a cultural void to the voters who flocked to hear him in ethnic neighborhoods. But the heart of his appeal was unabashedly racist, feeding on the resentment of those in the lower-income brackets who saw government-assisted improvement in the lot of blacks as a threat to their own.

Throwing the election into the House of Representatives had been the stated goal of the third-party effort when the Dixiecrats took their states out of the Democratic column in 1948. But while the defections to Wallace would be primarily among Democrats, he had no prospect of rallying majority support in any state outside the South, and could only contribute to the basic realignment already taking place in both parties.

Many of the Dixiecrats had followed the lead of Strom Thurmond and joined the Republicans, giving the party the respectable local political base it had never had in the days when the one-party system provided a bulwark against the black vote. Now that the barriers were down, Southern conservatives were free to join their peers in the national party traditionally committed to business-oriented interests similar to their own, while moderate Democrats formed a working coalition with blacks who could provide the balance of power in elections for state and local office.

Wallace's national campaign entourage was made up of well-educated Alabamians who had gravitated to the center of power when, as was still possible in the Deep South, an unabashedly racist appeal allowed the scrappy little governor to put together an unbeatable state political machine. The redneck credentials of the candidate himself were suspect: while born poor, the son of a failed small farmer, he had attended the state university, graduated from its law school, and served as a district judge. And he had taken a moderate stand in his first run for governor, only to lose to a racist opponent; it was then that Wallace made his famous vow "I'm not going to be outniggered again."

Among his handlers at least one would have to be rated a Southern patrician. Grover Hall had inherited the editor's chair at the *Montgomery Advertiser* from his father, who won a Pulitzer Prize fighting the Ku Klux Klan in the 1920s. In *An Epitaph for Dixie* I characterized him as perhaps the region's most eloquent editorial writer:

Hall is too intellectually honest to contend that there is anything approximating equality of treatment for Negroes in Alabama. . . . But his approach to the very real racial problems that beset his state largely consists of a running campaign intended to prove Negroes are even worse off in New York and Chicago. . . . This may be soothing, but it is irrelevant; the *Advertiser* circulates in Alabama, not in Harlem, and Alabama's problems, as Hall himself conceded when he deplored the fact that dynamite was being delivered to Montgomery front porches along with the morning paper, have now advanced far beyond simple questions of racial attitudes.

It seemed to me that the presence of this elegant, witty man in the Wallace camp provided an example of the alienation racial polarization was producing all along the social scale. For Hall it was hardly a matter of expediency; it cost him his job at the *Advertiser* when the owners could no longer tolerate his support of the feisty little governor, and it rendered Hall unfit for a similar position at the interpositionist *Richmond News-Leader* proffered by its genteel proprietors. Wayne Greenhaw, a friend and Montgomery newspaper colleague, thought Hall succumbed to the strain of romanticism endemic among Southerners of his caste:

Hall saw in Wallace an embodiment of the great Southern childhood myth of the warrior astride a great white charger doing battle for the love of the maiden. In Wallace's case the maiden was the people of Alabama first and the people of the South second. . . . For Hall, Wallace was Ivanhoe.

This seemed to me a prodigious stretch of the imagination, but Hall seemed to confirm it. "Part of my feeling derives from my love of Alabama and pride in the Kickapoo juice in the breed's blood," he wrote in a letter to a friend, and by way of attesting that this had little if anything to do with racism, he said of the Alabamian who was a leading integrationist on the U.S. Supreme Court: "I feel the same way about Hugo Black."

The contrast between Hall's patrician persona and that of the rambunctious candidate was a source of sardonic amusement for both when they dealt with bemused representatives of the national media. Hall recounted with glee an incident that occurred when he accompanied Wallace to Washington for his first appearance on the network TV program "Meet the Press."

On the eve of the broadcast the governor startled the editor by asking him to provide him with an instant foreign policy so he could respond to questions on his world-view. Hall, who had just read an article on current diplomatic issues in *The Wall Street Journal*, ripped it out and handed it to Wallace, who read it through several times, folded it, and tucked it in his breast pocket. Hall described to Greenhaw the aftermath of his short-order briefing:

> After the show, Wallace strutted into the lobby where Hall waited. He lighted a cigar, pulled out the clipping, wadded it and threw it into a waste can. "I don't need a foreign policy," he said. "All they wanted to know about was niggers, and I'm the expert."

Nixon was willing to concede the Deep South to Wallace but had well-founded hopes of carrying the upper tier of Southern states. When he took his campaign to North Carolina, the *Charlotte Observer* commented:

> If his speech here Wednesday was any indication, Richard M. Nixon's "Southern Strategy" is that Southerners are "just folks" like everybody else. . . . It crossed no Mason-Dixon lines of the mind and it certainly didn't try to out-Wallace George Wallace. . . . This was Nixon's first foray into the South and it was supposed to give some indication of how he would make special efforts to woo the region's voters. But it could have been given in Bayonne, New Jersey. . . .

The Republicans had written off the black vote, and it could be assumed that the nonwhite minority would again provide the crumbling Democratic coalition its only solid bloc support. But it seemed likely that the vote would fall well below the record turnout for Lyndon Johnson in 1964. Pride in the presence of blacks in all ranks of the armed forces had robbed the antiwar protest of mass appeal, and the defection of Martin Luther King had left the party without a rallying leader—until Bobby Kennedy entered the race.

The spectacular climax of the younger Kennedy's career added another of the contrasting personas perceived by those who have dealt with his family dynasty. Sympathetic biographers believe that the trauma of his brother's death brought forth a spiritual quality that had not been apparent in the hard-nosed campaign manager and guardian of the presidential flanks who bore the brunt of the resentment caused by the administration's policies and practices. After a period of withdrawal and solitary grieving, he came back into the arena by establishing residence in New York and winning a base of his own in the U.S. Senate. By 1968 he felt free to take on Lyndon Johnson, the man he regarded as a usurper of the Oval Office.

But the passionate crusader for peace and social justice who emerged in the course of the campaign was not yet visible when I spent a long day with him in New York a few months before he entered the race. He was one of four persons deemed specially qualified to deal with racial issues who joined with Robert Hutchins and me to examine the social and political implications of the stalled effort to desegregate the public schools.

Kennedy had been the sponsor of the group of young social scientists who influenced the War on Poverty measures initiated in 1965. Now representing the largest concentration of urban minorities in the country, he had established nonprofit corporations to deal with the range of problems affecting Bedford-Stuyvesant, a deteriorating Brooklyn residential area where 400,000 poor people were jammed together, 80 percent of them black and 10 percent Puerto Rican. He had used his family connections to recruit executives from the New York business establishment to join with leading urban planners in creating one of the first of what came to be called "enterprise zones" intended to employ the resources of the public and private sectors to bring the poverty-stricken enclave into the mainstream.

In exchanges over extended morning and afternoon sessions, Kennedy displayed clear-eyed recognition of the inadequacy of many of the programs with which he had been identified. These, he conceded, had created overpaid jobs in ill-defined community action agencies that had only served to divert attention from the failure of the school system to meet the needs of poor minority children. "A hell of a lot of money is involved," he said. "I'm willing to make a fuss if it will accomplish some good."

On this occasion he was Bobby Kennedy, the pragmatic, forward-looking public servant. Three months later, to Gene McCarthy and his supporters, he was an unprincipled political renegade who had gone back on his declared intention to stay out of the primaries after his colleague had demonstrated the president's vulnerability. As the beleaguered Lyndon Johnson saw it, "Robert Kennedy had openly announced his intention to reclaim the throne in the name of his brother. And the American people, swayed by the magic of his name, were dancing in the streets."

If there was in fact a spontaneous celebration, it was initially confined to college campuses, where the myth of Camelot had been enshrined after his brother's assassination. To Theodore White, who watched Kennedy launch his initial appeal to his natural following among the young, he came through as "hysterical, high-pitched, hair blowing in the wind, almost demoniac, frightening. In short, the ruthless, vindictive Bobby Kennedy again, action without thought, position without plan." The Washington columnist William V. Shannon found that he offered "such an astonishing perspective on public affairs it is hard to say on the basis of it whether Kennedy is seeking the presidency or the leadership of a new Children's Crusade."

The assassination of Martin Luther King after Lyndon Johnson's withdrawal from the race opened a wellspring of passionate support for Kennedy in black ghettos simmering down from outbreaks of grief-stricken violence. White, who joined his barnstorming tour a few weeks later in Indiana, found that he had developed a standard stump speech that differed little from Nixon's in content: "The difference between them was one of spirit. Whatever Robert Kennedy said rang with a passion, a cry, a call on emotions."

In the Negro ghettos of Indiana (as in the Mexican and in black districts of California) . . . he was the Liberator, come to free the oppressed. For, above all other themes in his campaign, beyond the program, the fire that burned most hotly in him was for the underprivileged. . . . The enemies of Robert Kennedy had already made him a saint in the black wards of America.

In states where the black vote was negligible, as in Oregon, he could still be bested by Gene McCarthy, whose youthful supporters were fired by resentment of the late-blooming Kennedy candidacy. But in the primary in California he edged out McCarthy and for a brief moment appeared to be the front-runner in the contest for the Democratic nomination.

At the victory celebration in a Los Angeles hotel Bobby Kennedy delivered what turned out to be his valedictory. His somber tone constrasted with the jubilance of his followers as he spoke of "what has been going on with the United States over the period of the last three years—the divisions, the violence, the disenchantment with our society. . . . Whether it's between blacks and whites, between the poor and the more affluent, or between age groups, we must stay together."

Then, as he left the ballroom, the malignant fate that stalked his family caught up with him. A deranged gunman was waiting in a crowded hallway, and Bobby Kennedy joined his brother and Martin Luther King in the hall of martyrs.

In April Hubert Humphrey had entered the race as the anointed candidate of Lyndon Johnson, which guaranteed Humphrey support of the Democratic leadership but saddled him with the implacable opposition of the party's anti-Vietnam faction. With the removal of Bobby Kennedy as a contender, and with McCarthy boxed in by his fellow Minnesotan, there was a scramble among an assortment of lesser contenders, with Senator George McGovern of South Dakota inheriting most of the Kennedy delegates.

To an extent the Vietnam issue had been muted by President Johnson's conditional move to open peace negotiations with the North Vietnamese. But while official representatives of Washington and Hanoi were finally meeting in Paris, they were bogged down with procedural details. The haggling had begun with Johnson's rejection of sites proposed by Hanoi, and it continued over composition of the delegations and even the shape of the negotiating table.

When Bill Baggs and I returned from Hanoi to report on our exploratory exchanges with the North Vietnamese leaders, we found the conflict between factions in the State Department and the White House still unresolved. After spending a week in Foggy Bottom helping prepare briefing papers for Ambassador Harriman, and meeting in closed session with the Senate Foreign Relations Committee, Baggs and I were convinced that the president was still not willing to accept the full-scale cease-fire the North Vietnamese had insisted on as the minimum prerequisite for a negotiated settlement of the war.

Concluding that an account of the imbroglio within the administration ought to be available before the Democratic convention, we hastily put together a book, *Mission to Hanoi*, subtitled *A Chronicle of Double-Dealing in High Places*. Copies were in the hands of the media a week before the delegates convened, but our revelations attracted little attention. By the time the Democrats headed for Chicago to choose their presidential ticket the TV screens and newspaper headlines were dominated by the antics of a frenetic remnant of the Anti-Vietnam War Mobilization.

The responsible leaders of the movement, and the serious young people who had enlisted in the political campaign on behalf of McCarthy and Kennedy, had been displaced in the news coverage by followers of the Youth International Party. The signals were being called by Jerry Rubin, hailed by Norman Mailer in his panegyric *The Armies of the Night* as "the most militant, unpredictable, creative—therefore dangerous—hippie-oriented leader available on the New Left."

Trading on that reputation, Rubin generated widespread coverage when he announced a Festival of Life to be held in a downtown park, and promised that the Yippies would put LSD in the municipal water supply and send thousands of naked youngsters running through the streets. Fewer than two thousand showed up for the festival, and a goodly number of those were undercover police. But when the motley band moved down to Grant Park, across the street from convention headquarters in the vast Conrad Hilton Hotel, the magnifying lens of television was waiting, and so were twelve thousand city police, five thousand National Guardsmen, and six thousand Regular Army troops standing by in reserve.

Mayor Richard Daley, the Irish puritan who presided over City Hall, was outraged by Rubin's presentation of a list of demands that included a declaration that "we believe that people should fuck all the time, anytime, whomever they want." He took seriously the Yippie leader's announced intention to "create a situation in which the Chicago police and the Daley administration and the federal government and the United States would self-destruct."

When the inevitable confrontations occurred, there were few if any true militants in the thin ranks of the Yippies and their camp followers. But under the selective eye of the television cameras the clashes resembled the riots Daley's police had put down during the long, hot summers—except that virtually all the participants and the great majority of the bystanders were white. The Yippies had no more appeal for Chicago's blacks than they did for Mayor Daley.

I was approaching the Conrad Hilton on my way to McCarthy headquarters when the police commanders on the ground lost control of the forces facing the swirling crowd outside the hotel, if in fact they tried to exercise it. Had I not been wearing *Miami News* press credentials I might well have wound up with the hapless youths who were flung into paddy wagons as the blue-helmeted police charged into the crowd swinging billy clubs.

The best guess in the wake of the action in the downtown area was that active provocateurs probably numbered no more than forty, and were armed against the tear gas and night sticks of the police with nothing more lethal than stink bombs and an occasional brickbat. Not a single shot was fired by either side; fire hoses were never used; no one was killed, or injured seriously enough to require hospitalization; the police and demonstrators treated at first aid stations were numbered in the low hundreds.

But the "police riots," as they were properly labeled, provided the stuff of ready-made TV news spectaculars. The confrontations were well removed from the securely guarded Stockyards Amphitheater where the convention met, and most of the delegates were unaware of them until they had access to repeated broadcast replays of the videotaped coverage. The maneuvering inside the hall, and in the hotel suites where the party leaders huddled, revolved around the effort to put some distance between the presumptive nominee, Hubert Humphrey, and Lyndon Johnson.

But the president was having none of it. He demanded, and got, a platform plank that praised him for initiating the Paris peace talks while inferentially endorsing the adamant stand against a cease-fire that had rendered them meaningless. In his acceptance speech the dispirited Humphrey had no choice but to go along. His tribute to the wounded giant was one of the few times Lyndon Johnson was mentioned by those who spoke at the convention he still dominated.

Hubert Humphrey was the first Democratic presidential candidate—although he was not to be the last—who would look back on what should have been his moment of triumph and lament, "I was a victim of that convention." He always believed that he could have bested Nixon if he had had a fair start, "but it's difficult to take on the Republicans and fight a guerrilla war in your own party at the same time. Chicago was a catastrophe."

That view was shared by most Democratic leaders, and throughout September they avoided the erstwhile happy warrior as he stumped the country under a pall of gloom. At the end of the month the polls showed him 15 points behind Nixon. Worse still, at 38 percent, he was only 7 points ahead of George Wallace.

In October the momentum began to shift. Humphrey bit the bullet and moved perceptibly away from Johnson on Vietnam, declaring that he would initiate a complete bombing halt in order to get the peace process moving. It was enough to bring back many disaffected McCarthy and Kennedy supporters, and he launched a counteroffensive on the other flank. In a speech in Detroit to an audience dominated by auto-workers, he took dead aim at George Wallace:

> Let's lay it on the line. George Wallace's pitch is racism. If you want to feel damn mean and ornery find some other way to do it, but don't sacrifice your country. George Wallace has been engaged in union-busting wherever he's had the chance . . . and any union man who votes for him is not a good union man.

That was a rallying cry for longtime Humphrey supporters among the labor leaders, many of whom sympathized with the hard-hats who were turned off by the anti-Vietnam protesters. Political action committees in the union locals were set to work following up the distribution of twenty million pieces of literature branding Wallace an enemy of workingmen and workingwomen. Veteran organizers with appropriate backgrounds carried the message in person to ethnic voters, and emphasized the racism issue in door-to-door drives to turn out the vote in black neighborhoods.

Nixon's strategy was to stay above the fray. He had endorsed the negotiating process initiated by the president, and this gave him a plausible excuse not to reveal what he billed as his own plan for guaranteeing peace with honor; it would not be appropriate to make it known, he said, while Johnson was still in charge of the nation's foreign policy. The wedge Wallace drove into the Democratic coalition relieved Nixon of the necessity of taking a position that might be construed as overtly racist, and he did not go beyond a general commitment to restore law and order in the ghettos.

But his lead over Humphrey in the polls continued to shrink until by mid-October both Harris and Gallup had Nixon's lead down to 42–40, a statistical dead heat. Still, Nixon continued to resist the urging of his aides, kept his own combative nature in check, and stayed on the high ground. His tightly organized campaign was designed to protect him against direct questioning by the media, and he refused to respond to Humphrey's challenge to head-to-head debate even after his now fired-up opponent began referring to him as "Richard the Chicken-hearted."

Under the slogan he adopted from a placard held aloft by a schoolgirl at an Ohio rally, "Bring Us Together," one of the most meanspirited partisans in recent history skillfully used paid television advertising to project the image of a healer. He bore too much baggage from his Red-baiting past to convince a majority of the voters that a new Nixon had risen from the ruins of the Republican Party. But when the votes were counted he had just enough to ensure victory—43.4 percent against 42.7 percent for Humphrey, a margin of 499,704 out of a total vote of 73,186,819. George Wallace's nearly 10 million votes, 13.53 percent of the total, tilted enough key states into the GOP column to give Nixon a majority in the Electoral College.

. . .

In the wake of the debacle at the Democratic convention in Chicago, *Center Magazine* published "A Symposium on the Limits of Dissent." In my contribution I recounted the scene on the last night of the convention when police came into the Conrad Hilton and threatened to arrest youthful campaign workers quartered on floors assigned to Gene McCarthy's headquarters. In the early morning hours, after the defeated candidate faced down the raiding party's senior officers, I walked along with McCarthy when he crossed Michigan Avenue to check on his and Kennedy's supporters who had taken refuge among the demonstrators herded into Grant Park. We passed through the line of National Guard troops who had replaced the Chicago police, and it suddenly struck me that the confrontation was now confined to one side of the generation gap:

> The soldiers standing shoulder to shoulder with their rifles across their chests were of an age with those who writhed along their front scattering taunts and jeers and obscene invitations. These were boys from Skokie and Peoria and East St. Louis largely bypassed by the affluence that underwrites a protest movement that has taken on the sound of revolution but so far has not achieved much more reality than the television dramas upon which all these young were suckled.
>
> Here was the limit of dissent. The obtuseness of the Mayor and the brutality of his police were facts. But it was also a fact that no government could allow dissidents to disrupt its vital processes. There would always be a line somewhere manned by very young men in combat fatigues under orders to hold at any cost—and if they were pressed long enough and hard enough the time would come when the elevated gun barrels would come down and live rounds would slide home. This would be the ultimate tragedy, and the ultimate irony, for if reality ever overtakes the rhetoric the old and corrupt will be somewhere else when the young provide their own executioners.

The gun barrels came down five months later, on the campus of Kent State University. Seconds later four students were dead and six wounded. Milton Viorst, bracketing the turbulent decade, wrote in *Fire in the Streets*:

. . . the 1960s, as suddenly as they had begun at Greensboro, ended at Kent State. This is not to say that the counterculture vanished, or that radicalism died. . . . But as an era when masses of people, most of them young, regularly took to the streets to challenge the practices of society, the 1960s ended with a thirteen-second fusillade in a small Ohio town. The decade ended because the civil rights movement, which was responsible for its conception, no longer contributed the seed to enrich it. . . .

RETROGRADE
NIXON AND THE SOUTHERN STRATEGY

Conscience and the Constitution both require that no child should be denied equal educational opportunity. That Constitutional mandate was laid down by the Supreme Court in Brown v. Board of Education in 1954. . . .

All too often, the result has been a classic case of the remedy for one evil creating another evil. In this case, a remedy for the historic evil of racial discrimination has often created a new evil of disrupting communities and imposing hardship on children—both black and white—who are themselves wholly innocent of the wrongs the plan seeks to set right. . . .

—PRESIDENT RICHARD NIXON,
Special Message to Congress on Equal Educational Opportunities
and School Busing, March 17, 1972

GARRY WILLS indulged a classics scholar's long view laced with irony in *Nixon Agonistes*, his 1970 postmortem on the election of the thirty-seventh president of the United States. But he was not being ironic when, with the new administration well launched, he wrote: "Even now, commentators do not see that Nixon is the authentic voice of the surviving American liberalism."

To Wills, Nixon was a true product of the contradictions that had developed as Americans attempted to adapt their heritage from British political thinkers to the vastly different conditions that emerged on this continent in the course of the Industrial Revolution. The controlling American faith was rooted in an outdated version of marketplace competition, and it was not confined to economics:

Proving oneself in the free arena of competition is the test of manhood, truth and political wisdom. . . . It is because Nixon is so totally this sweaty moral self-doubting self-made bustling brooding type, that he represents the integral liberalism that once animated America and now tries to reassert itself.

The concept of the self-made man has been the key to American liberalism. The central tenet of the great historical school of liberal thought has been a belief in self-regulation. If one simply removes imposed controls, the economy can be self-regulating (Smith), as the ecological balance (Malthus) and the animal world (Darwin) are self-regulating. If one removes controls man can be self-regulating (Locke); even ideas can be self-regulating (Mill).

But the cluster of mutually reinforcing arguments that grew out of this notion could not be made to correspond to reality. They ran into the same difficulty that plagued the idea of self-determination used to justify the foreign policy that resulted in military intervention in Vietnam. The trouble, Wills said, was "the impossibility of finding a 'self' to do the regulating."

Adam Smith's invisible hand, which was supposed to protect the interests of owners, consumers, and workers by balancing supply and demand, had proved to be not only invisible but also nonexistent in substantial areas as the economy was reshaped by rapid changes in technology and demography. Richard Nixon, Wills contended, was simply the latest product of the failure of both political parties to recognize this essential fact and develop strategies for adapting democratic institutions to deal with it.

Like most of those who had seen the new president close up, Wills, who had covered the campaign as a journalist, came away with respect for his intelligence, political acumen, and dogged perseverance, and with renewed reservations about the character flaws that had been evident throughout his rebounding career. As his narrow election margin indicated, Nixon had never been able to arouse a personal following, and most of the media seers rated him no better than the best of the poor choices made available by the fragmented political parties.

For Walter Lippmann, usually billed as the nation's public philosopher, endorsement of Nixon carried a note of desperation. Lippmann had concluded that the center might not hold and that the Republicans, with their limited regard for civil rights, were better fitted to deal with the result. The nation, he wrote, had entered upon "a time when the central institutions of the traditional life of man are increasingly unable to command his allegiance and his obedience."

> There are no easy answers and there are no quick solutions for the discontent that will have to be dealt with, and we would be hiding our heads in the sand if we refused to admit that the country may demand and necessity may dictate the repression of uncontrollable violence.
>
> It is better that Mr. Nixon should have the full authority if repression should become necessary in order to restore peace and tranquillity at home. . . .

Lippmann's fears proved unfounded, although the erosion of public confidence in traditional institutions continued, and domestic tranquillity remained hard to come by outside the nation's small towns and the homogenous enclaves where the affluent zoned out all but their own kind.

Upon taking office, Nixon damped down anti-Vietnam agitation with a flurry of peaceful gestures. Henry Kissinger, a presumptive dove, came over from Nelson Rockefeller's stable of advisers as the new national security chief, and was put in charge of the U.S. delegation at the Paris negotiations. A year after the election, when three hundred thousand antiwar protesters came to Washington, for a "peace mobilization," youthful marshals recruited from Gene McCarthy's campus legions joined city police to contain New Left militants who sought to disrupt the orderly mass lobbying effort.

Nixon also reached far outside his constituency to install Daniel Patrick Moynihan in the White House. One of the key participants in the formulation of the War on Poverty, Moynihan seized the opportunity to develop, under the aegis of the new president's proclaimed "New

Federalism," an approach to welfare reform that had not come to fruition under Lyndon Johnson.

Thus emerged what the capital press corps certified as a "new Nixon." James Reston of *The New York Times*, the bellwether of the pack, declared, "Mr. Nixon has taken a great step forward. He has cloaked a remarkably progressive welfare policy in conservative language. . . . He has repudiated his own party's record on social policy at home."

For a while that seemed to be the case. Under the media's usage of the term, Moynihan had originally qualified as a liberal since he was identified with the activist policies that had been the Democratic hallmark since Franklin Roosevelt's day. He was one of the leaders of Americans for Democratic Action, which became the keeper of the New Deal flame, and was among the Ivy League academics who first appeared on the Washington scene when Jack Kennedy summoned the best and brightest to serve on the New Frontier. Now he would be labeled a "neoconservative" by *The Nation* and a "neoliberal" by *The New Republic*.

He had been frozen out of politics when he was pilloried by blacks as a result of their misreading of the Moynihan Report. In 1965, when the backfire began to jeopardize President Johnson's relationship with the black leadership, Moynihan became subject to what he called the "process of exclusion" that returned him to his academic career. But he still had a compelling interest in political affairs, evidenced in 1968 when he published *Maximum Feasible Misunderstanding: Community Action in the War on Poverty*, a sometimes sulphurous account of the manner in which social scientists conditioned by the radical youth movement placed what he regarded as the fatal imprint of the New Left on the War on Poverty.

Moynihan's little book reflected the anger and frustration of a temperamental Irishman who had been on the losing side of a bruising political turf battle. Incorporating a university lecture series, it often lapsed into professional social science jargon, but it pulled no punches in attacking the notion of induced "maximum feasible participation" by the poor in conducting federally funded poverty programs.

The genesis of this bottom-up community action approach was traced to the "Mobilization for Youth" program developed to deal with the mounting problem of juvenile delinquency in New York City ghettos. A product of the Columbia University School of Social Work, it was described by Moynihan as

> a plan devised by a group of middleclass intellectuals to bring about changes in behavior of a group of lowerclass youth who differed from them in ethnicity and religion, in social class and attitudes, in life-styles and, above all, in life prospects.

Moynihan brought a unique authority to his indictment, which was at the heart of the case he made against the attempt to employ radical populist theory to replace existing institutions that, however imperfectly, had long served the urban poor. Although he bore the cachet of a top-drawer Ivy League social scientist, he had actually grown up in a poor Irish neighborhood in Harlem, the child of a single mother deserted by his alcoholic father when he was very young. His experience with poverty matched that of his black Harlem schoolmates; he, too, had shined shoes in Times Square. To finance his higher education he had worked as a bartender and longshoreman. As Garry Wills noted, he had lived the sociology he wrote about when he coauthored *Beyond the Melting Pot*, a study of New York's patchwork of ethnic life-styles.

That experience dictated Moynihan's insistence that funding for the War on Poverty should be used to expand and improve the work of existing schools and public and private social agencies that had long dealt with youngsters who were, in a description rejected by the radical social scientists, "inadequately socialized." The need, as he saw it, was to enable the system to better provide the acculturation and training that would permit socially handicapped youths to hold jobs and thus escape the stultifying net of welfare dependency.

Moynihan thought John Kennedy and Johnson shared that view, and had not realized that it was being subverted until it was too late to undo the damage. Neither the president nor the vice president was paying much attention in 1961 when Kennedy gave his blessing to a consortium of federal agencies, the Ford Foundation, and the city of New York that provided $12.5 million for pilot projects under the umbrella of the Mobilization for Youth. This opened the way for some of the most radical of the advocates of maximum feasible participation to find places on the staff of the President's Committee on Juvenile Delinquency. They were described by Moynihan as "waging war on the bureaucracy, attracting ideas and men from the outside, and colonizing them within the government. They sometimes referred to themselves as 'guerrillas.' "

As the programs ultimately grouped under the Office of Economic Opportunity (OEO) were being developed, these intellectual interlopers were "living off the administrative countryside, invisible to the bureaucratic enemy but known to one another, hitting and running and making off with the riches of the established departments." And Moynihan noted that

> The planning groups were made up exclusively of middle-class whites. No black had a place in the drafting of the poverty programs or the community action program guidelines. Yet it was the Negro community that was to be primarily affected. . . .

Maximum Feasible Misunderstanding is colored by Moynihan's resentment of fellow social scientists he accused of functioning as reformers first and professionals second. He charged that as they became progressively more radical, any desire to bring the poor into the system was supplanted by "near detestation of the system itself," echoing James Baldwin's taunt about integrating with a burning house.

Harry McPherson, a senior White House aide who had no such personal involvement, bore him out. McPherson recalled the internal struggle over poverty policy between "those who wished to acculturate the poor into the folkways of the middleclass and those who sought to arrange for the poor to seize power through community action programs." The result was the diversion of most of the limited resources of the OEO to new agencies "envisioned as radical alternatives to the traditional bureaus that served the caring and teaching roles of government."

By the end of 1966, the OEO was supporting community action programs in all fifty of the largest cities. Thousands of local blacks were hired at substantial salaries to organize neighborhood councils charged with formulating and implementing programs to meet needs identified by the poor themselves. The councils were ostensibly elected, with

voting restricted to those below the poverty line. But the actual participation of eligible voters hardly provided a feasible basis for operating
social agencies: 0.7 percent in Los Angeles, 2.4 in Boston, 2.7 in
Philadelphia, 4.2 in Cleveland, 5.0 in Kansas City.

Criticism came from the left as well as the right, and black veterans
of the civil rights movement joined in. Bayard Rustin spoke out against
"the bedlam of community action programs, which have made ghetto
political activity more difficult, not less." Kenneth Clark, a close observer of developments in Harlem, charged that programs designed to
take control away from the politicians became pork barrel operations in
their own right as they were

> taken over by sophisticated middleclass bureaucrats. In some
> cases upwardly mobile working class individuals became either
> the products or the puppets of the . . . controllers of these pro-
> grams. Sometimes the upwardly mobile indigenous became
> sophisticated poverty hustlers.

Reaction in city halls, state legislatures, and Congress followed; by
1967 big-city Democrats were leading the drive to cut back OEO
appropriations.

There were, of course, ideological overtones to the controversy, as
there always were in any political approach involving poverty and race
relations. But Moynihan thought it was the unreality of the leftward-
leaning "guerrillas" that doomed the War on Poverty:

> This is the eseential fact: *The government did not know what it
> was doing.* It had a theory. Or, rather, a set of theories. Nothing
> more. The U.S. government at this time was no more in pos-
> session of confident knowledge of how to prevent delinquency,
> cure anomie, or overcome that midmorning sense of power-
> lessness, than was it in possession of a dependable formula for
> motivating Vietnamese villagers to fight Communism.

In his second tour of duty in Washington, a single sentence in a memorandum to President Nixon taken out of context by his detractors did
further damage to Pat Moynihan's standing in the liberal community:

"The time may have come when the issue of race could benefit from a period of 'benign neglect.' " This was construed to mean that he advocated suspending the federal government's obligation to redress the deprivation blacks had suffered as a result of slavery and second-class citizenship.

What Moynihan did advocate was suspending the stultifying controls imposed on the poor in response to the ingrained conservative conviction that inability to earn a living resulted from lack of character. Under prevailing doctrine, if public charity was necessary to prevent starvation, it should be limited to those who could be certified as not being in need because they were lazy or dissolute.

The necessity of guaranteeing that only the deserving poor received the government's largess had shaped the welfare programs from their beginning under the New Deal. Bureaucratized social workers were charged with seeing to it that benefits were limited to those who had no possibility of earning a subsistence income. Particularly bothersome to moralists was the fact that single mothers who were kept out of the job market by the need to care for dependent small children could meet the means test if there was no able-bodied man in the house. As erosion of the ghetto family structure resulted in increasing illegitimacy, the perception that the government was subsidizing bastardy became a prime issue for the religious right.

In the state legislatures, laws were regularly proposed to remove from the rolls the mothers of illegitimate children. Cooler heads usually prevailed by pointing out that in thus imposing the wages of sin, the punishment would fall on the child, who was surely not a party to it. I remember attending a welfare conference where a veteran Alabama official offered a challenge to the theory of deterrence that produced nods of agreement from his colleagues. "It is my considered opinion," he said, "that at the moment of conception of a bastard child neither party is thinking about the welfare payment."

Moynihan proposed eliminating the means test, and the bureaucracy required to enforce it, by instituting a "reverse income tax." Those who reported to the Internal Revenue Service an income below the poverty level would be entitled to a sum that made up the difference. This had the virtue of reducing the disincentive effect of the existing system's requirement of total destitution. It would provide for partial payments to cover the income deficit for the working poor male unable to maintain a wife and children on the wages usually available to unskilled blacks.

Moynihan's proposal required that Washington assume sole responsibility for funding and administering welfare programs, thus fitting neatly into President Nixon's proclaimed New Federalism. Since it relieved the states of the burden of matching funds and administrative costs, it received overwhelming endorsement when he presented it to the National Governors' Conference. The lone defender of states' rights was Lester Maddox, Georgia's pick-handle segregationist, who presumably wanted to be rid of welfare altogether.

Elimination of the costly, unwieldy, and intrusive state and local welfare bureaucracy was welcomed by many of those who had applied experience with the social pathology Moynihan cited. New York City welfare commissioner Mitchell I. Ginsberg was struck by the irony of the new posture assumed by Richard Nixon:

> Here, coming from a Republican, is something that amounts to a guaranteed annual income. We'll have to call it something else, naturally. Something to make it sound like the free enterprise system. . . . We'll have to move toward compulsory national health insurance, too, and Washington will have to dream up something to call that. But I don't give a damn what they are called as long as they get done.

Nixon did create some new titles to camouflage programs proposed to meet the assumption embodied in the Moynihan approach—that the only effective way to reduce the welfare rolls was to open up job opportunities for those able to work. In the name of "black capitalism" he set up the Office of Minority Business, and pressed construction unions to adopt timetables for opening their ranks to minorities—an adaptation of affirmative action to guarantee minority employment that proved to be anathema to his party's right wing. "No Democrat ever so shredded market principles in peacetime," the disapproving conservative columnist George Will wrote. "It was the most radical intrusiveness by government since Prohibition."

But the programs designed to provide outreach to blacks never got more than lip service from the president. Roy Wilkins of the NAACP was soon dismissing them with a Southern folk saying: "He talk so good—but he *do* so po." By midterm the programs inspired by Pat Moynihan's second coming had quietly disappeared from the presidential agenda.

The Moynihan formula's emphasis on the use of existing ghetto institutions to implement poverty programs accepted the fact that, outside the rural South, most black welfare recipients lived in segregated inner city neighborhoods destined to stay that way, at least through the formative years of the children being born there. But acceptance of residential segregation as a governing fact in devising public policy marked a departure from one of the tenets of the liberal faith—that in a democratic society families should have the right to live anywhere they choose. The right obviously did not extend to blacks, since it was evident that no one would choose of his own free will to remain in the squalid quarters occupied by most of those resident in the inner cities.

The U.S. Supreme Court had ruled that restrictive real-estate covenants requiring owners to refuse to rent or sell property to blacks had no legal standing and could not be enforced, but this had little practical effect. Collusion among homeowners, landlords, real-estate brokers, developers, and lending institutions continued to maintain almost universal *de facto* segregation. In the 1960s more than 70 percent of all urban black families lived in substandard dwellings—those that did not meet public health requirements because of dilapidation and/or lack of minimum sanitary facilities. The percentage of whites in such dwellings was less than 20 percent. Market forces worked to maintain the pattern since the overcrowding produced as migrants and immigrants flocked into closed-off inner city neighborhoods made investment in slum housing highly profitable. Square foot for square foot, and in terms of services rendered, blacks typically paid more for housing than any other class of citizens. Moreover, virtually all of it was in areas deficient in parks, playgrounds, and public services and served by the oldest and most decrepit of public schools.

As far back as the New Deal it had been recognized that urban real-estate values had risen to the point that the market could no longer provide decent, affordable housing for most city dwellers. Creation of the Federal Housing Authority (FHA) in 1934 provided government-insured, low-rate, long-term mortgages to create a market for builders who met stipulated design and construction standards. The result was a growth in home ownership from 48 percent in 1930 to 63 percent in 1965, with most of the new dwellings in suburban neighborhoods that formed a "white noose" around the inner cities.

In 1937, in recognition of the fact that the FHA was of no benefit to poor families, federal funding was provided to permit local authorities to build public housing. These typically were three-story bare-bones apartment buildings designed for the "deserving poor," and rentals were established on the basis of income. Until 1947 there was no effort to ensure open occupancy, and all public housing developments were reserved exclusively for either whites or blacks, *de jure* in the South, *de facto* elsewhere. The black units were located in existing black neighborhoods.

It is significant that during this period the leading Senate advocates of subsidized public housing were the conservative Robert A. Taft of Ohio, the Dixiecrat Allen Ellender of Louisiana, and the liberal Robert Wagner of New York. The issue was not social reform—although castigation of callous slum landlords had been a feature of municipal politics for many years. Rather it was belated recognition of the failure of government at all levels to deal with the effects of demographic change. William L. Slayton, who headed the Urban Renewal Administration created by President Kennedy in 1961, noted that when he took office much of the urban landscape was in a "state of desolation":

> The slow but inexorable detritus of two centuries of settlement and uncontrolled development, plus fifteen years of stagnation in construction caused by the Great Depression and the demands of World War II, had brought our nation's urban areas to the dramatic deterioration of their physical plants with its attendant effects upon their homes, their businesses, and their cultural environment.

Until 1949 federally subsidized public housing was presumed to provide temporary quarters for upwardly mobile tenants who were in the process of improving their lot and who were expected to move on. But when the emphasis at the FHA shifted to urban renewal programs under which the land freed by slum clearance could be used for nonresidential purposes, the social criteria were abandoned and access to public housing was required for all displaced families—most of whom were black.

The relocation requirement introduced the race issue into public housing. Discrimination continued and became so blatant that, Slayton noted, "one often heard urban renewal derisively described as 'Negro removal.' " By 1962 President Kennedy was under mounting pressure from the civil rights leadership to alter federal housing policy. "To me, the issue is simple," Eleanor Roosevelt wrote in her newspaper column, "we cannot eliminate segregation in jobs, education or churches until we eliminate segregation in housing." It wasn't that simple to Kennedy, but he did issue an executive order establishing an antidiscrimination policy covering federally subsidized housing, including the "gentrified" middle-income housing created when slums were cleared.

Slayton made a manful effort to enforce the new policy, but its impact was limited to new housing constructed after the executive order was issued—leaving out all existing public housing, and actually applying to less than 20 percent of annual housing starts. Lyndon Johnson created the President's Committee on Equal Housing Opportunity, which recommended that the neutral policies still followed by most federal agencies concerned with housing be replaced by an affirmative commitment to nondiscrimination. But constitutional and political restraints prevented broadening the reach of the policy until 1968, when Johnson sent to Congress the first federal fair housing law.

The Potomac Institute collaborated informally with Slayton and other officials in the modification of housing policies, and before he left the Urban Renewal Administration to return to the private sector, he played for an assemblage of housing officials the recording of a satirical lyric composed by Harold Fleming. Sung to the tune of "St. Louis Blues," it represented the complaint of the civil rights leadership as personified by a slum resident:

I hate to see that dear old slum go down.
I hate to see that dear old slum go down.
There's no place for me in this whole damn town.

I'm movin' tomorrow just like I moved today.
Movin' tomorrow just like I moved today.
Here comes the bulldozer to push my house away.

I got the blues, got the blues, got the relocation blues.
I'm on the booze . . . 'cause I know I'm bound to lose.
I can't choose, can't refuse.
I got the relocation blues.

The use of federal funding and authority to promote the integration of the black minority into the larger society would continue, with requirements for "scatter-site" housing producing a mixture of middle-income black and white families in new or rehabilitated dwellings usually located in fringe areas where segregated neighborhoods had begun to overlap. With the support of federal and state antidiscrimination laws, middle-class blacks who conformed to the life-style of their white peers began to gain access to previously restricted housing in the suburbs. But despite the billions presumably invested in their clearance, the black slums endured and continued to deteriorate.

The evident failure of integrationist policies fostered increasing separatist sentiment among blacks, and there were some in the civil rights movement who accepted the pragmatic argument that poverty programs must be based on the assumption that segregation of poor blacks would continue for the politically foreseeable future.

Although it attracted little attention in the presidential campaign that marked the end of the Democratic ascendancy, a U.S. Supreme Court decision turning on that central question was handed down in 1968, and it became a prime factor in the drastically changed political climate that followed. In its own effort to deal with the reality of residential segregation, the Court issued new orders for the implementation of the *Brown* decision that ended the possibility of treating school desegregation as a regional issue.

In practice school integration had effectively come to a halt in the South under the "freedom of choice" policy approved by the federal courts. Finally taking note that its good-faith standard of compliance with the *Brown* mandate was being grossly abused, the Supreme Court issued a unanimous opinion that "the burden on a school board today is to come forward with a [desegregation] plan that promises realistically to work, and promises realistically to work *now*."

In turning down an appeal from Mississippi for more time, the Court ruled that "all deliberate speed is no longer constitutionally permissible," and set December 31, 1969, as a deadline for achieving a unitary system. When the order came down, nine of ten black children in the state were still attending all-black schools; a year later the proportion had dropped to one of ten. In the Southern and border states and in the District of Columbia, where 96.1 percent of black students had been in segregated schools before *Brown*, the proportion was down to 19 percent by 1971.

To bring about such wholesale change the Court for the first time began to take into consideration *de facto* as opposed to *de jure* segregation—that is, the existence of black and white schools where the law did not require them. This was the case with those attended by a great majority of urban children, since almost all were located in attendance districts defined by neighborhood. Without a change in the residential patterns that prevailed throughout the nation, children would have to be redistributed if the races were to be mixed effectively in the classroom.

In 1970 the *Swann* case, appealed from the Charlotte-Mecklenburg district in North Carolina, placed the issue, and the only feasible short-term remedy, before the Supreme Court. To comply with the new guidelines a district court had ordered the school board to redraw its attendance districts and provide buses to transfer children of both races to achieve a racial balance that would finally eliminate predominantly black schools.

By the time *Swann* landed on the high bench, Earl Warren, who held his brethren together through the wave of litigation that followed *Brown*, had been replaced by Richard Nixon's appointee as chief justice, Warren Burger. Although Burger wrote the opinion upholding the *Swann* ruling on behalf of a unanimous Court, it was clear that he was beset by trepidation. Departure from the concept of the neighborhood school, he wrote, might well be "administratively awkward, inconvenient and even bizarre in some situations, and may impose burdens on some." Nevertheless, he concluded, "desegregation plans cannot be limited to the walk-in school."

This was an attack on an institution that had achieved the status of an icon as the system of universal education developed throughout the United States. The threat to the presumed right of children to attend school in their own neighborhood precipitated a political paroxysm when the Supreme Court ruling against *de facto* segregation extended the impact of *Brown* beyond the Mason-Dixon line. In the massive 1978 study he titled *Must We Bus?*, Gary Orfield summarized the result:

> As [busing] plans were adopted, first in the South and then in some northern cities, opinion polarized against the desegregation orders. Within a year many political leaders, much of the mass media, and some members of the academic community had joined the opposition for the first time since 1954. . . .
>
> After a tumultuous decade of social and cultural change, a nation that had been torn by war, stunned by urban crisis, and shaken by assassinations, was not prepared to recognize or cope with metropolitan apartheid. People denied that the problem existed, claimed that it was being solved, argued that blacks and Latinos liked segregation anyway, or most often attacked the proposed solutions.

Swann, as it turned out, marked the forward thrust of the civil rights movement as far as poor blacks were concerned. "In the last third of the twentieth century, the school experience of black children had lost any geographical peculiarity," Meyer Weinberg wrote in *A Chance to Learn*. "Deprivation was the common experience throughout the country."

Looking forward to reelection, Nixon recognized that the Supreme Court had provided a prime opportunity to put into effect the "Southern Strategy" he had rejected in favor of moderation in the 1968 campaign. The climate was right for exploitation of rising white resentment against blacks and their political supporters, now being evidenced in all sections of the country. "Forced busing is wrong," the president told his speechwriter, William Safire, "and I don't care if it sounds like demagoguery— I want to say so loud and clear." He did that, and more.

To enlist the support of unreconstructed Southerners he moved to curtail enforcement of desegregation orders and promised to appoint judges to the federal bench who would undo the precedents set by the Warren Court. This produced what Orfield termed the most sudden shift on civil rights in the century:

> The conflict between the judicial requirements for busing and the President's active leadership of antibusing forces produced a severe institutional crisis in HEW and Justice. Bureaucracies created to enforce civil rights laws found themselves with controversial responsibilities in a political climate that had suddenly changed.

In a special message to Congress, Nixon set forth proposals he asserted would improve educational opportunities for minority children while eliminating what he characterized as the evils of busing. The message was a prime example of the discrepancy between rhetoric and reality that has continued to characterize the political debate over the means of dealing with the special problems of minority education.

Busing was not a sudden invention of the federal judiciary. It had been a part of the public school system since it was introduced as a means of improving the educational opportunities of children in rural areas. Assembling students over a considerable area made it possible to replace the one-room country schoolhouse with consolidated schools large enough to maintain a range of faculty and facilities. But in the Jim Crow states, black children had been left standing by the side of the road when the school bus passed. Evidence offered in the *Brown* litigation showed that Clarendon County, South Carolina, provided 30 buses for 2,375 white students attending 12 consolidated schools, but none for 6,531 blacks consigned to 61 dilapidated one- or two-room shacks.

The frustration and rage the president cited in his message to Congress had appeared only when busing was used to improve educational opportunities for minority children. Rapidly changing demography had long since brought the school bus to town; before desegregation was ordered in any city outside the South, more than half of urban schoolchildren were bused, and others were delivered by private automobiles or public transportation. For most Americans, the neighborhood school had become a fading memory; children who still walked to school were largely confined to affluent white suburbs.

The reality, however, did little to diminish the furor generated by the president's attack on busing, and it undoubtedly made a major contribution to his reelection. Kevin Phillips, who had served on Nixon's campaign staff in 1968, was now situated in the White House as the instigator, or at least the articulator of the Southern Strategy. He approached it as the means of bringing about a basic political realignment.

The object was to transform the Republicans into a national majority by luring into the fold two previously incompatible elements: conservative Southern Protestants alienated by the party's abolitionist heritage; and blue-collar workers, many of whom were Catholic, who resented the intrusion of blacks into their neighborhoods and workplaces. The coalition was subsequently reinforced by the hot-button "social issues" of birth control, abortion, and homosexuality that made political bedfellows of Catholic bishops and fundamentalist TV evangelists.

Tracing the effects of white backlash, Phillips concluded that a new populism was emerging, one that came from the right, not the left as before. In an interview with Garry Wills, he set forth the premise that has dominated Republican strategy ever since:

> The clamor in the past has been from the urban or rural proletariat. But now "populism" is of the middleclass, which feels exploited by the Establishment. Almost everyone in the productive segment of society considers himself middleclass now, and resents the exploitation of society's producers. This is not a movement in *favor of* laissez faire or any ideology; it is *opposed* *to* welfare and the Establishment.

The Southern Strategy required that the moderate pretensions of the New Federalism be abandoned in favor of a return to the Old Federalism under which racial segregation had been permitted wherever a white majority insisted on it. The Supreme Court was not yet disposed to temper desegregation rulings based on the *Brown* precedent, but it was possible for the president to vitiate the enforcement powers vested in the executive branch. He did so in a fashion that soon disposed of virtually all the poverty programs inherited from the previous administration.

His embittered predecessor, down on the LBJ ranch regaling Doris Kearns with the remarkable soliloquies recorded in *Lyndon Johnson and the American Dream*, told her, "There's a story in the paper every day about him slashing another one of my Great Society programs. I can just see him waking up in the morning, making that victory sign of his, and deciding which program to kill."

The great battles of the Kennedy and Johnson years had been fought in Congress to ensure federal intervention when local authorities refused to protect or advance the rights of blacks. Although the term did not come into general usage until later, the necessity for "affirmative action" by the legislative and executive branches to achieve desegregation was implicit in *Brown*. The 1964 Civil Rights Act pushed through by Lyndon Johnson as a memorial to Jack Kennedy forbade the payment of federal funds to school districts that continued discriminatory practices, and authorized the Justice Department to bring civil rights cases on its own motion. Vigorous enforcement by Johnson appointees at Justice and at Health, Education and Welfare followed.

While there were still Democratic majorities in both houses of Congress, Nixon cemented a working relationship with the congressional segregationist bloc by acceding to their demand that he fire the civil rights enforcement chief at HEW. Leon Panetta's offense was carrying out his statutory duty to withhold federal funds from schools defying court-ordered desegregation. He departed the federal service with a valedictory statement that applied across the whole of the civil rights front:

> Desegregated education has been upheld as legal principle, it has been pursued as public policy, with more success than many will admit, and it should not be undone where it is successful merely because of the rabid screams of those who would make political hay out of racial antagonism. . . . The issue is the future of the nation's race relations.

That kind of political hay ensured Richard Nixon's victory in the 1972 presidential election. By openly appealing to racist sentiment he abandoned any pretense of seeking the support of black voters, whose numbers were still increasing. Kevin Phillips had discounted their loss. "When white Southerners move, they move fast," he said in 1968, predicting that George Wallace's third-party candidacy would facilitate the process. "People will ease their way into the Republican Party by way of the American Independents." That, he pointed out, was how the followers of Strom Thurmond had made the transition after the Dixiecrat bolt in 1948. "We'll get two thirds to three fourths of the Wallace vote in 1972."

Running in the general election, Wallace had taken votes from the Democratic candidate, but if he made another third-party bid he would garner the votes of Southern segregationists whose support Nixon was counting on. In 1972 the Wallace role most useful under the Southern Strategy required his entry in the primaries, where he could weaken the ultimate Democratic nominee. The arrangement that brought about the little Alabamian's return to the fray as a born-again Democrat has a place in the annals of the dirty tricks that became standard in the Nixon White House.

Wallace had returned to the governor's office after the death of his wife, Lurleen, and was vulnerable to an IRS investigation of the income-tax returns of Gerald Wallace, his brother and former law partner who handled his private political transactions. This was duly launched in 1971, with Gerald Wallace soon complaining that the forty-seven IRS agents on his tail were "trying to beat George Wallace. You're not interested in my tax returns." In his 1989 biography *Nixon: The Triumph of a Politician 1962–72*, Stephen E. Ambrose recounted the outcome:

> In mid-1971 Nixon asked Wallace to fly with him from Mobile to Birmingham. What they talked about on that brief flight is not known. On January 12, 1972 the IRS announced that it was dropping its investigation of Gerald Wallace. The next day, George Wallace announced that he was entering the Democratic party primaries. The Democrats were disconcerted and alarmed. Larry O'Brien [the national chairman] disavowed the Wallace candidacy. George Meany [AFL-CIO president] denounced Wallace as a "bigot and racist." Nixon kept his reaction to himself.

Wallace, entering the race against twelve fairly prominent Democratic contenders, was confident that he could reinforce the message he had sent the national establishment his last time out. In Florida, where he confounded the pundits by coming in first, he no doubt had something more tangible than premonition when he predicted that if he won the primary, President Nixon would do something to halt busing within thirty days. It didn't take that long. Two days after the election, the president proposed a moratorium.

Wallace provided a striking example of the paralyzing effect the race issue has always had on the political process. His opponents in both parties were loath to express their low opinion of him and his tactics for fear of directing against themselves the passions he inspired. Richard Reeves, a veteran campaign correspondent, thought this accounted for Wallace's successful career as a political spoiler:

> Over the past few years I have talked with almost every Presidential-class candidate about the Alabama governor, and their assessments of him are just about identical. He is, in their minds, an ignorant and dangerous demagogue playing on the fears and darkest impulses of a segment of the nation. But even though national polls indicated that as many as two thirds of the American people were strongly anti-Wallace, these judgments stayed locked in the minds of Humphrey, the Kennedys, McGovern, Rockefeller. They said nothing—even when Wallace's national support was only at 10 percent and their united voices might have destroyed him. The inertial two thirds was not their problem; they were afraid of an aroused 10 percent.

How the Wallace campaign would have affected the outcome of the Democratic primary became moot when, as he circulated among his supporters in Maryland, another deranged gunman wormed his way through the crowd and fired a bullet into his belly that took the feisty Alabamian out of the race and left him confined to a wheelchair for the rest of his life. As Wallace lay paralyzed in the hospital, Richard Nixon called to offer his sympathy. The prone Wallace, an Air Force veteran of World War II, offered a snappy military salute when the president arose to depart, and it was duly returned. Wallace had every reason to believe that his cause was marching on.

When George Wallace carried the Michigan primary, George Mc-Govern, who ran third, behind Hubert Humphrey, made no effective move to denounce Wallace's blatant tactics. McGovern was restrained, I thought, by instinctive, deep-rooted civility. No one spoke out more consistently on controversial issues, but McGovern did so in the reasoned manner of the history professor he had once been at South Dakota Wesleyan in his native state. Entering politics in 1951 as a liberal Democrat, he served in Congress until he was defeated in a 1960 race for the Senate. President Kennedy appointed him director of Food for Peace, and in 1962 he won his state's other senate seat and became an outspoken opponent of the Vietnam War.

No one ever had any reason to doubt George McGovern's idealism or his courage. He had demonstrated the latter as a decorated Air Corps pilot in World War II, and he would display the former, often to his detriment, in his run for the presidency. After the debacle of the 1968 Democratic convention, where Edward Kennedy designated him the inheritor of his brother Bobby's delegates, McGovern became chairman of the Commission on Party Structure and Delegate Selection, charged with opening the party to those who complained that they had been excluded from its inner councils. The changes the commission wrought assured his nomination in 1972, and guaranteed his defeat.

McGovern had been helpful in the planning and organization of the *Pacem in Terris* convocations, and I had a high regard for him. Blair Clark, who as a representative of Gene McCarthy's supporters had been named cochairman of the McGovern primary campaign, took me to meet with him in Washington, and I came away with the feeling that, whether he intended it not, the McGovern Commission recommendations were a triumph for the youthful advocates of participatory rather than representative democracy. The effect this would have on the traditional Democrats whose support he would need in the general election did not seem to be a matter of much concern.

The last chance of holding together key elements of the old Democratic coalition vanished at the national convention in Miami. The new party rules required that each state organization must include in its delegation appropriate representation by youth, minorities, and women. And in 1971 the proportion of youthful delegates was increased by ratification of the Twenty-sixth Amendment to the Constitution enacted by Congress and reluctantly signed by Richard Nixon. With the voting age lowered to eighteen, college students became eligible for full participation in the nominating process.

The protest movements that gained blacks and youths seats at the Democratic convention had raised the consciousness of another faction that considered its members politically disadvantaged although they had been enfranchised for half a century. When the youthful and black delegates moved to support the demands of the insurgent women's caucus, George McGovern's supporters lost control of the convention. Theodore White thought the defining moment of a new interest-based coalition emerged with

> the explosion on the convention floor of that issue which torments modern women most—abortion, for the first time publicly debated at a convention in the presence of television. Forced to floor debate by their caucus, opposed by the governing McGovern majority as a political disaster about to happen . . . shouted down by voice vote at the command of McGovern whips—nonetheless, there was the issue, now out in the open. Should not a woman have personal control over her own body's reproductive processes as fully as a man?

Emboldened, the women's caucus on Thursday afternoon organized an impromptu vice presidential drive for Frances "Sissy" Farenthold, a Texas delegate, and by midnight had mustered 404 votes for her—not enough to put her on the ticket, but enough to astound the convention and prompt George McGovern to withdraw his commitment to the deserving party veteran Lawrence O'Brien and appoint the first Democratic party chairwoman, Jean Westwood. Each concession they won increased the pressures from the dissident factions, producing still more flip-flopping in the course of what White, looking back on his quarter century of political coverage, rated "the most mismanaged campaign in modern history."

· · ·

Richard Nixon had no opposition in his bid for renomination, and very little in the general election. He had finessed the war issue with a plan calling for phased withdrawal of American ground forces, ultimately leaving it to the South Vietnamese to defend themselves. Fatally flawed though it proved to be, the "Vietnamization" policy served its immediate political purpose by permitting substantial numbers of American troops to return home. Late in October Henry Kissinger topped off the ploy by announcing from the Paris negotiating table that an honorable peace treaty was in sight.

With continued American air support, the shaky South Vietnamese regime was able to stave off the inevitable defeat until 1975, but this was possible only because as early as 1969 Nixon secretly authorized bombing raids on Laos and a ground incursion across the border into neutral Cambodia that diverted the North Vietnamese by spreading the conflict to all of the former French colonies in Southeast Asia. But by the time this clandestine maneuvering was revealed to the American people it had become a minor item in the panoply of deception that brought down the Nixon administration.

It is an ironic fact that the secret plotting and illegal acts on the domestic side that led to Nixon's forced resignation one step ahead of impeachment began in the course of an election he had no chance of losing. The sub rosa operations conducted by the "dirty tricks" squad maintained by CREEP—the acronym for the Committee to Re-elect the President—had little if anything to do with the defeat of his Democratic opponent by one of the widest margins in history. Nixon's electoral vote was 520 against 17 for George McGovern.

But it was more a case of self-destruction by the Democrats than of triumph by the Republicans. The Southern Strategy had produced the landslide electoral vote, but it had provided Nixon with no coattails. The Democrats retained control of both the Senate and the House, and there were few in Washington who still doubted that the old Nixon known as "tricky Dick" had been in the White House all along.

James Reston, explaining away his own temporary delusion, would write an appropriate epitaph for the political chameleon who was re-certified as president of the United States: "There is scarcely a noble principle in the American Constitution that he hasn't defended in theory or defied in practice."

INTERLUDE
JERRY, JIMMY, AND JESSE

In the panhandle of Florida during the primary election campaign, I'd had my first real understanding of how much it would mean to Southerners to have one of their own elected President. Governor George Wallace had told Floridians that a vote for him would "send a message to Washington." A vote for me, I told them, would send a President there. . . . We in the South were ready for reconciliation, to be accepted as equals, to rejoin the mainstream of American political life. This yearning for what might be called political redemption was a significant factor in my successful campaign.

—JIMMY CARTER,
Keeping Faith: Memoirs of a President, 1982

IT SEEMS LIKELY that no president of the United States has been subjected to more professional and amateur psychoanalysis than Richard Nixon, although as far as I know he has never stretched out on an analyst's couch. While he was still riding high in the White House he decided to preserve his private conversations, if not his inner thoughts, and the small portion of that record made public has fascinated those seeking insight into the Jekyll and Hyde aspects of his public career.

In 1971 he had the Secret Service install voice-activated recorders to capture on tape all telephone and personal exchanges with those he dealt with in the Oval Office or the hideaways where he did most of his brooding and plotting. This record, compiled without the knowledge of virtually all of the other participants, was to be used in preparing his version of the historic events that took place on his watch, and in the quarter century since he was drummed out of office he has successfully fought to keep it out of the public domain.

The existence of the recorders was known only to the few in the White House who could be said to enjoy the president's confidence, which was limited at best. The tapes first came to public notice in 1974, when, under court order, selected passages were made available to the judge presiding over the trial of the members of the CREEP team arrested in the course of a bungled burglary attempt at the headquarters of the Democratic National Committee in the Watergate building.

Excerpts from the tapes revealed that the president had orchestrated a massive cover-up of the involvement of senior White House officials in the Watergate burglary. The evidence of improper use of government agencies at his direction led the House Judiciary Committee to set in motion impeachment proceedings, and before further action could be taken, Nixon resigned.

Only sixty of the four thousand hours of recorded conversations were made public at the trial. The rest have remained sequestered in the National Archives, heard only by the professional staff that processed all 950 reels and made them ready for public release. Millions of dollars spent on court action by Nixon have kept them embargoed, and in 1992 a federal court declared them the property of the former president.

However, there have been leaks that have prompted further revelations by some of those who served prison terms as a result of the Watergate trials. They show what one of the key participants, Charles W. Colson, termed the black side of the natures of the president and his fellow conspirators. In an article in *The New Yorker*, Seymour M. Hersh cited examples of Nixon's abandonment of even minimum standards of taste as he tried to act like the raunchy man's man he clearly wasn't.

"The tapes show him to be a racist," Hersh wrote. "Pejorative words and phrases dominated much of his private talk. Jews were 'kikes,' blacks were 'niggers,' and reporters were 'press pricks.' " When officials of a professional organization told the president they provided scholarships for blacks, he responded, "Well, it's a good thing. They are just down from the trees."

This behavior fits the dictionary definition of racism as "a belief or doctrine that inherent differences among the various human races determine cultural or individual achievement, usually involving the idea that one's own race is superior and has the right to rule others." It was no longer considered proper to display such sentiments publicly, but there was no reason to doubt that this continued to be the belief of a considerable majority of white Americans in the 1970s, although their right to rule others had been proscribed by law and was no longer officially acted on.

Nixon had been reared by a Quaker mother who practiced her religion's preachment of racial tolerance, and he continued to give lip service to the ideal. But like other moral restraints, it could not prevail when it ran counter to what he perceived to be his political interest. He was never to deviate from the dictum taught by Murray Chotiner, the California lawyer who introduced him to elective politics: A successful campaign must be negative, predicated on the idea that most people vote *against*, not *for*. A candidate, therefore, should expose as little of his own position as possible, while concentrating on real or trumped-up aspects of his opponent's life and record that most people are disposed to resent.

It followed that the Southern Strategy would prove irresistible to Richard Nixon when his political calculus demonstrated that resentment against government action deemed to favor blacks at the expense of whites had reached the point where handing over the black vote to the Democrats would be a detriment to his opposition in a national election.

Gerald R. Ford, who took over the White House on August 9, 1974, upon Nixon's abdication, was the temperamental opposite of the furtive, inward-looking man he replaced. An amiable former college football player, he had plodded upward through the Republican ranks as an extroverted hail fellow well met called "Jerry" by his most casual acquaintances. His commonplace persona made him believable when he pledged an administration of "openness and candor."

But that impression could not survive the absolution he granted Nixon a month later, for Ford was an unelected president who had been put in line for the office by the man he granted a blanket pardon "for all offenses against the United States." In October 1973 Nixon had selected him for the vice presidency when it was vacated by the forced resignation of Spiro Agnew, the truculent hatchet man who gave voice to Nixon's running campaign against the media's "nattering nabobs of negativism." Agnew was brought down by the revelation of petty boodling going back to his career as a maverick governor of Maryland.

There was nothing in Ford's record to indicate that he would deviate in any way from the policies put in place by his benefactor. Elected to Congress in 1948 from a safe Republican district in Michigan, his seniority made him House minority leader in 1965. In that post he delivered 85 to 90 percent of the votes of Republican House members against Great Society legislation. He maintained partisan solidarity when the Republicans regained the White House, and when Nixon sought to vent his frustration at the Senate's rejection of his anti–civil rights Supreme Court nominees, Ford obligingly launched an abortive effort to impeach Justice William O. Douglas.

Nixon had not quite finished off the Office of Economic Opportunity when he was distracted by Watergate, but his staff was still working on the last vestiges of the War on Poverty when Gerald Ford took over. On his fifth day in the Oval Office, he found on his desk an action memorandum from Kenneth Cole, the White House domestic affairs chief, recommending the final disposition of the agency.

From 1969 onward, Cole noted, Nixon had considered OEO "inappropriate," and had provided for its termination in the 1974–75 budget. This would be "consistent with philosophy that Community Action is more properly a state/local program and save the Federal Government over $300,000,000." The new president initialed the box indicating approval.

Ford's open, unassuming personal style altered the bunker mentality the White House staff had evidenced under Nixon, but that was the only noticeable change during his brief tenure. The abandonment of poverty programs in the name of states' rights was entirely compatible with his record in the House. In A Ford, Not a Lincoln, a title taken from the president's description of himself, Richard Reeves wrote:

Amendments, motions to recommit and other parliamentary parlor tricks make it possible for Rep. Ford to assert that he voted for final passage of every civil rights bill during his tenure.

Or he can let people know that up until the final votes, he fought to block every piece of civil rights legislation. He did both. . . . Whatever Ford's deepest feelings about civil rights— and friends said he had no deep feelings either way—he was able and willing to use that issue and others to trade for the valuable status of having no enemies in his own party.

On the campaign trail in Michigan, Reeves heard Ford bring up busing sixteen times in seventeen minutes without being asked, "repeatedly implying that the Democratic Party and any fellow travelers were dedicated to dragging blue-eyed children into the deepest wilds." As president, he erected an official monument to his opposition to desegregation when Boston police were unable, or unwilling, to handle violent demonstrations outside the city's public schools. Mayor Kevin White, as had the mayor of Little Rock, requested help from the force of U.S. marshals the Justice Department had used in the South to contain similar protests against federal court orders.

Ford declined the request, saying, "The court decision in that case in my judgment was not the best solution to quality education in Boston. I respectfully disagree with the judge's order." The president's tacit endorsement of mob action to defy the federal courts ignored the precedent set by a unanimous Supreme Court in the Little Rock case, and guaranteed continuation of turmoil in the ethnic neighborhoods of the one-time abolitionist stronghold.

The recalcitrance of the Nixon/Ford administration effectively nullified the Supreme Court's mandate requiring affirmative action by all branches of the federal government to end official discrimination against blacks. As it was implemented under Presidents Kennedy and Johnson, the interpretation of constitutional principle implicit in *Brown* had cleared the way for considerable progress by the black middleclass, but two decades after its enactment it was clear that it had brought about little change in the status of the poorly educated and socially disadvantaged majority of the minority.

Walker Percy, the most philosophical of the Southern novelists, thought the reason for this was demonstrated by the first lesson to be drawn from the history of his own region:

Where there is a racially distinct minority whose well-being depends to a degree upon law and to a degree upon the good nature of the majority, the minority will be buggered precisely to the degree that the law allows—even when there is considerable good nature at hand. No man can hold out for long against another man's helplessness. Sooner or later one will be seduced and the other will be buggered.

Once they were forced to face up to it, most white Southerners recognized that this was a fact of the life they had accepted as ordained. Despite the social barriers of segregation, the shared experience of blacks and whites in the ordinary affairs of daily life had created a reservoir of good will that eased the rapid and dramatic changes that came when the law no longer allowed discrimination in public schools and colleges, places of public accommodation, and employment.

Blacks who had the benefit of the generally effective if materially inferior urban schools, and had been conditioned by the middleclass values that prevailed in families far down the income scale, found ready acceptance in the marketplace. Dark faces began to be commonplace in downtown office buildings and behind hotel registration desks, bank tellers' windows, and the display counters of the most exclusive stores. With money in their pockets, the upscale black employees became valued customers for goods and services, and as their numbers increased there was upward progression into middle management.

The Southern cities still had poverty-stricken ghettos, although they were not as rigidly contained as those outside the region, and many blacks were trapped in pockets of poverty left behind in rural areas where farming no longer provided them a livelihood. Here, as elsewhere in the nation, Percy's law applied: Poor blacks were buggered by middleclass members of both races—and Washington no longer required or encouraged effective effort to bring them under the protection of antidiscrimination laws still on the books but far short of universal application.

. . .

A quarter century after the chief state school officers of the South assembled to consider the Ashmore Project's appraisal of the region's segregated educational system, I stood before their successors in a conference room at the Atlanta Biltmore Hotel. The Fund for the Advancement of Education had convened the first meeting of these elected officials in deepest secrecy, under oath to deny that it ever took place if word leaked that the possibility of desegregation had been mentioned in their presence. The successor gathering was aggressively public—a session financed by the National Institute of Education to consider means of carrying word of the future needs of education to the grass roots. And now each school chief was accompanied by a black deputy who obviously was not a token. In the keynote address I said:

> No one can seriously argue that the race problem is solved, but I do think it is taking on very different dimensions. . . . It is fair to say that we have reached a point where we can assume that racism—which until recently was the absolute determinant in your educational arrangements—is now a secondary problem, and a soluble one. If we look at the whole of the educational structure it would appear that the future of public education in the South is not significantly different from that facing schools and colleges everywhere in the nation.

The first question in the discussion period came from a black. "There surely have been a lot of changes on the surface," he conceded, "but do you think that, deep down, things are really different?" Yes, I replied, there has been a profound change:

> Twenty-five years ago the great majority of Southerners, white and black, believed the two races were fundamentally different. Now we know this is not so. And that's the root of the problem— blacks have turned out to be just like us, and we're no damned good.

This backhanded assertion of common humanity drew only thin smiles from most of the superintendents, but the laughter of their deputies shook the room.

The *Brown* decision was still pending in 1954 when I made my initial appearance before the schoolmen, and Senator J. William Fulbright had submitted to the Supreme Court a characteristically erudite *amicus curiae* brief based on a premise I had no doubt was shared by every member of my audience:

> The people of Arkansas endure against a background not without certain pathological aspects. They are marked in some ways by a strange disproportion inherited from the age of Negro slavery. The whites and Negroes are equally prisoners of their environment.

But, virtually overnight as history is reckoned, that environment had changed in a fashion that demonstrated that the pathological aspects of the interracial relationship were no longer operational in critical areas of daily life. In the days of the Ashmore Project the closest the staff could get to the Biltmore at mealtime was the office of the Southern Education Foundation a block away, where we shared catered barbecue sandwiches with our black colleagues. Now Atlanta had a black mayor, a black police chief, and a black Chamber of Commerce president, and a Georgia governor had united white and black Democrats in a fashion that would soon send to Washington the first Southern planter to occupy the White House since Zachary Taylor.

James Earl Carter, who insisted on being called "Jimmy" even in his official capacity, was an enigma to most Americans, including those who voted for him. In his public style he seemed to work at conforming to the stereotype that usually went with his status as a prosperous peanut farmer and small-town warehouse proprietor. He emphasized his cornpone accent and big, toothy smile, and instead of receiving visiting media representatives in the relatively sophisticated surroundings of Atlanta, he exposed them to Plains, his hometown down in Sumter

County, which not only looked like a television set but seemed to be populated by soap opera characters.

In action, however, Jimmy Carter came through as an Annapolis graduate with advanced training as a physicist and systems engineer. His acknowledged idol was Admiral Hyman Rickover, the Jewish martinet known as father of the nuclear submarine fleet in which Commander Carter performed his Navy service. He wore his Southern Baptist piety proudly, but he not only professed but acted on broad social concerns that required tolerance for those who could be judged, by the standards he set for himself, as sinful and weak.

These contradictions intrigued William Lee Miller, a former colleague of mine at the Center for the Study of Democratic Institutions, who covered the 1976 presidential campaign from the perspective of a professor of religious history with a special interest in ethics. A Northern Presbyterian who said he was born, at most, only once, Miller summarized his conclusions in the title of his book *Yankee from Georgia*.

To Miller, this deeply sincere fundamentalist displayed all the characteristics associated with the New England ethos. Carter, he wrote, acted on the traditional Yankee assumption that

life should be predictable, managed, planned. . . . Straighten things out; be competent; save money, save time; time is money. Save money, use it wisely, because for a Puritan to do so is Godly, and for a Yankee to do so is remunerative.

When the Civil Rights revolution ended the long moral isolation of the South and burst open the regional crust, Brother Jimmy, the Puritan-Baptist and warehouse owner, was ready to step forth into the world bearing the marks of an older, almost forgotten America.

Carter came along after my time in the South, and I did not know him, or any of the closed inner circle of Georgians who ran his campaign and accompanied him to Washington. Most of my friends among the politicians and journalists didn't like him. The political writers were particularly put off, as their Washington counterparts would be when he arrived there as a self-proclaimed outsider and continued to act like one. "The 'interfering spirit of righteousness' in American religious culture has set on edge the teeth of most of the country's better writers," Miller observed, "including many who write about politics for newspapers."

But there was more to it than adverse reaction to what many regarded as an excess of piety. Southern leaders who had taken a stand against segregation looked with suspicion on Carter, a latecomer to the cause. When, as a state legislator, he made his first run for governor in 1966, Georgia moderates were trying to resurrect Ellis Arnall, a former governor who had stood up to old Gene Talmadge and his son Herman. Carter's surprisingly strong showing in the first primary was credited with clearing the way for the election of a troglodytic segregationist, Lester Maddox.

Carter won the office by defeating another moderate, Carl Sanders, in a campaign in which Carter openly courted those who had defected to George Wallace's third party. Accused of "segging it up," he told Vernon Jordan, the black Atlanta lawyer who would later head the national Urban League, "you *won't* like my campaign, but you *will* like my administration." He delivered on the promise. His first act on taking office was to hang a portrait of Martin Luther King, Jr., in the lobby of the statehouse, and there were no lapses in his effort to live up to the principle set forth in his inaugural address:

> I say to you quite frankly that the time for racial discrimination is over. . . . No poor, rural, weak or black person should ever have to bear the additional burden of being deprived of the opportunity of an education, a job, or simple justice.

At this point in his career Carter's convictions coincided with his ambition. To win the White House in 1976 he would have to do what the Republicans' Southern Strategy held could not be done—carry the black vote nationally while holding Southern whites in the Democratic ranks. He faced that challenge head-on in the first significant Southern primary. George Wallace, pointing out that Franklin Roosevelt had also campaigned from a wheelchair, rolled into Florida waving the antibusing banner, and was handily put away by Carter, who ran well ahead of the field.

Out of office as Georgia governor because of the state's constitutional term limit, Carter had spent the preceding months in a lonely pilgrimage around the country seeking out small audiences of presumably influential people. One with such minimal national name recognition could hardly expect to make many converts, since those who practice politics rarely commit themselves so early to so long a shot. But with those who were willing to listen, Carter managed to put himself in the futures book by undercutting in advance the principal charge his opponents would use against him when the campaign went public—that he was a parochial upward-striver of dubious antecedents seeking to exploit post-Watergate disillusionment with Washington insiders.

I was away when he came to Santa Barbara to lead a dialogue session at the center, but months later, when his candidacy began to be taken seriously, *The Nation* asked me for an appraisal. Turning to the tape recording of Carter's wide-ranging exchanges with the center's skeptical intellectuals, I wrote:

> He is not satisfactory to those on the left who believe that the materialistic American society is hopelessly corrupt and will respond only to radical restructuring. He is a moderate reformist who makes no promise of ideological innovation, holding that we can follow the welfare route to attain a tolerable degree of social justice within the limits of representative democracy and marketplace economics.
>
> But he is a systems engineer by temperament and training, and there is no doubt that he would undertake a massive effort to shape up the flabby, inefficient federal bureaucracy—not necessarily to reduce its size but to improve the delivery of services. In that sense, then, he is equally unsatisfactory to those on both the left and right who believe the Republic's salvation requires the dismantling of the central structures of government and the transfer of autonomy to institutions closer to the people.

It could hardly be said that Jimmy Carter won a mandate in an election in which his popular vote was 40,828,929 against 39,148,940 for Gerald Ford, and his electoral majority only 297 to 240. The president he unseated was the only unelected incumbent in the nation's history, and the nominee of a divided party badly scarred by the Watergate scandals.

Ford had been weakened in the primary by the challenge of an unsullied Republican superpatriot newly risen in the West, Governor Ronald Reagan of California.

Carter, who was a tireless but hardly inspiring campaigner, also benefited from having an opponent with even less charisma. Ford, a physically awkward and frequently inept public speaker, was subject to the kind of ridicule that can be fatal to a candidate trying to appear presidential. Lyndon Johnson said Jerry Ford had played too much football without a helmet, and Gene McCarthy suggested that he was bound to have a peculiar world-view since he had played center and was used to seeing things upside down.

Carter, of course, was equally vulnerable. Any Southerner, even one with less conspicuous down-home characteristics, had an automatic handicap when campaigning outside his native region. "Southern political personalities, like sweet corn, travel badly," A. J. Liebling, *The New Yorker's* media critic, once observed. "They lose flavor with every hundred yards away from the patch. By the time they reach New York they are like golden bantam that has been trucked up from Texas—stale and unprofitable."

Skeptical newshawks were posed to pounce on the inevitable lapses in Carter's public statements. As a white Georgian appealing to black voters in the North, while attempting at the same time to lure working-class whites back into the Democratic fold, he had to tiptoe through a minefield of conflicting prejudices. Blacks rose up in wrath when he made an offhand remark about preserving "ethnic purity" in urban neighborhoods. On that and similar occasions he was rescued by the testimony of Atlanta's black congressman Andrew Young, who bore impeccable civil rights credentials as a leading disciple of Martin Luther King, Jr.

The Reverend Martin Luther King, Sr., helped out when Carter created a flap in fundamentalist circles, and aroused cries of hypocrisy elsewhere by seeming to admit in a *Playboy* interview that he sometimes felt a pang of lust for strange female flesh, although he never acted on it. Daddy King cleared up the theological point: "They can't kill you for looking. Old as I am, they *still* look good. When I see a good-looking woman, I look, and I wipe my mouth . . . and I wish I could . . . but I'm a preacher!" However this absolution may have sounded in other circles, it was highly effective at an interracial peanut roast in an Atlanta park in the year of Our Lord 1976.

In the Democratic coalition that prevailed in the general election, only the black bloc retained the solidarity once attributed to the whole of the South. There was a record 64 percent turnout of registered black voters, and 94 percent voted for Carter and his running mate, Walter Mondale. As a result, for the first time since the Dixiecrat rebellion in 1948, the Democrats carried every Southern state except Virginia.

When Carter was asked after the election whether he had incurred any political obligations, he said he had only one major debt—to Andy Young. He paid that off by appointing him ambassador to the United Nations, where, with the president's approbation, he denounced American racism, Western colonialism, and South African apartheid.

Other black appointments followed in record numbers as Carter pursued his announced intention to have minorities proportionately represented in his administration. In his first appointments to top-level jobs eight blacks were given places with cabinet rank. And he sent word to Southern senators that when they submitted recommendations for federal judicial appointments he expected to name at least one black judge in each of their states.

With the inauguration of Jimmy Carter, the minority made a penetration into the ranks of federal decision-makers at least commensurate with its numbers in the electorate. Moreover, this new level of inclusion aroused few cries of protest in the South, or anywhere else. But in practice it produced little more than a temporary halt in the effort to roll back the few Great Society programs that had survived eight years of Republican rule.

The national white majority now accepted the proposition that blacks were entitled to a higher place in American society, and, in the abstract, at least, most seemed to agree that the government had an obligation to ensure that they had full opportunity to attain it. But political support ran out when government action to achieve that end required additional expenditures, or was perceived as a threat to the advantages the status quo provided for whites.

The political rights gained in the course of the civil rights movement were secure, public accommodations were generally open to all comers, and blacks who had the financial means could move out of the segregated ghettos. But, as Martin Luther King, Jr., had come to recognize, this would avail little for poor blacks unless it was accompanied by measures that ensured access to the education and training required for truly gainful employment.

The breakthrough on the political front was brought about by a combination of moral suasion, confrontation, and boycott that provided the only effective leverage available to those outside the system. In the 1970s a young preacher who was on his way to becoming King's most conspicuous disciple began applying the formula to gain public and private support for a grass-roots effort in urban wastelands where there was precious little grass.

Jesse Jackson had settled in Chicago as director of the failed SCLC program King launched there near the end of his life. But he soon broke away to form an organization of his own, calling it Operation PUSH, the acronym for People United to Save Humanity. A native of my South Carolina hometown, Jackson billed himself as a simple country preacher, but as he quickly demonstrated, he was in fact a highly so-phisticated master of public relations.

In Greenville, a growing city that hardly qualified as a country place, he had become a local celebrity as the star quarterback on the black high school's football team. The white coach at Furman Univer-sity, who could not use him on his own squad, arranged an athletic scholarship at the University of Illinois. Attracting little attention there, he transferred to North Carolina AM&N at Greensboro, where he again became a football hero, and a leader of the student lunch counter sit-ins that launched SNCC. Later he attended the University of Chicago's Divinity School.

In Chicago's heavily black South Side he established PUSH head-quarters in a handsome old synagogue left behind by the flight of middleclass Jews to the suburbs. There his fervent, old-style preaching rallied a faithful following, and he used it to back up confrontations with the white political and business establishment. Poor as many of them were, the collective purchasing power of blacks had become a significant factor in marketing foodstuffs, beer, liquor, automobiles, clothing, and the like, and the threat of boycott against purveyors who did not qualify for PUSH's stamp of approval resulted in increases in black employment, and the placing of franchises with black businessmen.

By the late 1970s he had recognized that these concessions were going to mean little unless the deterioration of the black ghetto family could be halted. Drugs had become a major problem, and with their spread had come a marked increase in youth gangs, teenage pregnancy, and unsafe streets. Concluding that salvaging the youthful perpetrators and victims of this subculture would require the concerted effort of parents and schools, backed by the community at large, he began to concentrate his efforts on a ghetto organizing project he titled PUSH/Excel—Push for Excellence. I soon found myself involved in its evolution.

One Saturday morning in 1978 I sat in a dugout behind home plate at Dodger Stadium, grateful for the shade as the sun burned through the smog and spread a film of sweat over eddying clumps of varicolored humanity spread across the bright green grass of the infield. Amplifiers stacked around the pitcher's mound beamed the thumping rhythms of a rock band into the stands, where other thousands edged back out of the glare. Ubiquitous television crews certified this as a first-string media event, and a thicket of microphones followed the Reverend Jesse Jackson as he moved about among his flock.

From time to time the musicians paused and a resonant Southern accent as familiar to most Americans as that of the president of the United States echoed across the field. The star was easy to spot, seeming to rise a head taller than those who accompanied him, his neat, medium Afro framing a smooth brown face accented by a bold, down-curving mustache. In these opening hours of an all-day gathering he was explaining the procedure to be more or less followed at the First Annual Excelathon—a series of improvised contests between teams of schoolchildren, professional athletes, and assorted movie and television personalities.

The outfield scoreboard proclaimed that all proceeds would go to benefit the Push for Excellence Program in the public schools of Los Angeles. The list of sponsors parading across the screen was a compendium of the city's leading figures in entertainment, politics, and business, attesting that Jackson had become, as such figures were rated in those parts, a hot property—hotter than the stocky, bearded man in the planter's straw hat who stood beside him, Excelathon cochairman Marlon Brando; possibly even as hot as California's surrealist governor, Jerry Brown, who would soon materialize in the infield.

I was among those brought to Dodger Stadium by the young preacher's formidable persuasive powers, exercised not on me but on a wealthy Los Angeles friend of mine, Joseph W. Drown, who maintained a substantial family foundation. A generous supporter of children's causes, Drown had been impressed by the school program and had pledged a grant of one hundred thousand dollars. But he wanted to be sure that his money was not diverted to maintain the entourage, like that of a prize fight champion, that accompanied Jackson wherever he went, and he had enlisted me to help see that his wishes were carried out.

Drown had stipulated that his gift should be used to organize a fund-raising operation that would ensure a continuing income for the school project. He was a member of the board of the Center for the Study of Democratic Institutions, and had been impressed when we launched a direct-mail campaign that signed up more than a hundred thousand members, whose annual contributions became a major source of income. He had expected the initiation of something similar at PUSH when he turned over the first fifty thousand dollars of his grant. Seeing no sign of movement in that direction, he demanded an accounting and informed Jackson that he would use the remaining fifty thousand dollars, and any further contribution that might be required, to fund the campaign he had asked me and Peter Tagger, the center's direct-mail consultant, to set up for PUSH/Excel.

I had no doubt that there was a potential for such an undertaking after seeing Jackson in action in inner city schools in the months before the Dodger Stadium event. His ability to reach out to audiences of all kinds was demonstrated by his success in playing changes on the basic sermon that had placed him at the top of the media's celebrity scale. Before ecstatic teenagers assembled in school auditoriums in Chicago, Kansas City, Shreveport, Buffalo, Chattanooga, and points between, he let his country preacher style run free, building a thunderous chanted response to his litany:

I am SOMEbody!
If my mind can conceive it,
And my heart can believe it,
I know I can achieve it!
My mind is a pearl,
I can learn anything in the world—
I am SOMEbody!

At Howard University, before a group of veteran public school administrators, most of them black and wary, he laced his presentation with professional jargon, as he did when he went before the National Education Association at its annual convention in Dallas, talking of the need for a new kind of community support organization to motivate disadvantaged students and engender a learning atmosphere. In Chicago he bluntly charged a group of leading white businessmen with supporting what he called three-tier education—suburban schools based on class, private schools based on race, and inner city schools based on alienation and rejection.

At the New Orleans Superdome, where the Louisiana State School Board was his sponsor, he talked across the swarming teenagers to the parents in the audience of more than sixty thousand, challenging them to impose the home discipline he insisted was essential to scholastic achievement. He gave the Republican National Committee and Americans for Democratic Action the same challenge: "It doesn't matter if the Democrats or the Republicans are running the government so long as our young people have no confidence in it." Before committees of Congress he left no doubt that he shared youth's dim view of most contemporary officeholders.

In all these guises his message was uncompromisingly moral. "The issue is not ethnic, it's ethical," was among the most frequent of his alliterative catchphrases. He preached salvation of the deteriorating public school system as the minimum requirement of a just and democratic society. And he skillfully exploited every passing headline that could be construed as a reminder that blacks were still far short of the stated goals of the civil rights movement.

He and Julian Bond were the first of the King disciples to charge President Carter with backing off from his commitment to the black voters who provided his margin of victory, and Jackson was in the forefront of the protest against court challenges to affirmative action and the antiwelfare trend reflected in the tax revolt that began in California and spread across the country. Not even such a peripheral matter as a Miami prize fight involving an obscure white South African escaped his notice: He greeted this presumed apostle of apartheid with a vociferous demand that the State Department rescind his visa.

It could not be said that Jackson's press was uniformly favorable. A good many of my colleagues were reflexively suspicious of one who talked always in moral terms, and rarely softened the defiant stance of the Freedom Marcher with a touch of humility. In Chicago his media-oriented jousts with the Cook County machine aroused suspicions of personal political ambition, and the sharp-penned columnist Mike Royko labeled him Jet-Mouth Jesse.

But a *Chicago Tribune* poll asking citizens at large to name the living black leader they most admired gave Jackson 56 percent, trailed by Coretta King, 14 percent, Barbara Jordan, 11 percent, and Andrew Young, 9 percent. Royko's *Chicago Sun-Times* colleague, sports columnist Bill Gleason, while chiding Jackson for reverse racism in the matter of the South African boxer, felt constrained to add:

> He is one of the few black leaders who will stand before the dictatorial young and tell them that they must take off their hats in school; that they must be courteous to their teachers, parents and other elders; that they must not listen to lewd and suggestive phonograph records; that they must have excellent attendance records in high school with the purpose of getting a college education; that they must not support "blaxploitation" movies; and they must learn to read even if they are sixteen years old. Jackson is a Puritan at a time when the people he has devoted his life to need Puritanism.

The power of Jackson's personal appeal, and his instinctive ability to manipulate the media, made him impossible to ignore. When he appeared on "Sixty Minutes," more than six thousand letters came flooding into CBS, the highest return for any segment in the program's history. The leading civil rights leader of an earlier era was one of those who saw the broadcast, and was moved by it. Hubert Humphrey, suffering from terminal cancer, sent what amounted to a deathbed appeal to HEW secretary Joseph Califano urging support for PUSH/Excel.

The program, subsequently anointed with a federal grant, came down to an evangelical effort to reinstate the Puritan ethic at the lowest level of American society at a time when it seemed to be waning among those more fortunately situated, from left-wing intellectuals to pragmatic politicians to tax-sheltered businessmen. Thus PUSH/Excel was endowed at birth with a full quota of articulate critics.

The eclipsed leaders of the radical movements of the sixties revived the charges once leveled against Pat Moynihan, accusing Jackson of blaming a racist society's victims for crimes perpetrated against them. But it was evident that he was challenging the "victimizers" everywhere he went, and he managed to praise the New Leftists even while he disowned them:

> We accept and support the economic, social and political goals of the counterculture. We are intimately a part of it. But we don't accept negative values as a necessary corollary. We cannot allow the noble goals of the counterculture to be synonymous with the use of drugs, alcohol and sexual promiscuity, violence and vandalism. If we do, we will be defeated no matter how noble our goals.

PUSH/Excel also encountered the contention of some social scientists that its leader's charismatic approach could produce only a transient and diversionary effect. In playing the role of a moralistic pied piper, it was argued, he could arouse the young, but their resolve would fade when the piper departed, leaving them to relapse into the hedonistic subculture that offered the instant gratifications of drugs, sex, rock, and television. And this, in turn, would ensure that his white supporters would rapidly recover from the attack of conscience induced by his indictment of their racist heritage.

The grants he was now receiving from major foundations and government agencies required that he augment his slapdash team with professional managers, and he reluctantly did so, although, as I found in dealing with them, he could never bring himself to delegate the authority they needed to be fully effective. Still, he did achieve results that demonstrated that he brought something more than charisma to the PUSH/Excel effort. In St. Louis, where he was given credit for bringing together representatives of state and local government to resolve a festering strike by black teachers, James E. Ellis wrote in the *Post-Dispatch*:

> . . . Jackson appears to have done the impossible—formulate an education program everyone can agree on. Students like it because it treats them as equal participants in the learning process. Educators like it because it stresses the importance of study and classroom discipline. Members of the middleclass like it because it's primarily a poor people's program that stresses self-help and middleclass values. Politicians like it because it's one of the last rallying causes of one of their own—the late Hubert Humphrey.

PUSH/Excel enjoyed at least pro forma endorsement by white leaders wherever Jackson took his road show. His supporters ranged from the most conservative Chamber of Commerce types to such professed antiestablishmentarians as Jerry Brown, and it could be assumed that their motives varied widely. But, from whatever point on the political spectrum they responded, the program's appeal was enhanced by rising opposition to school busing.

In Los Angeles, one of the major cities operating its schools under court desegregation orders, the liberal president of the Unified School District, Howard Miller, persuaded his colleagues to appropriate funds for PUSH/Excel by arguing that its promise of reducing disorder and enhancing the learning process met the stated objections of those who opposed redistribution of students to achieve racial balance. The program was sold as a cut-rate gesture toward improving conditions in schools with predominantly black and Latino enrollment, and it outlasted its sponsor, who was removed by a recall election initiated by an unmollified antibusing organization.

Operating now on a national scale, the school program continued to inspire enough hope to offset the reservations of sophisticated skeptics. "It will take several years before Push for Excellence can be fairly judged," said a sympathetic *New York Times* editorial. "For now, it is heartening that a respected civil rights leader is telling disaffected youth that 'to do less than your best is a sin'—and that some of them are listening."

Jesse Jackson had attained a personal stature whose significance was not lost on the beleaguered Jimmy Carter, beset by an economy caught in an inflationary spiral and faced with a reelection campaign in which race was bound to be an abrasive, and inescapable, issue. In 1979, when his declining fortunes caused Carter to summon leaders considered among the nation's wise men to Camp David to offer counsel on how to retrieve public confidence, Jackson was aboard the first helicopter to land, accompanied by the preeminent Washington insider Clark Clifford; John Gardner, head of Common Cause; and Lane Kirkland, president of the AFL-CIO.

Jesse Jackson and I were a generation apart, and only poetic license made possible the shared joke he sometimes used in introducing me as a fellow Greenvillian, saying that we had gone to separate schools together. But there was common experience to link me to the two black matrons I sat beside in the VIP box at Dodger Stadium on the day of the Excelathon: Jesse's mother, Helen, and his grandmother, Matilda Burns. We shared memories of a South that was no more, a predominantly pastoral society where, despite the barriers of slavery and segregation, the two races had been joined together at its creation.

Now those barriers had come tumbling down, releasing the energy and talent of the tall young man who walked in glory before us, grown from the child these women had endowed with their own indomitable spirit. "I've never been poor," their boy would tell an interviewer. "We just didn't have any money. But we never perceived ourselves as poor. We would never *concede* to poverty." Matilda Burns and Helen Jackson reminded me, as their counterparts always did, of William Faulkner's laconic tribute to his black neighbors: "They endured." And this, surely, was the bedrock upon which the civil rights movement was founded.

For those of my generation still living in the South there were constant reminders of how great the change had been. With pride touched with wonder, Mrs. Jackson told me of the recent funeral of her husband. To the final rites of this modest post office employee came the mayor of Greenville, the governor of South Carolina, and a warm personal message from Jimmy and Rosalyn Carter. If this were discounted as the expedient response of politicians to the bereavement of a recognized media star, it did not diminish the significance noted by the Reverend Otis Moss, who came from Cleveland to officiate:

> Charles Henry Jackson moved into the world and into history in an unspectacular way, and nobody sent out the Klan to stop him in his birth. But if the haters of his day had known the potential, the possibilities and actualities wrapped up in that birth the Klan would have changed its march, and the world would not have heard of Jesse. . . .

When Charles Henry Jackson and I were growing up in Greenville, whites could ignore the black residents except for those who touched their lives as servants, looking the other way when the "haters" moved to ensure that blacks stayed in their place. No doubt some haters were still around, but now it was they who were beyond the pale. In the South the closed white society had opened to blacks who shared its middleclass values, and now they enjoyed most of the amenities. If the dispensation did not yet extend to poor blacks, the condition was not unique to the region. A schoolmate of mine who devoted much of her time to cultural activities offered a view of community relations in Greenville that would apply in New York, Chicago, or San Francisco: "The only real distinction now is between the couth and uncouth."

Blacks and whites circled each other warily in the middle ground that had opened between the separate spheres in which most members of both races still maintained their private lives. The active separatist movement led by Malcolm X had waned after his assassination, but James Baldwin was still preaching his gospel, and the distrust of whites it implied was inherent in the experience of virtually all blacks. On the white side, offense was often given inadvertently by those who had not shaken off the condescension that had traditionally shaped the interracial relationship. Blacks found it difficult to ignore such slights, even when they recognized that they reflected obtuseness, not malice.

Jesse Jackson and I had spent too much time in this middle ground to be unaware of the pitfalls. He had mastered Martin Luther King's skill at tempering the abrasiveness of the confrontational style with the balm of redemption. In our relationship, however, it fell my lot to do the confronting, and tolerance was often strained on both sides.

The direct-mail operation we were setting up required tightly organized production, scheduling, and accounting procedures. In the initial phase Peter Tagger's consulting firm could handle these, but the time was coming when they would have to be integrated into the business management of PUSH, and this was impossible without changes in Jesse's operating style he adamantly refused to consider.

"You just don't understand how we operate," he told me. "You and Joe Drown are used to dealing with an organization that runs like a high-powered automobile, where you just punch the right button and the right thing happens. PUSH is a poor folks' operation. It's like an old, broken-down wagon pulled by a mule that knows where he's got to go but has to find his own way to get there."

Jesse considered prophecy his primary mission and had faith that all else would follow since his cause was just. It was not easy, I explained to Drown, to organize a prophet. And communication was made difficult, I sensed, because of the generation gap; when Jesse looked at me he saw the image of the generation of white Greenvillians who had, for the most part, either ignored him or put him down. When he finally yielded to my importuning and brought in experienced black professionals to administer the fund-raising operation, he opened a letter written after I met with the members of the new support staff with a passage that reminded me of my trespasses while he applied the healing balm:

It is always good to be lectured to by a wise old crabby White man. Since you have paid your dues with love, compassion and courageous commitment you have earned some special privileges.

At that point we had completed sample mailings to test the return from contributor lists obtained from other organizations, and had committed most of the remainder of the Drown grant for a mass mailing we were confident would create a base membership and yield a substantial net annual income without any further investment. Like all such lists of donors known to contribute generously to minority causes, the six hundred thousand recipients were predominantly Jewish. Then, while the letters were still in the mail, Jesse suddenly answered an inner call to take his healing mission to the warring Semites of the Middle East.

In the fall of 1979 the front pages of American newspapers displayed a photograph of Jesse embracing Yasser Arafat, the head of the Palestine Liberation Organization. There was virtually universal outrage among American Jews, their emotional identification with Israel intensified by Jimmy Carter's on again-off again effort to mediate between Prime Minister Menachem Begin and his antagonist in the recent Israeli-Egyptian war, Anwar Sadat. "As you can see," I wrote to Jesse, reporting a net loss from the mailing, "the flap that followed your Mideast tour was disastrous."

Jesse was no anti-Semite, but he had been irrevocably tarred by the brush. In a *Washington Post* interview with Judy Bachrach, she injected the issue into his explanation of his role as a Puritan prophet:

> "I have been bred," he says simply, "into accepting responsibility. And part of that is accepting responsibility for my person, my family and my race."
>
> And what about my race?
>
> Jesse Jackson smiles. "That's my race," he replies without a moment's hesitation. "The human race. In my Father's house there is but one race."

But it was, and would continue to be, a house divided.

DEAD END

TRIUMPH OF A GREAT COMMUNICATOR

> Reagan, speaking to the future of America with a vision of the past, gave hope of things to come. To those who shared the gospel of a better life with less government, he offered the promise of Goldwaterism without Goldwater. But even those who did not share this vision were apt to be stirred by Reagan. . . . Even when making a stump speech, he was not a shouter. Rather, he came into the family living room, on television, like the nice neighbor next door who was armed with simple and plausible answers to great and complex questions.
>
> —LOU CANNON, *Reagan*, 1982

JIMMY CARTER, the first governor to occupy the White House since the *Brown* decision, had firsthand experience with the disabilities still visited on poor black children as a result of stalled progress toward school desegregation. As president, he followed his systems engineering approach in dealing with the problem, calling for a basic reorganization of the scattered, uncoordinated federal agencies that dealt with the public schools:

> When I became president, in spite of the importance of the subject, education was still sometimes treated in Washington as an afterthought or nuisance, discussed at the cabinet level

mostly when it involved lawsuits concerning equal rights for black, Hispanic, handicapped, or female students.

His solution was to bring the concerned agencies together at the cabinet level. But the proposed Department of Education immediately ran into turf problems. Secretary Califano of HEW objected to removing his department's middle initial, and along with it thousands of bureaucrats under his jurisdiction. The opposition was sufficient to delay creation of the new cabinet office until October 1979, when Carter appointed as secretary of education an able California judge of the U.S. Circuit Court of Appeals, Shirley Hufstedler. She found a festering crisis on the racial front waiting for her.

Richard Nixon's efforts to appoint U.S. Supreme Court justices who would reverse what he called the Warren Court's "human engineering" had begun to bear fruit, and for the first time there was a retreat on the school mandate. His and Gerald Ford's appointees provided the 5-to-4 majority that effectively ended the use of redistricting as the primary means of eliminating segregated schools.

The excuse for tempering the previous stand came when a federal court found the Detroit school system guilty of unconstitutional segregation, but concluded that no remedy was possible in a district two-thirds black and growing blacker. The judge held that racial balance could only be achieved in a metropolitan district that incorporated schools in surrounding suburbs, and ordered its creation.

The Supreme Court overturned the ruling on jurisdictional grounds. The majority rejected the contention that these suburbs were creatures of the state that had employed delegated powers to impose land use requirements, building codes, and other restrictions that barred lower-income families, thus making the state a party to fostering the pattern of urban growth that made racial imbalance inevitable in the schools of metropolitan Detroit.

In the majority opinion, Chief Justice Burger declared the suburban districts beyond the reach of *Brown*, invoking the principle of localism he had reluctantly abrogated in *Swann:*

No single tradition in public education is more deeply rooted than local control over operation of the schools; local autonomy has long been thought essential both to the maintenance of community concern and support for public schools and to the quality of the educational process.

Whatever may be said of the legal argument, there could be no doubt that the result was as Justice Thurgood Marshall described it:

> The Court's answer is to provide no remedy at all for the violation proved in this case, thereby guaranteeing that Negro children in Detroit will receive the same separate and inherently unequal education in the future as they have been unconstitutionally afforded in the past.

The new dispensation began to undo successful desegregation programs in smaller cities where the attraction of suburbia for affluent families was steadily increasing the proportion of blacks within the city limits. As litigation proceeded over the next decade under the Detroit precedent, Little Rock, where it all began, provided a case in point. Orders issued in *Cooper* v. *Aaron*, which occasioned the showdown at Central High School, had remained in effect, and had been instrumental in the notable progress made toward eliminating segregation.

As in most Southern cities prior to *Swann*, desegregation in Little Rock had been so gradual the black schools had remained virtually intact. Once student reassignment became mandatory, the school board, with solid support from community leaders, instituted busing to achieve racial balance. *Newsweek*, in a gloomy 1981 survey of the deterioration of the nation's public schools, cited Central High as a shining exception:

> Today Central is once again a national symbol—as one of the best public high schools in America. Sixty-five percent of the seniors go to college, and fifty-seven percent of the student body is black. Central, indeed, provides solid proof that racial harmony and academic excellence are not mutually exclusive.

In 1957, when the litigation precipitated by Orval Faubus's defiance of the federal courts began, the Little Rock school district was 75 percent white. Twenty years later it was 71 percent black—and Henry Woods, the federal judge now presiding, was finding it increasingly difficult to devise a formula that would maintain racially integrated schools.

As in Detroit, the problem was rooted in the failure of the growing city to adjust its boundaries to encompass the metropolitan area of which it became the hub. Judge Woods approved a move initiated by the city's school board to consolidate three contiguous districts in order to restore a workable black-white ratio. In another court action the state government was required to make substantial funds available to further the integration process, and under the supervision of a special master appointed by Woods a number of promising innovations were initiated. But the suburban districts appealed, and in its final ruling the Circuit Court of Appeals stood on the Detroit precedent. In the end the embattled Woods recused himself with a declaration that applied to every federal judge similarly situated: "I am unable to successfully implement a plan to bring equity to children of this district. . . ."

> In my years as district judge in this difficult case involving the three school districts in Pulaski County, I have attempted to oversee the implementation of positive desegregation plans which would benefit all children in the public schools. . . . Whatever the plan finally mandated by the Court of Appeals, those who take as their part delay and obstruction will have won. For those people delay is victory, regardless of the cost to schoolchildren or the community.

From the beginning, failure to recognize the profound effect of rapidly changing demography on the public school system characterized the acrimonious debate over educational policy precipitated by *Brown*. It was commonly charged, and widely believed, that the threat of desegregation was responsible for massive white flight from urban school districts. The fact was that the movement of the affluent away from crowded city neighborhoods began when the automobile made it feasible, and had reached flood tide before the effort to eliminate racial discrimination in the schools began.

The departure of the upwardly mobile from inner city neighborhoods left a vacuum filled in large part by blacks displaced by the mechanization of agriculture, and by legal and illegal immigrants from Latin America and the Caribbean. The resentment these newcomers aroused as they spilled over into white working-class neighborhoods predated *Brown*. Resistance in those precincts was so embedded that, except for Boston and Los Angeles, no serious attempt to employ busing to eliminate predominantly black schools was ever undertaken in any major city.

By the time the Supreme Court turned its attention to *de facto* school segregation, the typical metropolis consisted of a ring of residential suburbs surrounding inner cities whose decaying housing stock was overpopulated by poor blacks and Latinos. The single-family dwelling, standing on its own patch of ground, had become the American ideal, and government support in the form of low-interest loans and subsidized public services was available for those who could afford the down payment.

The massive shift in the nation's demography was accompanied by profound changes in the life-styles of Americans. As it developed in the last century, the public school was designed to serve the nuclear family: a wage-earning father, a housekeeping mother, and one or more children living in a stable, homogenous community. But in the permissive, highly mobile era that followed World War II, this pattern was disappearing; by 1980 more than half the women of childbearing age were working full-time, and an increasing number of mothers at all income levels were single. "We have moved from a society dominated by one type of arrangement, the husband-provider nuclear family, to a more variegated society with many types of household, no one of which predominates," Daniel Yankelovitch wrote in *New Rules*.

The failure of the school system to adapt to the changing needs of its patrons was demonstrated in the rising level of dropouts in the ghettos, declining test scores in the suburbs, and drug- and alcohol-related juvenile delinquency at all levels of society. There was widespread recognition of the need for reform, but little support for the sort of massive effort this would require. A prime element in the myth of the neighborhood school was the sanctity of local control, and this was seized on by those who opposed federal action to deal with the fact that education of the quality provided at public expense for most white children was still beyond the reach of poor blacks and Latinos.

. . .

Jimmy Carter's establishment of the Department of Education was based on his recognition that federal policy was not keeping up with societal changes that had brought unprecedented pressures to bear on the public school system. This prompted my acceptance when I was asked to sign on as a consultant to an old friend, Assistant Secretary Elizabeth Carpenter, who had been the *Arkansas Gazette*'s Washington correspondent before she became a senior White House aide to Lyndon and Lady Bird Johnson.

With Secretary Hufstedler's encouragement, I was able to poke around the new agency inquiring how the department proposed to carry forward its mandate to equalize educational opportunity now that political pressure effectively prevented busing. This turned out to be what is called in Washington a blockbuster question—one people don't ask, not only because they're afraid of the answer, but because they don't want to be associated with the question.

There was general agreement among the senior professional staff that the question was in order; there was also general agreement that it was too hot to handle. In addition to the protective instinct of the civil servant to cling to the status quo, the educational bureaucrats had inhibitions brought over from the academy, where pedagogues, behavioral and social scientists, and philosophers had long been immersed in controversy over the nature of the learning process.

It was, in any case, not a propitious time to discuss domestic changes. Jimmy Carter's reelection campaign was imminent, and there were alarming signs of disintegration in the shaky Democratic coalition that brought him to office. His running battle with Congress over energy policy as the price of imported oil escalated prompted some party leaders to consider taking him on in the primaries, and he was receiving alarming signals from his supporters in the Jewish constituency, one of the party's prime sources of campaign funds.

Among the president's inheritances from previous administrations was a woefully bungled Middle East policy. Henry Kissinger's exercises in realpolitik had not eased the tensions between Israel and the surrounding

Arab nations, and had hardened the tendency of American Jews to use uncritical backing of Israel as a litmus test for politicians seeking their support.

Carter had passed with flying colors in 1976. "I considered this homeland for the Jews to be compatible with the teaching of the Bible, hence ordained by God," he wrote in *Keeping Faith*."These moral and religious beliefs made my commitment to the security of Israel unshakable." But after touring the region as president and meeting with Arab leaders, he concluded that there could be no settlement of the threatening military confrontation until Israel faced up to the unresolved questions raised by the existence of native Arabs in its own territory, and in the areas it had occupied on its borders in the course of the recent armed conflict.

It was an issue no Israeli politician was willing to face, and the most adamant of them all, Menachem Begin, had just become prime minister. When Carter, who made resolution of the Mideast crisis a personal mission, received indications from Anwar Sadat, the Egyptian leader, that he was willing to withdraw his nation's claim to some of the occupied territory, he decided to arrange a three-way parley with himself as a full participant. "I had to repair my damaged political base among Israel's American friends," he wrote, "and in the process build further support for our peace effort."

In September 1978, against the advice of his political advisers, Carter invited Begin and Sadat to meet alone with him at Camp David, and after thirteen days of bargaining, arm-twisting, and prayer, the president emerged with accords that enabled him to go before Congress and announce agreement on a framework for peace in the Middle East. Later that day there was a meeting at the White House with key American Jewish leaders he described as "delightful, full of fun and good cheer, and we welcomed it because it was so rare."

In his last year in office, trouble for the president came to a head in another part of the Middle East, the oil-rich empire of Iran. The United States had maintained Shah Mohammad Reza Pahlavi on his Peacock Throne, training and arming a sizable Iranian military force as a Cold War deterrent to possible designs on the region by the Soviet Union.

But in January 1979 Shiite Muslim fundamentalists led by the hot-eyed Ayatollah Ruhollah Khomeini toppled the shah and drove him into exile. New tensions spread throughout the area, shaking the balance of power that had guaranteed Israel's continued existence.

Neither foreign nor domestic crises could shake Jimmy Carter's confidence in his own destiny. His diary entry for June 12, 1979, summarized a meeting with his top aides called to notify them that he and Vice President Mondale would be standing for reelection in 1980:

> . . . I told them that they should screen their entire staffs, to tell everybody that we were faced with difficulty now, and that it was very likely to get worse in the future. If they couldn't take the pressure to get out. I felt personally confident that we were doing a good job for the country, that we would prevail again in this Congress as we have in the previous Congresses, that I would win in 1980 no matter who ran against me, and that I was going to fight to the last vote.

The public opinion polls indicated that Senator Edward Kennedy of Massachusetts had moved into position as his principal primary opponent, and in Washington the prevailing view was that he would probably unseat the incumbent. When asked about that possibility at a meeting with a group of congressmen, Carter made what he described as a "somewhat brusque comment" that gained wide circulation. Mondale told him his promise to whip Kennedy's ass was ill-advised, but the president noted in his diary, "Some of my staff members say it is the best thing for morale around the White House since the Willie Nelson concert."

The Democratic coalition now contained two new components that were based, not on the usual special interests, but on mythology. There was in the rising generation a substantial number of voters who had persuaded themselves that had Jack and Robert Kennedy not been assassinated, the trauma of the Vietnam War would have been avoided and the goals of the civil rights movement achieved. The durable myth made paragons of peace and justice out of the Cold Warriors and political pragmatists the record showed the Kennedys to have been. And it made their youngest brother, Ted, a formidable contender, despite his reputation as a boozer and woman-chaser.

For many members of the sixties college generation, an extension of the Kennedy myth kept alive the faith that individual rejection of the conventional values that ordered society could be translated into political power. This millennial vision still enjoyed currency on the campuses, and it prompted the candidacy of an entrant who talked as though he shared it, and may have. Edmund G. Brown, called Jerry, had become governor of California by virtue of conventional political support inherited from his father, called Pat, an ebullient, standard-issue Democrat whose constituents cast their ballots for his son because he was able to write "Jr." after his name.

I was one of them. I had known and admired Pat Brown since my days of campaigning with Adlai Stevenson, and I gazed with wonder upon Jerry, who seemed to me the product of a political system that had come loose from its partisan moorings. This had become evident when, between the two Browns, the state was governed, or presided over, by an aging actor making his initial entry into politics, Ronald Reagan.

In California, where the postwar boom and Cold War arms buildup had provided a steadily rising standard of living, and a tax base that provided perhaps the best public services of any state, the issues of race and poverty that marked the basic division between Republicans and Democrats had all but disappeared. This allowed Reagan to preach conservative laissez-faire doctrine while the state government continued to provide generous support for the kind of tax-supported education and welfare programs he deplored.

Like his Republican predecessor, Jerry Brown received an emotional charge from campaigning and was bored by governing, which Reagan delegated, and Brown ignored as best he could. Jerry was a visionary with a genuine talent for discerning the underlying issues raised by the technological revolution reshaping American society, but it was coupled with a disdain for people and politics that rendered him incapable of translating his vision into action.

Jerry had been trained in a Jesuit seminary before deciding he could not meet the requirements of holy orders, but the ascetic style of the seminarian remained with him. Unmarried at forty, he refused to move into the new governor's mansion built for Ronald Reagan and instead slept on a mattress placed on the floor of the barren apartment he rented near the state capitol. He also spurned the official limousine, drove his own old sedan, and when in San Francisco stayed overnight at a Zen meditation center. Spurning material things, as did his youthful admirers, he picked up on the current fads of advanced thinkers, particularly the philosophy of limits that proclaimed that small is beautiful.

None of this was very useful when he went up against the hard-nosed Jesse Unruh, a good ol' boy from Texas who, as Speaker of the California Assembly, controlled the legislature, and by default became the boss of what was left of the state Democratic Party. But while Jerry appeared to keep his gaze fixed on the far horizon, his awareness of political reality quickened when ambition prompted him to look upward to higher office, as I discovered when I inadvertently happened upon him as he began preparing for his race against Jimmy Carter.

I had been summoned by Jesse Jackson to join him for dinner at a hotel in the black ghetto that surrounds the campus of the University of Southern California. When I arrived, a member of the entourage informed me that Jesse was running late, which was hardly a surprise. I had once beat my way across Chicago in a raging blizzard to keep an appointment he had moved back the night before from 10:00 to 8:00 A.M., arriving at the office building behind the synagogue to find the doors locked and no one in sight. A janitor finally rescued me, and I was glowering in a corner of the lobby when, a little after nine, Jesse strode in wearing a long fur-collared overcoat and a Russian-style hat. "That's the trouble with white people," he said. "They're *always* on time."

In Los Angeles, after I finished dinner alone, word came that Jesse had returned and was upstairs waiting for me. I found him stretched out on the bed delivering a lecture on realpolitik to an attentive Jerry Brown. "What you've got to do to attract the black vote," he was saying, "is get yourself identified with Africa. That's the coming thing.

"Just go out there and visit as many countries as you can, get your picture in the papers with the top people. You've already got your position on civil rights, you're all right on education and the death penalty, and you've made a lot of black appointments. You don't have to make pronouncements on foreign policy. Just denounce apartheid and colonialism. Just being there in the right company certifies you as problack."

The governor followed his advice and shortly departed for a tour of the Dark Continent. To ensure maximum media exposure he took with him the star pop singer Linda Ronstadt, whose presence at his side at picture opportunities helped allay the inevitable suspicions that attended a middleaged bachelor with unusual personal habits. When the presidential primary opened with the Iowa caucuses in early 1980 the candidate irreverent correspondents labeled Governor Moonbeam was on hand, along with Ted Kennedy.

"All three candidates for the Democratic Party's nomination had been products of the insurgency of the sixties and seventies—Kennedy nostalgic, Carter contemporary, Brown futuristic," Theodore White wrote. "But by April 2 the nomination was securely Carter's."

Jerry Brown was the first to self-destruct. He didn't win a single delegate in the Iowa caucuses, and only 10 percent of the direct vote in New Hampshire. He decided to skip the intervening primaries and go for broke in Wisconsin, where he put on a bizarre Hollywood-style light and film clip show to accompany his own narration. He received only 12 percent of the vote there, and on April Fool's Day conceded: "It is obvious that the voters have spoken and given their verdict on my 1980 campaign. . . ."

They also had rendered their verdict on Kennedy's, although he wouldn't accept the arithmetic even after Carter's delegate majority had clearly put the nomination out of reach. The president had run well ahead in the early primaries, but there were indications that he was becoming increasingly vulnerable to the challenge he would face in the general election.

A series of crises in the Middle East virtually removed the president from the campaign trail. He had to see to the evacuation of ten thousand Americans in Iran who were placed in jeopardy when the shah fled and Ayatollah Khomeini began to dominate the splintered remnants of civilian government. The Soviet invasion of neighboring Afghanistan created paralyzing new foreign policy issues.

Recognizing that the exiled shah's presence in the United States would further inflame Khomeini and his followers, the State Department had arranged for asylum in host countries less vulnerable to the Iranian demand that he be returned for trial. In October Mexican doctors diagnosed malignant lymphoma, and David Rockefeller prevailed on Carter to admit the shah to the United States to undergo treatment at Memorial Sloan-Kettering Cancer Center in New York City.

On November 4 a mob surrounded the U.S. embassy in Teheran and declared that the sixty "foreign devils" inside the compound would be held hostage until Khomeini's demands were met. Thus began the hostage crisis that would consume much of the hands-on president's attention and energy, and force him to adopt the so-called Rose Garden Strategy for most of his reelection campaign.

On the eve of the New York primary, in an effort to rally support in the United Nations for retaliatory moves against Iran, the United States voted for a motion by Third World nations to deny Israel authority over Jerusalem, claimed as a holy city by Jews, Muslims, and Christians. The White House responded to the predictable uproar by announcing that the president had not been informed and the vote was repudiated.

This followed shortly after disclosure of Ambassador Andrew Young's private meeting with representatives of the Palestine Liberation Organization had forced the president to accept his resignation. The spreading controversy widened the breach between blacks and Jews that became a prime factor in Carter's struggle to hold together the Democratic coalition. He noted in his memoir that "black leaders believed that Ambassador Young had been unjustly condemned for merely doing his duty," and he acknowledged the even more damaging reaction in the Jewish community:

> The equivocation after the United States vote had served to emphasize the dramatic nature of the error. Later, this episode was the direct cause of my primary losses in New York and Connecticut, and it proved highly damaging to me among American Jews throughout the country for the remainder of the election year.

Teddy Kennedy, who was kept in the race less by his own ego drive than by the importuning of his extended family and the sentimental mourners for the lost Camelot, refused to concede that he had lost even when the primaries ended in June with 1,971 delegates pledged to Carter against his 1,221. He called for an "open convention," which, as Carter pointed out, could hardly qualify as democratic since it would mean abandoning the party rules and state laws adopted to eliminate the back room deals that had permitted party bosses to determine the choice of presidential nominees.

Carter correctly foresaw that "it was only natural that the other hopefuls, the news media, and those who wanted to continue the exciting contest would grab this banner of an open convention and run with it." The contrived struggle continued until the Democrats gathered in New York City in August for a national convention that seemed to me, looking on from the press pen, to provide an even sadder spectacle than the one that had foreshadowed Hubert Humphrey's defeat twelve years before.

The issue once again was loyalty—to the candidate named in the primary, and to the party rules, including the one that bound each delegate to vote on the first ballot for the one he had been elected to support. Carter had assured Kennedy of a chance to present his case to the convention, and his chosen advocate, the noted Washington lawyer, Edward Bennett Williams, spoke from the rostrum urging the president to emancipate his elected delegates. Rebuttal was provided by George McGovern, who saw the undoing of the party reforms he had fostered.

Carter turned back the challenge, winning a floor vote 1,708 to 1,174. Kennedy indicated that he was finally prepared to endorse the ticket, and came before the convention "not to argue as a candidate, but to affirm a cause." Then, virtually without reference to Carter, he delivered a stemwinding partisan speech in the rousing Kennedy style that had won his brothers a place in the hearts of a legion of voters.

In his acceptance speech, Jimmy Carter acknowledged that the emotional response evoked by his rival eclipsed anything he could be expected to inspire, saying, "Ted, your party needs—and I need—your idealism and dedication working for us." But in the traditional assemblage of party leaders around the anointed candidate, Kennedy could not resist a final gesture of deprecation, refusing to accept the hand Carter reached out to him. Instead, as White described it, "he lifted his hand in a seigneurial wave of good-bye, as if he had appeared at the wedding of his chauffeur, and was gone."

. . .

On the Republican side, the primary quickly shook down to a two-man contest between Ronald Reagan, who had inherited the Goldwater mantle, and George Bush, the gentlemanly Washington insider who bore the cachet of the moderate wing of the party. Bush, a former congressman and Republican national chairman, had much the better campaign organization, and he topped Reagan in the Iowa caucuses. But his momentum—Big Mo, as he called it in his prep school fashion—ran out in New Hampshire, and by the time the road show reached Michigan, the race was over.

Bush had made some headway against Reagan in the East and Midwest, dismissing the Californian's budget proposals as "voodoo economics," and challenging the simplistic anticommunism that constituted his foreign policy. In these areas Bush, who had been director of the CIA and Nixon's emissary to China, had credentials Reagan clearly lacked.

But at that stage of his political development, Bush's genteel background made him too fastidious to embrace the obstreperous new elements in the Republican coalition that were to provide Ronald Reagan with an unassailable political base—the antigovernment zealots to be found among unreconstructed Southern segregationists, and in such organizations as the fundamentalist Moral Majority, the National Rifle Association, and the right-to-life movement. Their strength and concentration were demonstrated when Reagan carried every state south of the Mason-Dixon line and west of the Mississippi.

Reagan's handlers, however, were aware that the heritage from Goldwater's damn-the-torpedoes presidential campaign carried an aura that put off centrist voters, in and out of the party. Reagan had perfected a speaking style that projected the amiable, easygoing side of his nature and tempered the harshness of the hard-line message he was actually delivering. But there was still a need for a moderate running mate, and he cheerfully handed the second prize to his recent detractor, George Bush, who had been standing by hoping for it.

It had been, and would continue to be, a strange, disjointed campaign. An incumbent president was normally given the edge because of the power, patronage, and media exposure the White House afforded, but circumstances—some of his own making, others beyond his control—had largely canceled these advantages for Jimmy Carter. When the general election campaign opened after Labor Day the polls showed Carter and Reagan in a virtual dead heat.

The day after the Democratic convention the president stopped by a meeting of two hundred black delegates and told them, "I have a secret weapon, and that is the black people of this country, who know they have a friend in Jimmy Carter." Blacks had been highly visible on the floor, but some subscribed to the Kennedy myth, and Jesse Jackson had been busy heading off defections. "We have the key to the White House door," he warned those who were wavering. "And we should hold that key until we get more judgeships. We should hold that key until we have at least three cabinet members. . . . We are the difference."

Neither candidate had any disposition to belabor the race issue. Adoption of the Southern Strategy had required the Republicans to write off the black vote, and their candidates had no need to indulge in a George Wallace–style appeal to whites. Code words that aroused a racist response without identifying the respondent as a bigot were now imbedded in the political vocabulary. "States' rights" still worked in the South, and "busing" and "affirmative action" touched hot buttons everywhere in the nation.

But Richard Wirthlin, the Republicans' staff pollster, detected a negative response on more general social issues, and recommended that Reagan appear before the national Urban League convention in New York. This was intended to offset the finding that he was acquiring an image as "an unsympathetic candidate lacking a personal concern for the people's problems of welfare, aging, health care, etc."

Reagan agreed, but panicked his handlers when he insisted on stopping off at the Neshoba County Fair in Mississippi en route to the Urban League engagement. He angrily rejected pleas that this was no time to make an appearance at the site of the most notorious atrocity of the civil rights era, the collaboration of local law enforcement officials with the Ku Klux Klan in the kidnapping and assassination of three voter registration workers, two of whom were Jewish. In his brief Mississippi appearance Reagan limited his comments to his standard promise to restore states' rights and local rule, but as Lou Cannon wrote:

> The visual statement on television next day was a sea of white faces at the Neshoba Fair with Reagan's words floating above them. By then Reagan was at the Urban League comparing himself to President Kennedy attempting to win Protestant votes in 1960. He urged his listeners not to consider him a "caricature conservative" who was "anti-black, anti-poor and anti-disadvantaged."
>
> . . . It was an otherwise uneventful speech, and Reagan escaped with polite applause and sighs of relief from his aides.

Cannon, the most thoroughgoing of the Reagan biographers, had covered his eight years as governor of California before joining *The Washington Post* for the presidential campaign and subsequent assignment as White House correspondent. His 1982 book *Reagan* recounted a series of blunders by the candidate when he spoke without a prepared text and larded his comments with purported facts that were often wrong and frequently fantastic.

Cannon thought this derived in part from Reagan's long career as a screen actor. In his mind, as he aged, "the myths which Hollywood promulgated as history became actual explanations of the past." This was pronounced in his dealing with racial issues. The income and celebrity that came with the status he achieved in Hollywood provided effective insulation against the realities of ordinary life.

Reagan seemed to me caught in a time warp, seeing the world as it existed before World War I in Dixon, his Illinois hometown. The minority was too small to create racial tensions in those bucolic environs, and he had few contacts with blacks in the years that followed, for they were excluded from the sports he broadcast during his radio career, and were given only menial roles in the movies made before he outlived his career as leading man and turned to politics.

Cannon cited a striking example of this kind of fantasizing in the primary campaign against Jerry Ford in 1976. In a speech at Charlotte, Reagan had astounded his audience when he said that segregation in the armed services had ended during World War II as a result of the Japanese bombing of Pearl Harbor:

It was corrected largely under the leadership of generals like MacArthur and Eisenhower. . . . One great story that I think of at the time, that reveals a change was occurring, was when the Japanese dropped the bomb on Pearl Harbor. There was a Negro sailor whose total duties involved kitchen-type duties. . . . He cradled a machine gun in his arms, which is not an easy thing to do, and stood at the end of a pier blazing away at Japanese airplanes that were coming down and strafing him and that was all changed.

He dismissed the correction when he was reminded that desegregation in the military did not begin until a decade after Pearl Harbor when President Truman, over the opposition of General Eisenhower and the rest of military brass, issued an executive order. "I remember the scene," Reagan told Cannon. "It was very powerful."

Reagan was on his way to earning his reputation as a great communicator, but Cannon described him as a great deflector—one who was able to shrug off his own bloopers with a rueful grin and simply ignore documented attacks brought by his opponents. His skills as an actor helped; he had spent his professional life before the camera and had learned to gauge live audience response when General Electric hired him to spread the gospel of free enterprise in the waning days of his Hollywood career. But the real secret of his success on the stump was his sincerity; it was evident that he believed what he said, preposterous as it might sound to those who held a more complex view of the real world.

In the general election campaign Carter modified the Rose Garden Strategy that had kept him close to the White House during the primaries, and opened with a September rally in Alabama. At Tuscumbia he was greeted on the way from the airport by Ku Klux Klansmen in full regalia waving "Reagan for President" signs. He took note of the white sheets to be seen in the crowd of more than fifty thousand, and drew an enthusiastic response when he charged the Klansmen with desecrating the Confederate flag:

There are still a few in the South . . . who practice cowardice and who counsel fear and hatred. They marched around the State Capitol in Atlanta when I was governor. They said we ought to be afraid of each other, that whites ought to hate and be afraid of blacks and blacks ought to hate and be afraid of whites. And they would persecute those who worship in a different way from most of us. . . .

As the first man from the Deep South in almost 140 years to be president of this nation, I say that these people in white sheets do not understand our region and what it's been through, they do not understand what our country stands for, they do not understand that the South and all of America must move forward.

Reagan, who received a garbled report of the encounter en route to a speaking engagement in New Jersey, dredged up another item from his store of fanciful history and tossed off a one-liner that drew gasps from his audience when he said of his opponent: "Now I'm happy to be here while he is opening his campaign down there in the city that gave birth to the Ku Klux Klan." Sensing the reaction, he told an aide as he left the stage, "I blew it." Lou Cannon reported on the aftermath:

Before the night was out, concerned Southern Republican leaders were calling Reagan headquarters, and the candidate found it necessary to apologize to the state of Alabama and the community of Tuscumbia, which was not the birthplace of the Klan. By now the campaign was reeling, and Reagan's own confidence was shaken.

Both candidates had been avoiding personal attacks, but now Carter, pressing to take advantage of Reagan's discomfiture, opened himself to the charge that he had crossed the line. At Martin Luther King's home church in Atlanta, Ebenezer Baptist, he said that if Reagan were elected there would probably never be a national holiday for the pastor's martyred son. And, he went on, "You've seen in this campaign the stirring of hate and the birth of code words like 'states' rights' in a speech in Mississippi; in a campaign reference to the Ku Klux Klan relating to the South. This is a message that creates a cloud on the political horizon. Hatred has no place in this country."

A reply on behalf of the Reagan camp was delivered by George Will, a conservative Washington columnist who had become a Reagan confidant:

Until last Tuesday, Jimmy Carter had contented himself with implying that Ronald Reagan is an equal opportunity warmonger who will incinerate everyone on earth, regardless of race, color or creed. But Carter has decided that moderation in pursuit of power is no virtue. Now he has said that Reagan is a racist.

The Reagan campaign team had been waiting for an opportunity to cry foul. The strategy had been to deflect Carter's anticipated effort to make Reagan the issue, and now they seized the opportunity to turn the tables. A Democratic strategist who had served in California campaigns warned that Reagan was a singularly elusive target for personal attack, and if Carter attempted it he would be in danger of forfeiting his own reputation "as a good and decent person who practiced Christian charity in his dealing with others."

But Reagan's continued success in sloughing off issue-oriented charges that revealed wide gaps in his understanding of the problems the nation faced at home and abroad frustrated Carter, and he abandoned the high ground. In a speech in Chicago, he declared that it would be "a catastrophe" if Reagan were elected. "You'll determine whether or not this America will be unified," he told the partisan audience, "or, if I lose the election, whether Americans might be separated, black from white, Jew from Christian, North from South, rural from urban."

It was a real issue, but it became a boomerang when Reagan responded not in anger, but in sorrow. Carter, he said, owed the country, not him, an apology. Asked if he thought Carter was "fighting dirty," he replied, "I think he's a badly informed and prejudiced man."

By the time the two finally faced off in a television debate, Reagan was able to defuse Carter's accurate description of his stand on national health insurance as "campaigning against Medicare" with what became the most memorable catch phrase of the campaign: "There you go again." It was uttered, Cannon said, almost sorrowfully, like an uncle rebuking a none-too-favorite nephew who was known to tell tall tales.

The polls showed a close race right up to the end, but when the returns were in, Reagan had 50.75 percent of the popular vote. Another 6.61 percent had been siphoned off by John Anderson, a genteel congressman who identified himself as a liberal Republican, a term that was becoming an oxymoron. That left Jimmy Carter with 41.02 percent.

The Electoral College vote, 489 to 49, showed the extent of the disaster the Democrats had suffered; the Carter/Mondale ticket carried only the home states of the candidates, Georgia and Minnesota, plus Maryland, Rhode Island, West Virginia, Hawaii, and the District of Columbia. The black bloc was the only intact remainder of the party's traditional coalition; 90 percent voted for their friend Carter, but the total vote was down.

Reagan racked up significant percentages among all the voting groups identifiable by ethnic or religious background. Protestants gave him a 57–36 margin, Catholics 47–43, and among Jews he won 1 of 4 of those who had voted for Carter in 1976, reducing the once over-whelming Democratic margin to 4 to 3. His name no doubt helped Reagan carry the Irish vote in every major state; a majority of Italians went for him in New Jersey, New York, and California. He carried the Polish-Slavic vote in New Jersey, Connecticut, Illinois, and Michigan. For the first time a Republican candidate made inroads into the Latino vote, pulling 25 percent.

The demographics of the ethnic vote were specially significant. A high percentage of the Reagan voters were counted as working class, enabling him to come close to a majority among union members, and to lead Carter 48–43 among blue-collar workers as a whole. Ethnics who had not attained upper middleclass status were still concentrated in big city neighborhoods, a fact that took on increasing significance as racial tensions mounted. Unlike the whites who had decamped to sub-urbia, they were, as Kevin Phillips described them, those who "felt the shove of fellow proles in the same block."

The bitterest pill of all for Carter was the loss of the entire South, except for Georgia. He blamed the split engendered by Ted Kennedy's attempt to unseat him, and the conspicuous lack of party loyalty among many Democratic officeholders. "The only reason a Southern congressman goes to a Democratic convention," he said, "is so he can walk out."

The president took his defeat gracefully, with only traces of bitterness showing up in his private diary entries. It was generally conceded that he was an honorable man who had lived up to the pledge that drew derisive comment from Washington insiders when he made it in the course of his first campaign: "If I ever lie to you, if I ever make a misleading statement, don't vote for me. I would not deserve to be your president." I doubt that many of those who voted against him would have used that as an excuse.

There was an air of contrition among many who came to call at the White House in the interval between the election and Reagan's inaugural. In his diary entry for December 16 the lame-duck president wrote:

> I met with the Advisory Committee on Women. . . . I've enjoyed getting to know these women leaders, some of whom were almost emotional in their approval of what we have tried to do and have actually done. If they and the blacks and Hispanics and the consumers and the environmentalists and others had been as friendly toward me a year ago as they are now that I'm going out of office, I would not have had any trouble getting reelected.

It would soon be evident that all these organized groups had lost the key to the White House. In January, when the Carters were packing up for their return to Plains, I wrote a note of condolence to Jesse Jackson: "I see by the morning paper that you had lunch yesterday at the White House. I guess it was something like the Last Supper. In any case, I expect you'll be dining elsewhere for a while."

POSTMORTEM
THE REAGAN COUNTERREVOLUTION

The belated achievements of "equality before the law" revealed a harsh truth that the long struggle for civil rights had obscured: guarantees of legal equality could not change the unequal condition of most black Americans. Almost at once the field of the debate shifted, and the older civil rights ideal has since stood as the most widely voiced objection to the race-conscious methods by which a fuller measure of equality has been sought in the post–civil rights era.

> —ANDREW KULL, "The 14th Amendment That Wasn't,"
> *Constitution*, vol. 5, no. 1

AT THE BEGINNING of the 1980 presidential campaign, Richard J. Whalen, a Republican strategist, predicted that Ronald Reagan would win because he gave his party a secret weapon—"the fact that Democrats fail to take him seriously." That was also true of seasoned political observers when he first came to Washington. Most shrugged off as leftover populist campaign rhetoric the declaration that provided the theme for the new president's inaugural address: "Government is not the solution to our problems. Government *is* the problem."

Washington insiders took this as a variation on the standard plaint of those who came to the capital as self-professed outsiders. Jimmy Carter held the course record with his 1976 denunciation of the "horrible, bloated, confused, overlapping, wasteful, insensitive, unmanageable bureaucratic mess in Washington." But the realities imposed by roller-coaster fluctuations in the economy had always stymied the reformist impulse, and for fifty years there had been no significant departure from basic policies of governance put into place in the New Deal period.

To offset the social and economic effects of the Great Depression, the Roosevelt administration had adopted some of the ideas advanced by the British economist John Maynard Keynes, and for a generation they had been relied on to flatten the curve of recession, control inflation, stimulate growth, and provide tax income to pay for goods not readily available in the private sector—housing for low- and moderate-income families, health care, urban transportation, and the like.

Democrats and Republicans, with some differences on priority and method, had been in general agreement that the Keynesian formula was essential to the functioning of a modern industrial society. They had agreed, too, that the central government must provide or encourage measures—unemployment insurance, welfare payments, old-age pensions, medical insurance, environmental protection, job and product regulation—that would protect individuals against circumstances beyond their control.

By the time President Eisenhower ended the Democratic rule that produced these policies, the government had been reshaped around them, and the general was not a man disposed to challenge the status quo. Richard Nixon professed to accept them with enthusiasm. In an interview shortly after taking office, he said of his declared support for the government's family aid programs, "There's nothing I feel more strongly about." Asked about his willingness to unbalance the budget to spur economic growth, he replied, "I'm now a Keynesian in economics," prompting Howard K. Smith to observe that for a Republican this was "a little like a Christian Crusader saying, 'All things considered, I think Mohammad was right.' "

There was no evidence that Reagan had ever given serious thought to economic theory, or, for that matter, practice. As a lethargic governor of California in a boom period he had followed the Democratic legislature's lead in maintaining existing programs, raising taxes when necessary to balance the budget. In the course of the presidential campaign he picked up on the brand of economics labeled "supply side" because it furthered his real purpose—to reduce the authority of the federal government to levels not seen since the Articles of Confederation created a shaky coalition of sovereign states empowered only to provide for the national defense. So far as government was concerned, Reagan was an abolitionist, not a reformer. Lou Cannon described the genesis of Reagan's operating theory:

> Reaganomics was not born in a classroom, nor did it spring full blown like Athena from the brows of economist Arthur Laffer and writer Jude Wanniski, though it owed much to these high priests of supply side economics. . . . While its claims were conflicting and its figures never susceptible to normal arithmetic, it was a thoroughly appropriate advocacy for Reagan. . . . Counsellor Edwin Meese, faithfully echoing Reagan's views, contended that improvement of economic conditions is "50 percent psychological." Others in the Reagan entourage were infected, like Meese, by the contagious optimism of their leader. Seen in this light, Reaganomics was less a program than a joyous secular theology not susceptible to examination by statistical data. Reagan believed in Reaganomics and was confident that his untried combination of programs would lead to a new prosperity. The Reagan inner circle believed in Reagan. And the others, whether believers or not, went along.

The consequences were not long in becoming apparent. There was happy talk among the president's supporters of a "Reagan revolution" to correct the inflation and slow growth they blamed on taxes and governmental intrusion into the marketplace. But when the administration submitted its first budget to Congress, the Nobel laureate economist James Tobin saw it as the product not of a revolution but of a "counterrevolution in the theory, ideology, and practice of economic policy":

> Wealth breeds wealth and poverty breeds poverty. . . . Here, as in other democracies, governments have sought to arrest the momentum of inequality by free public education, social insurance, "war on poverty" measures and progressive taxation. The U.S. budget and tax legislation of 1981 is a historic reversal

of direction and purpose. Existing institutions, commitments, and "safety nets" can't be rapidly dismantled, but the message is clear enough: Inequality of opportunity is no longer a concern of the federal government.

Back in the 1950s, when I wrote *An Epitaph for Dixie* and cited Cotton Ed Smith's three-plank platform—states' rights, tariff for revenue only, and white supremacy—it was regarded as an anachronism even in the South. Such a shameless appeal to racism, parochial chauvinism, and economic self-interest was written off as an obsolete product of the theater of the absurd nurtured by one-party politics. But dressed in different language, Cotton Ed's platform reemerged in 1980, and survived intact when Vice President George Bush succeeded President Reagan in an election that indicated endorsement, or at least acceptance, by a substantial majority of the voters.

States' rights, equated with localism and privatization, was a primary element of Reaganomics. The commitment to free trade as a corollary of free enterprise made protective tariffs a live election issue. And while no one outside the lunatic fringe still talked out loud about white supremacy, it was never possible to separate racism from doctrinaire insistence that the federal government should have no role in determining social policy.

I had occasion to reflect on the implications of this resurgence of states' rights philosophy on a fine spring day in 1988 when I returned to its fountainhead to sit beside an imposing black man on the platform at Clemson University's commencement exercises. My companion was General Colin Powell, national security adviser to the president of the United States and soon to become chief of the nation's armed services. Draped around our necks were the traditional hoods denoting the brevet doctoral status that had just been conferred on us.

The general was amused when I told him the only hoods I could recall seeing in those parts fifty years ago had been equipped with eyeholes. There were other, more profound reminders of the sea change in white attitudes that had made possible his presence as honoree at an institution he could not have attended in his student days. Clemson's foothill domain is studded with memorials to Dixie.

The showpiece is the carefully preserved mansion where John C.

Calhoun elaborated the doctrine of states' rights in defense of slavery. The first college building erected after his Fort Hill plantation became the Clemson campus commemorates then governor "Pitchfork Ben" Tillman, who rallied a populist following with a brutally repressive formulation of Calhoun's theory of white supremacy. Conspicuous among the newer structures is the Strom Thurmond Institute, named after the venerable alumnus who in 1948 headed the rump States' Rights Democratic Party protest against President Truman's civil rights program.

Then there is the massive seventy-five-thousand-seat "Death Valley" stadium that replaced the modest football field of my day. In the twenty-six years since Harvey Gantt was admitted to the university under court order, blacks had played a primary role in making Clemson a major power in intercollegiate athletics. When the Tigers moved up to No. 1 in national football ranking by defeating the University of Georgia Bulldogs there were only three whites on Clemson's starting eleven, four on Georgia's.

It didn't seem politic to mention to General Powell another memory that came flooding back when we repaired for lunch to an elegant VIP suite atop the stadium. A year after *Brown*, the sports editor of the *Arkansas Gazette* returned from a high school coaching clinic to report what he considered a harbinger. A University of Arkansas graduate who had become a star professional quarterback had been asked how he felt about playing with black teammates. The coaches were reassured by his answer: "When you get out there on the field, there's only one question: Can our niggers beat their niggers?"

When I mentioned this to the *Gazette*'s venerable proprietor, J. N. Heiskell, whose memory reached back to Reconstruction, he shook his head and said, "I had always hoped they wouldn't become our gladiator class." It was a prescient comment. In America as in Rome, the descendants of slaves had enjoyed their most conspicuous success as athletes, warriors, and entertainers.

Colin Powell was a living refutation of the belief in white supremacy embodied in the laws of the nation until it was challenged in the courts by black plaintiffs, and on the streets by black leaders of the civil rights movement. The military services provided the closest approximation of a meritocracy we have, and he could not have moved up through the ranks had he not demonstrated to the satisfaction of often prejudiced superiors uncommon qualities of intelligence, courage, diligence, and organizational ability.

But the general would not have had an opportunity to display those qualities had it not been for the affirmative action undertaken by Harry Truman, the president whose reelection prompted Strom Thurmond to lead what had since become a parade of defecting Southern Democrats into the Republican fold. Over the objections of General Eisenhower, then chief of staff, Truman exercised his authority as commander in chief to order the first mass institutional desegregation in the nation's history. The Army and the Air Force then had only one black officer with rank as high as colonel, the Navy had a total of four of any rank, and the Marines had one.

When Powell, who earned a commission in the Army Reserve at the College of the City of New York, was called up for duty in Vietnam, black and white soldiers were serving shoulder to shoulder. It was no longer possible to treat black officers as mere tokens to be kept as far away from white troops as possible, as they had been in the World War II Army I served in.

The military's hierarchical command structure made it possible to enforce the presidential edict; subordinate commanders might grumble, but they could not ignore a direct order. Powell recalled that he encountered a good deal of racial unpleasantness along the way, but the bigotry of some of his peers obviously had not hindered his rapid climb to the top.

The first black to attain four-star rank, Roscoe Robinson, recalled, however, that it had taken more than a decade to break through the glass ceiling senior commanders imposed to preserve the upper echelons for their own kind. "It took more than a presidential proclamation," he said. The sixteenth black to graduate from West Point, he was assigned to an all-black unit in Korea, and was subsequently barred from assignments that would have put him on the road to the top: "There were regions in the world blacks could not go to. There were very few blacks assigned to visible jobs at higher headquarters. None of these opened up until the sixties."

Like most career soldiers, Colin Powell considered himself apolitical, and when his prominence in Washington's inner circles led to a press conference question about party preference, he bluntly replied: "I don't have to answer that. I haven't answered it, and I'm not going to answer it. . . . I'm a military officer." He had not been identified with the civil rights movement, but he conceded that the Army's need to respond to the pressures it generated had facilitated his ascent to the apex of the command structure. By the time the Vietnam campaign escalated into a major conflict, blacks had finally won the recognition previously denied members of their race who had served with valor in every American war. It was a major breakthrough, and pride in the achievement denied Martin Luther King significant black support in his protest against the futile war in Southeast Asia.

Military service, with its shared dangers and hardships, had seemed to me to promise a useful advance in race relations. It could teach skills and inspire self-confidence in black youths with little education and no prospect of more. And service in an integrated unit could provide a salutary experience for white youths that could help dispel the myth of genetic black inferiority. But the prospect was soured when it turned out that the draft, as practiced in the Vietnam War, grossly discriminated against the poor of all races.

Student deferments allowed middleclass youths to sit out the war in college if they chose to, and most did. The great majority of the grunts who manned the front lines in Vietnam were blacks, Southern rednecks, and urban ethnics. The casualty rate among blacks was more than twice their proportion in the population. And when the survivors came home they were scorned, along with their white compatriots, by vociferous converts to the anti-Vietnam cause.

The draft had since been abandoned in favor of an all-volunteer professional force, and military life provided a useful common experience for the two races. A career as a noncommissioned officer offered one of the best prospects for income and security available to blacks without a college education; by 1990, annual pay for a master sergeant had risen to $31,000, plus allowances for personal and family expenses, medical care, and a generous pension. Blacks still accounted for only 7 percent of the commissioned officers, but they made up 22 percent of the 1.8 million enlisted personnel, nearly twice their percentage in the population.

When General Powell was ordered by President Bush to deploy a massive expeditionary force in the Persian Gulf, blacks made up nearly a third of the troops expected to bear the brunt of the casualties. The reaction to this apparent discrimination was reflected in the black community by polls that showed only 47 percent support for Operation Desert Shield, against 80 percent among whites.

When the issue was raised with Powell he replied, "That is not a question for the chief of the Joint Staffs. That is a question for the American people." In any case it became moot when the forces triumphed in short order with a minimum of casualties and all the fighting men and women were acclaimed as heroes—with Colin Powell touted by Republican leaders as the ideal choice to run as vice president when President Bush stood for reelection.

The fact that racial discrimination in the military had been largely eliminated with the evident approbation of the white majority certainly represented a major advance in race relations. But like the other gains made by the civil rights movement, it did not reach down effectively to the black underclass. A high school diploma or its equivalent was now mandatory for the kind of high-tech soldier, sailor, and airman the modernized armed forces required, and there was no place for those who dropped out of school and became subject to a different set of manhood rites prescribed by the armed gangs that dominated their inner city neighborhoods.

Ironically, inadequate schooling did not prove to be a barrier for black gladiators who possessed the physical attributes required for collegiate athletic competition. They were welcomed into institutions of higher learning despite evident lack of academic qualification, and a significant number moved on to lucrative careers in professional sports without attaining any semblance of a formal education during the years they were presumably enrolled in college classes. Less than a fourth of those who made varsity football and basketball teams were awarded degrees, and one of the professional stars told a congressional committee that he and a good many of his peers were still functionally illiterate when they received theirs.

In its early days Thorstein Veblen pointed out that football bore the same relationship to education that bullfighting had to agriculture. Yet football and basketball had become widely publicized, income-producing enterprises on the major campuses. What began as fun and games for the amusement of players and student spectators had become a public extravaganza designed to please fans who had no connection with the sponsoring institution.

The amateur status of college athletes was presumed to be guaranteed by limiting subsidy to the provision of room, board, and tuition. The intense competition in recruiting, however, encouraged higher expectations, and illicit means of meeting them were found as the college teams became a farm system for the professional leagues, where the stars counted their income in the millions. Although only 1 percent of black college athletes survived the weeding-out process and gained access to such wealth, they made up 74 percent of the players in pro basketball and 62 percent in pro football.

The system was defended as a means of providing education for poor minority youths who would otherwise be denied it. It did serve this purpose in some cases, producing responsible citizens who provided role models to fire the ambition of ghetto youth. But the system proved inherently corrupting. A 1991 study commissioned by the Knight Foundation found that during the 1980s half the institutions in its top division were cited for violating rules of the National Collegiate Athletic Association. Father Theodore Hesburgh, former president of Notre Dame, one of the great football powers, cochaired the investigation and called for concerted action to clear "the scum from the swamp of intercollegiate athletics."

The civil rights movement had provided blacks with the visibility long denied them, but for the most part they were viewed by whites through the mass media. This meant that while they could achieve wide recognition and be admired, even idolized, the social gap that divided the black and white communities remained largely intact. The breakthrough came as television achieved a national audience and became the primary creator of celebrity; the electronic medium's voracious appetite for common-denominator programming opened up the field of popular entertainment, which had been effectively off-limits to blacks when it was confined to theater, movies, and radio.

Prior to World War II a few black entertainers with extraordinary talent achieved star status as jazz made its way into the mainstream, but they remained on the periphery and were often exploited by white managers. Otherwise, mass audiences saw blacks only as figures of low comedy, and in the tradition of the minstrel show these were often portrayed by whites in blackface. This was the case with "Amos 'n' Andy," one of the most popular and durable radio programs, and *The Jazz Singer*, which introduced sound to motion pictures.

But as the civil rights movement opened the way for a dramatic increase in black purchasing power, the Madison Avenue advertising agencies discovered a new and neglected market for brand-name consumer goods. Since the needs of advertisers determine the audiences TV seeks, the networks began experimenting with programs designed to attract black viewers without offending whites. Bill Cosby, a comedian with a gentle touch, created and starred in what became the most successful situation comedy on television, fashioning it around a middleclass family distinguished from its white counterparts only by skin color.

In the multibillion-dollar music industry, which caters to the youth market, inhibitions quickly disappeared when black jazz was combined with white country music. The way was opened for black entertainers to stake out places at the top of the charts and add their own rap style; at the dawn of the 1990s Michael Jackson occupied the place once held by the archetypical redneck Elvis Presley as a generational icon.

The erosion of standards of propriety in pop entertainment produced stand-up comics like Richard Pryor and Eddie Murphy, specialists in satiric, off-color humor who attained top ranking on the nightclub circuit and were co-opted by the movies. Oprah Winfrey and Arsenio Hall found their place among the millionaire hosts of TV talk shows that featured celebrity guests and titillated audiences with freewheeling discussion of offbeat human behavior. Hollywood, where the box office is the final arbiter, even embraced Spike Lee, a talented young filmmaker who derived his ideology from Malcolm X. Lee graduated to big budgets when he demonstrated that his sensational, antiwhite movies could fill theaters.

. . .

In positive terms, the new visibility blacks had acquired applied largely to those who had achieved middleclass status. The rapid increase in their numbers in a single generation was the most significant achievement of the civil rights movement. The percentage of black families with annual incomes of fifty thousand dollars or more increased from 5.8 percent in 1967 to 13.8 percent in 1990. More than a million blacks were now counted among the affluent, and as many more were well enough off to afford the life-style of the middleclass. Forty percent of these lived in the suburbs, while most of the rest were to be found in gentrified enclaves effectively removed from the inner city ghettos.

This remarkable record of progress was made possible by the shift toward more permissive attitudes by whites, but it had not yet significantly affected the lot of the majority of blacks, who were still classified as working poor or underclass. Still, there was enough forward movement in the 1970s to justify the prediction in my book *Hearts and Minds* that the progression, if it could be maintained, "may yet be reckoned the most profound social change mankind has achieved without resort to violence."

My optimism had waned by the time the book reached print in 1982. With the return of the Republicans to power under Ronald Reagan it immediately became evident that another effect of the new visibility of blacks had been to reinstate, and further distort, corrosive racial issues that had intermittently dominated national politics since the founding of the republic. The rhetoric associated with the Republicans' Southern Strategy had a polarizing effect on both races, and reduced white support for government programs that had been instrumental in opening to blacks the kind of employment required to provide middleclass status in a market-oriented society.

Reaganomics depended on economic growth induced by minimal taxes and severely limited government regulation to provide an upward spiral of prosperity that presumably would lift the deserving poor out of poverty. It was assumed that an appeal to inherent family values, combined with stringent law enforcement, would serve to restore stability to inner city neighborhoods. But for this theory to work, employment with a prospect of advancement must be opened to blacks—

and this had been denied all but an exceptional few prior to the civil rights movement. Discrimination had been tempered in some major industries by the fair employment practices required of wartime military suppliers, but prior to the 1960s exclusion of blacks from all but menial jobs was standard practice in most areas of employment.

The breakthrough that opened the way for the economic emancipation of blacks came in 1961. The first of the steps that were to be lumped together under the rubric "affirmative action" was an executive order issued by President Kennedy reserving a percentage of federal contracts for minority-owned businesses, and authorizing procurement agencies to require that companies doing business with the government set aside job vacancies for qualified minority applicants.

The Civil Rights Act of 1964 extended these requirements to all companies with more than fifteen employees, and set up the Equal Employment Opportunity Commission (EEOC) to oversee compliance. Normal attrition was depended on to provide the openings set aside for minority employees, and most employers voluntarily accepted guidelines based on availability of qualified minorities in the local labor pool. Where there were credible claims of continued discrimination, class action suits were brought by the Justice Department, most of which were settled by negotiated consent decrees. The "equal opportunity employer" imprimatur awarded by the EEOC met with such public approbation that it gained the support of the major business associations.

There was comparable backing among the CIO unions, which, under the leadership of Walter Reuther of the United Auto Workers, had actively supported the civil rights movement. But policy made at the top did not necessarily convert the rank and file; to Reuther's embarrassment, the grand kleagle of the Ku Klux Klan turned out to be a member of the Atlanta UAW local. And there was all but universal resistance among AFL craft unions, whose apprenticeship requirements gave them control of employment at the entry level.

Richard Nixon put a Republican gloss on the effort to bring blacks into the economic mainstream by setting up the Office of Minority Business Enterprise in the Commerce Department to promote "black capitalism." And in response to urging by employers, the administration standardized the various employment requirements. The pattern-setting "Philadelphia Plan" was devised to meet the complaint of building contractors that they could not comply with EEOC requirements under conditions imposed by their unions.

In Philadelphia restrictive union hiring practices were exemplified by the plumbers' and pipefitters' local, which included only 12 blacks among its 2,335 members. A settlement negotiated by the Justice Department called for step-by-step increases, with a goal of 22 to 26 percent. Similar goals and timetables were incorporated in the regulations governing all federal procurement and contracting; by 1970 the new dispensation affected corporations that employed more than a third of the nation's work force. Extended throughout the private sector by further legislation and executive orders, this would be labeled a "quota system" by Nixon's Republican successors, and used as a code term for a concerted attack on all forms of affirmative action.

As long as economic growth continued to produce new jobs, there was very little real conflict of interest between white and black job applicants at the entry level. In an expanding economy a white man turned down for a job to make way for a minority or a woman could readily find an equivalent opening elsewhere. Small businesses were exempt from EEOC regulations, and in larger work forces with regular turnover minority and female newcomers were readily absorbed.

In the case of promotion, however, head-to-head competition was inevitable. Higher-paying jobs required skills gained through experience, and seniority had long been a determining factor, usually written into union contracts and civil service regulations. Since in most cases whites had been on the promotion track before there were any black employees, blacks were ruled out if seniority was the sole criterion.

"Retroactive seniority," the device used to offset this built-in discrimination, was upheld in 1976 by a divided U.S. Supreme Court. The majority opinion, written by Justice William Brennan, found that without such a dispensation a black worker

will never obtain his rightful place in the hierarchy of seniority according to which these various employment benefits are distributed. He will perpetually remain subordinate to persons who, but for the illegal discrimination, would have been, in respect to entitlement to these benefits, his inferiors.

Dissenting, Justice Lewis Powell agreed that this was the case, but held that the remedy would penalize

> the rights and expectations of perfectly innocent employees. The economic benefits awarded discrimination victims would be derived not at the expense of the employer but at the expense of other workers.

In *Chain Reaction: The Impact of Race, Rights, and Taxes on American Politics*, Thomas and Mary D. Edsall cited a case history that proved both justices correct. The Birmingham Fire Department did not hire its first black fireman until 1968, and held out until 1974 before hiring a second. Resistance was finally broken by court action in 1981, two years after the city elected a black mayor. The department agreed to a consent decree providing that until proportional parity was attained every white hired or promoted would be matched by a black who could meet standard test requirements.

In 1983 a black lieutenant was appointed, although his qualifying test score was 122, against 192 for a competing white applicant. Conceding that blacks had been unfairly treated in the past, the white loser said, "Somebody needs to pay for this. But they want me to pay for it, and I didn't have anything to do with it. I was a kid when all this went on." The black winner countered, "The fact is, sometimes [whites] have to pay up. If a wrong has been committed, you have to right that wrong."

It was not, of course, possible to level a playing field without some loss of advantage for those who were in a favored position. Although only a small minority of whites were affected by the negotiated settlements worked out by the EEOC, the perceived injustice provided additional fuel for the ideological backlash touched off by busing. The Republican Party, the Edsalls wrote,

> was able to stake out a conservative civil rights stand that won strong majority support. Advocacy of "equal opportunity"—the original clarion call of the civil rights movement—became the

center-right position, the core of a new conservative egalitarian populism. . . . The importance of race in the chain of events that brought Ronald Reagan to the White House cannot be overestimated.

Reagan, who had cast himself as a great commoner, was ideally suited for exploitation of the real and fancied grievances that resulted when white men, working as carpenters, plumbers, sheet-metal workers, iron-workers, steamfitters, policemen, and firemen, became the focus of the antidiscrimination drive waged by the Civil Rights Division of the Justice Department. And these were traditional constituents of the Democratic Party.

The ideological push for repeal of fair employment policies enacted by Congress, approved by the Supreme Court, and widely accepted by employers turned on the contention that they constituted preferential group treatment at the expense of individual merit. But where it was deemed to serve a worthy public purpose, the government had long provided comparable group entitlements in the form of veterans' benefits, crop subsidies, tax credits to businessmen, and the like. The practice did not become controversial until the groups involved were minorities and women who had been denied equal treatment in the educational system and the workplace.

As the basis for court action supported by the Justice Department, it was contended that applying such standards constituted "reverse discrimination" against white males. Where a limited number of openings was involved this was a plausible argument, and it was the focus of the *Bakke* case, which brought the issue to a head before the Supreme Court in 1977.

Alan Bakke, a white man turned down for admission to the Medical School of the University of California at Davis, claimed violation of meritocratic principle when he did not receive one of a hundred openings although his grades and test scores were higher than those of applicants who filled the sixteen places set aside for minorities.

But professional schools had never used grades and test scores as the sole measures of eligibility for admission. The dean in charge at

UC Davis testified that he had employed other standards to modify numerical ranking in at least a hundred cases—including those in which consideration was given to relatives of a retired chancellor, a former president of the county medical society, and the chairmen of legislative committees that passed on the university budget. There was in fact no campus in the land—and no private enterprise, for that matter—where meritocracy so narrowly construed could be said to prevail.

The black student who occupied the slot denied Bakke obviously was given special treatment. Whether this kind of discrimination was justified, Thurgood Marshall contended in a memorandum circulated to his brethren, turned on the justices' appraisal of the place occupied in society by the black minority from which qualified applicants were drawn:

> I wish to address the question of whether Negroes have "arrived." Just a few examples illustrate that Negroes certainly have not. In our own Court, we have only three Negro law clerks here, and not so far have we had a Negro officer of this Court. On a broader scale, this week's *U.S. News & World Report* has a story about "who runs America." They list some 83 persons— not one Negro, even as would-be runner-up. . . . The dream of America as the melting pot has not been realized by Negroes—either the Negro did not get into the pot, or he did not get melted down.

Marshall's blunt reminder that blacks remained a uniquely visible minority no doubt contributed to the Solomonic judgment finally handed down. The pro–civil rights majority of the Warren Court had been whittled away, and four justices found that Bakke had suffered unconstitutional discrimination. Four others held that he hadn't, leaving Justice Powell, the only Southerner on the bench, to cast the deciding vote and write an opinion that watered down the principle of affirmative action but allowed it to stand.

Powell held that the specific numbers called for in the UC Davis policy could be construed as a quota, and on that technicality approved Bakke's admission. But he also upheld the right of a university to exercise broad discretion in determining admissions policy, conceding that action to increase the number of minorities in the learned professions clearly served a worthy public purpose.

With the advent of new Republican appointees the Court began to yield to efforts by the executive branch to weaken the enforcement provisions of civil rights laws, but Congress continued to hold firm, enacting legislation that plugged loopholes opened by the courts. The practical reason was that few employers and administrators joined in the demand for change. The political reason was that women, who constituted a majority of the electorate, now had an interest in the issue as compelling as that of the minorities.

When Reagan called for a halt to the federal effort to achieve a racially integrated society, more than 30 percent of the blacks had achieved the upward mobility that led to middleclass status, and, like their white counterparts, they would temporarily benefit from the tax cuts and lowered inflation rates attributed to Reaganomics. Many of those who had risen above the immediate need for government assistance emulated their white peers in looking the other way when they encountered the unfortunates who fell through the tattered welfare safety net, and in increasing numbers began to live on the streets.

But for the majority of blacks the change in direction was catastrophic. Those classified as working poor lived on the margin just above the poverty line, trapped there by their inferior education and limited skills. Most of the jobs available to them outside the shrinking manufacturing sector paid less than the annual average of $15,017 a national cross section polled by Gallup estimated as the minimum necessary in 1989 to sustain a husband, wife, and two children. Most had no health insurance, and they did not qualify for Medicaid. Nor were their families entitled to such income supplements as the food stamps provided for those on welfare.

Effective abandonment of the effort to break up the ghettos by subsidizing low-cost, scatter-site housing left many of the working poor confined to black neighborhoods where the life-style was determined by dysfunctional families blighted by generations of welfare dependency. Those who qualified for government support fell below a poverty line set in 1989 at $12,675 annually for a family of four. When Reagan left office, Americans in this category had increased by 6 million, for a total of 30.2 million. More than a third were children; half of the children were black, one in three Latino.

The disintegration of the black family in the crime-ridden ghetto environment could hardly be questioned as the illegitimacy rate for black children rose to 63 percent. In Washington, D.C., now 70 percent black, four times as many black men were jailed in 1989 as were graduated from public schools. In the segregated inner cities the family role for young black males was commonly limited to fathering children they promptly abandoned. A grim distillation of government statistics was presented to the NAACP at its 1990 convention:

> One of four black men in their twenties is either in jail, in prison, on probation or parole.
>
> Violence is the No. 1 cause of death for black males between the ages of fifteen and twenty-five; their murder rate is ten times that of their white counterparts.
>
> Black men in poor, inner city neighborhoods are less likely to live to the age of sixty-five than their counterparts in Bangladesh. Black males are the only U.S. demographic group that can expect to live shorter lives in 1990 than they did in 1980.

These figures added up to a national urban crisis of the first magnitude. Yet a president whose tenure was characterized as *Sleepwalking Through History* by one of its chroniclers, Haynes Johnson, continued to turn a deaf ear to pleas for action to deal with the plight of the cities. This seemed to me a flight from reality that exceeded anything I had known in the days when the Southern mythology still sustained Jim Crow.

On the economic front Reagan set out to reverse the effort to deal with poverty through income redistribution. His tax reforms included cuts in the upper brackets that transferred $25 billion in disposable income from the less well off to the wealthiest fifth of the population. Welfare had always been a particular object of his scorn, and entitlement programs for the poor suffered 60 percent of the initial budget reduction. Court action was initiated to undo the civil rights policies the Supreme Court had approved in the years since *Brown*.

Justice Department lawyers attempted to overturn court orders requiring school desegregation, and sought to dilute the enforcement provisions of the Voting Rights Act. The president exercised his authority to cancel guidelines for implementing open housing, and another executive order restored federal tax exemptions for segregated private schools—a violation of the 1964 Civil Rights Act so flagrant that more than 100 of the 176 lawyers in the Civil Rights Division at the Department of Justice resigned in protest.

When this head-on attack was rebuffed by a slender majority of the Supreme Court, Reagan used his appointive power to vitiate the enforcement agencies. Thwarted by Congress in the effort to abolish the Civil Rights Commission, he loaded it with appointees who created a deadlock that rendered it impotent. And, having placed the Justice Department in the control of attorneys who opposed affirmative action on principle, he appointed a black lawyer of similar persuasion to head the EEOC.

Clarence Thomas, who took over as chairman in 1982, proclaimed his conviction that "distributing opportunities on the basis of race or gender . . . turns the law against employment discrimination on its head. Class preferences are an affront to the rights and dignity of individuals." The policy under which the agency had initiated class action suits to further negotiated settlements was abandoned in favor of prosecuting individual cases of discrimination. The limited but protracted litigation that resulted created a mounting backlog of complaints, and the cases that did go to trial provided redress only for individuals who initiated the action. The effect was to halt the use of goals and timetables until action by Congress, upheld by the Supreme Court, forced reinstatement of the original policy.

The appeal of populist politics, whether of the right or the left, is to the voter's immediate self-interest, and it dismisses those who advocate broader policies as elitists who scorn the common folk. While it can be used to win elections, it can also make it impossible for the winner to govern effectively. Reagan's pledge to cut taxes as a means of taking the government off the backs of the people drew a widespread popular response. But reduced tax income produced mounting deficits even though support for government activity was sharply curtailed in areas other than defense, where expenditures were sharply increased in response to the flag-waving chauvinism that characterizes right-wing populism.

As far as welfare and entitlement programs were concerned, the budget deficit was an intended result, seen as a means of guaranteeing against reinstatement of curtailed expenditures. But reduced income also made it impracticable for the Reagan and Bush administrations to deal effectively with the issue of law and order touted as their No. 1 domestic concern. Reagan had declared an all-out war on crime, and Bush pledged an escalation with the emphasis on drugs. But neither provided funding to pay for the expansion of the criminal justice system such an undertaking required.

Emphasis on law and order was bound to evoke a popular response. No one could question the evident fact that criminal activity spawned in the ghettos constituted a clear and present danger. Unsafe streets and public transportation had become commonplace, and violence had begun to spill over into middleclass neighborhoods. Funded by huge profits from the drug traffic, teenage gangs armed with automatic weapons engaged in turf battles in many cities, with a mounting death toll of innocent bystanders.

The Reagan/Bush devotion to tougher law enforcement was largely evidenced in the push for enactment of laws that reinstated the death penalty for homicides and required longer prison sentences for lesser offenses. Federal judges were appointed who were willing to roll back the constitutional protections afforded the accused, and they were usually upheld by the Supreme Court, now headed by the hard-line Chief Justice William Rehnquist.

The most disturbing aspect of the emphasis on tougher criminal penalties was its application to the juvenile court system. Children who violated the law were normally tried as "delinquents" in separate courts where judges proceeded on the assumption that rehabilitation was possible for those who had not yet become hardened criminals. Most were given probation and returned to society under court supervision, while the more recalcitrant were incarcerated in institutions where the emphasis was on education rather than punishment.

Although the rate of violent crime among juveniles actually declined by 19 percent from 1978 to 1988, the incarceration rate increased by

50 percent. The get-tough policy at the federal level was emulated by the states, where laws were rewritten to provide that under-age youths could be tried as adults and sentenced to regular prisons—the transfer age dropping to fourteen in seventeen states and to thirteen in Mississippi.

Michael Mahoney, a former official of the Illinois Youth Center, explained why: "Politicians . . . seize upon some crime that has caught the public eye. Then they pass a law to make the punishment tougher, and the public nods its approval." Frank Reynolds, the presiding juvenile court judge in Philadelphia, pointed to the end result:

> The people in this country, having destroyed the children through neglect, have decided that they are not going to do anything to repair the damage. The alternative then is to just lock them up, and that's what they're doing.

Juvenile delinquency had become commonplace in all classes of society. The 1990 statistics showed that 70 percent of all juveniles arrested were white—but, as in all criminal justice categories, blacks bore the brunt of the punishment. Only 35 percent of the whites arrested wound up in custody, against 46 percent of blacks. That worked out to 287 incarcerated white juveniles per 100,000, against 1,009 blacks.

Tougher criminal justice procedures did not necessarily require significant federal expenditures, but it would cost a great deal to provide the additional police, prosecutors, judges, and prisons their enforcement would require. That burden fell upon state and local governments already hard-pressed by the cutback in federal matching funds for highways, urban renewal, welfare, and education. The failure to provide means to underwrite the rhetoric of the war on crime began to hamstring the police, bog down the courts, and fill the prisons to overflowing.

In California, a 1990 report by the state bar association found the overburdened criminal justice system on the point of collapse. Criminal case filings had risen by 114 percent between 1978 and 1988, and the prison population had more than quadrupled, from 24,000 to 101,000. Overcrowding in institutions filled to 185 percent of rated capacity forced a liberal parole policy, but two thirds of those released in 1988 were back behind bars within two years, bringing the total of incarcerated parole violators to 35,000. With all of this, the violent crime rate continued to rise, with a 12 percent increase recorded in 1989.

The result could be seen graphically on the front lines, where beleaguered citizens depended on the police for protection of life and property. In 1989 only 16.8 percent of the felonies committed in Los Angeles County resulted in felony arrests; only 9.7 percent of these reached court on felony charges; and only 5.4 percent resulted in jail sentences. The spiraling incidence of offenses left the police with no time to properly investigate any but major crimes. And prosecutors often reduced these to misdemeanors to obtain guilty pleas and relieve the burden on the courts.

District Attorney Ira Reiner explained why his office routinely offered probation or reduced prison sentences in return for guilty pleas: "If more than 5 percent go to trial the system shuts down. The system is functioning—and I suppose you could put quotes around 'functioning'—because only 5 percent go to trial."

Three years later the steadily rising crime rate, coupled with steadily declining state and county appropriations for the prosecutor's office, threatened to cut the percentages still further. Reiner's successor Gil Garcotti told the county board of supervisors that a proposed 16 percent cut in his budget would force him to abandon prosecution of felony auto theft, burglary and narcotics cases, and virtually end prosecution of misdemeanors.

Comparable statistics were reported in every state with a large metropolitan population. The situation in New York had become so desperate the city's first black mayor, David N. Dinkins, announced a "battle plan against fear." It called for the addition of 7,900 police officers to provide neighborhood foot patrols. This would add $1.8 billion to the budget of a municipality that for a decade had been verging on bankruptcy, and there was little prospect of help from the state capital, Albany, where state deficits were piling up.

The failure of the Reagan/Bush war on crime was directly related to inability to make headway with the concurrent campaign against drugs.

The federal government could hardly use the states' rights doctrine to palm off its responsibility for the flow of narcotics across the nation's borders, and this continued unabated despite beefed-up interdiction efforts by the Customs Service, Border Patrol, and Coast Guard. Equally unsuccessful was the offshore program employing foreign aid and support by U.S. armed forces to induce governments in Asia and Latin America to destroy the sources of heroin and cocaine.

This supply-side approach had no perceptible effect on the incidence of drug addiction. Narcotics continued to be readily available on ghetto street corners, in the schoolyards of middleclass suburbs, and in the haunts of aging yuppies for whom cocaine became the "recreational drug" of choice. Despite occasional raids on wholesalers, resulting in the seizure of millions of dollars' worth of narcotics, the street price remained relatively low.

Means were developed to step up the effect of cocaine through a freebased derivative called crack. There were also "designer drugs" that could be manufactured out of readily available chemicals. And back in the remote hills, descendants of moonshiners who had defied the federals in the Prohibition era were now growing marijuana—believed to rank as the leading cash crop in my upscale home county, Santa Barbara.

Victims of drug addiction could be found at all levels of society, but the casualty rate was highest among the black underclass. The use of narcotics, although common among jazz musicians, had not been widespread in the black community until white youths in the sixties proclaimed a drug culture as a mark of their liberation from the constraints of middleclass society. This had the effect of creating a popular demand comparable to that which created the illicit liquor trade during Prohibition. Since hard drugs provided the illusion of instant power, and opiates an escape from reality, they had a special allure for the powerless, and poor blacks made up a disproportionate share of the expanding market.

A substantial part of the enormous profits from the drug trade remained in the hands of the Asian and Latin American cartels that produced the basic components, and most of the rest went to criminal organizations that took over wholesale distribution. Blacks were few at the relatively protected upper levels of operations; they shared in the take primarily at retail, where ghetto youths provided a ready source of dealers willing to ignore the high risk of doing business on streets that became combat zones in the war on drugs.

As long as they could escape the narcotics squads and the gun-toting competitors who sought to take over their turf, these flashy young-sters held the only high-paying jobs available in their neighborhoods. Their poverty-stricken customers joined the criminal ranks as prostitutes, burglars, shoplifters, and armed robbers in order to maintain their habits. By 1988 they accounted for 38 percent of all drug arrests, and many of the 454,724 blacks who made up nearly half the inmates of the nation's prisons were convicted of drug-related felonies.

In 1980 the United States ranked third among industrialized nations in percentage of incarcerations per capita, but by the end of the decade it had moved into first place, imprisoning 426 persons per 100,000, against 333 in South Africa and 268 in the Soviet Union. Broken down by race, the rate for black American males stood at 3,109 per 100,000, four times that of black South Africans in a country racked by racial turmoil.

The Reagan/Bush commitment to a supply-side approach to dealing with the drug epidemic virtually precluded any effective effort on the demand side. This would require emphasis on preventing and curing addiction; instead, the federally mandated war on drugs devoted 70 percent of its resources to the criminal justice system.

A similar pattern was imposed on state and local governments as matching funds for activities other than law enforcement were reduced. From 1980 to 1990 federal contributions to the cities declined by 64 percent, and it was here that most medical and social services for the indigent were maintained. The result was a steady increase in the in-cidence of drug addiction, accompanied by a decrease in the facilities required to deal with it. By 1990, treatment was available for only 20 percent of the addicts who needed it.

Deploying police forces in a fashion that focused on the inner city, and placed blacks of all classes at risk of harassment, had the effect of erasing many of the gains the civil rights movement had made in tempering the bias of what was still a predominantly white criminal justice system. Black police had become commonplace in the South, their numbers had increased beyond token status in the North and West, and they headed departments in major cities. But as the drug trade spawned organized street gangs and high-powered automatic weapons replaced switchblades and Saturday-night specials, combat mentality began to take over among officers of both races.

Anyone wearing a police uniform or displaying a detective's badge was at risk when he went into the ghetto to investigate a complaint or make an arrest. This led to hassling the innocent as well as the legitimately suspect, and as discipline began to break down there was increasing transgression of the uncertain line that sets apart the proper employment of force from the use of firearms and billy clubs to administer the punishment many policemen believed the courts no longer imposed.

Encounters of this kind usually took place out of view of the white community, but a prime case in Los Angeles in early 1991 was exposed to the national television audience after a high-speed auto chase ended in a neighborhood outside the ghetto. Videotape taken by an amateur photographer who happened to be nearby showed that the unarmed black driver, Rodney King, offered no resistance, but was clubbed to the ground and brutally kicked and hammered with batons by three officers. At least nineteen others, including a sergeant, stood by and made no move to interfere.

The usual cover-up as the police closed ranks in the face of criticism was not possible in this case. Daryl Gates, who cherished his reputation as the nation's toughest police chief, could do no better than insist that "we can turn up absolutely nothing that would suggest [a racial motive] except for the officers were white and the suspect was black."

That was sufficient explanation for the battered victim, an amiable alcoholic with a record of nonviolent criminal offenses, who was obviously drunk when he attempted to evade arrest. Rodney King made no reference to racism per se when he was released from jail without charge and allowed to exhibit his injuries at a press conference. The men in blue who broke his leg and shattered bones in his eye socket and the base of his skull no doubt concurred when he said: "They consider themselves different humans than we are. . . . They're all a family. And they're a big family. And they're one family, and we're another family."

That was a sentiment shared by Patrick J. Buchanan, the pit bull of Washington commentators who would carry it into the coming presidential campaign as the candidate of the Republican right wing. "In our polarized and violent society," he wrote,

> most Americans have come to look upon the cops as "us," and upon King, a convicted felon, as "them." He is the enemy in a war we are losing, badly, and we have come to believe the cops are our last line of defense. If the cops beat him brutally, many will say that even though the cops went too far, they are our troops. . . .

The Bush administration's reaction to the furor followed the party line. The Justice Department announced that the assistant attorney general for civil rights, John R. Dunne, would undertake a review of the 15,000 complaints of police brutality filed during the past six years. But, Dunne warned, states' rights necessarily limited his approach. "We're not the 'front line' troops in combating instances of police abuse," he said, merely a "backstop" for internal discipline and state and local prosecutors. There had not been much backstopping under the Reagan/Bush administration; in the past year the department had received 7,690 complaints, conducted 3,050 investigations, and sought only 46 indictments.

In a speech to the Fraternal Order of Police, President Bush called for additional death penalty laws, as did the 1991 crime bill he sent to Congress, and referred to prison furloughs in a fashion that prompted a *Los Angeles Times* reporter to observe that he "sounded every bit the once and future candidate, turning out one by one the successful buzz-words of the 1988 campaign and signaling the reprise he is likely to produce for next year's presidential race."

At the beginning of the new decade the problems posed for state and local governments by the devolution of federal responsibility were compounded by economic recession. While the Bush administration could ignore or discount the declining economic indicators, the effect of decreased state and local tax revenue was inescapable for governments bound by constitutions that prohibited the deficit financing that kept Washington going. A balanced budget was required in every state except Vermont, and by the end of 1990 thirty were deep in the red. Twenty-six had raised taxes, and all were slashing expenditures.

In New York, Governor Mario Cuomo, facing a $6 billion deficit, sought a $1.2 billion increase in taxes and a 10 percent reduction in school aid and health benefits—and had the outer doors of his office smashed in by the vanguard of 20,000 protesters, mostly black and Puerto Rican, who marched on the state capitol for a "Budget Storm" rally. In California, faced with an 11 to 12 percent rise in school enrollment and welfare rolls caused by population increase, the deficit projections soared to $14 billion. Connecticut, with the highest per capita income in the nation, had a shortfall of $2.4 billion—a third of all its spending—and Governor Lowell Weicker forced through the state's first income tax.

In Michigan, trying to cover a $1.8 billion deficit in the 1991 budget, Democrats in the legislature pushed through a supplemental appropriation measure providing cuts of 17 percent in welfare payments, 22 percent for foster parents, and 18 percent for Medicaid health providers—this on top of the 9.2 percent reduction in 1990 funding for state programs. The new Republican governor, John Engler, vetoed the bill, demanding that the cuts be increased by another 10 percent. "The Democrats," he said, "continue to defend a welfare state that doesn't work."

The end product of the Reagan/Bush economic policy was not only a staggering deficit in the federal budget, but also a mounting deficit in public services at the state and local levels. But the ancient doctrine of laissez faire was now presumably cemented in place by the pollsters' finding of approval ratings for President Bush running as high as 91 percent in the wake of a cut-rate military victory over Iraq in the conflict among oil-rich fiefdoms in the Middle East. Under the headline "Putting Civil Rights on Automatic Pilot," *The Washington Post* summed up the administration's post–Gulf War approach to domestic issues: "The conservative ideological crusade is over. The builders are gone and the maintenance crew is in charge."

AFTERMATH
POLARIZATION OF THE PRIMARIES

In the Democratic party, an unfamiliar and un-American racism dominates the choice of delegates, as does a mechanical division of Americans by sex. Special interests, from the most greedy to the most idealistic, pour more money into politics than ever before, finding the primaries the most vulnerable point in the American process. . . . Most of the delegates, who were supposed to be free to vote by their own common sense and conscience, have become for the most part anonymous faces, collected as background for television cameras. . . .

—THEODORE H. WHITE,
America in Search of Itself

THE ECONOMIC roller coaster was on the downturn during the early years of the Reagan administration. While the "stagflation" that had plagued Jimmy Carter was tempered when the oil shortage eased, inflation was still running near 10 percent and unemployment was rising. In a February 1983 "Letter from Washington" in *The New Yorker*, Elizabeth Drew found it striking

> how quickly what was termed "the Reagan revolution" was over, and how evident the seeds of its destruction were all along. . . . By misinterpreting his mandate (with the help of a large number of commentators) and operating at the far end of the ideological spectrum, the president squandered his advantage. . . . In Au-

gust of 1981, Republicans, according to their own accounts, went home for the recess "in a state of euphoria"—their president was sweeping all before him—and returned in September "in a state of panic. . . ." A program that didn't add up in the presidential campaign didn't add up when it was submitted to Congress, and emerged (after Democrats and the White House bid up its price) even more mathematically askew.

Speculation that Reagan would not run for reelection was widespread. Lou Cannon wrote in an epilogue to his 1982 biography, "It was an axiom in the White House that Reagan, like so many of his modern predecessors, would be a one-term president." Cannon added his own prediction that the visibly aging president would not run again.

But if there was panic among Republicans at large, the amiable fellow who put in a short day in the Oval Office seemed impervious to it, as were the true believers in his inner circle who discounted the bad news even when complaints began turning up in the columns of the tribune of supply-side economics, *The Wall Street Journal*, where Norman C. Miller wrote:

> It is fundamentally unfair for the administration to concentrate almost exclusively on cutting assistance to the poor while simultaneously providing an excessive array of tax breaks to affluent persons and corporations.

The president's pollster, Richard Wirthlin, told Cannon he was finding that a growing majority of Americans shared that view.

But those who spoke for Reagan continued to insist that any complaint about social injustice was based on a misreading of statistics. "The number of people remaining in poverty is very small, and it grows smaller every year," wrote Martin Anderson, one of the president's domestic policy advisers. "The war on poverty has been won, except for a few mopping-up operations." That view could be sustained only if poverty were equated with starvation, and even here Democrats in Congress were holding public hearings that turned up evidence that nutritional deficiencies among poor children were approaching levels not seen since the Depression. Ed Meese responded: "I don't know of any authoritative figures that there are hungry children. I've heard a lot of anecdotal stuff, but I haven't heard any authoritative figures." After all, he said, getting in a swipe at the cheating "welfare queens" who played leading roles in the Reagan demonology, "people go to soup kitchens because the food is free and that's easier than paying for it."

The president himself had the final word when he made what turned out to be his farewell appearance before to the NAACP at its 1981 national convention, declaring that those who said that his domestic policy discriminated against poor blacks were "either ignorant of the facts or . . . are practicing, for political reasons, pure demagoguery." It was a notable display of chutzpah, since Nancy Reagan was the only person on the platform who hadn't said so.

There is no evidence that the blind eye the personally benign Reagan turned on the plight of poor blacks could be attributed to bigotry. Rather, it seemed to me an inevitable consequence of the prevailing attitude in the White House cited by Terence H. Bell, the respected professional educator who was appointed Secretary of Education. In Meese, the President's ideological gatekeeper, he found himself faced with "a man who literally detested the federal government," Bell wrote in *The Thirteenth Man*, a memoir published after he was forced out of office. "He viewed the upcoming Reagan presidency as a magnificent opportunity to smash the government programs that had created a 'welfare state.' " At less rarefied levels, however, the gentlemanly Mormon was shocked to hear executive branch functionaries refer to the late civil rights leader as "Martin Luther Coon," and dismiss Arabs as "sand niggers."

Blacks were again frozen out of the White House, and this time there was no one to hear their complaints who had any possibility of obtaining the president's ear, as there had been when Richard Nixon served as vice president and could at least offer sympathy. Under the rules of partisan politics followed by the Republican leadership, the administration owed nothing to a constituency that gave 90 percent of its votes to its opposition. And the Democrats, presumably bound to respond to those who had supported them, had lost their majority in the Senate in the course of the Reagan landslide, and suffered sharp losses in the House.

Ronald Reagan's personal popularity, which turned out to be largely unaffected by widespread doubts about the efficacy of Reagonomics, paralyzed the political process. As long as the administration held to the position that the federal government had no role to play in providing equality of opportunity for the disadvantaged, the Democrats in Congress could no longer devise means of dealing with social problems posed by the growing black underclass and the flood of unassimilated immigrants from Latin America and Asia. Even after the Democrats regained their majority in the Senate in the 1986 midterm election, opposition to affirmative action orchestrated from the White House made it virtually impossible to muster the two-thirds vote required to override an every-ready presidential veto.

Moral suasion backed by mass demonstrations of the kind Jesse Jackson had used to move the white power structure was no longer effective. It was not in Jackson, however, to give up his cause, and the celebrity it had earned for him. In the days when he made frequent appearances at President Carter's side, Jackson had denied political ambition, saying he sought no appointment, only an "anointment from the Lord" that would enable him "to converse with the president, and to make recommendations, and to advise, to impact on the world—without losing my integrity." But as the 1984 presidential election approached, the prophet concluded that his mission now required him to embrace the things that were Caesar's.

Jackson entered politics at the top, announcing his candidacy for president in November 1983, thus becoming one of eight Democrats lured into the fray by Reagan's presumed vulnerability. Senators Reubin Askew of Florida, Alan Cranston of California, John Glenn of Ohio, Gary Hart of Colorado, and Fritz Hollings of South Carolina had regional identity, which made them contenders for the vice presidency if they struck out on the top spot. The other two were veterans of previous presidential elections, Fritz Mondale and George McGovern.

Jackson's candidacy quickly demonstrated his ability to unite rank-and-file blacks while splitting the black leadership. No one, including the candidate, thought he had a chance of winning the nomination; the tactical consideration was that television coverage of the campaign would provide their most effective advocate a platform from which to press the concerns of blacks, and give him a broker's role at the national convention. But most of those who held elected office thought a black candidacy would weaken the coalition with white Democrats upon which they depended, and they were joined by other mainstream leaders who resented the manner in which Jackson upstaged them when the media's attention turned to racial issues.

His entry in the Democratic primaries was opposed by Coretta King; Andrew Young, now mayor of Atlanta; Mayor Coleman Young of Detroit; Julian Bond, a member of the Georgia State Senate; Benjamin Hooks, executive director of the NAACP; and Vernon Jordan, director of the Urban League. Only two first-string black politicians offered initial endorsement: Mayor Richard Hatcher of Gary, Indiana, and Representative John Conyers of Michigan.

There was little doubt that Jackson would attract a solid majority of the black vote running against a phalanx of white Democrats, but that would not be sufficient to carry a single state, and the number of delegates he could amass under proportional representation would limit the leverage he might exert at the convention. The influence blacks could exercise in their own right was determined by the residential segregation that concentrated black voting strength in urban precincts and rural Southern counties with a residue of unemployed sharecroppers. Blacks constituted numerical majorities only in districts where the need for government services was most acute, and the means of providing them most limited—areas abandoned by the affluent suburbanites who now made up a controlling majority in state and national elections.

The black politicians who found places in city halls, county courthouses, state capitols, and Congress could function effectively only in coalition with whites. And as the moral fervor of the civil rights movement receded, their leverage was reduced even as their numbers increased. When black leaders gathered in Atlanta to observe the twenty-third anniversary of the death of Martin Luther King, the political dilemma they faced was summed up by Cornel West, head of African-American studies at Princeton:

The power of the civil rights movement under King . . . was its universalism. Now instead of being viewed as a moral crusade for freedom, it's become an expression of a particular interest group. Once you lose that moral high ground, all you have is a power struggle, and that has never been a persuasive means for the weaker to deal with the stronger.

At the end of his life King had recognized that hard truth and launched an effort to broaden the movement's base by bringing together the poverty-stricken of all races. The mule that headed his funeral cortege had been intended as a symbol for the "Poor People's March on Washington" he was organizing when he was brought down by an assassin's bullet. But after witnessing the pathetic result when his successors at SCLC attempted to carry out his plan, I wrote:

> The March was a fiasco and probably would have been even if King had lived to lead it. . . . The concept of a poor people's movement was based on the dubious assumption that common misery could produce common purpose. In the case of blacks, the reverse had been true. The disadvantaged of a different color or culture had always resisted joint effort—poor whites out of an unwillingness to acknowledge any degree of equality with blacks, Latinos, Indians and Orientals because linguistic differences and pride of identity caused them to resist acculturation.

When he plunged into the presidential race, Jesse Jackson set out to put a political spin on King's idea. He announced that he would seek a basic realignment within the Democratic constituency to make it a "Rainbow Coalition." He was campaigning, he said, not as a black candidate, but as one who sought a fundamental change in the party to make it responsive to needs of blacks, women, and Latinos that remained unmet because of the dominance of white males committed to the status quo.

Jackson contended that the black vote had been held below its potential because the white partners in the Democratic coalition, particularly in the South, had permitted practices intended to limit minority candidates' ability to win local and state elections. He produced arithmetic to demonstrate that a voter registration drive, which would be a key element of his campaign, could change the outcome of the presidential contest. Only eleven million blacks were registered out of almost eighteen million qualified to vote; if fourteen million were registered, along with two million more Latinos, he insisted, "Reagan cannot win— and no one can ignore their demands." He spelled out what that could mean for the Democratic leadership:

> How the candidates treat us and the issues we raise will deter-mine our response. We must have a reciprocal relationship. The issues that are crucial to us . . . cannot be put on the back burner. Anyone who doesn't work on these takes our support for granted, and is at risk. Never again can the ticket write us off. If we have just expanded the number of Democrats without expanding our role in democracy, we will have failed.

In the early primaries, where his practiced platform manner and highly charged moral message stood out in contrast to the drab, issue-oriented offerings of his competitors, Jackson enjoyed a respectful response from white audiences. He was expert at adapting his country preacher style to his audience, although he never abandoned the moral thrust of what were essentially sermons. In joint appearances with the other candi-dates—which were called debates but rarely were—he was able to match, or gloss over, their expertise on heavyweight items such as Eu-romissiles and industrial policy.

Elizabeth Drew, who followed him around New Hampshire, re-counted the reaction when he addressed "an audience of comfortable white college women . . . and had their total attention and, in the end, enthusiasm. Jackson does make a strong moral case, and he puts on a great show." He had a similar effect when he appeared before seven hundred New England high school students assembled for a mock po-litical convention. As the Democratic road show moved from primary to primary he would demonstrate his appeal to idealistic young people at high schools and colleges all across the country.

But while he presented a beguiling figure in person, his rhetoric came across as hot on television, which usually picked up on him when he was exuding intensity, and he could be seen by whites as threatening. Most of those who responded affirmatively to his appeal did not vote for him, and those who did saw him as extrapolitical, a candidate who could not win but provided a means of safety voting one's conscience.

Nationwide, Jackson drew 90 percent of the black vote, but nowhere did his support significantly exceed the proportion of blacks in the total. In Pennsylvania, for example, he carried Philadelphia, but his statewide vote was only 17 percent. In his home state, South Carolina, he ran ahead of the leading contenders, Mondale and Hart, but his total was only 25 percent, and his lead was made possible by a 50 percent vote for an uncommitted—which meant white—slate of delegates.

By May it was clear that no Rainbow Coalition had emerged, and Jackson began complaining openly about his lack of white support, blaming it in large part on the media. He was in fact a black candidate, and that reality limited his freedom of action. If he was to have a political future he could not afford to force the kind of divisions in the party that would make certain President Reagan's reelection; and if he followed the lead of the lesser contenders and withdrew, he would forfeit the opportunity to press the party leadership into making concessions to his constituency.

Gary Hart, fading fast as the campaign moved on to California, suggested in a Los Angeles television interview that he might accept Jackson as his running mate. But the offer, if it could be considered one, was hastily withdrawn when the reaction set in. Jackson, who had never managed to assuage the bitterness he had aroused among Jews with his overtures to the Palestine Liberation Organization, had inadvertently stoked up the fires again.

In a casual airport conversation with Milton Coleman, a black *Washington Post* reporter, he had referred to New York as "Hymietown" in explaining his difficulty in expanding his support there. Coleman reported the conversation to his colleagues, and the politically incorrect term was attributed to Jackson in a story written by someone else. The Black Muslim leader Louis Farrakhan accused Coleman of betraying a black brother, and in a radio broadcast seemed to be threatening him with death. As he had in the case of Farrakhan's earlier diatribes against Jews and their religion, Jackson disavowed the threat, but he did not disassociate himself from the Muslim leader, who continued to speak at his rallies.

Vice President George Bush seized the opportunity to exploit the breach in the Democratic coalition. Speaking before a Jewish organization, he declared that Reagan and his administration "denounce the intrusion of anti-Semitism into the American political process," and attacked Mondale and Hart for not having been more critical of Jackson. Both had denounced Farrakhan, but neither had run the risk of alienating blacks by confronting Jackson.

The furor did not die down, and Mondale, who was in sight of the nomination, began to bear the brunt. When Farrakhan referred to Israel as the product of an outlaw conspiracy and termed Judaism a "gutter religion," some Jewish leaders demanded that Mondale disassociate himself from Jackson. Mondale responded by denouncing Farrakhan's statement as "venomous, bigoted, and obscene," and called on Jackson to repudiate him. Jackson waffled, and days passed before his campaign organization issued a statement in his name calling Farrakhan's statements "reprehensible and morally indefensible."

When the Democrats convened in San Francisco, Fritz Mondale had 2,107 elected delegates. Gary Hart, with 1,230, would remain in contention, but the head-counters who calculated the trading possibilities were convinced that the prize was Mondale's. He was the logical choice, the best-equipped candidate by background and temperament. A product of Hubert Humphrey's old Minnesota Farmer-Labor-Democratic alliance, he had been his state's attorney general, had succeeded Humphrey in the Senate, and had served as Jimmy Carter's vice president. Mondale retained the loyalty of the leaders of the traditional Democratic factions, and his civil rights record would have ensured black support in the primaries had Jackson not been in the race.

Needing a bold gesture to liven the drab image he projected on television, and at the same time reach out to one of the major voting groups alienated by Reagan's civil rights stand, Mondale chose a woman, Representative Geraldine Ferraro of New York, as his running mate. Although Mondale had discussed it with him before he made it, the choice turned out to be especially offensive to Jackson.

This marked the advent of what was to become standard practice for Democratic contenders, the abandonment of geography in favor of ethnic identity in balancing the ticket. When Mondale publicly summoned prospective choices for interviews at his Minnesota retreat, aside from the Italian Ferraro they were Dianne Feinstein, the Jewish mayor of San Francisco; Henry Cisneros, the Latino mayor of San Antonio; and Michael Dukakis, the Greek governor of Massachusetts. Jackson was riled because the black who filled out the spectrum was not he but Wilson Goode, the mayor of Philadelphia, who had supported Mondale in the primary.

Physically exhausted by his poorly organized, nonstop campaign and embittered by the Farrakhan controversy, Jackson arrived in San Francisco to receive word that some party leaders were now arguing that if Mondale repudiated him he would gain more votes among whites than he would lose among blacks. It was a dubious proposition, and Mondale ignored it, continuing his effort to unite the party—which Jackson's intransigence was making increasingly difficult.

When he was left out of consideration as running mate, Jackson complained that he was eliminated because of pressure from Jews, and accused the press of "Aryan arrogance." At a time when he was advocating moves toward Cuba and the Soviet Union that represented a radical departure from existing bipartisan foreign policy, he demanded a voice in Mondale's selection of the secretaries of state and defense, and suggested that he might be an ideal choice to head the State Department.

But he was in a poor trading position. The black political leaders who had withheld public endorsement of Mondale for fear of alienating Jackson's supporters were now climbing aboard the winner's bandwagon. Mondale had more black delegates at the convention than Jackson did. The presentation of clearly unacceptable demands in order to use their rejection to raise an issue was standard practice, but at this stage of Jackson's quest for influence there was an aura of blackmail in his announcement that his followers should wait for a signal from him before committing themselves to support the Democratic ticket. With the colors reversed, it was the kind of black-and-white proposition the Dixiecrats had presented to party leaders when they adopted a civil rights platform and nominated Harry Truman.

There was the usual skirmishing before the platform committee, this time with blacks under Jackson's leadership pressing for planks calling for minority quotas in employment and education, and Jews calling for their ban. An issue was drawn on the double primary and other voting requirements that pitted Jackson supporters against white Southerners. Gary Hart's representatives negotiated with the Jackson people on the possibility of merging forces in the hope of bringing about a deadlock, but Mondale's backers headed off any such deal by making cosmetic concessions to Jackson. The floor fight ended when the term "verifiable measurements" was substituted for the dread word "quota," and Mondale's aides, who had conceived it as a face-saving gesture for Jackson, agreed that this was "a victory for the Rainbow Coalition."

A major blow for party unity was struck by the inspired selection of Mario Cuomo to deliver the keynote address. The New York governor was one of the country's great orators, whose persona symbolized the party's liberal tradition. The proud ethnic background of a second-generation American—he referred to his own career as "an ineffably beautiful tribute to the democratic process"—gave thrust to the moral charge he brought against the president. While Reagan referred to America as a shining city on a hill, Cuomo said,

> There's another city, another part of the city, the part where some people can't pay their mortgages and most young people can't afford one, where students can't afford the education they need and middleclass parents watch the dreams they hold for their children evaporate. In this part of the city, there are more poor than ever, more families in trouble. There is despair, Mr. President, in the faces you don't see, in places that you don't visit in your shining city.

Delivered in low key, but with an undertone of muted passion, the address gave a forward cast to traditional Democratic policies by contrasting them with the Republican commitment to a socially constricting status quo. It provided a model of what Cuomo prescribed as the means of offsetting Reagan's polished and appealing rhetoric, "not so much with speeches that will bring people to their feet as with speeches that bring people to their senses."

It was by any reckoning a great piece of oratory, but at least in terms of immediate effect, Jesse Jackson managed to top it when he took the platform to acknowledge his nomination. He fed speculation over whether he would finally endorse the Mondale-Ferraro ticket by insisting that the vote count be completed without the usual move to make the nomination unanimous once a majority was attained. He didn't hint at the answer until he pronounced his opening lines:

> Tonight, we come together bound by our faith in a mighty God, with genuine respect for our country, and inheriting the legacy of a great party. This is not a perfect party. Yet we are called to a perfect mission; our mission to feed the hungry, to clothe the naked, to house the homeless, to teach the illiterate, to provide jobs for the jobless, to choose the human race over the nuclear race. . . .
>
> There is a proper season for everything. There is a time to sow and a time to reap. There is a time to compete and a time to cooperate. I ask for your vote on the first ballot . . . a vote of conviction, a vote of conscience. But I will be proud to support the nominee of this convention for president of the United States.

Jesse Jackson was back in line. One reason was made evident when the votes were finally counted: Mondale, 2,191; Hart, 1,200; Jackson, 465. He had nowhere else to go. But there were other reasons. At the end of the speech, which swooped and soared over familiar Jackson terrain, moist-eyed white and black delegates were holding hands, swaying in unison to the sound of a gospel singer slowly intoning "Ordinary People."

In the course of his sermon he had said, "My constituency is the damned, disinherited, disrespected, and the despised. They have voted in record numbers. . . . The Democratic Party must send them a signal that we care." The prophet and the politician warred in the soul of Jesse Jackson, but I don't think he has ever doubted that he was the ordained bearer of that message.

Jackson went on to campaign loyally for the Democratic ticket and press his voter registration campaign, and on Election Day Fritz Mondale received the usual 90 percent of the black vote. But the effect of his actions in the primary had been to widen the fissures in the Democratic coalition. The very potency of the image Jackson projected on television made him a symbol that invoked the latent racism and genuine fears fostered by the Republicans' Southern Strategy, which now had an ideal executor in Ronald Reagan.

Reagan had used the bully pulpit afforded by the White House to persuade a majority of the American people that the federal government was, as he constantly reminded them, the root of all their problems. The fact that he was able to do so after he had ostensibly been in charge of it for four years and had actually increased its scope—and its indebtedness—was evidence of the power television conferred on a politician able and willing to fully exploit its image-making capacity. After the president's kickoff reelection campaign speech, Elizabeth Drew, who had been dubious about his chances, wrote:

> Reagan's sense of theatre is unmatched in politics, his use of language unique, and his capacity for arrogating to himself the symbols and values Americans hold dear—flag, family, God, patriotism, national strength—awesome. He is the master weaver of the national myths.

In the myth he had woven for himself, Reagan was seen as a great commoner, although he was in fact a rich man who preferred the company of those who were even richer, and had obtained a divorce in order to marry a high-fashion wife. He was able to offset the handicaps his life-style might have entailed by expertly appealing to the angers, resentments, and patriotic and religious inclinations of middleclass and working-class voters. His pollster was delighted with the result, noting that by 1984 his soundings showed that "blue-collar voters applaud Reagan's building up of America's defense, that they like his appeal to traditional values, and his opposition to affirmative action and quotas—and that they simply like Reagan."

In the face of this impervious popularity, Fritz Mondale found it impossible to campaign on the issues. In his acceptance speech he pointed to the perils posed by the escalating national debt and committed himself to the only feasible means of bringing it under control. "We are living on borrowed money and borrowed time," he said, noting that Reagan had seemed to agree when he promised to reduce the budget deficit by two thirds by the end of his term. There was, Mondale pointed out, only one means by which that goal could be met: "Mr. Reagan will raise taxes, and so will I. He won't tell you. I just did."

It was a fair comment, based on the assumption that the next president would be forced to face fiscal reality, but the mesmerizing effect of Reaganomics on the voters had removed reality as a factor in presidential campaigns. For the next eight years the budget would be even more drastically unbalanced while the national debt mounted into the trillion-dollar range. The pledge of no new taxes had become a talisman that ensured the Republicans their longest reign in sixty years.

Ronald Reagan's policies and public image were now indistinguishable, and he had no need to make further gestures to maintain the fervent support of the right-wing elements his success had made dominant in the Republican coalition. He was against abortion and for prayer in public schools and the use of public funds to support private schools, including those still segregated; he was against government funding for birth control programs that included the use of contraceptives; and he had agreed that creationism should be offered in the school curriculum along with evolution. Although he was the first president in memory who did not regularly attend church (he said it was to avoid distracting the congregation), he was acclaimed by the fundamentalists who marched under the political banner of the Moral Majority. No doctrinaire Christian had any reason to doubt where Ronald Reagan stood on the so-called social issues.

George Bush inherited Reagan's policies but was indelibly stamped by his own elitist background. The prep school style of a Yale clubman clung to him, and it still showed through after he sought to add a Texan patina when he entered upon the political career expected of the son of a moderate New England Republican with a seat in the U.S. Senate. Transplanted to Houston, where old money was not a handicap if there was enough of it and it bore the scent of oil, Bush was able to win a safe Republican seat in Congress. But when he tried for the Senate, his appeal dissipated in the great open spaces of the Lone Star State.

Unlike Reagan, who believed in what he stood for, Bush seemed to have no fixed convictions. From the beginning of his career his political reactions had been expedient; in Texas, he had first supported school desegregation, and then, when busing produced a groundswell of opposition, reversed himself. In his first run for president he had done a U-turn on Reaganomics, deriding supply-side theory in the primaries, then embracing it without reservation when it became the price of the vice presidency.

There was no hint of a dissent from any Reagan policy or action during the next eight years, and he pulled no punches when he served as hatchet man for the president in the run against Mondale. But Bush never gained the trust of the Republican right wingers, who simply could not accept a patrician Yankee as one of their own. It was this that brought him up short in 1988 after his ingrained civility seemed to break through in his declaration that as president his goal would be "a kinder, gentler society."

If this was also intended as an effort to broaden the Republican base by appealing to moderates in both parties, it was short-lived. Bush became increasingly dependent on holding the Reagan constituency in place after the Democrats nominated a centrist candidate, Michael Dukakis, who would run on his record as the socially progressive, fiscally conservative governor of Massachusetts.

Bush's handlers devised a campaign for him that employed the Southern Strategy with all stops out. The object was to destroy Dukakis by painting him as the left-wing, tax-and-spend, soft-on-crime liberal he clearly wasn't. Since Bush was far from an inspiring speaker, the campaign was built around photo opportunities contrived so that TV news editors couldn't ignore them, although they were set up to provide minimum exposure of Bush to interrogation by their correspondents.

He turned up in flag factories to play the patriotic card by contrasting the persona of a decorated World War II Navy pilot with that of the unassuming Dukakis, who had no war record and who as governor had not opposed a measure to ban the Pledge of Allegiance in public schools. Television cameras trailed Bush when he went out in a boat to dramatize Boston Harbor's pollution, which he blamed on Dukakis, although it was primarily due to the curtailment of environmental protection funds by the Reagan administration. And Bush made a baleful television celebrity out of Willie Horton, a black rapist furloughed from a Massachusetts prison, who was featured in TV ads as blatantly demagogic as anything I had witnessed in the days when Southern politicians exploited race prejudice to rally the rednecks.

Although Dukakis entered the race running even or slightly ahead of Bush in the polls, he was never able to respond effectively to the Republican attacks even when they were palpably wide of the mark. And once again the Democratic candidate was running as the nominee of a badly divided party, made even more so after Jesse Jackson broke out the banner of the Rainbow Coalition for a second run in the Democratic primaries.

This time Jackson relied less on an emotional moral appeal and more on a reasoned argument that the affluent could not continue to write off the growing underclass without imperiling their own well-being. After watching him in the bellwether Iowa caucuses, where he drew a warm response from a preponderantly white constituency, Roger Simon wrote in the *Baltimore Sun:* "It was a new Jesse; the Jesse who refused to perform. The Jesse who says: I no longer have to preach at every stop to get your attention. It is time to stop concentrating on how I say it, and start listening to what I say."

When the campaign moved on to the industrial centers of the Midwest, his attacks on the antilabor stance of the Reagan administration had resonance with blue-collar workers who had gone over to the Republicans in previous elections. In Illinois, Michigan, and Wisconsin his vote totals were well in excess of the percentage of black voters— enough so that, as other contenders were eliminated, he found himself in a two-man contest with Dukakis.

But whether it was because of his race, or because of foreign policy positions unacceptable to a majority of the voters, his white support dwindled once he was no longer running against the field. In the final primaries his margin of white voters had shrunk until it embraced only those on the far left. And, once again, the nonblack poor failed to respond to the Rainbow Coalition appeal. Latinos in Texas gave Dukakis 79 percent of their votes, and in California they favored him almost 2 to 1.

After Dukakis had won enough delegates to ensure his nomination, Jackson put a personal twist on the power broker's role, insisting that he was entitled to consideration for the vice presidency even though the polls showed him with an unfavorable rating so high that his presence on the ticket would guarantee a Democratic defeat. With Jackson no one could ever be sure, but I thought that this probably was intended only to reassure his followers that the implied threat of a black boycott still ensured them a voice in party policy. But, in responding, the Dukakis camp failed to recognize a fact of political life Democratic candidates now had to deal with—the hypersensitivity of blacks, who, with good reason, did not trust the professed good intentions of whites.

When he rejected Jackson's bid, as he had to do, Dukakis neglected to inform him in advance of his public announcement that his running mate would be a white Southerner, Senator Lloyd Bentsen of Texas. It was an oversight that would have been accepted, if not ignored, had it involved a white contender, but Jackson could use it to fire up his constituency's resentment by invoking the image of the plantation South:

> At this point my constituency has no place on the team. I cannot
> be expected to go out into the field, pick up voters, bale them
> up, and deliver them to the big house where policy is made
> and priorities are set around the table, and not be part of the
> equation.

He was, of course, an inescapable part of the equation, but that worked both ways: He still had nowhere else to go. So he settled for Dukakis's guarantee of funding for a first-class nationwide voter registration drive that would keep him in the news. In return he delivered another stem-winding speech when the time came to anoint the candidates. *The Washington Post* called it an awesome political feat. Jackson had "managed at once to maintain his posture of challenge to the system and yet to bring his supporters back into it, to make it safe and respectable for them in their own terms to support the Dukakis-Bentsen ticket."

Analyzing the returns after Ronald Reagan's landslide victory over Fritz Mondale, Elzabeth Drew had observed, "Reagan's success in running an essentially substanceless, carefully controlled campaign has been much criticized, but it will undoubtedly also be emulated, since it worked." By dividing the electorate along racial lines, Mondale was given 90 percent of the black vote, while Reagan led among white males 68 to 31, giving him a lead among most identifiable groups except women. Despite the presence of Geraldine Ferraro on the Democratic ticket, Republican support had increased among women voters.

The Southern Strategy didn't work as well for George Bush—his electoral majority was only 426 to 111—but Lee Atwater, the bright young South Carolinian who served as Bush's campaign strategist, had demonstrated that it could be effective even with a lackluster candidate if his opponent could be demonized. Rewarded by appointment as chairman of the Republican Party, he began laying the groundwork for Bush's reelection.

As Atwater saw it, the problem was to retain Bush's right-wing support, which was only lukewarm, while allowing the new president to follow his moderate instincts. The virtually unanimous media condemnation of the Willie Horton TV ads was a warning that overt appeal to racism could backfire. The problem, then, was to evolve a strategy that would allow the administration to continue to pursue Darwinian social policies without appearing to be indifferent to their effect on blacks in particular and the poor in general.

The successful appeal of Martin Luther King for white support, translated into political action by Presidents Kennedy and Johnson, had been directed to the concept of fairness—a part of the heritage of most members of the white majority even though they often ignored it in response to appeals to their self-interest. In terms of constitutional theory, fairness was synonymous with justice, and had provided the basis of the Supreme Court's desegregation rulings. The Southern Strategy upon which the Republican ascendancy depended required a reversal of the policy established by *Brown*. So, beginning with Nixon, there had been a search for Supreme Court appointees who were prepared to turn the prevailing doctrine of fairness on its head.

There were now justices on the Court who condemned measures designed to benefit the minority of citizens as unfair to the majority, who would bear the brunt of the monetary cost and lose some of the special advantages they enjoyed. Although they had not yet prevailed, they were gaining ground in the citadel where the concept of affirmative action was first translated into law.

In the 1950s the present chief justice, William Rehnquist, serving as a law clerk to Justice Robert Jackson, in a memorandum to his boss denounced the effort of blacks to obtain the voting rights denied them in the one-party South: "I take a dim view of this pathological search for discrimination. It is about time the Court faced the fact that the white people of the South don't like the colored people." In his subsequent career as practicing lawyer, Justice Department attorney, and associate justice he opposed school desegregation, ending discrimination in places of public accommodation, and equal rights for women—that is, any application of the equal-protection clause of the Fourteenth Amendment to secure minority rights.

In a 1979 article in the *Washington University Law Quarterly,* Justice Antonin Scalia, who became Rehnquist's most consistent supporter on the Court, added an ethnic twist to the usual arguments against "restorative justice." "My father came to this country when he was a teenager," Scalia wrote, "and not only had he never profited from the sweat of any black man's brow, I don't think he had ever seen a black man." It would be making a mountain out of a molehill, he said, to treat any racial debt Italian, Irish, or Jewish immigrants might have incurred as comparable "with that of those who plied the slave trade, and who maintained a caste system for many years."

To whites who accepted this ethnic distinction, those who supported affirmative action were guilty of reverse discrimination. Drawing distinctions based on race, it was contended, was no less opprobrious when employed to admit a deprived minority to the mainstream than when it was used to keep them out. Although it was rarely acknowledged as such, this was a revival of the argument used to invalidate the original civil rights laws enacted by Congress after the Civil War.

In 1875 the Supreme Court held that statutes requiring that blacks must be served in places of public accommodation—the hotels, lunch counters, theaters and transportation of that day—were not covered by the Constitution's equal-protection clause. Justice Joseph P. Bradley of New Jersey, writing on behalf of an 8-to-1 majority, declared that there must be some stage in the freedman's emancipation when "he takes on the rank of mere citizen and ceases to be the special favorite of the laws, and when his rights, as a citizen or a man, are to be protected by the ordinary modes by which other men's rights are protected."

The concept of a "color-blind" Constitution was enshrined in the cases that led up to the separate-but-equal ruling in *Plessy* v. *Ferguson*. But the term first appeared in the opinion of the lone dissenter, Justice John Marshall Harlan of Kentucky, a former slaveowner and the only Southerner on the bench in the post–Civil War years:

> The white race deems itself to be dominant in this country. And so it is, in prestige, in achievements, in education, in wealth and in power. . . . But in the view of the Constitution, in the eye of the law, there is in this country no superior, dominant ruling class of citizens. There is no caste here. Our Constitution is color-blind. . . .
>
> The destinies of the two races in this country are indissolubly linked together, and the interests of both require that the common government of all shall not permit the seeds of race hate to be planted under the sanction of law. . . .
>
> [Under the majority ruling] there would remain a power in the States, by sinister legislation, to interfere with the full enjoyment of the blessing of liberty; to regulate civil rights, common to all citizens, upon the basis of race; and to place in a condition of legal inferiority a large body of American citizens.

A hundred years later Justice Harry Blackmun echoed Justice Harlan when he wrote in his separate opinion on *Bakke*:

> . . . in order to get beyond racism, we must first take account of race. There is no other way. And in order to treat some persons equally we must treat them differently. We cannot— we dare not—let the equal-protection clause perpetuate racial supremacy.

One of the most striking of the paradoxes that abounded in Washington was the use of the sevenfold increase in elected black officeholders brought about by the civil rights movement as an argument against affirmative action. This was cited as an example of "empowerment," the buzzword that reinstated Justice Bradley's thesis that blacks now had all the rights government could properly provide, and were in position to advance their own welfare through individual and collective action.

This kind of social Darwinism had a special attraction for blacks who abandoned their peers to enlist in the Reagan revolution. The idea that standing in society depended on moral and intellectual fitness was particularly gratifying for those who had risen from humble beginnings, as was usually the case with blacks who gained a place in the mainstream during the post-*Brown* years. They could hardly deny that they had benefited from the government's effort to provide equal opportunity, but they could discount it.

Shelby Steele, a leading black conservative, argued that affirmative action served primarily to assuage the guilt feelings of whites, while denying blacks the right to be judged, as he put it in a book title, on *The Content of Our Character*. For the race as a whole, he said, this was debilitating

> because it makes our suffering and victimization into an identity, so that we are encouraged to think of ourselves as victims. Once this identity is in place we are weakened, since we assume that we must be repaid for our historic suffering and that these reparations will be the power that delivers us. No worse illusions can afflict a people struggling to overcome the scars of oppression, since they throw us back into the same dependency on the whim of others that made us suffer in the first place. In this way, today's black suffering only reenacts yesterday's black inferiority. The irony is that once we identify with our suffering, we lose the power to end it.

Steele, a professor of English at San Jose State University, offered this exercise in pop psychology in a *Los Angeles Times* article supporting President Bush's nomination of Clarence Thomas for the Supreme Court. Steele contended that opposition to Thomas by the NAACP and other civil rights organizations, largely based on his anti–affirmative action record as EEOC director, demonstrated that

> they have fallen into what might be called the liberalism of redress. Here the focus is so singularly on the redress due the

sufferer that he is all but absolved of obligations to himself and society. . . . In the liberal cosmos, self-help threatens redress, so Thomas must be rejected precisely because he did help himself.

"After all," Steele asserted, "there was no affirmative action back in segregated Pin Point, Georgia." But there was. It was provided by the Catholic Church, which rescued Thomas from inferior black public schools, provided white nuns for his primary and secondary schooling, and made it possible for him to attend Holy Cross University; and by Yale University, which set aside the place he occupied in its law school.

It took nothing away from the content of Thomas's character, which undoubtedly contained an impressive measure of self-reliance, to note that his experience had little in common with that of the mass of poor blacks, who still had no access to the kind of tutelage and discipline provided him as a result of institutional response to the civil rights movement.

In the public relations campaign orchestrated by the White House on his behalf, Thomas was cast as a Horatio Alger character whose rise was solely due to his pluck. The effort to frame his views in terms of self-help vs. redress succeeded so well that the Democratic leaders downplayed the issue of affirmative action and challenged the appointment largely on the ground that Thomas, who had spent most of his career as a Republican-sponsored bureaucrat, had displayed little capacity as either legal scholar or practitioner and had voiced dogmatic opinions that raised questions of judicial temperament.

The White House strategy was to have Thomas deny or discount the views turned up in the nominee's paper trail of doctrinaire speeches and articles in which he elaborated a version of natural law that "allows us to reassert the primacy of the individual," thereby giving protection to economic freedom and property rights that he, along with his patrons Ronald Reagan and George Bush, insisted the Supreme Court had undervalued.

"If applied the way Judge Thomas seems to suggest," said Professor Laurence Tribe of Harvard Law School, this philosophy "would outlaw minimum wage laws, child labor laws, and laws protecting the right of reproductive choice. Invocation of the natural law in the history of the

Court has much more often been used to subjugate and subordinate people than to liberate them."

This was the real issue raised by an appointment intended to ensure a reactionary majority on the Court for decades to come. Thomas's nomination was clearly the opening gun in the president's 1992 re-election campaign. While denying, but in effect conceding, that there should be a Supreme Court quota to guarantee a minority seat, Bush put forward a black nominee whose views on civil rights conflicted in every important respect with those of the justice he would replace, the Court's first and only black member, Thurgood Marshall.

Announcing Thomas's nomination just four days after Justice Marshall resigned because of age and declining health, Bush told Thomas, "You've made it this far on merit, but from here in it's politics." The first part of the statement was as dubious as the president's assertion that his nominee was the best man available for the job, or Thomas's claim that he had never even discussed the Supreme Court ruling on abortion. The forty-three-year-old Thomas would never have been given a place on the federal bureaucracy's fast track had he not, out of conviction or expediency, subscribed to the right-wing politics enshrined in the Reagan/Bush White House. Although it is doubtful that he needed it, the president was justified in warning him he was now in the middle of a political fray. The scenario prepared by his handlers for the confirmation hearing was designed as a ploy to discomfit the Democratic leadership and weaken its support in the black community.

Thomas's protracted but listless sessions before the Judiciary Committee ended in a 7-to-7 split along party lines. But on the eve of the vote by the full Senate, where the administration had lined up enough defecting Democrats to guarantee Thomas's approval, there was a leak to the media of a confidential statement by a black law professor at the University of Oklahoma who testified that Thomas had sexually harassed her while she served as his legal adviser at the Department of Education and the EEOC.

Anita Hill was a reluctant witness whose testimony had been obtained by the FBI at the request of the committee, and the members had agreed not to make this dirty linen public at an open hearing. But when it became evident that Thomas was going to be confirmed without any follow-up on Ms. Hill's deposition, a firestorm of feminist protest broke out against what was seen as a bipartisan failure of white males to take seriously the issue of sexual harassment. Thomas's presumed Senate majority eroded to the point where the White House found it prudent to delay the vote until the matter could be fully aired.

The committee scheduled a public hearing that produced three days of TV drama that would have been X-rated had it not consisted of privileged testimony and cross-examination. As Chairman Joseph Biden said, an explosion was inevitable "when you add the kerosene of sex, the heated flame of race, and the incendiary nature of television lights." The result was the most dramatic political confrontation since the Watergate hearings, and it attracted a huge national audience.

The rise of Anita Hill, one of thirteen children of poor black farmers in Oklahoma, paralleled that of Thomas; she, too, was a graduate of Yale Law School who generally shared his conservative political views. After she left Washington to take up her career as a legal scholar she had earned the respect of her professional colleagues, hundreds of whom came forward to attest to her integrity. The comely professor was unshakable as she detailed the unwelcome sexual advances she said Thomas had made while he was head of the agency charged with protecting female employees against such harassment.

Thomas's rebuttal consisted of a categorical denial of her charges, and an impassioned attack on the Senate Democrats he charged with joining a conspiracy of liberal interest groups who sought to destroy him because of his conservative views. And he played the race card by claiming that Anita Hill had employed demeaning sexual stereotypes to further the "high-tech lynching of an uppity black."

The committee Democrats, as Jesse Jackson said, were left "sitting there paralyzed as soon as he raised the race issue." Thomas's tactics had the effect of reducing the issue to the question of which of the two was lying. The nominee had an obvious motive for doing so, since even his Republican champions conceded that if he were guilty as charged he was unqualified. Hill's testimony and that of her corroborating witnesses provided convincing evidence that she had neither personal nor ideological reasons for making false charges.

But the Republican hatchet men, swinging freely without effective challenge by the Democrats, followed a White House script that portrayed her as an ideological conspirator, or a scorned woman seeking revenge, or an advanced neurotic who couldn't tell fantasy from reality. Provided with this smorgasbord of presumed motivation, the polls showed that 60 percent of the citizenry gave Thomas the benefit of the doubt—findings that were reflected in the Senate's 52–48 vote to confirm the nomination.

George Bush had succeeded in putting the civil rights leadership on the defensive. There were not many blacks who shared Thomas's doctrinaire views, but there was widespread support for the proposition that they might as well accept a black conservative since there was no chance that Bush would send up any nominee who would support civil rights as defined by the Warren Court. Claude Lewis, a columnist for *The Philadelphia Inquirer*, declared, ". . . an all-white Court would be more seriously flawed than an all-conservative Court."

But there was, of course, much more to it than that. Charles R. Lawrence III, a black law professor at Stanford, cited reactions that were usually concealed from whites:

> There is [a] story here that is perhaps the most difficult for those of us in the Afro-American community to talk about. It is the story of black male violence against, and degradation of black women. This is a story of our own internalization of racist myths, a story of black men taking the anger that wells up within us when we are humiliated and degraded by whites and turning it on the women within our own families and communities. It is a story that leads many in our community to believe Anita Hill even as we wish we could say, "This cannot be true." There has been an unwritten code of silence that says we must not speak of this story outside of our communities because white men will use it against us. This is why so many blacks who believe Hill's story continue to . . . blame Professor Hill for being the messenger who had been the bearer of the bad news.

The Thomas nomination, as it had been designed to do, contributed to the further unraveling of the Democratic coalition, and reduced the ability of blacks to influence public policy. This was graphically demonstrated by the Senate vote. Eleven of fifty-seven Democrats joined the Republicans to provide the two-vote majority. Eight of these were from the South—two from Louisiana, two from Georgia, and one each from South Carolina, Alabama, Virginia, and Oklahoma. All had found majorities favoring Thomas among their black constituents, whose support had previously kept them in the Democratic column on civil rights issues.

The division among blacks on the Thomas appointment turned on a conflict between two of their own, and was hardly likely to produce any significant shift of black votes to Bush, who would carry into his reelection campaign the baggage left behind in the White House when Ronald Reagan returned to the sanctuary provided by his wealthy friends in Bel Air, Los Angeles's most exclusive suburb.

Privation of the poor, and the steady increase in the ranks of the underclass, were now coupled with an economic squeeze on the middleclass that provided inescapable evidence of the failure of Reaganomics. President Bush trapped by his own "read my lips" campaign commitment against any tax increase, offered no solution to the dislocations caused by the slowing of economic growth and the rise in unemployment. Congressional refusal to grant his continued insistence on a reduction in the capital gains tax that would be of benefit only to those in the upper-income brackets revealed the extent to which trickle-down economics had lost the appeal it enjoyed when Ronald Reagan first renamed it and peddled it as the sovereign remedy for the nation's ills.

Bush's use of the presidential veto to block any move by the Democrats to deal with the economic downturn produced a congressional gridlock that forced him to yield to the insistence of the Republican leadership that he accept a deal that would permit tax increases—disguised under the euphemism "revenue enhancement"—in return for cuts in federal spending. But this served only to enrage his right-wing constituency, while it did nothing to improve the economic situation.

However, the chickens coming home to roost at the White House were lost to sight after the president launched a short, phenomenally successful war against a highly touted Iraqi military force led by a baleful dictator. The quick victory in the Desert Storm campaign unleashed a burst of patriotic fervor sustained by flag-waving parades for homecoming military units that served to launch the Fourth of July celebration in May and keep it going into September. The president's approval rating in the opinion polls soared to unprecedented levels, leading most Washington political observers—including Democrats rated as leading contenders for their party's nomination—to the conclusion that George Bush was unbeatable. It turned out to be an egregious misreading of political reality.

TURNAROUND
THE DEMOCRATS RISE AGAIN

The American people have summoned the change we celebrate today. You have raised your voices in an unmistakable chorus. You have cast your votes in historic numbers. And you have changed the face of the Congress, the presidency, and the political process itself. . . .

—Inaugural address, WILLIAM JEFFERSON CLINTON, forty-second president of the United States, January 20, 1993

CONVENTIONAL POLITICAL WISDOM in the United States now emanates from a Greek chorus of media commentators, most of them resident in Washington, the rest available by satellite for TV talk shows. Some still indulge in printed commentary, but the style is set by talking heads fully conditioned to speak in brief sound bites. And since static television programming requires the semblance of controversy as a substitute for action, they are usually paired off as purported liberals and conservatives.

A supporting cast is drawn from politically identifiable figures in government, the universities, and the think tanks that have proliferated in the national capital. Those who become regulars are shortwinded enough to function effectively under constraints of time and political balance that preclude any semblance of genuine dialogue. Many of these contribute their talents without charge in return for the kind of TV celebrity that can be converted into book contracts, lecture fees, and stipends provided by lobbyists. Cumulatively, the Washington talk shows reflect, without challenge or effective analysis, the current status of the public and private interests that shape government policy.

The conventional wisdom generated in this fashion proved to be notably faulty in the course of the 1992 elections. Fallacious assumptions endured despite contrary evidence turned up by the army of reporters who took to the field with the opening of the primary season. The beginning premise was that Ronald Reagan had created a Republican majority that embraced much of the middleclass, and it was expected to hold together despite his successor's lack of personal appeal for its right-wing core. For the Democrats to prevail, it was held, their party would have to move to the center—and few thought that was possible in light of the cleavages that had developed around issues of race, gender, and poverty.

These assumptions persuaded those usually mentioned as potential Republican candidates that this was not the year to challenge an incumbent president. But a tribune of the party's extreme right wing, Patrick Buchanan, decided to take leave from his talk show and newspaper column and enter the race against the man he charged with betraying the Reagan revolution. The response, backed by freehanded contributions to Buchanan's campaign fund, ended any prospect that George Bush might be able to follow his natural inclination and mount his campaign on the high ground.

When he announced his entry in the New Hampshire primary, Buchanan accused Bush of succumbing to the "politics of compromise and capitulation." The final infidelity, he said, came when Bush agreed to a watered down civil rights bill. After his appointment of Clarence Thomas to the Supreme Court, Buchanan had expected the president "to knock that quota bill right out of the park. Bush caved . . . I just said good-bye."

Buchanan resurrected pre-Eisenhower isolationism, adopting the chauvinist "America First" slogan as a campaign catchphrase. He created a firestorm that attracted media coverage by complaining that American Jewish leaders—"Israel's amen corner"—had driven the United States into the Persian Gulf War, which he had opposed. Calling for racial quotas to halt the immigration of "Zulus," he contended that if the country had to have immigrants it would be much easier to assimilate white Europeans than black Africans. When, in a clear test of racist sentiment, the former Ku Klux Klan leader David Duke won a near-victory in a Louisiana Republican primary, Buchanan observed that Duke was "talking about the things that are on people's minds. Every time he says, 'I think white people have equal rights, too,' he puts his message across." That was also Pat Buchanan's message, a key part of the reactionary appeal that went across well enough in the early primaries to put the Bush campaign into a tailspin from which it never recovered.

A leading political oracle, William Schneider of the conservative American Enterprise Institute, who also served as an analyst for the *Los Angeles Times* and CNN, summed up the outlook for the Democrats:

> It's Cuomo versus Clinton. That's the conventional wisdom about the way the 1992 Democratic presidential campaign is shaping up. What's odd is that New York Governor Mario M. Cuomo hasn't even gotten into the race yet. And Arkansas Governor Bill Clinton is still down in the single digits in the polls.

Cuomo's principal asset was high name recognition as an eloquent spokesman for New Deal liberalism. But he could never make up his mind to face the bruising battles that lay ahead, and when the primary lists began to close, none of the six declared candidates could register more than a trace in the polls. In addition to Clinton, they were Senators Paul Harkin of Iowa and Bob Kerrey of Nebraska, former senator Paul Tsongas of Massachusetts, Governor Douglas Wilder of Virginia, and former governor Jerry Brown of California.

The forty-six-year-old Arkansan moved out in front by virtue of the recognition he had gained inside the party, where most of the leadership had long since placed him in the futures book. He had been running for public office most of his adult life, and had become a consistent winner. It could be assumed that the ultimate goal of a career politician would be the top job in his profession, so Clinton's entry in a wide-open presidential primary was no surprise. As a Southerner with an impeccable civil rights record, he was a good bet for a place on the ticket, and either the first or second spot would provide national exposure that would put him in the running next time if George Bush proved to be unbeatable.

But when front-runner status began to give Clinton high visibility during the warmup for New Hampshire, the media had trouble getting him into focus. The first problem was that he was from Arkansas, a venue generations of comedians had employed as the source of the standard stage version of the country bumpkin. The stereotype obviously didn't fit a graduate of the Georgetown University School of Foreign Service, a Rhodes scholar at Oxford, and an honor graduate of Yale Law School.

Although he had the amiable manner of a good ol' Southern boy, Bill Clinton was in fact the most sophisticated candidate in the race— better equipped by a unique combination of education and experience than anyone put forward by either party since the Democrats nominated Adlai Stevenson, for whom the term "egghead" was coined. For Clinton it was translated as "policy wonk," meaning one who knew more about any relevant political subject than the person who raised it.

As they began examining his record, the correspondents found that for at least four years the young governor had been shoring up the frayed Democratic coalition by convincing many of its leaders that he could win the support of the middleclass voters Reagan had lured into the Republican fold. Using the platform of the bipartisan National Governors' Conference, which he served as chairman, and that of the moderate Democratic Leadership Council he helped found, he had positioned himself squarely in the center of the political spectrum— rejecting both Reagan/Bush laissez-faire, which was clearly working against the interests of the middleclass, and the "tax and spend" philosophy attributed to conventional Democrats. Addressing his peers at the 1991 meeting of the Democratic Leadership Council, he drew nods of approval when he declared:

> Too many of the people who used to vote for us, the very
> burdened middleclass we're talking about, have not trusted us
> in national elections to defend our national interests abroad, to

put their values in our social policy at home, or to take their tax money and spend it with discipline.

Addressing the voters, he built his exposition of central, essentially economic issues around a pledge to do his best to

give you a government that represents all of America, that doesn't get out of touch. One that is probusiness and prolabor, progrowth and proenvironment, one that believes you can be for civil rights and civil order, that believes you can be profamily and prochoice.

This could be, and was, called straddling, but it was also a call for a return to activist government that rejected the polarities fostered by the Republicans' antigovernment strategy. And the response of those the worsening recession made receptive to the promise of change indicated that he was cutting a wide swath by the time he faced his first test at the polls in New Hampshire.

With George Bush being mauled by Pat Buchanan, the tacticians at the Republican National Committee decided to make a preemptive start at destroying Clinton's credibility. The race issue was not available as a wedge, since Jesse Jackson, recognizing that the black leadership was opposed to his kind of divisive political campaigning, had remained on the sidelines. This cleared the way for Governor Wilder, a black pragmatist who billed himself as a fiscal conservative. But when the candidates headed South to work the black churches, Wilder proved less at home with the congregations than Bill Clinton, and he was never a factor.

The "character issues" that were to haunt Clinton throughout the campaign first surfaced when allegations of philandering and draft dodging were peddled to the Washington press corps by the Republican National Committee's "research" team. Both charges were old hat in Arkansas, as the investigative reporters who flocked to Little Rock discovered, and for the first month or so no more than innuendo made it into general circulation.

Rumors of what was called a "zipper problem" were inevitable in the case of the handsome, virile young governor; even decrepit old political lions were surrounded by nubile groupies ready to demonstrate Henry Kissinger's thesis that power is the ultimate aphrodisiac. The story that Clinton had maintained a liaison with Gennifer Flowers, a local nightclub singer, had been circulated by his Republican opposition in his last gubernatorial campaign, but had been spiked by her denial and threat of libel action.

This time a supermarket tabloid refreshed her memory with a six-figure payment, and arranged to have her appear at a New York press conference to claim that she had been bedding down with the governor for the twelve years he had been in the governor's office. Once her tale was in circulation beyond the checkout counters, the respectable media abandoned the pretense that they would not be used by politicians to spread personal gossip, and gave Gennifer a front-page ride. Clinton, with his wife, Hillary, at his side, went on television with a flat denial, but it was the kind of salacious story that, with an occasional boost from those who planted it, took on a life of its own.

The governor, like a considerable majority of the baby boom generation, had opposed the war in Vietnam, and when student deferment was no longer available tried to obtain a place in one of the military reserve units that permitted part-time service on the home front. His opponents in previous elections had attempted to use his anti-Vietnam record in their effort to portray him as a New Left radical, but there was no mileage in it even in so patriotic a redoubt as Arkansas. There, as everywhere else, evasion of combat service had been standard practice for middleclass youths whose relatives had even a smidgen of political influence.

When the issue surfaced in the presidential race it was bolstered by documents obviously obtained from confidential government files. These could be interpreted as indicating that Clinton had lied in the course of maneuvering for a reserve appointment. He produced his own records, but they were inconclusive, and the impression that he was dissembling was enough to foster the image of a duplicitous politician—"Slick Willie," as his Arkansas critics labeled him. When Clinton charged that Republican campaign operatives were behind this effort, a TV reporter demanded proof. "Down home," the governor said, "when we find a turtle on the top of a fence post, we know somebody put it there."

Six weeks before the New Hampshire primary, Clinton's front-runner status was certified by cover stories in both *Time* and *Newsweek*. Then, on January 27, Gennifer Flowers held her press conference, and on February 6 *The Wall Street Journal* broke the draft story. A survey by the Center for the Study of Media and Public Affairs showed that in the weeks leading up to the election Clinton had more coverage on the network evening news—most of it unfavorable—than all his opponents combined.

Putting his untested young campaign crew into high gear, he countered with a voter canvass that exhausted the pack journalists, most of whom had written him off. Operating on the presumption that a great many voters really didn't care about either issue, and that those who did would not believe that he was a draft-dodging womanizer after dealing with him face to face, Clinton seemed bent on pressing the flesh of every resident of New Hampshire, including children. Between them, he and Hillary succeeded in reaching enough voters to ensure a second-place finish—which was all that had been expected since the New England candidate, Paul Tsongas, had favorite-son status. On the night of the election Clinton suggested that the reporters replace Slick Willie with a new label: the Comeback Kid.

S. Robert Lichter, the Media Center's codirector, summed up the results of the primary:

> Now, Paul Tsongas has emerged from the debris as the latest beneficiary of a media boomlet . . . the only candidate to receive high marks on the evening news for both his personal qualities and his electability—a winning ticket in the media momentum sweepstakes. Journalists prize unlikely candidates who tell voters what they don't want to hear, and Tsongas has become the John Anderson of 1992.

Lichter noted that there had been a similar phenomenon on the Republican side, where Bush had committed the cardinal sin of running behind the media's projections. Although Buchanan wound up well behind Bush, he was given the lead in the "expectations race, a standard defined by journalists rather than voters."

> Thus the media are back in the thick of the action, creating and destroying front-runners, substituting their own expectations for delegate counts in calling the race, holding up the candidates' dirty linen to the cameras, and generally acting very much as they did four years ago.

The heads of the major news operations had sworn that they would never again be used to convey the kind of demagoguery employed to destroy the candidacy of Michael Dukakis, but the only distinction Lichter could find was that this time the damage was bipartisan: "Although Clinton has received the most negative television coverage among the Democrats, Bush has gotten by far the worst press of any candidate."

The media interpretation of the Democratic contest as a two-man race between Clinton and Tsongas was quickly drained of substance. After the round of Southern primaries, where the Arkansan won most of the delegates, Kerrey and Wilder dropped out, and Harkin was left with only the forlorn hope that he could be resuscitated by the labor vote in the Midwest. Clinton's sweep of Illinois and Michigan in early March finished off Tsongas and Harkin, and only Jerry Brown stood between him and the nomination.

Brown had been a loose cannon on the deck ever since he stood in front of Independence Hall in Philadelphia to launch a campaign that attempted to equate the Founding Fathers with New Age dreamers and New Left radicals. As usual, he zeroed in on what was in fact a basic issue the others were dodging—the corrupting influence of special interest money and the uses of the new communications technology it paid for. And, as usual, he threw it away by wrapping it up with such practical absurdities as a flat tax and radical antiestablishment formulations attractive only to fringe voters.

Brown kept his shoestring campaign alive with a symbolic refusal to accept any contribution over $100, coupled with an appeal for small donations pledged by calling an 800 number he recited like a mantra when a TV camera came within range. Casting about for anything he could use in his ad hominem attacks on Clinton, be dragged in the race issue by announcing that he would choose Jesse Jackson as his running mate. This was obviously a meaningless offer, since there was no way Brown could win the nomination, so Jackson thanked him kindly but declared that at the moment he was a noncandidate—leaving the door sufficiently open to remind the media that he was still in the wings.

Although Clinton had virtually clinched the nomination with his Midwest victories, he still faced the demolition derby provided by the New York primary, and in Connecticut he was edged out by Brown when diehard Tsongas fans ignored his withdrawal and voted for him anyway. In New York the nation's most brutal political coverage feeds on ethnic and religious voting blocs that automatically condemn any candidate who makes a gesture toward one of the others. For Clinton, a moderate Southern Baptist, it was like campaigning in a meat grinder. But, in a splendid irony, it also proved to be the end of the road for Jerry Brown.

Kevin Phillips, the Nixon political strategist who apprenticed in New York's Irish precincts, once said that "the whole secret of politics is who hates who. . . . You make plans from certain rules of exclusion—you can't get the Jews *and* the Catholics." For Jerry Brown, with Jesse Jackson hung around his neck, the rule of exclusion applied among both Jews and blacks. Clinton, who had the support of all but the most rabid antiwhite black leaders, carried substantial majorities among both, and Brown finished behind Tsongas, who was present only as a bittersweet memory.

By June the major party contenders in the general election had been chosen, but the drumfire of denigration for both Bush and Clinton continued in the media after their party rivals were vanquished. In the last significant primary Clinton piled up a substantial margin in vote- and funding-rich California, although Jerry Brown was on the ballot, playing the spoiler's role in his home state. In previous national elections the extraordinary sweep the Comeback Kid had achieved in the course of winning twenty-eight of thirty-six state primaries would have been accepted as evidence that he was very much in the running for the final prize.

But the *Los Angeles Times* headlined its summing up: CLINTON SEEKS

BRASS RING, FINDS IT STILL OUT OF REACH. Conceding that he had demonstrated that he was "far better prepared than any of his rivals for the nomination," the article warned that "despite an astonishing decline in Bush's fortunes, Clinton faces the daunting task of trying to reestablish his credibility and recapture the attention of voters disillusioned with him and with the political process."

As one who occupied a place on the fringe of the substantial body of well-wishers identified as FOB—Friends of Bill—I had followed the primary campaign with more than the usual interest of an unreconstructed Yellow Dog Democrat. Clinton was still in high school when I moved away from Arkansas, but I had seen him in action after he appeared on the political scene. The personal and professional ties formed during my years at the *Gazette* had proved binding, and, as a consultant to Hugh Patterson, the publisher, I was a frequent visitor to Little Rock. Like the other FOBs, I had considered it only a matter of time before this extraordinarily talented young man made a run for national office.

When I first met him he had served two terms as the state's attorney general and had just been elected governor—a boy wonder who had surrounded himself with bright young men and women not yet free of the illusions fostered by the generational rebellion of the sixties. Clinton had challenged not only the special interests that dominated the state government but also the political traditions deeply rooted in the state's collective psyche. What he saw as necessary reforms many Arkansans regarded as manifestations of hubris—as they put it, a matter of being too big for his britches. At the end of his term he was replaced by a feckless Republican.

During the next two years Clinton prepared for the first of his spectacular comebacks. Ms. Hillary Rodham, who had flaunted her maiden name as a feminist symbol when she entered law practice in Little Rock, had become Mrs. Clinton when she appeared with her penitent husband as he traveled Arkansas' seventy-five counties to confess the errors of his youthful ways and seek redemption. A majority of the voters embraced the wayward son, forgave the Yankee wife he had brought home from Yale Law School, and kept the handsome young couple in the governor's mansion until they packed up and moved to Washington.

My personal contacts with Clinton were casual. Age separated me from his social orbit; he could hardly be expected to spend any of his few off-duty hours with one who considered Elvis Presley an abomination, found the Beatles absurd, and stayed as far away as possible from rock music and its high-decibel offshoots. But I did have access to the *Gazette*'s political reporters and commentators, and I still had a place at the table near the bar at the Little Rock Club, which served as a forum for informed political speculation and caustic appraisal of the performance of public officials.

Clinton's abortive first term taught him that he could only govern by consensus—a consensus, that is, of the public and private interests that controlled the Arkansas legislature. As in most states, membership in the General Assembly was officially conceived as a part-time occupation and compensated accordingly, although in fact most of a legislator's time and energy were consumed by politics. This effectively limited the office to those whose income could be maintained or enhanced through their political connections.

The two-year term and limited powers imposed on governors by Arkansas' antiquated Constitution required a perpetual populist campaign for an incumbent who hoped to overcome the obstruction that departure from the status quo faced in the legislature. Change would require funding for financially undernourished public institutions, and constitutional limitations limited the possibility of significantly increasing state revenue to inherently unpopular sales or other consumer taxes.

Populist campaigning, of which Bill Clinton proved to be a master, can be and often is characterized by demagoguery, but he seemed to be as free of it as any politician I had known. He had one great advantage: Race was no longer a live political issue in Arkansas. Orval Faubus had abandoned race-baiting during the latter years of his long tenure; Winthrop Rockefeller left a moderate imprint on the state's Republican organization; Dale Bumpers and David Pryor, now U.S. senators, were members of the generation of Southern governors who perfected the interracial coalition that maintained Democratic control of most state and local offices.

Clinton had a natural ability to establish personal rapport with all classes and conditions of citizens. He was without malice, his interest in their personal well-being was genuine, and although he did a great deal of talking, it was evident that he also listened. When he dealt with those opposed to a course he was advocating, his mastery of the details of the matter under consideration—and his estimate of the political consequences—were usually infallible and often overwhelming.

Governing by consensus meant governing by compromise. The steady improvement in the state's economic growth rate and its educational, health care, and criminal justice systems resulted from the trade-offs the governor made with interests that had to be brought together to accomplish such change. Those who regarded as unthinkable any concession on issues involving human rights or the natural and cultural environment charged him with selling out. Interests that came out second best in the trading accused him of bad faith. And some of my aging contemporaries, who had once been political insiders, could not conceal their resentment at having been replaced by a new generation in the corridors of power.

Yet on basic issues he demonstrated that he placed a limit on compromise, and when it was reached, he stood firm. A notable example was the dogfall with a key segment of his natural constituency, the teachers who made up the Arkansas Education Association (AEA). A task force chaired by Hillary Clinton put together a comprehensive package of school reform measures that included a tax increase to provide higher pay, which the teachers welcomed. But it also required mandatory competency testing to weed out substandard teachers, which they bitterly resented. Between them, the Clintons twisted enough arms to get the legislation approved, but the AEA refused to endorse him in a subsequent election.

It seemed to me that in his twelve years as governor Bill Clinton displayed the quality Harry Truman once defined as the ultimate test of political leadership—the ability to get people to do what they don't want to do, and like it. But Clinton's success, and the fact that his relaxed style and unbounded optimism made it look easy, also fostered resentment. The national attention he and his talented wife began to attract gave rise to the parochial charge that they were only interested in furthering his presidential ambitions.

When investigative reporters came to Arkansas looking for the

Achilles heel of the Washington outsider who had confounded the conventional wisdom, the same, predictable sources of adverse comment turned up in all their accounts. Accusations of dissembling and waffling were readily available on both flanks of the centrist governor. Local partisans wired into the Republican National Committee proffered tips as to alleged influence peddling by Bill and Hillary Clinton, and the media outriders put these in circulation although there was no credible evidence that the governor had ever made a political trade that worked to his or his wife's personal profit, or against the public objective he sought.

The sum total of all the checking and probing was confirmation of a fact that for a decade had been reconfirmed biennially by the vote of a substantial majority of Arkansans: Bill Clinton was a consummate politician. That was enough to provide a leitmotif for those who were trying to discredit him with voters elsewhere who didn't know him and had been conditioned by twelve years of relentless antigovernment propaganda orchestrated from the White House.

Despite Jerry Brown's effort to use overtures to Jesse Jackson to arouse black separatists in the inner cities, Clinton had made impressive headway in his effort to bring together urban blacks and disaffected blue-collar ethnics. When he was asked what he considered the most important element of the Michigan primary vote that secured his nomination, he cited his experience in addressing black and white working-class voters in Macomb County, where the exodus from Detroit had produced a heavy concentration of "Reagan Democrats." He felt, he said, that he had touched the "deeply human core to all these problems, a shared wound to the American psyche. . . ."

> I just have this feeling, this absolute conviction, that [these] people even below their thinking level are aching to be brought together across the racial divide.
>
> If I can't do it, I don't think I can win the race. More importantly, if I can't do it, I don't think I can govern the country.

The separatist issues kept alive in the inner cities by antiwhite agitators such as Lewis Farrakhan and Al Sharpton did not seem to be having much effect after Jerry Brown got his comeuppance in New York. Then a white jury found the Los Angeles police officers charged with beating Rodney King not guilty, and the city's black and Latino precincts erupted in rioting that left fifty-two dead, ten thousand businesses destroyed by arson, and a billion dollars' worth of property damage. Rancorous racial divisions fed by television coverage of atrocities involving both whites and blacks left Los Angeles in a state of shock and sent waves of apprehension through every major city.

As he shaped his campaign to appeal to middleclass voters, Clinton had been accused of glossing over the problems of urban poverty with their special connotation for the black underclass, and Jesse Jackson took up the drumbeat as he faced TV cameras among the ruins of South-Central Los Angeles. This renewed the prospect that he might form an alliance with Jerry Brown, who had made it clear that he intended to use his pledged delegates as a claque to challenge the centrist agenda the Democratic Party chairman, Ron Brown, was preparing for the national convention.

Clinton mounted a preemptive strike that served notice that he could not be whipsawed by the kind of loaded convention-eve demands Jackson had made on the past two Democratic presidential candidates. The Los Angeles riots had heightened racial sensitivity among blacks of all classes, and Jackson had found it prudent not to disavow those who condoned violence. The night before Clinton addressed a Washington, D.C., meeting of the Rainbow Coalition, an award had been given to a young rap singer, Sister Souljah, who employed the incendiary antiwhite lyrics common to the rap form. In a *Washington Post* interview she had made her views known in more comprehensible language:

> . . . if black people kill black people every day, why not have a week to kill white people? . . . So, if you're a gang member and you would normally be killing somebody, why not kill a white person? . . . It's rebellion. It's revenge. You ever hear of Hammurabi's Code? Eye for an eye, a tooth for a tooth?

Reconciliation was the theme of the Rainbow Coalition session Clinton was invited to address, and he questioned how it could be pursued in light of the award that had just been made: "You had a rap singer here last night named Sister Souljah. Her comments before and after the Los Angeles riot were filled with a kind of hatred that you do not honor today. . . ." Reading her quotes from the *Post* interview, he said, "If you took the words 'white' and 'black' and reversed them you might think David Duke is giving that speech."

Jackson complained that the candidate had used the occasion to make a racist appeal to his white supporters. Clinton replied: "I started out this race determined to bring people together across racial lines, and I'm going to speak out against anybody who is not doing that." Will Marshall of the Democratic Leadership Council was delighted with the result. Jackson, he said, had provided a media-focused opportunity for a successful challenge to "the assumption by white liberals that they don't have the moral standing to hold blacks to commonly held standards—or risk being called racists if they do."

When black politicians with the rank of Mayor Michael White of Cleveland and Congressman Mike Espy of Mississippi spoke out in support of Clinton, Jackson was reminded that he had run out of political bargaining chips. And Democratic Chairman Ron Brown, the wily black lawyer who had been his campaign manager four years before, had a pat hand when he dealt with Jackson on Clinton's behalf. The prophet would be given a place under the TV lights at the national convention, but the price would be an advance pledge to support the party ticket and refrain from any denigration of the nominee.

In the late spring I was asked by Clinton to send along suggestions for focusing public attention on real issues rather than the tactical skirmishes exemplified by his standoff with Jesse Jackson. The horse race aspect of the contest had kept interest alive until he secured the nomination, but media attention diminished sharply when he scheduled a series of substantive topical addresses to develop the positions he would take when he faced the incumbent president in the fall.

The problem had become acute when Ross Perot, an eccentric Texas tycoon, began floating trial balloons for an independent candidacy. He established his stance as a political outsider by announcing during his kickoff appearance, on "The Larry King Show," that he was prepared to spend up to a hundred million dollars of his own money to finance a populist campaign. Described by the Texas political commentator Molly Ivins as "a feisty little billionaire with jug ears who sounds like a chihuahua," Perot had enough built-in curiosity value to ensure access to the rest of the network talk shows, where he used snappy comebacks in lieu of details when asked how he would go about single-handedly driving the special interests out of Washington.

All he needed, he proclaimed, was a summons to duty by the "real people" manifested without the corrupting intervention of party primaries and conventions. A call to his Dallas phone bank would enable supporters to enlist in the effort to put his name on the general election ballot as an independent. If they met the legal requirements in all fifty states he would make himself available to "lift up the hood" on the government, and get to work on balancing the budget and restoring economic growth. It was, he reiterated, just that simple for a fellow who had learned the requirements of the new age of high technology while piling up a three-billion-dollar personal fortune in the computer business.

With his pledge to finance his campaign out of his own pocket he had tapped into the broad vein of disillusionment with the political process exploited from the left by Jerry Brown, and by adopting Paul Tsongas's priority on budget balancing he rallied the disaffected on the right. He also appealed to widespread distrust of the media by berating his interviewers, and in short order achieved a favorable poll rating that topped those of the major party candidates. A *Washington Post* expert on political style, Mary McGrory, observed that when Clinton launched his campaign "it was good to be tall and smiley; now, however, it is high chic to be short and short-tempered, as is proven by the fact that Ross Perot has shoved him into third place."

In June I sent Clinton a memorandum titled "The Three-Way Race." The Republican Party line contended that the media, because of its alleged liberal bias, was favoring Clinton over Bush, a durable shibboleth that had evoked sardonic laughter from every Democratic presidential candidate I had known. After Clinton had eliminated his effective primary opposition, David Broder, generally regarded as the most authoritative of the Washington pundits, wrote:

The closer Bill Clinton gets to the Democratic presidential nomination, the more nervous—if not despairing—many of his fellow partisans become. To hear them talk, they're not sure whether their convention will serve as a prelude to an election or a political execution.

In my memo I noted that Clinton's problem with the media resulted in large part

> from the fact that only 15 percent of the reporters and commentators sampled in this week's *Los Angeles Times* media poll believe you have a chance to be elected. It follows that the others are virtually constrained to seek out, or fabricate, evidence that their judgment is correct.

It was the judgment of Clinton and his campaign staff that, aside from capturing the media spotlight, Perot's tentative bid was doing Clinton little harm and might be helping him, since Perot seemed to be mounting a personal vendetta against President Bush, whom he held primarily responsible for the failures of the central government. Perot included the Democrats in his indictment in terms not different in kind from those used by Clinton when he allocated a share of guilt to Congress.

I had no disposition to question the tactical decisions of a campaign staff that had brought Clinton through the serial crises created by the character issues. My impression of the extraordinary competence of the FOBs working full time on Clinton's behalf, and the energy and dedication of the talented youngsters hired to do the legwork, was reinforced when I went to Little Rock to discuss contributions to Clinton's acceptance speech with George Stephanopoulos, his communications director.

It seemed to me that the Perot candidacy would have to be dealt with at the national convention, a tricky business since Clinton would need the votes of those who were reflexively responding as the maverick Texan gave voice to their anger and frustration. Most of the draft passages I submitted were intended to employ Clinton's centrist position as the base for attacks on Bush's ineffective laissez-faire policies, and on the radical-right ideology implicit in Perot's proposal to install one-man rule in defiance of the divided powers provided by the Constitution.

I was delighted to have my contributions invalidated by Perot's unexpected withdrawal. He had concluded, he said, that his candidacy might result in a three-way split in the vote that would throw the election into the House of Representatives, and he wanted no part of such a divisive result. Moreover, it now appeared to him that the Democratic Party had pulled itself together in a fashion that would make it possible for its nominee to achieve the economic reforms he believed essential. There was no mention of Bill Clinton, and nothing to sustain the inevitable speculation that a deal must have been made, since the timing of the withdrawal guaranteed that the convention would be the coronation Ron Brown had planned.

There was really nothing left to speculate about when the delegates entered upon an endless round of parties interspersed with pro forma sessions in the gigantic television set that had been erected in New York's Madison Square Garden. Clinton had already announced his vice-presidential selection, defying the conventional wisdom by naming Senator Albert Gore, Jr., of neighboring Tennessee, whose youth, background, and regional appeal paralleled his own. The "double Bubba" ticket presented two Ivy League–honed career politicians who qualified as liberals on human rights and moderates on economic issues. And Gore brought with him another personable blond wife and a passel of tow-headed children to whom the TV cameras were as kind as they were to the Clintons.

The TV news anchors and commentators looked down from their glass boxes on the happy tumult on the floor of the convention and groused because it was virtually impossible to stir up any conflict in the united party. Perot's announcement had quashed the rumor that Jesse Jackson was about to jump ship and join the Texan, and no one took Jerry Brown seriously when he tried to drum up a phony free-speech issue by refusing to accept his place on the agenda when Ron Brown invoked the party loyalty pledge taken by all those assigned to speak during the broadcast networks' limited coverage.

The diversity of the delegates' backgrounds reflected the multicultural nation the United States was becoming, but the confrontations this had produced in the past were out of order. When Jesse Jackson mounted the podium to manfully salute Bill Clinton he called on his own constituency, the neglected poor, "to turn pain to power, pain to partnership, not pain into polarization." Turning to his white brethren, he said, "If we pursue that ethic, that love ethic . . . we will win and deserve to win."

When the convention reached its climax with the nomination of two good ol' Southern boys, the seconding speeches brought forth a parade of blacks bearing wound stripes from the civil rights movement. Congressman John Lewis, leader of the fateful march across the bridge at Selma, was there to remind that Bill Clinton and Al Gore were "sons of the South" who had never lost sight of Martin Luther King's vision of the beloved community. And Barbara Jordan's organ tones rolled out King's injunction from the Birmingham Jail: "We will have to repent in this generation not merely for the vitriolic words and actions of bad people, but for the silence of good people." She followed with a pointed challenge to blacks whose integrationist faith had lapsed:

> We are one, we Americans, and we reject any intruder who seeks to divide us by race or class. We seek to unite people, not divide them, and we reject both white racism and black racism. This party will not tolerate bigotry under any guise.

Plain-spoken Maxine Waters, representative of the Los Angeles congressional district that bore the brunt of the recent rioting, had an equally pointed message on behalf of the pragmatists who had worked their way up to positions of political leadership in the nation's black precincts:

> Four years ago I seconded the nomination of Jesse Louis Jackson. Tonight I rise to second the nomination of Bill Clinton. . . .
>
> I understood that you have to start early. I knew, looking at the [primary candidates], that it had to be Bill Clinton. . . .
>
> Let me tell you where the power really lies. When a Maxine Waters endorses a Bill Clinton, the power to convince him, to work with him, is awesome power.

Up in their glass boxes, removed from the surges of emotion that swept across the floor, the TV pundits complained that the whole thing had been a contrived spectacle devoid of content. Spectacle it had been, as all campaign events must be in the television age, but in this instance the medium was the message, leaving no doubt that a new generation had arrived to take over the places of power, bringing with it leaders conditioned by the vast, interrelated changes in technology, demography, and popular culture that had taken place in their formative years. The FOB Hollywood producers who stage-managed their fellow Arkansan's coronation boiled the message down to the name of the little town where Bill Clinton was born: Hope.

Restoration of hope in a dispirited electorate would require change—change in the way the government functioned, and in the way the voters had been responding to the stresses of a contracting economy. It was as heralds of a new day that Bill Clinton and Al Gore took the show on the road. Accompanied by their wives and children, they immediately set forth in a bus caravan aimed at the heartland, stopping wherever small-town Americans waited, sometimes for hours, to greet them. The TV cameras caught a heartwarming response from the grass roots that impressed even the jaded occupants of the trailing press buses.

The Democratic presidential candidate's display of energy and genuine rapport with ordinary citizens provided a telling contrast with the depressed George Bush, isolated in the White House by an ill-timed Rose Garden Strategy, deflated by the precipitous drop in his poll ratings, and surrounded by a rattled and ineffective staff.

Pat Buchanan's aborted primary campaign had served to spring the trap that had been set for the president when William F. Buckley, Jr.'s, influential *National Review* declared that conservatives could no longer support him "unless he makes a major, explicit, and convincing turn to the right." Edwin J. Fuelnor, Jr., president of the Heritage Foundation, had followed up in his "Report on the State of Conservatism 1992": "Conservatives today are virtually unanimous in their disapproval of the Bush administration. . . . George Bush is more a weathervane than a compass."

The president's expedient stance on the "social issues," uncomfortable as it obviously was for him, had alienated the moderates, particularly prochoice women. To hold together any semblance of a campaign organization he had no option but to yield control of the national convention to right-wing ideologues who barely concealed their contempt for him. When the Republicans convened in Houston in August it was as though Buchanan had won the primary election and chosen television evangelist Pat Robertson as his running mate.

Speaking at the opening of the convention, Buchanan seemed to treat his endorsement of the president as a response to God's will. He managed this by treating the Democratic candidate's lawyer wife as a symbol of the feminist/minority cause he denounced with an invocation of religious bias as pointed as that employed by the Know-Nothings a century ago when they used Catholic immigrants as partisan whipping boys:

> There is a religious war going on in this country. It is a cultural war, as critical to the kind of nation we shall be as the Cold War itself, for this is a war for the soul of America. Clinton and Clinton are on the other side, and George Bush is on our side.

To Pat Robertson, an "insidious plague has fastened itself on the families of America," and the Democrats were its carrier:

> When Bill and Hillary Clinton talk about family values, they are not talking about either families or values. They are talking about a radical plan to destroy the traditional family and transfer its functions to the federal government.

In literature circulating at the convention and by mail across the country, Robertson demonized the women's movement, citing it as the leading threat to the nation now that godless communism was in abeyance.

> The feminist agenda is not about equal rights for women. It is about a socialist, antifamily political movement that encourages women to leave their husbands, kill their children, practice witchcraft, destroy capitalism, and become lesbians.

When George Bush accepted the mantle of his party he was committed to conducting a campaign that would employ the Buchanan/Robertson version of family values as an umbrella to cover opposition to all forms of government action intended to protect the civil rights and entitlements of minorities and the female majority. This, of course, was an affirmation of Republican policies in effect for the past twelve years, but now it bore the overt stamp of bigotry Richard Nixon and Ronald Reagan had managed to avoid.

. . .

The general election campaign followed the tracks laid down at the party conventions. Clinton, as best he could, stayed on the high ground, with few lapses in the standards of civility the media had clamored for, and the party leaders had pledged, after the desecrations of 1988. Without a Teflon-coated persona to deflect blame for the protracted recession bequeathed by his predecessor, Bush again resorted to a negative campaign that consisted primarily of an effort to discredit his opponent by any means, fair or foul.

Ross Perot, his ego drive displaying distinct signs of paranoia, tried to derail both candidates by reentering the race in the homestretch. First he hired professional managers, publicists, and advertising agencies, and sent out paid workers to fashion his volunteer support groups into a standard campaign organization. But when it became evident that this was costing him the nonpolitical outsider status that provided his only real appeal, he fired all the professionals, and sat down to prepare a campaign he could keep under his own absolute control. This consisted of sixty million dollars' worth of paid TV broadcasts, for which he wrote the script and appeared alone as a talking head surrounded by mind-boggling charts.

It was a remarkable fact that in the most completely television-driven presidential contest the nation had yet seen, this was the only significant infusion of paid advertising. To get past the screen of network newscasters and commentators that limited direct access to the voters, it had become standard practice for candidates to retain Madison Avenue agencies to shape their images, package their messages, and buy airtime for their delivery. But by 1992 the great expansion of channels provided by cable television had broken the networks' monopoly on political broadcasting.

This followed when it was realized that topflight politicians could provide the free, celebrity-caliber talent upon which the plethora of low-budget talk shows depended. And Clinton expanded the outreach beyond the limited audiences attracted to news-oriented programs by appearing on talk shows intended primarily as entertainment. I was one of the print-oriented journalists who had been complaining for years that the line between TV news and entertainment had become hopelessly blurred, and I was given pause when Clinton turned up on the late-night Arsenio Hall show wearing shades and playing the saxophone.

But it was quickly demonstrated that in terms of political propriety I was simply out of date. What seemed to my generation beneath the dignity of a presidential candidate was regarded as entirely acceptable by those who had grown up in the television age, or were in the process of doing so. The response was so favorable that Clinton canceled a long-scheduled half-hour paid broadcast, and George Stephanopoulos explained that this had nothing to do with the campaign budget: "If you gave me three million dollars today, I wouldn't spend a penny on TV. We can't get any more [exposure] than we are getting."

Clinton successfully adapted to TV the populist style he had employed in Arkansas to rally the support he needed to overcome or minimize policies imposed by special interests. In his small state he could actually make personal contact with a majority of voters if he worked at it day in and day out. That was not possible in the case of a national constituency, but he could use surrogates from the talk show studio and call-in audiences to project the image of one who stayed in touch with ordinary citizens, listened to them, and knew what they, and he, were talking about. This was how he had offset the slings and arrows aimed at him by journalists and their manipulators, and the overt attacks on his character by George Bush and Ross Perot. And, Clinton promised, he had no intention of changing his ways after he won the election.

A sign on the wall at Clinton headquarters that became a famous campaign artifact admonished the strategists: "It's the Economy, Stupid!" Prime Republican targets for attack were provided by the everyday experience of most Americans. The tattered safety net intended to ease the dislocations of recession no longer protected most workers, and privation had begun to spread upward through the middleclass. But to exploit the vulnerability of the Republicans on economic issues, Clinton had to spell out alternatives to failed policies—and in doing so he restored to the political agenda the basic issues of governance that had been glossed over in the name of laissez faire.

Professional economists were now roughly divided between the Cambridge and Chicago schools, with those who leaned toward the

Democrats identified with the Massachusetts Institute of Technology and Harvard, while the intellectual godfathers of Reaganomics had their roots at the University of Chicago. Peter Temin, chairman of MIT's Economics Department, summarized the basic difference: "We believe the market is good for most things, but not for everything, as opposed to a more Chicago view, where they think the market is good for everything." Practically all of Clinton's advisers were identified with the Cambridge school, and their recommendations required an active role for government on a broad front to deal with a fundamentally changed economy no longer contained by national boundaries.

The economists pointed to structural changes in the market and the workplace that had slowed economic growth, increased unemployment, and downgraded jobs. This had resulted in a decline in the real income of all Americans except those in the higher brackets, and for most it had begun to mean a lowering of living standards that for almost half a century had been steadily improving for most of the nation's productive workers.

The political equation called for short-term measures to provide immediate relief for the unemployed and deal with the unrest in the ghettos, but if the structural imbalances in the economy were to be dealt with there would have to be a longer-term approach that would require a redirection of public and private investment and changes in tax and regulatory policy. Any effective program would require a reduction, or at least a curtailment, of the mounting federal deficit.

Oversimplified political rhetoric reduced the issue to a choice between additional tax revenues and a drastic reduction in government programs. But as a practical matter any further curtailment of spending for social programs was bound to increase the level of unrest among the poor that exacerbated the urban crisis and militated against the economic growth both sides agreed was essential to any long-range solution. Bill Clinton insisted that a way could and must be found to deal with unmet social problems as well as the economic dislocations that would not be affected by any easing of the current recession.

In ordinary times it would have been considered impossible to enlist significant support at the top level of society for a populist campaign that exploited the resentment of the many against the real and perceived special privileges of the few. But in mounting his centrist approach Clinton had picked up potent allies in the upper reaches of the American establishment, where many who normally supported the Republicans had been disillusioned by the government's failure to come to grips with social and economic issues that now had adverse consequences in their own spheres of operation.

These apostate Clinton supporters were typified by the hundred chief executive officers of leading corporations and educational institutions who made up the membership of the foundation-supported Business–Higher Education Forum. In 1990 they had produced a publication, *Three Realities*, that ran directly counter to public opinion as measured by the polls that gave George Bush a high approval rating.

The report, supported by extensive research, found that reality in the case of the underclass demonstrated the total failure of conventional approaches to the problems of poverty, "whether generous-spirited or hard-nosed." They had not taken into account "the degree to which the least favored have fallen victim to the past, are profoundly alienated by the present, and have little hope for the future."

The insistence that welfare should be reduced or eliminated because it causes a "culture of dependency" was dismissed as not only unreal but inhumane:

> Public assistance serves a population grievously in the need of help: infants, children, and female heads of households already destitute. To suggest that society take away what little they have in order to motivate them to reach for more is perverse. It is, indeed, unconscionable.

The forum's recommendations seemed old-fashioned when considered in the light of what had passed for political discourse in recent years. They were preceded by a reminder that, while the nation's strength lies in its diversity, its motto is *e pluribus unum*—from the many, one. The civil rights movement, functioning initially in the interests of blacks, the most conspicuous victims of discrimination, was credited with political reforms that made possible a start toward bringing all disadvantaged groups into the mainstream. But further progress would require action on the economic front, and here only a concert of interests could prevail:

. . . victory in the struggle for economic equity will require
new sacrifices and new energies from all of us. The standard to
which we must rally can best be defined by minority leaders.
But they cannot succeed alone. Our common task is to convince
our young people that oppression can be lifted, that discrimination can be eliminated, and that poverty can be overcome. . . .

The forum gave this hortatory injunction substance by setting forth
recommendations that would require the kind of national economic,
social, educational, and health care policies that had become virtually
unmentionable in Washington. In doing so the CEOs were surely aware
that implementation would require a return to the progressive tax structure reversed by Reaganomics, and a basic reallocation of responsibility
and resources within the federal system.

They were in position to see at firsthand that supply-side nostrums
were not producing the growth a healthy economy required. Laws of
supply and demand conceived when suppliers and consumers dealt with
each other face to face had not been adapted to a global economy being
transformed by a technological revolution. In their generation these
CEOs had seen the marketplace internationalized, the nature of manufacturing and service enterprises and the work force profoundly altered,
financial institutions shaken to their foundations, and unprecedented
threats posed for the physical and social environments. The bottom line
as they read it showed a high cost for meeting the demands posed by
these changes—and a prohibitive cost for continued failure to do so.

Beneath the hoopla and often overblown rhetoric these premises provided the solid basis for the Clinton campaign, and they were accepted,
at least in part, by enough voters to give him an opportunity to put
them into effect.

Perot's heavy investment in TV advertising helped him garner 19
percent of the popular vote, but it was scattered among the states and
was drawn equally from Clinton and Bush; its primary importance was
as a measure of the extent of disillusionment with the political process.
Clinton's 43 to 38 percent popular vote margin over Bush gave him a

victory in the Electoral College that indicated the collapse of the Republican coalition, and at least a partial restoration of the Democrats' traditional support base.

The Democrats reclaimed four states from the Republicans in the Confederate South, and would have had more without Perot on the ballot, for in the seven states where Bush led, he topped 50 percent only in Mississippi. Clinton ran well ahead of Bush in suburbia, working-class neighborhoods, and among the young. The racial/ethnic/ religious divisions in the nation at large were indicated by Clinton's majorities among the groups identified in the exit polls. Only among white males did he fall below 50 percent, but there was a downward curve among the others: Blacks gave him 82 percent; Jews, 78; gays, 72; liberals, 68; Latinos, 62; the poor, 59; union members, 56; and big city voters, 55.

James Carville, the chief strategist of the Clinton campaign, summed up the result: " "We've been given a chance, not a mandate." The media's dispensers of conventional wisdom had never given him even that until it became impossible to ignore the collapse of Bush's candidacy and the irrelevance of Perot's. "I kept finding reasons to doubt that Clinton would make it," David Broder confessed. "The columns continued in that vein right up through mid-October."

Although Clinton's approval rating had reached 71 percent, the highest inaugural-month rating in thirty years, the negative tone of the chorus of TV pundits who traffic in the views of Washington insiders was hardly affected. If Jimmy Carter's honeymoon with the Washington press corps was a one-night stand, Bill Clinton never even made it to the bridal suite.

But if he had hoped for a better reception, the new president was not surprised by the one he got. When the editors who prepared *Time*'s Man of the Year cover story asked him what enduring legacy he would bring to the White House, Clinton said it was that he had taught the people of Arkansas to think long-term: "It's what I want most to do nationwide. It won't be easy and it will require a constant dialogue with the country, but it has to be done, and I mean to do it." James McGregor Burns, biographer of Franklin Roosevelt and Jack Kennedy, got a one-word reply when he asked Clinton how he proposed to deal with the kind of congressional deadlock that had thwarted his Democratic predecessors: "Persistence."

PROGNOSIS
A BATTLE FOR THE DISAFFECTED

We are in an odd situation. At one level of intelligence, or consciousness, Americans know their political language is false and their ideas
are sentimental, [but] it is the only language we have—drained of
content though it may be.

—WILLIAM PFAFF, *Barbarian Sentiments:*
How the American Century Ends

IN THE SUNDAY, January 17, 1993, edition of *The New York Times*
Magazine, Michael Kelly and Maureen Dowd, White House correspondents for the nation's most influential newspaper, rendered a judgment that reflected the prevailing view of the mass media:

William Jefferson Clinton becomes the 42nd President of the
United States three days from now an oddly unknown man. He
has succeeded remarkably well in being many things to many
people, but that leaves the question of who he really is.

Is he the New Democrat or the same old thing?. . . . There
is a fundamental tension between the glib politician and the
dedicated student of public policy, the man always looking for

approval and the man who knows that wrenching changes are required to put the country on a new course.

The effect was to perpetuate by inference the "character issues" that had provided the basis of the Republican presidential campaign, and of Ross Perot's sideshow—discounting in advance any policy the new president might put forward by questioning whether he was what he purported to be—a pragmatic centrist, or an impostor who, out of guile or weakness, was fated to emerge in office as a tax-and-spend Old Democrat.

At first the questions did not carry much weight in the country at large, where the populist inaugural celebration and Clinton's trenchant maiden speech before Congress prompted a positive response. But doubts about the new president's true identity had become fixed in the conventional wisdom, which, as Robert Parry pointed out in *Fooling America*, defines "the limits of permissible thinking within the journalistic and governmental communities of Washington."

Like most such canons, the conventional wisdom did not keep pace with the changing tenor of the times. The truism that an activist president's success depended upon putting the basic elements of his program through Congress in the first hundred days of his administration dated back to Franklin Roosevelt's time. The last such triumph had been recorded by Lyndon Johnson, and it was negated by the time he faced reelection.

When Johnson, riding the momentum of his 1964 landslide, launched his Great Society program, the University of Michigan's annual survey of voter attitudes showed that 62 percent believed that the central government could be trusted to do what was right most of the time. In 1992, when Bill Clinton edged into office with a shaky plurality, the Michigan poll showed that only 26 percent still held that view.

The reality that would determine Clinton's political fate was highlighted by the *Los Angeles Times* in its own depth polls of voter sentiment, but given little weight in the usual media analysis of the president's shortcomings:

> The idea that the government could do anything well, or anything to help them, runs into a web of suspicion and cynicism

so dense and self-reinforcing that it is virtually impenetrable. Much of the complaint about government . . . is reflexive, timeless, impervious to argument.

During the transition period, bored correspondents languishing in Little Rock generated speculation on the effect of the president-elect's campaign promise to see to it that minorities and women were appropriately represented in his administration. Clinton's approach to filling out his cabinet was hardly novel; for Democrats, beginning with Jack Kennedy, the party's commitment to civil rights had required inclusion of increasing numbers of those previously excluded. But grist for the media mill was provided by crossfire from conservatives, who complained that Clinton was applying quotas at the expense of merit, and by leaders of his own party's interest groups who protested that selections from their ranks were either too few, or did not include the candidates they preferred.

Only the most doctrinaire critics seriously questioned the competence of those finally named, and they did conform to Clinton's centrist stance, ranging from center left to center right on economic issues. Those who would be in charge of welfare and the environment were widely experienced and as moderate as could be expected in areas polarized by philosophical differences between the two parties. While minorities were proportionately represented, feminists insisted that women were not, and, citing a comparable interest in civil rights, they laid claim to the key office of attorney general, which would not be filled until Clinton had settled into the White House.

There were two inherently divisive issues—abortion and gay rights—on which civil rights constituencies expected action by the new president. No one with Clinton's experience could have been unaware that he was moving into a political minefield when he announced his intention to use his executive powers to change the rules barring gays and lesbians from military service, to remove the "gag rule" that prevented discussion of abortion by publicly funded health providers, and end the ban on the use of fetal tissue in medical research.

I had had no contact with Clinton or his political strategists since the early days of the general election campaign, but it seemed to me the only question raised by such action so early in his administration was tactical. No one with a commitment to civil rights could condone the kind of discrimination inherent in these practices, and cases involving both the abortion rules and the homosexual ban were already before the courts, and in the headlines. I assumed that Clinton had decided to face these issues early on in the hope of putting the controversy behind him before he had to face Congress on the economic and social proposals at the heart of his program.

On the abortion ruling, this proved to be the case; the protest from the pro-life leaders was pro forma, the Democratic majority held firm, and there were enough pro-choice Republicans to quell any effective congressional counteraction. But on the right of gays to serve in the military he ran head-on into the Joint Chiefs of Staff, aided and abetted by one of the most potent of the Democratic barons who held sway in the Senate, Sam Nunn of Georgia, who from the outset had displayed a marked lack of enthusiasm for the Clinton candidacy.

Clinton may have hoped that such bold and decisive action would at least provide rebuttal to the charge that he always waffled when faced with controversy. Instead, the openings it provided his political enemies were cited by the pundits to support their contention that he had surrounded himself with political neophytes and was himself dangerously ignorant of the ways of Washington.

Mark Shields found the president and his young White House staff "incredibly inept"; John McLaughlin saw "slowness and vacillation"; Tim Russert declared that "the president is stumbling"; to Jack Germond and Jules Witcover he didn't display "the common sense of a gnat." The Los Angeles Times saw hope "rapidly turning to chilly uneasiness, even dismay," and The New York Times harrumphed, "He needs to show that he, not Slick Willie, is the ringmaster." Looking back eight months later, David Shaw, who covered the media for the Los Angeles newspaper, concluded that no president in recent history "had been subjected to a greater barrage of negative media coverage than Bill Clinton suffered."

Civil rights issues concerned with overt discrimination against blacks enjoyed a degree of immunity to partisan attack on the Hill, but they had become part of a trinity that also included gender and religion—both of which had been invoked by the president's stands on abortion and gay rights. This quickly doused any hope Clinton may have entertained that he was moving away from the minefield when he nominated a Jewish woman from the corporate bar as attorney general.

His cabinet appointments were also intended to demonstrate generational change, and in looking for someone in his own age group he came up with the mother of a young child. As was commonplace under the badly drawn and indifferently enforced immigration laws, the eminently qualified Zoe Baird turned out to have been the employer of an illegal alien as a live-in nursemaid who made it possible for her to pursue her career as a leading corporation lawyer.

The uproar that greeted the revelation caught Clinton off guard, and unnerved Senate Judiciary Committee members. The conclusion that it would not be politically safe to confirm Ms. Baird forced her to withdraw, an outcome loaded with irony. It had nothing to do with the plight of immigrants whose dubious legal status left them open to exploitation. In this case Ms. Baird, who treated her servants generously, had been sheltering a Peruvian couple who were promptly deported when she paid the delinquent tax.

The cries of outrage came primarily from working mothers in income brackets below Ms. Baird's half-million-dollar level. They had paid the Social Security taxes the law required, while she had done so only after making the short list for Cabinet appointment. Resentment against women who could afford quality day care without strain on their financial resources was sufficient to derail the appointment of a second upperclass working mother, federal judge Kimba Wood, even though she had met all the legal requirements for the West Indian immigrant who looked after her children.

The issue was seen as one of special privilege not available to less affluent families for whom maintenance of middleclass living standards now required two breadwinners. The working mothers whose protests inundated Capitol switchboards were frustrated by the unavailability of reliable day care for their children comparable to that provided by live-in domestic servants they could not afford. But E. J. Dionne, Jr., a *Washington Post* expert on mass mores, thought that something more than a class issue was involved:

We've gone through a social revolution these past thirty years over the role of men and women. There's a lot of discomfort about the sort of families we're creating (or not creating). . . .

These are wrenching issues, and Zoe Baird, Judge Wood (and for that matter Hillary Clinton) become convenient symbols. We often prefer stereotypes—"the yuppy woman from hell" vs. "the moral majoritarian stay-at-home mom"—to trying to sort our way through the personal and social meaning of choices we make all the time.

A century ago that inveterate skeptic Mark Twain identified an inherent characteristic of the democratic political process: "We all do no end of feeling, and we mistake it for thinking. And out of it we get an aggregation which we consider a boon. Its name is Public Opinion." The communications revolution had since added visual imagery to the flow of information upon which political judgments depend, enhancing the visceral reaction. Russell Baker once observed that on the night in 1960 when a confident, eloquent John F. Kennedy faced an apparently shifty Richard Nixon in the first televised campaign debate, "image replaced the printed word as the natural language of politics."

Economics, claiming rationality as its guiding principle, was still relied upon to impose a degree of reality on the political process over the long haul. But in terms of immediate reaction, reason was frequently overcome by the ideology that determined traditional partisan divisions. And it often disappeared entirely when politicians were forced to deal with the civil rights trinity.

The illegal-alien flap caused feminists who had applauded the president for his stand on abortion to accuse him of selling out their cause when he failed to back up Ms. Baird and Judge Wood. And when he came up with a childless nominee for attorney general, the touchiest of the gender issues, homosexuality, came in by a side door.

Janet Reno, the highly praised chief state prosecuting attorney in Miami, was a fifty-six-year-old, six-foot-two, Harvard Law School graduate safely past childbearing age. But the fact that she had never married left her open to the suspicion, openly aired by an opponent in her last election, that she must be a lesbian. When the question was raised again after she received the nod from Clinton, she replied: "Mr. Thompson [her defeated opponent] always worries about my sexual preference. But the fact is that I'm just an awkward old maid with a very great affection for men."

The media's intensive examination of her record as the four-term chief prosecutor in the multiracial center of international drug traffic turned up no one who questioned her integrity. The black leaders who complained of the failure to convict white policemen charged with beating a black man to death blamed it on the jury, and conceded her exemplary record on minority rights in a city beset by racial tension.

This removed race as a consideration, and her reputation as a tough prosecutor was an asset on Capitol Hill. During the Reagan/Bush years criminal-law enforcement had been established in the conventional wisdom as the primary means of dealing with unrest in the ghettos. Bill Clinton had acknowledged this with a proposal to increase the police available to deal with inner city crime, and now he had a nominee who, unlike the first two, was a living symbol of law and order. There was no doubt that Janet Reno would be unanimously confirmed after she testified before the Judiciary Committee:

> The most important problem in America today is violence, and people want those who hurt and maim and kill and brutalize put away and kept away for as long a time as they possibly can be. That's my goal.

The most divisive impact of the civil rights trinity came on the issue with the most limited constituency. Opinion polls measuring reaction to Clinton's announced intention to require an end to the military's ban on homosexuals showed that 70 percent believed sexual relations between persons of the same gender was wrong. This was hardly surprising, since virtually all religious denominations still taught that homosexual practice is a sin.

In the course of the civil rights movement, however, free choice of sexual relations between consenting adults had gained constitutional protection, permitting gay men and women to come out of the closet in increasing numbers. They still encountered social stigma, but in housing, public accommodations, and employment they had gained acceptance comparable to that of women and blacks. In practice, most heterosexuals evidenced no objection to homosexuality unless it was flouted as a challenge to their own standards of behavior.

Only in the military were gay men and lesbians still treated as outlaws; to enter the service of their country they had to lie about their sexual orientation, and if it became known, they were subject to automatic discharge no matter how unblemished their records. The irony was that homosexuals had been serving, often with distinction, in all ranks of the American armed services since they were organized. The generals and admirals who protested the presidential directive were very well aware of this, but insisted that the morale of their troops would be seriously impaired if it were officially acknowledged that persons who served alongside them might be gay.

To justify their stand the military leaders had to contend that homophobic prejudice was so widespread in their commands it could not be contained by existing regulations banning unwanted sexual advances, or even gestures. But the efficacy of these means of enforcing discipline sufficient to prevent threats to good order had been demonstrated by integration of the racially segregated services in the face of presumably implacable white prejudice.

In 1948, the top brass, and their supporters in Congress, had cited the opinion polls when President Truman ordered desegregation of the armed services, and they had shown virtually the same level of public disapproval. Every argument offered in support of the ban on gays had been raised by military commanders and politicians, and had been proved invalid by experience. A Rand Corporation study commissioned by the Pentagon predicted the same result in the case of gays.

This posed a painful dilemma for General Colin Powell, who had to recognize that latent racial prejudice would be accentuated if he supported gay rights in defiance of his white colleagues on the Joint Chiefs of Staff. He was not alone in that concern. "Although some black leaders have publicly supported lifting the ban," the *Los Angeles Times* reported, "the army of voters and lobbyists swarming over Capitol Hill in the gay-rights push has been conspicuously white—and devoid of high-profile support from mainstream black- and Latino-run civil rights groups." Initially, the NAACP took no position on the issue, and a Latino leader said her organization just had too many other things to deal with.

Those who backed away were reminded by Colbert L. King, a black *Washington Post* editorial writer, that they were turning a blind eye to their own history. A former Army officer and an admirer and friend of General Powell, King was convinced that more than homophobia was involved in the bigoted response to columns he wrote in support of gay rights. If the president's order was overturned by congressional action, he predicted, "gays and lesbians will surely become the 'niggers' of the '90s":

> African Americans should be the last group on earth to let that happen. With the Joint Chiefs, the far right, political demogogues, some macho brothers, and a host of white guys lined up against them, gays and lesbians won't gain much support by having me on their side. They would be far better off with Colin Powell. Everything I know about our own struggle for freedom, dignity and our right to fully participate in this country, including its armed forces, tells me their side is where we belong.

When I read King's plaint my memory unreeled a scene in Little Rock's Jewish country club a generation ago, when the *Arkansas Gazette* was under boycott for supporting desegregation of the public schools. As in most Southern cities, the small Jewish community was largely made up of prosperous descendants of German immigrants who had settled in the state before the Civil War. The leading department and specialty stores were owned by prominent old families, and they had continued advertising in the *Gazette* when the Citizens' Council threatened to extend the boycott to include them. But most of the Jewish business, professional, and cultural leaders had stayed on the sidelines when their Christian peers began organizing a protest movement against Governor Faubus's closure of the city schools.

My host at the country club, a physician, was a conspicuous exception, and it became increasingly obvious that his presence, coupled with mine, was discomfiting his fellow members. We were excluded from the usual camaraderie in the bar, but we had the solicitous attention of the black bartender, and we lingered perhaps too long. The evening came to an abrupt end when my friend suddenly stood, glared around the room, and declared, "You people remind me of the story of two Jews facing a Nazi firing squad. When the commander called out,

'Ready, aim—' one of them cried, 'Wait, for God's sake, don't shoot!' And the other turned on him and said, 'What are you trying to do—stir up trouble?' "

It was, I suppose, inevitable that a generation later blacks should be divided over a civil rights issue that did not directly affect their immediate interests and might work against them. But the bigotry aroused by the trinity of sex, religion, and race exempted no one who professed to love or even tolerate his neighbor.

While the country was in an uproar over the issue of gays in the military, *The New Yorker* published a Valentine's Day cover portraying a bearded, black-hatted Hasidic Jew kissing a responsive black girl. Cries of outrage arose in Brooklyn's Crown Heights, where protracted racial encounters had involved the most rigorously traditional of the orthodox sects.

The magazine's editor, Tina Brown, replied that the "dreamlike vision of comity and love speaks for itself," and the artist, Art Spiegelman, explained that his painting was "knowingly naive." He was, he said, fully aware of the religious taboo against a Hasidic Jew's embracing even his own wife in public:

> But, once a year perhaps, it's permissible for a moment to close one's eyes, see beyond the tragic complexities of modern life, and imagine that it might really be true that "All you need is love. . . ."

There had never been a time when there was more talk about racism, and, it seemed to me, less understanding of its causes and effects. In the 1980s a majority of white Americans had been persuaded that racial prejudice was no longer a deterrent to progress for the black minority. Once that notion became part of the conventional wisdom, those who opposed measures offered in the name of civil rights could claim immunity from any suggestion of bigotry.

Faced with imminent death from a brain tumor, Lee Atwater, the talented young South Carolinian who headed the Republican Party apologized for having employed the crimes of a furloughed black rapist as a demagogic device to discredit the Democratic presidential nominee, Michael Dukakis. "I said that I would 'strip the bark off the little bastard' and make Willie Horton his running mate," he wrote in *Life*. "I'm sorry for both statements. The first for its naked cruelty, the second because it makes me sound racist, which I am not."

Lee Atwater was not racist if the tests were those an overwhelming majority of whites could not have passed in the South Carolina of my youth, and to a lesser extent his. He approved the franchise for blacks, and solicited their votes; he had no objection to sitting with them at mealtime; and as a jazz guitarist he acknowledged his cultural debt. I don't know whether he could have included blacks among his best friends, but I am sure he would have been pleased to do so had any turned up who were not alienated by his race-baiting campaign tactics. "He was something worse than a bigot," Carolyn Williams wrote in a *Washington Post* obituary. "He was a man who pretended to be a bigot in hope that it would sell."

Disavowal of racism had become the mark of respectability everywhere in the nation. Once the vote was secured for blacks it also became a practical necessity for politicians with a significant black constituency. Senator Strom Thurmond complained to his biographer Nadine Cohodas that he had been misunderstood by his critics: "Some of them got in their mind that I was just a racist. Well, honestly, in my heart, I've never been a racist."

If racism denoted implacable hatred of blacks, there was no reason to question the old Dixiecrat's sincerity. No doubt he had always treated blacks kindly when he dealt with them in person. He just didn't believe in civil rights—but neither, if their polemics were taken seriously, did those in the black community who preached the separatist gospel. They insisted that the improved educational opportunities and economic gains the movement had produced were meaningless; government action could not redress the real grievances of the minority, and served only to assuage the guilt feelings of the more sensitive whites and lull the righteous anger of the oppressed.

The first direct test of the civil rights trinity on Capitol Hill came when Roberta Achtenberg, an openly avowed lesbian, came up for confirmation as assistant secretary of Housing and Urban Development. Like all the Clinton nominees, she could not be challenged on the basis of professional background and applied experience, but Jesse Helms, an openly avowed homophobe, forced a record vote on the floor. Ms. Achtenberg was approved 58–31, with opposition limited to 26 Republicans and 5 Democrats from the Southern Bible Belt.

There was no significant challenge to Clinton's black nominees until Lani Guinier came up for confirmation as assistant attorney general for civil rights. A classmate of the Clintons at Yale Law School, her experience included service as a top assistant in the Justice Department's Civil Rights Division during the Carter administration, and as a voting rights specialist for the NAACP Legal Defense Fund. Since 1988 she had pursued her specialty as a law professor at the University of Pennsylvania.

A white male with comparable credentials would have aroused the opposition of the organized factions opposed in principle to any form of affirmative action. It followed that as soon as Ms. Guinier's nomination was sent to the Hill, the Republicans began publicizing tendentious excerpts from her extensive writing in law journals, claiming that her paper trail represented a radical, un-American departure from the legal mainstream.

She was accused of advocating forms of proportional representation for blacks that would violate the principle of majority rule. But she had dealt only in the abstract with an unsettled issue that had concerned legal scholars and practitioners since the Supreme Court affirmed the principle of one person, one vote as the basic guarantee of voting rights.

The central question she addressed had been raised in court action initiated in Etowah, Alabama, where application of the one-person, one vote doctrine resulted in eliminating the gerrymandering that had effectively nullified black participation in the election of county commissioners. As a result, two blacks were elected, but the white majority on the commission stripped the minority members of the power to control road maintenance in their districts, a prime function of the office. The Bush administration joined the NAACP in arguing that electors were denied their voting rights if the majority in a legislative body could thus incapacitate their chosen representatives.

The basic issue remained unsettled when the Supreme Court voted 6–3 that the Voting Rights Act applied only in elections and did not extend to officials once they were in office. Ms. Guinier's position was surely well inside the mainstream if it could be supported by a Republican attorney general. But my examination of representative excerpts from her writing revealed an even greater irony.

Her research into the limitations encountered by elected minority representatives, and the solutions adopted to deal with them, took her back a long way—back to a political philosopher who addressed the issue while seeking a means of fending off the congressional majority's drive to abolish slavery. That was John C. Calhoun, described by C. Vann Woodward as "the South Carolina Machiavelli . . . who called his doctrine 'the concurrent majority.' "

> It provided various veto or "negating" devices by which minorities could defend themselves against majorities, and long after the ill-starred cause on which he lavished his remarkable genius had passed away, his idea took on new life among his successors.

It was in fact alive and in full force and effect in the U.S. Senate when Lani Guinier's fate hung in the balance. Senate rules fashioned by Southern Democrats to prevent passage of civil rights legislation had just been invoked by the Republican minority to block the president's short-range economic stimulus proposal. Only forty-one votes were required to maintain a filibuster, and there were forty-three Republican members. As long as Minority Leader Bob Dole could hold his followers together he could keep key Clinton programs from coming to a vote.

Ms. Guinier's consideration of the possible utility of some form of a concurrent rather than a simple majority stopped far short of providing the minority with the absolute veto exercised by Dole's flock. Like most law journal articles, hers were speculative, raising possibilities for consideration without proposing hard-and-fast solutions. In the *Michigan Law Journal* she explained:

> I simply invite voting rights activists and litigators to consider a different conceptual, remedial and pragmatic approach. I am not articulating a grand theory of politics. Nor do I argue that these propositions are statutorially or constitutionally required.

But Clint Bolick, a former Reagan administration lawyer who led the charge against Ms. Guinier on the talk show circuit, insisted that she had rejected majority rule and was in fact "Clinton's quota queen." That well-worn code word was sufficient to guarantee the opposition of the Jewish lobby, solidify the Republican opposition, and frighten wavering Democrats.

Democratic solidarity quickly dissipated, and Clinton was importuned by his supporters on the Hill to avoid forcing them to take a stand in the civil rights minefield. When the vote count indicated that the nomination could not be approved, the president capitulated. But Ms. Guinier refused his request that she voluntarily withdraw, insisting that she should be given the right to present her case to the committee—and, via television, to the nation.

After an agonizing confrontation with his friend, Clinton withdrew her nomination, offering the excuse that he had finally read her law review articles and found that he could not agree with her thinking on majority rule. It was the latest, and potentially the most damaging, of what his critics, and a good many of his supporters, were now calling self-inflicted wounds.

I could find nothing in my reading of excerpts from Ms. Guinier's writing to sustain the president's interpretation. Neither could Attorney General Reno, who had not only read the articles but had extensively interviewed the nominee before concluding that she was eminently qualified for the office. At a televised press conference the Justice Department arranged to give her an opportunity to outline the testimony she would have offered on Capitol Hill, Ms. Guinier said:

> I have always believed in one man, one vote. Nothing I have written is inconsistent with that. I have never been in favor of quotas. I think I represent an important and mainstream tradition that this administration is also committed to—that is, vigorous enforcement of the civil rights laws as enacted by Congress.

I demurred only when she expressed confidence that reason would have prevailed had she been allowed to argue her case before the battery of lawyers who made up the Judiciary Committee. She was, I thought, faced with the situation Thurgood Marshall described when he wrote in his last dissenting opinion, "Power, not reason, is the new currency in this Court's decision-making." It was a judgment that applied with equal force in the other two branches of government.

Janet Reno, who stood by Ms. Guinier to the end, recognized that harsh truth: "I told her I would support the president in his ultimate decision because I think he was trying to determine what was best for the future of civil rights enforcement." He was also trying to salvage the basic elements of his legislative program, which in its first test had been rejected by the unanimous vote of the Republicans in both houses of Congress.

Civil rights leaders were outraged that a leading ornament of the movement had been made a sacrificial lamb. But those who met with the president at the White House after he had announced his decision agreed that he had no choice but to avoid a protracted fight he had no chance of winning. In her valedictory statement, Lani Guinier said of her law school classmate: "We disagree on this but we do agree on many things. He believes in racial healing and so do I." Members of the congressional black caucus were decidedly less charitable, but they, too, could count votes.

In their appraisal of the president's prospects as he moved toward the critical showdown with Congress on his fiscal and social policies, the virtually unanimous verdict of the Washington pundits was that their prophesy of failure had proved to be self-fulfilling—the self being Bill Clinton. In the summer issue of *The American Prospect*, academic presidential experts Richard Neustadt, Walter Dean Burnham, James McGregor Burns, and Richard Valelly took a longer and less conclusive view. But there was no real disagreement with the finding of David Lauter of the *Los Angeles Times*:

> The problems of adapting to Washington have worsened because of the President's own character, attitudes and work habits—including his penchant for a decentralized, democratic management structure. . . .
>
> The system has also accentuated Clinton's own tendency

to waver from one issue to another, failing to maintain a consistent line of argument that will convince voters of the correctness of his position.

That was fair comment. Clinton himself came close to endorsing it when he conceded that he had not been able to keep his focus on the central elements of his program, and made a spectacular move to reorganize the White House staff by replacing young George Stephanopoulos with David Gergen, a middleaged Republican spin doctor.

Gergen, an amiable North Carolinian with an Ivy League polish, was himself a major contributor to the conventional wisdom, having become an editor of *U.S. News & World Report* and a fixture on the "McNeil-Lehrer News Hour," after serving as a communications expert in the Nixon and Reagan administrations. His appointment was seen not only as a means of placating a hostile press corps but as a signal that Clinton was now ready to reach out to the Republicans.

But to *The New York Times* the appointment was not a belated attempt at bipartisan fence-building, but an unconscionable abandonment of principle: "It points up a deterioration of political values and an erosion of journalistic standards in the capital. . . . It amounts to nonpartisanship run amok." The editor of the *Times* editorial page, Howell Raines, was an Alabamian who won his spurs covering the civil rights movement in the South, and I thought I could detect the reaction of one who had encountered too many double-talking politicians in his home country, and too many sycophantic journalists when he served as the newspaper's Washington bureau chief.

But the central fallacy of the conventional wisdom was the conclusion that Clinton had "lurched to the left" in an effort to placate his liberal constituency. A better case could be made that he had lurched to the right when he yielded to the insistence of conservatives in his own party that he could not move forward with his activist program unless he gave a higher priority to deficit reduction.

The cacophony of media coverage had deprived the terms "left," "right," and "center" of any real meaning. For a president elected with only 43 percent of the popular vote, compromise was necessarily the order of the day as a joint committee sought to reconcile the amended versions of the administration budget finally approved by single-vote margins in the House and Senate. But the nature of the compromise depended on where one placed the political center.

If the centrists were those who insisted that no new revenue could be considered without first enacting massive spending cuts to guarantee deficit reduction, Clinton could not join them without finally abandoning commitments to his constituents he had already agreed to water down. Those in the middle- and lower-income range would be the principal losers under the drastic curtailment of economic and social programs the deficit hawks demanded as the price of their support.

The conventional wisdom reckoned success and failure in terms of power, and in the opening rounds of the budget battle the Republicans had clearly won. But not much attention was paid to what would follow if they continued to prevail in the struggle over economic and social policy. The minority's unanimous party-line vote in both houses could only be read as presaging continuation of the gridlock a substantial majority had voted against in the general election.

The driving force of Clinton's partisan opposition in Congress was a doctrinaire commitment to laissez faire. The Republican field commander, Bob Dole, made no bones about it. Gridlock, he said, was a bad thing only if you were trying to change something. The minority leader had committed his troops to keeping things as they were at the end of the Reagan counterrevolution. But there was reason to doubt whether the status quo was any more popular in June than it had been in November.

Six months after the presidential election the Los Angeles Times poll measured changes in support for the three factions that had split the popular vote. Clinton still had 37 percent support; the Republicans were down to 19 percent; Ross Perot was off 3 points, at 16 percent; and 26 percent could cite no political grouping they were prepared to join.

Political identity was not being defined by issues but by attitudes. More than half of Perot's supporters agreed that government should play an active role in meeting the needs of the people, while the Republican faithful, now shown to be 92 percent old-stock whites, remained committed to laissez faire. The dominant characteristic of the Perotistas was their suspicion of authority, whether it be that of big government, big business, or organized religion, which meant that many did not trust their authoritarian leader. "Most of them are actually following the message, not the man," said Frank Luntz, a Republican pollster who had worked for the Perot campaign. Nonpartisanship was also running amok outside the Washington beltway.

Lani Guinier's resurrection of Calhoun's theory of the concurrent majority was directly related to the situation black politicians found themselves in as Clinton struggled to preserve the basic elements of his program. The election had increased their numbers in Congress by 50 percent, but the standoff between the putative Democratic majority and the coalition of Republicans and resurgent Dixiecrats threatened to preclude the trading necessary to preserve entitlements regarded as essential for their inner city and poor rural constituents.

In Calhoun's day the polarizing issue had been the abolition of slavery, and when compromise became impossible the political system collapsed. Another civil war was hardly in prospect as racial issues again became a determinant in congressional infighting, but it was evident that the concurrent majority that had emerged in response to the civil rights movement no longer existed.

In the 1970s the Republicans had recaptured the White House by winning majority support for curtailment of a positive role for government in dealing with the urban crisis signalized by the Long Hot Summers. The result had been to virtually preclude any realistic effort to adapt federal programs to changing conditions within the black community—a need pointed out to the incoming president by Daniel Patrick Moynihan, the expatriate Democrat installed as counselor in the Nixon White House:

> The era of equal opportunity, nondiscrimination, integration, and such is coming to an end. . . . Before long blacks will be demanding 11 percent of all public places and services—in universities, civil services, legislatures, military academies, embassies, judges. This is not what the civil rights movement expected to come about, or hoped to see, but it does appear to be the outcome nevertheless.

What building contracts and police graft were to the nineteenth-century Irish, the welfare departments, Head Start, and black studies programs will be to the coming generation of Negroes. They, of course, are very wise in this respect. These are expanding areas of economic opportunity. By contrast, black business enterprise offers very little.

The integrationist thrust of the civil rights movement had been blunted, Moynihan contended, by the government's failure to recognize the differences that separated assimilated middleclass blacks from those who were "abnormally dependent, demographically under siege, unusually self-damaging in their behavior, with an appalling lack of educational achievement." This had produced a class problem concealed within the race problem. And that could be dealt with only if "the nation sets out in earnest to dissolve the great black urban lower class (and the rural slums that feed it) that the militant middleclass now uses as a threat to the larger society."

Moynihan's advice was ignored as President Nixon turned instead to a political strategy that depended on exploitation of real and perceived conflicts of interest between the white majority and the black minority. After the Republicans regained the White House in 1981 black politicians found the threat of violent upheavals in the inner cities the only certain means of attracting the attention of the nation's white leaders.

"Black power!" became the battle cry of the militants who challenged Martin Luther King's integrationist doctrine. But the issue really wasn't power, in any collective sense, since there was no way a small minority could impose its will on a resistant majority. The inchoate demand for individual empowerment reflected resentment of the implication of inferiority in the social exclusion that still prevailed even for blacks whose achievements and standards of personal conduct equaled, or exceeded, those of their white peers.

In some of the most telling testimony heard in the school desegregation cases, Kenneth Clark had demonstrated that even the most fortunately situated black children, consciously or unconsciously, yearned to be white. Richard Wright, driven into exile in France by the discrimination he portrayed in his novels, adopted Nietzsche's term "frog perspective" to characterize the view of blacks who had thrust upon them the assumption that they existed on a lower social and moral plane. In *White Man, Listen!* he wrote:

> A certain degree of hate combined with love is always involved in this looking from below upward. And the object against which the subject is measuring undergoes constant change. He loves the object because he would like to resemble it; he hates the object because his chances of resembling it are slight, remote.

In a memoir, *A Taste of Power,* Elaine Brown, who became a Parisian expatriate a generation after Wright, made a point of her childhood longing to be white. The frustration this inspired stayed with her after she took a white lover and immersed herself in the sophisticated circles that opened to her in the 1960s. Liberation came only when she joined the Black Panthers and "tasted power, finally coming to the point [where] I realized I was someone of value . . . [and] rejected anyone who said I wasn't."

In Oakland, Huey Newton, one of the founders of the movement, became her lover. In 1974, when Newton fled to Cuba, Elaine Brown succeeded him as head of the national Black Panther movement. Under her leadership the Panthers briefly became a positive influence—but only after she had moved them into the mainstream. Chapters in major cities established storefront operations to provide food and medical care for poor children, and in Oakland they supported a model school, launched a voter registration drive, and were given credit for helping elect the city's first black mayor.

Then, in 1977, Huey Newton returned from exile and reinstated the drug culture, gun-toting militance and rampant sexism that had characterized the early movement. Elaine Brown and her seven-year-old daughter were forced to flee for their lives. But a decade later, when Newton was gunned down in the course of a drug transaction, she came back from Paris to attend his funeral. Despite the abuse she had suffered at black hands, her love for him had not abated, nor had her rage at the society that made him an outcast.

In 1993, on a first-class tour of the United States to promote her book, she was untouched by the brief resurgence of good feeling that followed Bill Clinton's election. In Boston she sensed "an attitude" on the part of the bellboy who escorted her to her room, and in Beverly Hills she was offended by a desk clerk who didn't recognize her as a guest. "You wouldn't believe the rage I've felt," she told an interviewer. "And I've only been here three weeks. I actually hate this country. It's such an insult to be black in America."

It had been generally assumed that the alienation inherited from the nation's racist past could be dealt with by integrating the segregated minority into the larger society. That was the goal of the civil rights movement, and the intended result of the new legal status it achieved for blacks. Opening the educational system was expected to complete the process of acculturation, so that black identity would have no more significance than that accorded the ancestry of other citizens of a nation of immigrants. But it had not worked out that way.

The majority of poor black children had been left behind in deteriorating urban public schools, while parents who could afford to do so, black as well as white, removed their children to private or suburban schools. On college campuses more or less voluntary racial segregation prevailed in living accommodations and amenities. It was said that outside the gymnasium and athletic field, the only interaction between blacks and whites took place in the classroom—and there it imposed a severe strain on the collegial spirit. Ideological battle lines were defined by the insistence of blacks that their identity be recognized by changes in the curricula, answered by the charge that this not only constituted discriminatory special treatment but was also a threat to academic freedom.

The new diversity in greatly expanded student bodies forced recognition that white male domination of higher education had resulted in serious omissions in studies of American history and culture. In 1960 college enrollment had been 94 percent white, with a third of the remaining 6 percent enrolled in black institutions. Although coeducation had become standard, there had been similar neglect of the historic role of women, and most established scholars recognized that in both cases they were faced with a legitimate demand.

In his 1969 presidential address to the Organization of American

Historians, C. Vann Woodward conceded that American scholarship had been limited by the white majority's conviction "that European culture, *their* culture, was so overwhelmingly superior that no other could survive under exposure to it." The result was treatment of American history that tended to strip blacks of their African heritage. But changing a curriculum has been likened to moving a graveyard, and frustration at the response of the academic hierarchy produced campus cults that not only demanded institution of ethnocentric and feminist studies but also condemned traditional humanities and liberal arts as irrevocably distorted by Eurocentric tradition and male chauvinism.

The choleric manifestations of Afrocentrism and feminism became a political *cause célèbre. Illiberal Education*, Dinesh D'Souza's contribution to the conservative canon, charged that the effort to bring minorities and women into higher education had undermined meritocracy, and went on to assert that catering to their whims had saddled the universities with programs that "promulgate rigid political views on civil rights, feminism, homosexual rights and other issues pressed by activists who got these departments set up in the first place."

Reviewing D'Souza's book, Elizabeth Fox-Genovese, director of the Emory University Institute for Women's Studies, defended specialized programs but conceded that

> a rising tide of thought control, special pleading, cultural separatism and intellectual dishonesty is inundating our campuses and subverting the true purposes of education, not to mention freedom of thought and racial integration.

The issue identified as "political correctness" did not remain confined to academia. George Bush added it to the Republican campaign arsenal, proclaiming that "political extremists roam the land, abusing the privilege of free speech, setting citizens against one another on the basis of their class or race." That was true of some black separatists, but their capacity to divide the country was minuscule compared to that of whites who employed the mass media to reply in kind.

In any city in the land you could turn on the radio at peak listening hours and hear call-in show hosts invoking a chorus of bigotry with the charge that Bill Clinton had sold out the white majority by yielding to demands for special privileges for blacks, gays, and feminists. And Ross Perot was a ubiquitous presence on network television, purchasing half-hour blocks of prime time to augment the free ride his message was given on the talk shows.

"Let's face it," *The New York Times* columnist William Safire wrote, "we have a third party, financed by Ross Perot. . . . Nativism is its wellspring, populist revolt is its style, autocratic technocracy is its essence. . . ."

Perot has demonstrated that $100 million plus a large dose of chutzpah buys you a place at the starting gate. He has shown that name recognition can be gained virtually overnight; that call-in shows can catapult a candidacy from the ridiculous to the menacing.

If American society is divided by horizontal class lines, there is also a vertical division based on race that begins at the point where the affluent are set apart from the poor. Analysis of 1990 census data showed that blacks in significant numbers lived in upscale urban and suburban neighborhoods, but intimate contact with their white neighbors was minimal. Generations of Southern demagogues had claimed that such residential race mixing would result in wholesale miscegenation, but the 53 million marriages recorded in the 1990 census included only 240,000 with a black spouse.

In the upper strata of society racial attitudes, reinforced by ethno-centrism on both sides, still inhibited interaction and provided fertile ground for political exploitation. But in the ghettos the issues were still those that had existed throughout the nation's history. The greatly ex-panded opportunities available to middleclass blacks remained as far beyond the reach of most underclass youths as they had been for their sharecropping forebears. Segregation was still the dominant fact of life below the poverty line, and the issue was quite literally survival.

In his campaign, Clinton had carefully avoided proposals targeted directly at the festering problems in the inner cities. If they could be persuaded to vote, the poor blacks who lived there could provide effective political support, but the threat of racial violence emanating from these neglected communities also worked against any candidate who embraced their cause in the name of social justice.

The result was spelled out in the conclusions of leading social scientists who contributed to *The Urban Underclass,* a 1991 Brookings Institution study. "Universalism" was the key term that emerged from the mass of statistical evidence. Despite the surge of antitax sentiment, broad-based programs such as Medicare and Social Security had remained securely imbedded in the unbalanced federal budget. But problems peculiar to poor blacks had long since lost priority. Any approach to meeting their needs would have to be, as J. David Greenstone put it, "politically feasible, that is, be supported outside the inner cities."

Kevin Phillips, whose focus on the common denominator of self-interest had made him the most reliable Washington appraiser of political attitudes, concurred:

> To the extent that you tell the middleclass you are going to tax the rich so that you can give more to the middleclass, they will love you. But if you tell suburbia you are going to tax them more so you can give more to low-income school districts, they are not going to do it.

Head Start was the only Great Society program of consequence to survive the rising tide of right-wing populism. The preschool program was never adequately funded, but it managed to gain popular support to the point where it even received the blessing of Presidents Reagan and Bush. President Clinton was pledged to increase its reach to include all eligible children, and increased funding was included in his pared-down budget.

Head Start met the political test the administration applied to most of the recommendations it made to Congress—that they have sufficient popular support to overcome ideological opposition. "Poor children, who cannot readily be blamed for their plight," Greenstone noted, "are relatively popular beneficiaries." And Head Start also had the political virtue of being effectively divorced from any prospect of directly advancing racial integration.

Busing was a dead letter, and the Supreme Court had opened the way for district courts to rescind orders requiring the elimination of segregated schools. Eligibility for Head Start required that children must come from families below the poverty line, and if it were opened to all such, the great majority of new black recruits would be found in urban districts from which 96.7 percent of white students had decamped.

As he rounded into the second year in office, it was unclear how well Bill Clinton was succeeding in his declared goal of persuading the American people to take a longer-range view of public policy. Congress had imposed a higher priority on budget-balancing than he had projected, forcing him to cut back on proposed economic stimulus programs to offset the continuing effects of structural job loss. But the outlines of a new industrial policy had been put in place, and he had restored the burden of increased revenue on upper-income taxpayers, while exempting the poor and minimizing the impact on those in mid-income brackets.

He was still plagued by the skepticism of the media, which continued to portray him as a blundering neophyte out of his depth in big league politics. But when Congress closed out the 1993 session, *Congressional Quarterly*'s scorecard showed that Clinton had prevailed on 90 percent of the votes on which he took a stand—the highest success rate since the first year of the Eisenhower administration forty years before.

In the course of wheeling and dealing with Congress, he had reaffirmed his centrist position—prevailing against the Republicans on basic elements of his social programs, and successfully outmaneuvering the labor unions on the left and Ross Perot on the right, to put through the North American Free Trade Agreement with a vote margin that refuted the dire predictions of the pundits.

As he moved to take his case directly to the electorate, the polls showed that he was rallying majority support for health care reform, the centerpiece of his design for redirecting the nation's social policies. Government-directed universal medical coverage would provide an essential benefit for the underclass but the emphasis was on meeting the needs of the middleclass. Welfare and educational reform were still on the presidential agenda, but as a *Los Angeles Times* headline put it, the White House was "Fighting a Quiet War on Poverty."

Some of the initiatives clearly are focused on relieving poverty— programs aimed at decreasing homelessness and stimulating business in depressed communities for example. Other new programs, including national service, are couched in rhetoric about helping a broad spectrum of the population but are targeted at low-income individuals and poor communities.

Clinton's critics labeled this a "stealth policy." Those on the left discounted the programs as palliatives designed to distract attention from his sellout to business interests in the name of job creation, while the Heritage Foundation spoke for the right wing when it charged that the administration was really bent on "throwing money at every welfare program we've ever had . . . old ideas that the administration is trotting out even when they are proven failures."

But Labor Secretary Robert Reich pointed out that the focus on encouraging private sector job creation was

> what we were elected to do. The putting-people-first campaign was all about investing in the work force. There is a difference between this and the older Democratic philosophy of redistributing wealth from the rich to the poor. It's about giving everyone in society the capacity to be a constructive member of society.

Representative Craig Washington of Texas reflected the prevailing view of the Congressional Black Caucus: "It's a smart approach. The people who have the least clout and the least influence . . . are poor people. If you stick something out there like a sore thumb, it would never get passed. It's more important to do something to help the poor than to beat your horn about it."

Appraisals of Clinton's performance in terms of the conventional political orientation of Democrats and Republicans had become virtually meaningless in the face of pressures emanating from the electorate. Passage of a package of gun control measures he had sponsored, Clinton said, had nothing to do with ideology; the Congressional response demonstrated that "Americans are finally fed up with violence that cuts down another citizen with gunfire every twenty minutes." Wherever they chose to place the blame, city dwellers were faced with inescapable reminders of the cost to the whole community of failure to deal with the root causes of crime and violence in the inner cities.

The mounting negative force of these unmet needs were demonstrated in the 1993 off-year elections in Los Angeles, which epitomized the dislocations afflicting all major cities. The coalition of liberals, Jews, blacks, labor and downtown business interests that had kept a moderate Democrat, Tom Bradley, in the mayor's office for twenty years went down to crushing defeat. His successor was Richard Riordan, an obscure Republican multimillionaire who had moved ahead of twenty-eight candidates with a Perot-style television blitz paid for by six million dollars of his own money.

An exit poll on the day of Riordan's runoff victory over the Democratic organization's candidate, City Councilman Michael Woo, provided what the *Los Angeles Times* termed "a downcast portrait of the city's political landscape":

> It is a portrait of an electorate deeply divided by race and by what it expects of the next mayor, but unified in its doubts about the honesty of both candidates, its distaste for the campaign's negative tone and its deep skepticism that improvement will occur. . . .

With a different cast of characters, that portrait would be replicated in mayoral elections in Detroit and New York later in the year.

Maxine Waters, who represented riot-torn South-Central Los Angeles in Congress, put a human face on the source of municipal angst:

> Look on any street corner—any street corner in my congressional district or in any other urban center—and you will see him. He is a member of our lost generation.
>
> He is between 17 and 30 years old, the product of a dysfunctional family. Unskilled and without a job, he is living from girlfriend to mother to grandmother. He's not reflected in the unemployment statistics and surely isn't on the tax rolls. If he's

driving, it's without a license. If he's bunking in public housing, you won't find his name on the lease. He has a record—misdemeanors if he is lucky, felonies more likely. He was the most visible participant in the Los Angeles uprising, but otherwise he seems almost invisible to society.

For too many young men in my district, and in other cities around this country, there is precious little hope. They have given up on themselves and they have given up on us. If we know what's good for us—and him—we had better start paying him some attention.

Bill Clinton came before the American people as a healer, committed to bringing together a divided nation. Martin Luther King, he said, had been the teacher of his generation: "He taught us about the pain and promise of America, about the redemptive healing of faith and discipline, about love and courage. . . ." As a politician in a poor Southern state, Clinton had also recognized the end of racial discrimination as a pragmatic necessity—not only to meet the pressure exerted by newly enfranchised blacks, but also to free whites of the crippling legacy from the racist past. Blacks now posed a similar challenge for the nation.

When they were isolated and powerless, their existence as a mass of exploited workers had refuted the majority's professed moral precepts; the civil rights movement that made them a positive factor in national life had tested the basic tenets of governance. Now the movement had run its course and black leaders no longer held the moral high ground. But the effects of the social Darwinism reinstated as public policy could not be ignored if there was to be a restoration of the level of civility upon which democratic government ultimately depends.

The death of Thurgood Marshall during the week of the Clinton inaugural had provided a poignant reminder of the practical consequences of the nation's failure to live up to the moral standards prescribed in its founding documents. He was laid out on Capitol Hill in the great hall of the marble temple emblazoned with the slogan "Equal Justice Under Law." Congress had ordered Abraham Lincoln's catafalque brought to the Court to serve as his bier, and scores of thousands filed by to pay their respects to one of the last survivors of those who carried the civil rights banner in the days when there was no mass movement to support them,

For me, Justice Marshall symbolized the gallantry that went into the effort to change the legal contours of the nation's race relations. When I first encountered him he was a lonely figure standing tall in Southern courtrooms before hostile white judges and juries, arguing the case for his people he would ultimately make undeniable. He was sustained in that hazardous practice by a sense of irony and an ingrained civility that never deserted him.

The *Newsday* columnist Murray Kempton thought the origin of those qualities could be seen in an anecdote from the days when young Thurgood worked during college vacations as a waiter at the Gibson Island Club on Chesapeake Bay, where his father was chief steward:

> One night, when the younger Marshall was at his station, a visiting congressman from Iowa, high flown with insolence, wine and ignorance of the customs of the region, called out, "Come here, nigger."
>
> And then Ellison Durant Smith, the senator from South Carolina, rose up to demand in thunder, "What did he call you, Thurgood? I will not hear that word spoken in this club."
>
> The offender was driven into the night, exiled for a private racial slur by the wrath of Cotton Ed Smith, the most tireless race-baiter on the Senate floor. The "n" word was Smith's common currency for the campaigns he debased; but he would not tolerate its utterance in the company of gentlemen.

Marshall could tell that tale without rancor. It came from the vast stock of anecdotes he drew upon to instruct his learned brethren on the Supreme Court. "They are his way of preserving the past while purging it of its bleakest moments," Justice William Brennan said. "They are also a form of education for the rest of us. Surely Justice Marshall recognizes that the stories made us—his colleagues—confront walks of life we had never known."

Entertaining no doubt as to his own identity, Marshall ignored the circumlocutions that reflected the effort to end usage blacks believed, with good reason, to be redolent of white contempt. He never accepted "black" and continued to use "Negro" in his opinions until his final years on the bench, when he adopted "African-American" but pointedly rejected "Afro-American."

It was said even by admirers that Marshall's opinions could not be considered the work of a great legal scholar. That was the note James Jackson Kilpatrick, the father of interposition, struck in reviewing a hagiography written by the black columnist Carl Rowan. Yet, however he may have intended it, Kilpatrick paid proper tribute when he wrote, "His passion was not for law. His passion was for justice." Those who had come to the Court lately made a distinction between the two that cast Marshall in the role of dissenter.

He held on as long as he could, telling those anxious for a vacancy, "I have a lifetime appointment and I expect to serve it. I expect to die at 110, shot by a jealous husband." But in 1991 declining health forced him to step down, making way for Clarence Thomas, a black lawyer of another generation who had won appointment by repudiating everything Marshall stood for.

It was a measure of the changing political climate that the justice who moved from majority to minority came to the bench after winning twenty-seven of thirty-three cases he argued before the Court, many of them brought in the days when most of the justices were rated as conservative. When he put aside the advocate's role he demonstrated that the usual political labels had little application in the areas of the law where he consistently took his stand.

"Marshall's focus has always been more inclusive than African-Americans," said Nicholas deB. Katzenbach, who served as attorney general in the stormy days of the civil rights movement:

> His concern is with all people who do not enjoy the full benefits of a free society. . . . Fundamentally, he is in his passion for the individual a conservative, a democrat who cannot tolerate the arbitrary acts of governmental bureaucracy in its unconcern for individual rights.

Kenneth Clark rode with Marshall when he headed South to Charleston to try *Briggs*, the Clarendon County case he would pursue to his final victory in *Brown*. Late that night, as the train pounded down through

Virginia, Marshall looked up from his briefs and said, "You know, Kenneth, sometimes I get awfully tired of trying to save the white man's soul."

The task of redemption remained unfinished, and as a new president came up from the South to address it he was faced with the question I had left open a generation ago when the rise of the civil rights movement marked the end of the era I memorialized in *An Epitaph for Dixie*: "There is reason to wonder, certainly, whether the American political system as it has evolved under the impact of the expanding cities is anywhere giving us the kind of public and private leadership our age demands."

BIBLIOGRAPHIC NOTE

THE CIVIL RIGHTS movement and the reaction to it have produced a vast and varied literature. The hundreds of volumes on my shelves, representing only a small sampling, range from scholarly tomes to polemical tracts, and all—including a considerable number dismissed by the critics as without literary merit—have been useful in my effort to appraise the popular response to the legacy of racism that still shapes the political process.

Since a memoir does not require annotation or a formal bibliography, many writers who have influenced my view must go unacknowledged. Authors and their work are identified in the text only in cases of direct quotation or extensive paraphrase. This also applies to my own writing, which I have relied upon not only to refresh my memory but also to convey an unadorned sense of my reactions, and those of my contemporaries, at the time when history was being made. Passages from my published work, condensed but substantively unchanged, are carried over as appropriate to the chronology.

This volume grew out of the conviction that an understanding of the racial tensions prevalent throughout urban America requires an examination of the civil rights movement in the context of the shifting currents of public opinion that determined its outcome. Only a small minority of white Americans were actively involved in the evolution of the inclusive policies that opened the mainstream to middleclass blacks. The reaction of the rest was determined by attitudes reinforced, or modified, by the impressions conveyed by newspapers, magazines, television, and books.

Media coverage became a determinant when the political rebellion launched by the Dixiecrats in the aftermath of World War II reopened the public debate over legal and de facto segregation that had been dormant for fifty years. The moral issues posed by racial discrimination became inescapable, and for the first time black leaders empowered by the civil rights movement were speaking out in their own right. This guaranteed a deeply emotional response by members of both races. I don't think I overstated the case when I wrote in 1968:

> The issue holds the undisputed American course record for public and private ambivalence. Nothing in our national experience remotely compares with the unresolved racial dilemma for the production of bloodshed, emotional trauma, rank injustice, supercharged rhetoric, dubious theology, unsound academic research, bad legal theory, and perverse political practice.

As one fated by place of birth and choice of profession to deal with manifestations of the race issue, I was soon aware of the limitations this has imposed on the written record, including my own contributions to it. Prior to the 1950s most of my writing was published in newspapers as reportage or social and political commentary tempered by policies determined by those with whom I shared editorial responsibility. Since then I have published fourteen books and numerous articles in national magazines that dealt, directly or in passing, with racial issues.

The Negro and the Schools (Chapel Hill: University of North Carolina Press, 1954) was commissioned by the Fund for the Advancement of Education with the understanding that it would not argue the case for or against desegregation. *The Man in the Middle* (Columbia: University of Missouri Press, 1966) was the text of the Paul Anthony Brick Lectures sponsored by the Philosophy Department, which specified that they should deal with ethics. *Arkansas: A History* (New York: W. W. Norton, 1978) was commissioned by the American Association for State and Local History as one of the States and the Nation Series commemorating the Bicentennial. These volumes bore some scholarly trappings.

The books most frequently quoted or paraphrased here are more subjective, cast in the form of thematically related essays: *An Epitaph for Dixie* (Norton, 1957), *The Other Side of Jordan* (Norton, 1960), and

Hearts and Minds: The Anatomy of Racism from Roosevelt to Reagan (New York: McGraw-Hill, 1982). All were focused on the effect of the civil rights movement on the changing contours of race relations.

I have left unchanged the style of racial identification in passages taken from these works. The evolution in the treatment of the minority in publications of general circulation is important as a reflection of the rising consciousness of blacks, and as a demonstration of the ability of the black leadership to impress their sensitivity on the editors and publishers who determine linguistic usage.

Until the 1960s blacks usually were portrayed in print and on radio and television by demeaning stereotypes that certified their inferior social status. When I was breaking in as an apprentice journalist, the style sheets in effect on most newspapers designated members of the minority as "negro," with a lower-case "n." "Colored," having been incorporated in the title of the NAACP back in 1913, was acceptable, but "black" was proscribed, along with such palpably offensive terms as "nigger," "darky," and "coon."

The first change in usage in response to black complaints I can recall resulted in the capitalization of "Negro" to put it on a par with racial terms such as "Irish," "Italian," and "Japanese," which were often hyphenated with American. Next came a demand for courtesy titles. The general practice called for the full name of an adult in the first reference, and thereafter the surname was preceded as appropriate with an abbreviated professional or political title, or "Mr.," "Mrs.," or "Miss." But except for professional titles, Negro surnames were denied this mark of respect.

As usage became less formal these courtesy titles were eliminated for all males but were retained for white females. The offense implicit in their denial to even the most respectable Negro matron was compounded by the fact that colored females were rarely mentioned at all. News relating to family affairs was confined to what were then called "society" pages, and these remained unassailable bastions of white supremacy.

The psychological effect of these public marks of social inferiority was a matter of special concern for civil rights leaders, who recognized that raising black consciousness was essential to their cause. Ralph Ellison, who chose *Invisible Man* as the title for a novel depicting black life at midcentury, noted that "Negro Americans are in a desperate search for identity. Their whole lives have become a search for the answers to the questions: Who am I? What am I? Why am I? and, Where?"

The proliferation of young black writers in recent years has added an edge of anger to their depiction of an implacable white majority— which to some degree is refuted by their own entry into the publishing mainstream. Their work, like that of their white contemporaries, is usually charged with sexual overtones and fits readily into an expanding market for the literature of alienation.

The result has been a marked revision of the standards of style and taste in publications of general circulation. The demands of blacks were followed by those of women when they began to organize in political factions. White women had been accorded a respected, even revered, place in American society, but as feminist leaders adopted the confrontational tactics of the civil rights movement they demanded an end to special treatment. The titles "Miss" and "Mrs." reserved for them denoted a marital status that did not apply to the increasing number of divorced women, professionals who chose to retain their maiden names, and those who rejected any implied restraint on their sexual freedom of choice. Thus the newly coined "Ms." came into being, although it has fallen out of favor as the demand for equal treatment with males led to the elimination of the last vestige of the courtesy title.

But the evolution of color- and gender-blind media treatment ran counter to the use of bloc identification as a source of political leverage. This has made it difficult to act upon the premise that any identifiable group is entitled to determine its proper designation. Some blacks, seeking to enhance the ethnic identity previously downplayed, demand to be referred to as "African-American" or "Afro-American." American Indians, after being geographically displaced for five centuries, have introduced "Native American." The lack of satisfactory terms to cover the variety of recent immigrants from nations to the south and west of the United States has left editors divided between "Hispanic" and "Latino" and facing uncertain distinctions between "Asian" and "Pacific Islander." And the homosexual rights movement, having gained acceptance for "gay," now has factions that have reinstated "queer" and "dyke" for their satirical shock value.

In this form of protest against discrimination, as in most, blacks can make a special case. The injustice and psychological harm done by the traditional white imputation of inferiority to African ancestry was translated into social and legal sanctions of a different order than those applied to others not born to the prevailing culture; only blacks have constituted a permanently identifiable minority. But the effort to exalt an African identity remote in both time and space is largely a political gesture divorced from the reality facing a people whose forebears arrived here with the first settlers. It is as divisive as if the minority with which I am identified insisted on being called "British-Americans."

Like most aging writers, I have a curmudgeonly reaction to revisions that reduce the precision of language, and this volume will provide evidence that I have generally lagged behind the avant-garde of linguistic liberation. Abandonment of the smug and prudish Victorian standards that were still in effect when I became an editor has resulted from movements I have generally supported. But I am not sure whether this has enhanced, or diminished, the quality of the political dialogue on the central issues of race.

As one who has had to deal with contemporary events without the benefit of moral certitude, I can only offer in expiation of the ambivalence some readers will doubtless ascribe to this work the dictum of the Nobel laureate Czeslaw Milosz: "You cannot strive for coherence where coherence is not possible. Today, in our time, somebody who doesn't learn to live with contradictions is lost."

ACKNOWLEDGMENTS

ONE OF MY FIRST visitors after I settled in at the *Charlotte News* at the end of World War II was John Popham, who had just returned from service with the Marines in the Pacific. He had expected to resume his career covering municipal politics for *The New York Times* but had been diverted by Turner Catledge, the Mississippian who presided over the news operation. Catledge had concluded that profound changes of national import were impending in the South.

Thus Johnny Popham, whose credentials included a beguiling tidewater Virginia accent, described as sounding like sorghum fired from a Gatling gun, became the first and, by all odds, the best-informed national correspondent to cover what would become the civil rights movement. By the time other outside journalists were attracted to the region by the Dixiecrat rebellion prompted by Harry Truman's reelection, Popham had established warm personal relationships with politicians, newspaper people, preachers, and professors from the Potomac to Eagle Pass—including the leaders of the black community, who were largely invisible to whites.

Traveling more than fifty thousand miles a year by automobile, usually on back roads where he could stop off to commune with poor whites and blacks in relaxed circumstances, Popham established linkage among those actively engaged on both sides of the movement, cultivating sources that provided the balanced information and insight he freely dispensed to anyone who could use it.

A remnant of that linkage still endures in the dwindling group of survivors of the civil rights era who gather annually in Atlanta for a reunion called the Popham Seminar. A principal keeper of the flame is John Ansley Griffin, a benign sociologist who believes that under-standing the forces that reshaped Southern society can be derived from the informal, often raucous exchanges of his old, dear friends.

The ranks have thinned since we began gathering at Griffin's house twenty-three years ago. Ralph McGill, the editor of the *Constitution*; Harold Fleming, director of the Potomac Institute, to whom this book is dedicated; and Bill Baggs, editor of the *Miami News*, are dead. But Popham, Claude Sitton, who succeeded him as *Times* Southern cor-respondent, and Bill Emerson, who was on the front lines for *Newsweek*, are still in full voice, and the seminar has expanded to include a hotel hospitality suite full of journalists and academics who were engaged in later phases of the movement, and, in some cases, still are.

This is an appropriately long-winded acknowledgment of my debt to the garrulous colleagues who through the years have contributed to, and often challenged, the conclusions I set forth in this memoir. In addition to those whose advice I have absorbed by osmosis, I have asked five others to vet the book in manuscript and give me the benefit of varied perspectives. They are

- Julian Bond, a veteran of the movement led by Martin Luther King, who narrated the PBS series "Eyes on the Prize" and is now a professor of history at the University of Virginia
- Blair Clark, former director of CBS News and editor of *The Nation*
- John Egerton, author of *The Americanization of Dixie*, who is just adding to the list of his distinguished works a new book that traces the origins of the civil rights movement to pre–World War II days
- Eugene Roberts, former national affairs editor of *The New York Times* and editor of *The Philadelphia Inquirer*, who is now a professor of journalism at the University of Maryland
- Sander Vanocur, who arrived at Little Rock as a fledgling correspond-ent for NBC, went on to cover the White House, and became national political correspondent for ABC.

I am also indebted to Virigina Fleming for making available the unfin-ished history of the Potomac Institute her husband was writing at the time of his death. William Slayton, the first director of the Urban Renewal Administration, provided important material from his files.

Senator Daniel Patrick Moynihan, a key figure in the development of federal anti-poverty programs under Presidents Kennedy, Johnson, and Nixon, has been generous with his time, augmenting the perceptive observations in his memoir *Maximum Feasible Misunderstanding.* Judge Henry Woods of the federal district court at Little Rock provided background on the landmark Central High School litigation over which he presided.

Finally, I have been fortunate to have Simon Michael Bessie as my editor and publisher at Pantheon Books. In the course of his distinguished career he has published many of the key authors who have chronicled the interaction of race and politics since World War II. The understanding and support he provided, along with the backstopping of his assistant, Abigail Strubel, have been essential in seeing this work through to print.

INDEX

Clifford, Clark, 87, 140, 211, 272
and elections of 1948, 56, 70–71, 72, 73, 75, 80
Clinton, Bill, xviii–xx, 378–96, 399–400, 402–3
abortion issue and, 380–82, 383
appointments of, xix, 380–84, 388–92, 393
as Arkansas governor, 360–63
Ashmore's contacts with, 360, 361, 365, 367
civil rights and, 354, 380–92, 395–96, 405–6
crime and, xix, 384
in elections of 1992, xviii, 353–60, 363–77
gay rights and, 380–82, 384–87, 388–89
health care and, xviii, xix–xx, 376, 402
Clinton, Hillary Rodham, xviii, 356, 357, 360, 362, 363, 371, 383
CNN, 353
Cohn, David, 93, 95
Cohodas, Nadine, 388
Cold War, 71, 205–6, 282
Cole, Kenneth, 255
Coleman, Milton, 331
Coleman, William T., Jr., 109
Colson, Charles W., 253
Columbia University, 233
Commission on Civil Rights, 66
Commission on Interracial Cooperation, 25, 26, 33
Commission on Party Structure and Delegate Selection, 249
Committee of Law Teachers Against Segregation in Legal Education, 97
Committee to Re-elect the President (CREEP), 251, 253
Common Cause, 272
Communist Party, U.S.A., 17, 71, 77
Community Action Program, 183
Conference of Concerned Democrats, 210
Conflict and Crisis (Donovan), 57
Congressional Quarterly, 402

Congress of Industrial Organizations (CIO), 86, 308
Congress of Racial Equality (CORE), 146, 148, 172, 179, 180, 189–90, 194
Connecticut, budget deficits in, 323
Connor, Theophilus Eugene "Bull," 26
Constitution (Kull), 297
Constitution, U.S., 66, 343
constitutional amendments
First, 114
Fourteenth, 342
Twenty-sixth, 250
Constitutional Rights Conference, 162
Content of Our Character, The (Steele), 344
Conyers, John, 328
Cooper v. *Aaron*, 278
Corcoran, Tom, 22
Cosby, Bill, 306
Cotton States and International Exposition (1895), 12–13
Council of Economic Advisers, 183
Council of Federated Organizations (COFO), 172
Counsel to the President (Clifford), 73
Court Years, The (Douglas), 101, 103
Cranston, Alan, 327
crime, criminal justice system, xix, 43, 316–23, 384
Crisis, The, 15–16, 86
Crucible of Race, The (Williamson), 39–40, 42
Crump, Edward H. "Boss," 164
Cuba, 333
Cuomo, Mario, 323, 334, 353
Currier, Stephen, 145–46

Dabbs, James McBride, 63, 113
Dabney, Virginius, 62, 63, 105
Daedalus, 189
Daley, Richard, 224
Davies, Ronald, 126, 129, 131
Davis, Benjamin O., 52
Davis, Jeff, 64
Davis, Sammy, Jr., 137
day care, 382–83

ABOUT THE AUTHOR

HARRY S. ASHMORE began his career in his native South Carolina as political writer and state capital correspondent for the *Greenville News*. As executive editor of the *Arkansas Gazette*, he was awarded the Pulitzer Prize for his editorials, and the newspaper won the award for distinguished public service in the Little Rock school-integration controversy. He is also a recipient of the Freedom House and the Lillian Smith awards.

Mr. Ashmore joined the Center for the Study of Democratic Institutions when it was established in 1960 to appraise the impact of demographic and technological change on American society, and then served as its president. He is the author of ten books dealing with the civil rights movement, as it made race relations a dominant political issue.

He has been a correspondent for the *New York Herald Tribune*, editor in chief of the *Encyclopaedia Britannica,* and publisher of *Center Magazine.* He was advisory vice-chairman of the American Civil Liberties Union from 1958 to 1984, and he is a member of the executive board of the National Committee for an Effective Congress.

A graduate of Clemson University, and a Nieman Fellow at Harvard, he has honorary degrees from Oberlin, Grinnell, the University of Arkansas, and Clemson. He and his wife, Barbara, live in Santa Barbara; they have one daughter, Anne.